First World War
and Army of Occupation
War Diary
France, Belgium and Germany

14 DIVISION
41 Infantry Brigade
Rifle Brigade (The Prince Consort's Own)
8th Battalion
20 May 1915 - 31 July 1918

WO95/1895/1

The Naval & Military Press Ltd
www.nmarchive.com
Published in association with The National Archives

Published by

The Naval & Military Press Ltd

Unit 10 Ridgewood Industrial Park,

Uckfield, East Sussex,

TN22 5QE England

Tel: +44 (0) 1825 749494

www.naval-military-press.com

www.nmarchive.com

This diary has been reprinted in facsimile from the original. Any imperfections are inevitably reproduced and the quality may fall short of modern type and cartographic standards.

Contents

Document type	Place/Title	Date From	Date To
Heading	WO95/1895-1		
Heading	14th Division 41st Infy Bde 8th Bn Rifle Bde May 1915-Jly 1918		
Heading	14th Division 8th Rifle Brigade Vol 20.5-29.6.15		
War Diary	Ostrohove	20/05/1915	20/05/1915
War Diary	Pont De Briques	21/05/1915	21/05/1915
War Diary	Latten	21/05/1915	21/05/1915
War Diary	Merckegham	22/05/1915	26/05/1915
War Diary	Zuytpeene	27/05/1915	27/05/1915
War Diary	Fletre	28/05/1915	28/05/1915
War Diary	Bailleul	29/05/1915	06/06/1915
War Diary	Rozenhill Huts	07/06/1915	10/06/1915
War Diary	Pioneer Fm	11/06/1915	12/06/1915
War Diary	Rozenhill Huts	13/06/1915	29/06/1915
Miscellaneous	Field Return		
Miscellaneous	For information of the A.G.'s Office at the Base. Officers and men who have become casuals, been transferred or joined since last report.		
Miscellaneous	Field Return		
Miscellaneous	For Information Of The A.G's Office At The Base		
Miscellaneous	Field Return No of Report 3		
Miscellaneous	For information of the A.G.'s Office at the Base. Officers and men who have become casuals, been transferred or joined since last report.		
Miscellaneous	Field Return	12/06/1915	12/06/1915
Miscellaneous	For information of the A.G.'s Office at the Base. Officers and men who have become casuals, been transferred or joined since last report. Place Pioneer Farm.	12/06/1915	12/06/1915
Miscellaneous	Field Return	19/06/1915	19/06/1915
Miscellaneous	For information of the A.G.'s Office at the Base. Officers and men who have become casuals, been transferred or joined since last report.	19/06/1915	19/06/1915
Miscellaneous	Field Return	19/06/1915	19/06/1915
Miscellaneous	For information of the A.G.'s Office at the Base. Officers and men who have become casuals, been transferred or joined since last report. Place Vlamertinghe.	26/06/1915	26/06/1915
Miscellaneous	Field Return		
Miscellaneous	For information of the A.G.'s Office at the Base. Officers and men who have become casuals, been transferred or joined since last report. Place Vlamertinghe.	30/05/1915	30/05/1915
Heading	14th Division 8th Rifle Brigade Vol II 1-29.7.15		
War Diary	In Trenches East of Ypres Round Railway Wood	01/07/1915	09/07/1915
War Diary	In Billets 2 Miles S.L Of Poperinghe	10/07/1915	24/07/1915
War Diary	Bde Reserve Dugouts 1mile No. of Ypres	25/07/1915	29/07/1915
Miscellaneous	For Information Of The A.G.'s Office At The Base	10/07/1915	10/07/1915
Miscellaneous	Field Return		
Miscellaneous	Field Return	10/07/1915	10/07/1915

Miscellaneous	For Information Of The A.G.'s Office At The Base	10/07/1915	10/07/1915
Miscellaneous	Field Return	17/07/1915	17/07/1915
Miscellaneous	For Information Of The A.G.'s Office At The Base	17/07/1915	17/07/1915
Miscellaneous	Field Return	24/07/1915	24/07/1915
Miscellaneous	For Information Of The A.G.'s Office At The Base	24/07/1915	24/07/1915
Miscellaneous	Field Return		
Miscellaneous	For information of the A.G.'s Office at the Base. Officers and men who have become casuals, been transferred or joined since last report. Place Ypres.	31/07/1915	31/07/1915
Miscellaneous	Field Return		
Miscellaneous	For information of the A.G.'s Office at the Base. Officers and men who have become casuals, been transferred or joined since last report. Place Ypres.	31/07/1915	31/07/1915
Miscellaneous	Field Return		
Miscellaneous	For information of the A.G.'s Office at the Base. Officers and men who have become casuals, been transferred or joined since last report. Place Ypres.	31/07/1915	31/07/1915
Miscellaneous	Field Return		
Miscellaneous	For information of the A.G.'s Office at the Base. Officers and men who have become casuals, been transferred or joined since last report. Place Ypres.	31/07/1915	31/07/1915
Miscellaneous	Field Return		
Miscellaneous	For information of the A.G.'s Office at the Base. Officers and men who have become casuals, been transferred or joined since last report. Place Ypres.	31/07/1915	31/07/1915
Miscellaneous	Field Return		
Miscellaneous	For information of the A.G.'s Office at the Base. Officers and men who have become casuals, been transferred or joined since last report. Place Ypres.	31/07/1915	31/07/1915
Miscellaneous	Field Return		
Miscellaneous	For information of the A.G.'s Office at the Base. Officers and men who have become casuals, been transferred or joined since last report. Place Ypres.	31/07/1915	31/07/1915
Miscellaneous	Field Return		
Miscellaneous	For information of the A.G.'s Office at the Base. Officers and men who have become casuals, been transferred or joined since last report. Place Ypres.	31/07/1915	31/07/1915
Miscellaneous	Field Return	03/08/1915	03/08/1915
Heading	14th Division 8th Bn Rifle Brigade Vol III From 28th Jly To 8 Sept 15		
War Diary	Gingerhead Chateau & Ypres	28/07/1915	29/07/1915
War Diary	Hooge	29/07/1915	31/07/1915
War Diary	Bivouac 1 mile E Of Poperinghe	31/07/1915	02/08/1915
War Diary	Ypres	03/08/1915	10/08/1915
War Diary	Rest Bivouac G.V	11/08/1915	12/08/1915
War Diary	Canal Bank North Ypres	13/08/1915	17/08/1915
War Diary	Canal Bank 1.1.b	18/08/1915	22/08/1915
War Diary	I.4.a & c	23/08/1915	06/09/1915
War Diary	Watou	07/09/1915	08/09/1915
Map	Map		
Miscellaneous	For information of the A.G.'s Office at the Base. Officers and men who have become casuals, been transferred or joined since last report. Place Ypres.	07/08/1915	07/08/1915
Miscellaneous	Field Return	07/08/1915	07/08/1915

Miscellaneous	For information of the A.G.'s Office at the Base. Officers and men who have become casuals, been transferred or joined since last report. Place Ypres.	15/08/1915	15/08/1915
Miscellaneous	Field Return	15/08/1915	15/08/1915
Miscellaneous	For information of the A.G.'s Office at the Base. Officers and men who have become casuals, been transferred or joined since last report. Place Ypres.	21/08/1915	21/08/1915
Miscellaneous	Field Return	21/08/1915	21/08/1915
Miscellaneous	For information of the A.G.'s Office at the Base. Officers and men who have become casuals, been transferred or joined since last report. Place Ypres.	28/08/1915	28/08/1915
Miscellaneous	Field Return	28/08/1918	28/08/1918
Miscellaneous	For information of the A.G.'s Office at the Base. Officers and men who have become casuals, been transferred or joined since last report. Place Ypres.	04/07/1915	04/07/1915
Miscellaneous	Field Return	04/09/1915	04/09/1915
Miscellaneous	For information of the A.G.'s Office at the Base. Officers and men who have become casuals, been transferred or joined since last report. Place Ypres.	04/09/1915	04/09/1915
Miscellaneous	Field Return		
Miscellaneous	C Form (Duplicate) Messages And Signals		
Heading	14th Division 8th Rifle Brigade Vol IV Sept & Oct 15		
War Diary	Watou	09/09/1915	13/09/1915
War Diary	Ypres	14/09/1915	21/09/1915
War Diary	A28.d.9.9.	22/09/1915	25/09/1915
War Diary	H.11.d.9.9	25/09/1915	28/09/1915
War Diary	Trenches	29/09/1915	12/10/1915
Miscellaneous	For information of the A.G.'s Office at the Base. Officers and men who have become casuals, been transferred or joined since last report. Place Ypres.	08/10/1915	08/10/1915
Miscellaneous	Field Return	08/10/1915	08/10/1915
Miscellaneous	For information of the A.G.'s Office at the Base. Officers and men who have become casuals, been transferred or joined since last report. Place Ypres.	08/10/1915	08/10/1915
Miscellaneous	Field Return		
Miscellaneous	For information of the A.G.'s Office at the Base. Officers and men who have become casuals, been transferred or joined since last report. Place Watou.	11/09/1915	11/09/1915
Miscellaneous	Field Return	11/09/1915	11/09/1915
Miscellaneous	For information of the A.G.'s Office at the Base. Officers and men who have become casuals, been transferred or joined since last report. Place Ypres.	18/09/1915	18/09/1915
Miscellaneous	Field Return	18/09/1915	18/09/1915
War Diary	Arras Reserve Billets	09/04/1916	11/04/1916
War Diary	Trenches I.49-I.60	12/04/1916	18/04/1916
War Diary	Wanquetin	19/04/1916	24/04/1916
War Diary	Arras Trenches I49-I.60	25/04/1916	30/04/1916
Miscellaneous	8th Bn Rifle Brigade		
Miscellaneous	8th Battalion The Rifle Brigade Roll Of Officers		
War Diary	Arras	01/05/1916	12/05/1916
War Diary	Maroeuil	12/05/1916	16/05/1916
War Diary	Savy	17/05/1916	21/05/1916
War Diary	Mont St Eloy	22/05/1916	27/05/1916
War Diary	La Targette	27/05/1916	31/05/1916
Miscellaneous	8th Batt. Rifle Brigade		
War Diary	La Targette	01/06/1916	02/06/1916

War Diary	Ecoivres	03/06/1916	09/06/1916
War Diary	Maroeuil	10/06/1916	19/06/1916
War Diary	Ecoivres	20/06/1916	21/06/1916
War Diary	St Nicholas	22/06/1916	27/06/1916
War Diary	Trenches K.1. 102-111	27/06/1916	30/06/1916
Miscellaneous	8th. Battalion The Rifle Brigade List of Casualties for June 1916		
Miscellaneous	8th. Battalion The Rifle Brigade Roll Of Officers	30/06/1916	30/06/1916
Heading	War Diary of 8th Bn. The Rifle Brigade From; 1st July 1916 To 31st July 1916 Volume 15		
War Diary	Trenches E Of Roclincourt K.1.102-111	01/07/1916	03/07/1916
War Diary	Duisans	04/07/1916	09/07/1916
War Diary	Trenches E Of Roclincourt	10/07/1916	15/07/1916
War Diary	St Nicholas	16/07/1916	21/07/1916
War Diary	Trenches E Of Roclincourt	22/07/1916	23/07/1916
War Diary	102-111 Map Ref 51B 1/40,000 Form G.b.c.1 /2.4 To A.30.c.4.5	23/07/1916	27/07/1916
War Diary	Trenches E Of Roclincourt 102-111	28/07/1916	29/07/1916
War Diary	In The March	30/07/1916	31/07/1916
Miscellaneous	8th. Battalion Rifle Brigade Casualties July 1916		
Heading	41st Brigade 14th Division 1/8th Battalion The Rifle Brigade August 1916		
Heading	War Diary of 8th (s) Bn. The Rifle Brigade From: 1st August 1916-To: 31st August, 1916 Volume XVI		
War Diary	In The March	01/08/1916	01/08/1916
War Diary	Lonquevillette	02/08/1916	07/08/1916
War Diary	Dernancourt	08/08/1916	17/08/1916
War Diary	Trenches	18/08/1916	26/08/1916
War Diary	Dernancourt	27/08/1916	30/08/1916
War Diary	Laleu	31/08/1916	31/08/1916
Miscellaneous	8th. Battalion The Rifle Brigade Roll Of Officers		
Miscellaneous	8th. Batt. Rifle Brigade Casualties August 1916		
Heading	War Diary of 8th Bn. The Rifle Brigade From: 1st September, 1916 To 30th September, 1916 Volume XVII		
War Diary	Laleu	01/09/1916	10/09/1916
War Diary	Dornancourt	11/09/1916	11/09/1916
War Diary	Fricourt Camp	12/09/1916	12/09/1916
War Diary	Delville Wood	13/09/1916	15/09/1916
War Diary	Switch Trench	16/09/1916	16/09/1916
War Diary	Fricourt	17/09/1916	17/09/1916
War Diary	Dernancourt	18/09/1916	22/09/1916
War Diary	Lucheux	23/09/1916	26/09/1916
War Diary	Wanquetin	27/09/1916	27/09/1916
War Diary	Riviere	28/09/1916	28/09/1916
War Diary	Grand Rullecourt	30/09/1916	30/09/1916
Miscellaneous	For information of the A.G.'s Office at the Base. Officers and men who have become casuals, been transferred or joined since last report. Place In the Field.		
Miscellaneous	Field Return		
Miscellaneous	For information of the A.G.'s Office at the Base. Officers and men who have become casuals, been transferred or joined since last report.		
Miscellaneous	Field Return		

Miscellaneous	For information of the A.G.'s Office at the Base. Officers and men who have become casuals, been transferred or joined since last report.		
Miscellaneous	Field Return		
Miscellaneous	8th. Battalion The Rifle Brigade		
Miscellaneous	For information of the A.G.'s Office at the Base. Officers and men who have become casuals, been transferred or joined since last report. Place In the Field.		
Miscellaneous	Field Return		
Miscellaneous	For information of the A.G.'s Office at the Base. Officers and men who have become casuals, been transferred or joined since last report.		
Miscellaneous	Field Return		
Miscellaneous	For Information Of The A.G's Office At The Base		
Miscellaneous	Field Return		
Miscellaneous	For information of the A.G.'s Office at the Base. Officers and men who have become casuals, been transferred or joined since last report. Place In the Field.		
Miscellaneous	Field Return		
Miscellaneous	For information of the A.G.'s Office at the Base. Officers and men who have become casuals, been transferred or joined since last report. Place In the Field.		
Miscellaneous	Field Return		
Miscellaneous	8th. Battalion The Rifle Brigade Roll Of Officers	30/09/1916	30/09/1916
Miscellaneous	8th. Battalion The Rifle Brigade Roll Of Officers		
War Diary	War Diary of 8th Bn. The Rifle Brigade From: 1st October, 1916 To 31st October, 1916 Volume XVIII		
War Diary	Riviere	01/10/1916	03/10/1916
War Diary	Trenches A.23.b.7.5	04/10/1916	21/10/1916
War Diary	Riviere	22/10/1916	25/10/1916
War Diary	Berneville	26/10/1916	26/10/1916
War Diary	Grand Rullecourt	27/10/1916	29/10/1916
Miscellaneous	8th. Batt. Rifle Brigade	31/10/1916	31/10/1916
Miscellaneous	8th, Battn. Rifle Brigade		
Heading	War Diary of 8th (S) Bn. The Rifle Brigade From: 1st November,1916 To: 30th November, 1916 Volume 18		
War Diary	Grand Rullecourt	01/11/1916	30/11/1916
Heading	War Diary of 8th Bn The Rifle Brigade 1st To 31st December 1916 Volume 20		
War Diary	Grand Rullecourt	01/12/1916	14/12/1916
War Diary	Beaumetz	15/12/1916	15/12/1916
War Diary	Wailly	16/12/1916	21/12/1916
War Diary	Riviere	22/12/1916	27/12/1916
War Diary	F. 2 Sector	28/12/1916	31/12/1916
Miscellaneous	8th Bn. The Rifle Brigade Roll Of Officers	31/12/1916	31/12/1916
Miscellaneous	8th Battn. The Rifle Brigade		
Heading	War Diary of 8th (S), Bn The Rifle Brigade From: 1st January, 1917 To: 31st January, 1917 Volume 20		
War Diary	Trenches R.23.51c	01/01/1917	03/01/1917
War Diary	Beaumetz	04/01/1917	09/01/1917
War Diary	Trenches R23 (51c)	10/01/1917	15/01/1917
War Diary	Riviere	16/01/1917	17/01/1917
War Diary	Trenches R 23 (51c)	25/01/1917	27/01/1917
War Diary	Simencourt	28/01/1917	31/01/1917
Miscellaneous	8th Battn. The Rifle Brigade		
Miscellaneous	8th Battn. The Rifle Brigade List of Officers Serving	31/01/1917	31/01/1917

Heading	War Diary of 8th (S) Bn. The Rifle Brigade From: 1st February, 1917 To: 28th February, 1917 Volume XXII		
War Diary	Simencourt	01/02/1917	01/02/1917
War Diary	Grand Rullecourt	02/02/1917	28/02/1917
Miscellaneous	Please Tell All Ranks Now Sorry I Was To Have No Opportunity Of Wishing Them "Good Bye"		
Miscellaneous	8th Bn. The Rifle Brigade Roll Of Officers	28/02/1917	28/02/1917
Heading	War Diary of 8th (S) Bn. The Rifle Brigade From: 1st March 1917 To: 31st March 1917 Volume XXIII		
War Diary	Grand Rullecourt	01/03/1917	16/03/1917
War Diary	Gouy	17/03/1917	18/03/1917
War Diary	Dainville	19/03/1917	22/03/1917
War Diary	Arras	23/03/1917	24/03/1917
War Diary	Trenches G35.d.3.6 51b 3ws	25/03/1917	28/03/1917
War Diary	Ronville Caves	29/03/1917	31/03/1917
Miscellaneous	8th Bn. The Rifle Brigade	31/03/1917	31/03/1917
Heading	War Diary of 8th Bn. Rifle Brigade From April 1st 1917 To April 30th 1917 Volume 24		
War Diary	Ronville Caves (arras)	01/04/1917	01/04/1917
War Diary	Trenches G.35.d.3.6.51b	02/04/1917	03/04/1917
War Diary	Arras	04/04/1917	08/04/1917
War Diary	G.35.d.3.6 51b	09/04/1917	10/04/1917
War Diary	Harp	10/04/1917	10/04/1917
War Diary	West Of Wancourt	10/04/1917	12/04/1917
War Diary	Arras	13/04/1917	13/04/1917
War Diary	Monchiet	14/04/1917	14/04/1917
War Diary	Grand Rullecourt	15/04/1917	23/04/1917
War Diary	La Cauchie	24/04/1917	24/04/1917
War Diary	Blairville	25/04/1917	26/04/1917
War Diary	N.7.b.2.2 Sheet 51b S.W	27/04/1917	29/04/1917
War Diary	Trenches N7b2.2 Sheet 51b S.W	30/04/1917	30/04/1917
Miscellaneous	8th Bn. Rifle Bde		
Miscellaneous	8th Bn. Rifle Bde	30/04/1917	30/04/1917
War Diary	N.7.b.2.2 (51B France) O.19.C.2.9	01/05/1917	03/05/1917
War Diary	Nepal Tr.	04/05/1917	04/05/1917
War Diary	N.7.b.2.2	05/05/1917	13/05/1917
War Diary	Telegraph Hill	14/05/1917	14/05/1917
War Diary	N.24.c.0.5 (51b)	15/05/1917	19/05/1917
War Diary	O19.2.3	20/05/1917	20/05/1917
War Diary	O19.2.3 (51b)	21/05/1917	24/05/1917
War Diary	N.24.c.0.5	25/05/1917	25/05/1917
War Diary	Rest Camp M.10.d. (51b)	26/05/1917	31/05/1917
Miscellaneous	8th Bn. The Rifle Brigade	31/05/1917	31/05/1917
War Diary	M 10.d (51b)	01/06/1917	04/06/1917
War Diary	N7.b.2.2 (51b)	05/06/1917	11/06/1917
War Diary	Monchiet	12/06/1917	12/06/1917
War Diary	Laherliere	13/06/1917	13/06/1917
War Diary	Bertrancourt	14/06/1917	30/06/1917
Miscellaneous	8th Bn The Rifle Brigade	01/06/1917	01/06/1917
Miscellaneous	8th Bn. The Rifle Brigade	30/06/1917	30/06/1917
Miscellaneous	8th Bn. The Rifle Brigade Roll Of Officers	30/06/1917	30/06/1917
War Diary	Bertrancourt (Somme)	01/07/1917	07/07/1917
War Diary	Terramesnil	10/07/1917	11/07/1917
War Diary	Berthen	12/07/1917	31/07/1917
Miscellaneous	8th Bn. The Rifle Brigade Roll Of Officers On Strength	31/07/1917	31/07/1917
Miscellaneous	8th Bn. The Rifle Brigade Casualties	31/07/1917	31/07/1917

Heading	War Diary of 8th (S) Bn,, The Rifle Brigade From : 1st August 1917 To: 31st August, 1917 Volume XXVIII		
War Diary	Berthen	01/08/1917	05/08/1917
War Diary	Hondeghem Area	06/08/1917	07/08/1917
War Diary	Hazebrouck Area	08/08/1917	15/08/1917
War Diary	Dickiebusch	16/08/1917	18/08/1917
War Diary	Zillebeke	19/08/1917	20/08/1917
War Diary	Dickiebusch	21/08/1917	24/08/1917
War Diary	Inverness Copse	24/08/1917	27/08/1917
War Diary	Dickiebusch	28/08/1917	28/08/1917
War Diary	Meteren	29/08/1917	31/08/1917
Miscellaneous	8th. Bn. The Rifle Brigade	31/08/1917	31/08/1917
War Diary	Meteren	01/09/1917	02/09/1917
War Diary	Neuve Eglise	03/09/1917	10/09/1917
War Diary	Trenches N.E. of Messines	11/09/1917	19/09/1917
War Diary	Support N.E. Messines	20/09/1917	20/09/1917
War Diary	Neuve Eglise	21/09/1917	30/09/1917
Miscellaneous	8th Bn. The Rifle Brigade Appendix To War Diary	30/09/1917	30/09/1917
War Diary	Neuve Eglise	01/10/1917	05/10/1917
War Diary	Reninghelst	06/10/1917	08/10/1917
War Diary	Dickiebusch Area	09/10/1917	10/10/1917
War Diary	Stirling Castle (Bde Reserve)	11/10/1917	11/10/1917
War Diary	Strling Castle	12/10/1917	16/10/1917
War Diary	Bedford House	17/10/1917	19/10/1917
War Diary	Ridge Wood	20/10/1917	21/10/1917
War Diary	Reninghelst	22/10/1917	22/10/1917
War Diary	Meteren	23/10/1917	31/10/1917
Miscellaneous	8th Bn, The Rifle Brigade Appendix To War Diary-October 1917 Roll Of Officers	01/11/1917	01/11/1917
Miscellaneous	8th Bn, The Rifle Brigade Appendix To War Diary-October 1917		
War Diary	Meteren	01/11/1917	10/11/1917
War Diary	St Martin-Au-Laert	11/11/1917	29/11/1917
War Diary	Brandhoek	30/11/1917	30/11/1917
Miscellaneous	8th Bn. The Rifle Brigade Appendix To War Diary-November 1917 Roll Of Officers	30/11/1917	30/11/1917
War Diary	Brandhoek	01/12/1917	01/12/1917
War Diary	Passchendaele	02/12/1917	08/12/1917
War Diary	Brandhoek	09/12/1917	17/12/1917
War Diary	Nr Brandhoek	18/12/1917	19/12/1917
War Diary	Nr St Jean	20/12/1917	22/12/1917
War Diary	Nr Passchendaele	22/12/1917	27/12/1917
War Diary	Esquerdes	28/12/1917	31/12/1917
Miscellaneous	8th. Bn. The Rifle Brigade Appendix To War Diary		
Miscellaneous	8th. Bn. The Rifle Brigade Appendix To War Diary Roll Of Officers	31/12/1917	31/12/1917
War Diary	Esquerdes	01/01/1918	02/01/1918
War Diary	Sailley Le Sec	03/01/1918	21/01/1918
War Diary	Mezieres	22/01/1918	22/01/1918
War Diary	Roye	23/01/1918	23/01/1918
War Diary	Beines	24/01/1918	24/01/1918
War Diary	Clastres	25/01/1918	25/01/1918
War Diary	Urvillers	26/01/1918	27/01/1918
War Diary	Line Urvillers	28/01/1918	31/01/1918
Miscellaneous	Appendix to War Diary 8th Bn, The Rifle Brigade	31/01/1918	31/01/1918
Miscellaneous	8th. Bn. The Rifle Brigade	31/01/1918	31/01/1918

War Diary	Trenches Near Itancourt	01/02/1918	03/02/1918
War Diary	Clastres	04/02/1918	08/02/1918
War Diary	Trenches Near Itancourt	09/02/1918	19/02/1918
War Diary	Itancourt	20/02/1918	21/02/1918
War Diary	Essigny	22/02/1918	28/02/1918
Miscellaneous	8th Bn. The Rifle Brigade	28/02/1918	28/02/1918
Heading	41st Brigade 14th Division 8th Battalion The Rifle Brigade March 1918		
Heading	War Diary of 8th Bn. The Rifle Brigade From :1st March 1918 To : 31st March 1918 Volume XXXVI		
War Diary	Essigny	01/03/1918	05/03/1918
War Diary	Trenches Urvillers	06/03/1918	13/03/1918
War Diary	Clastres	14/03/1918	18/03/1918
Heading	8th Rifle Brigade		
War Diary	Clastres	19/03/1918	21/03/1918
War Diary	Jussy	22/03/1918	22/03/1918
War Diary	Flavy	23/03/1918	23/03/1918
War Diary	Cugny	24/03/1918	24/03/1918
War Diary	Beines	24/03/1918	24/03/1918
War Diary	La Vignette	25/03/1918	25/03/1918
War Diary	Thiescourt	25/03/1918	26/03/1918
War Diary	Estrees St Denis	27/03/1918	27/03/1918
War Diary	Gournay	28/03/1918	28/03/1918
War Diary	Nogent	29/03/1918	29/03/1918
War Diary	Hebecourt	30/03/1918	30/03/1918
War Diary	Vers	31/03/1918	31/03/1918
Heading	41st Inf. Bde. 14th Div War Diary 8th Battn The Rifle Brigade April 1918		
Heading	War Diary of 8th (S) Bn, The Rifle Brigade From : 1st April 1918 To: 30th April 1918 Volume Xxxvi		
War Diary	Hourges	01/04/1918	02/04/1918
War Diary	Blangy	03/04/1918	03/04/1918
War Diary	Bois de' Aceroche	04/04/1918	04/04/1918
War Diary	Aubigny	05/04/1918	07/04/1918
War Diary	St Fucien	08/04/1918	12/04/1918
War Diary	Coupele Vieille	12/04/1918	13/04/1918
War Diary	Lisbourg	14/04/1918	18/04/1918
War Diary	Sains Les Fressin	18/04/1918	23/04/1918
War Diary	Fressin	24/04/1918	26/04/1918
War Diary	Guarbecque	26/04/1918	27/04/1918
War Diary	Lisbourg	28/04/1918	28/04/1918
War Diary	Fressin	29/04/1918	30/04/1918
Heading	War Diary of 8th (S) Bn, The Rifle Brigade From:1st May 1918 To: 31st May, 1918 Volume XxXVII		
War Diary	Fressin	01/05/1918	01/05/1918
War Diary	Embry	02/05/1918	14/05/1918
War Diary	Steenbecque	15/05/1918	27/06/1918
War Diary	Bernieulles	27/06/1918	30/06/1918
Miscellaneous	To Brig-Gen R.C. Maclachlan , D.S.O.		
War Diary	Bernieulles	01/07/1918	17/07/1918
War Diary	Riviere	18/07/1918	21/07/1918
War Diary	Trenches R 23 (51c)	22/07/1918	24/07/1918
War Diary	Bernieulles (Pas-de-C)	18/07/1918	27/07/1918
War Diary	Bernieulles (P-De-C)	28/07/1918	31/07/1918
Miscellaneous	8th Bn. The Rifle Brigade Appendix To War Diary-July 1918	31/07/1918	31/07/1918

Miscellaneous	D.A.G 3rd Echelon	31/07/1918	31/07/1918

14TH DIVISION
41ST INFY BDE

8TH BN RIFLE BDE

MAY 1915-JLY 1918

[illegible] 3 8 18

41

14th Division 121/5496

8th Rifle Brigade

Vol I. 20.5 — 29.6.15

July '18

Instructions regarding War Diaries and Intelligence Summaries are contained in F. S. Regs., Part II. and the Staff Manual respectively. Title pages will be prepared in manuscript.

WAR DIARY 8th Bn Rifle Brigade

or

~~INTELLIGENCE SUMMARY.~~

(Erase heading not required.)

Army Form C. 2118.

Place	Date	Hour	Summary of Events and Information	Remarks and references to Appendices
[illegible]	20.5.15	3am	[illegible] arrived in camp. 28 officers [illegible] other ranks	
PONT de BRIQUES	21.5.15	12 noon	as above left for WATTEN. found transport [illegible] 3 officers 103 other ranks	
WATTEN	21.5.15	5am	marched to MERCKEGHEM arriving at 8am. 31 officers 925 other ranks	
MERCKEGHEM	22.5.15	9.30am	Bde Route March	
"	23.5.15		Church Parade, clear up billets	
"	24.5.15	9.30	Bde Route March	
"	25.5.15		Bn at disposal of [illegible] coys	
"	26.5.15		Bn at disposal of [illegible] coys	
"	26.5.15	7.30am	Bn marched to ZUYTPEENE in Brigade and billetted	
ZUYTPEENE	27.5.15	8am	Bn marched to LE COZ de PAILLE [illegible] miles N of FLETRE for night.	
FLETRE	28.5.15	9am	Bn marched to billets 1 mile east of BAILLEUL and billetted	
BAILLEUL.	29.5.	7.15pm	B & C Coys started four days instructional tour in trenches, attached to 5th North South Staffs respectively	
			A & D coys being instructed by 6th North South Staffords	
	30.5.		As above. [illegible] wounded in head	
	31.5.		As above. Rfn Cavanagh [illegible] wounded in [illegible]	
	1.6.		B & C coys march out at 11.30pm relieved by 6th North Staffs with A & D coys	
	2.6		A & D coys tour of instruction in trenches. Remainder digging G.H.Q line	
	3.6		— — —	
	4.6			
	5.6			
	6.6	8am	Bn marched to [illegible] HUTS near LA CLYTTE.	
[illegible] HUTS.	7.6	8pm	Bn marched into trenches and took over from 85th Bde	
	8.6		In trenches. [illegible] wounded	
	9.6		[illegible] casualties. Rfn [illegible] Rfn [illegible] killed. [illegible]	
	10.6		Bn marched into DICKEBUSH and [illegible] Bde Reserve.	

1577 Wt. W10791/1773 500,000 1/15 D. D. & L. A.D.S.S./Forms/C. 2118.

Instructions regarding War Diaries and Intelligence Summaries are contained in F. S. Regs., Part II. and the Staff Manual respectively. Title pages will be prepared in manuscript.

WAR DIARY
or
INTELLIGENCE SUMMARY.
(Erase heading not required.)

Army Form C. 2118.

Place	Date	Hour	Summary of Events and Information	Remarks and references to Appendices
PIONEER FM.	11.6.15		Bn in Brigade Reserve resting. Had to find digging party for 9th K.R.R. in N10. Lt Carson Walton and Sgt Percy [?] shot by the same bullet whilst lying behind the trench with their digging party.	
	12.6.15		Bn handed over to 1st Bn Cheshire Regt who marched in about 600 strong, made up with fresh drafts from England, commanded by Capt W. B. Ramsden brought in from S. W. Borderers.	
		7pm	Bn marched in to ROZENHILL HUTS	
ROZENHILL HUTS.	13.6.15		Church parade under Brigade chaplain in wood in morning. Remainder of morning spent in cleaning up camp, which was very dirty, water very difficult to obtain.	
	14.6.15		Marched into billets about 2 miles west of POPERINGHE. Billets very scarce half the Bn lying out. LANCASHIRE Yeomanry and 14th Divisional Cyclist Company billeted next us further west.	
	15.6.15		C.O. warned to reconnoitre trenches held by 3rd Division east of YPRES. Capts Ballaine [?] and Cavendish also sent up for this later.	
		9pm	Bn with remainder of Brigade marched into C camp huts 1 mile S.W. of VLAMERTINGHE arrived there at midnight. Bivouaced for the remainder of night. Heavy bombardment,	
	16.6.15		preliminary to attack by 3rd Division, commenced by guns all round at 2.50am continued till 4.15am.	
		?pm [?]	Bn warned to be ready to move at a moments notice.	
		12.20pm [?]	Bn ordered to proceed into G.H.Q. line just east of YPRES.	

Instructions regarding War Diaries and Intelligence Summaries are contained in F. S. Regs., Part II. and the Staff Manual respectively. Title pages will be prepared in manuscript.

WAR DIARY
or
INTELLIGENCE SUMMARY.
(Erase heading not required.)

Army Form C. 2118.

Place	Date	Hour	Summary of Events and Information	Remarks and references to Appendices
			On arrival there at 9pm found 9th RB and 5th Ox and Bucks still in occupation, took over temporary trenches on their right. All transport and machine guns of Brigade crowded together unloading in KRUISTRAAT for 1 hour. No casualties.	
		4pm	14th Bde moved up to reinforce 3rd Div attack, Bn took over 9th RB and Ox + Bucks trenches.	
		11pm	Warned to stand by in case reinforcements required, not called out.	
	17.6.15		In G.H.Q. line in Reserve. Very good line of trenches.	
	18.6.15		8th Bn K.R.R. came into trenches on our right instead of holding railway line on our left.	
			7th RB holding railway behind 7th K.R.R., who were in support to us.	
	18.6.15		A quiet day except for occasional shelling which did no damage. Stood by all night in case of attack, 14th Bde taken out of line in early morning.	
	19.6.15		Quiet day till 3pm when 2 whizz bangs came over, burst over HdQrs, killed 1 wounded 3, including Sergeant Major Fry hit in elbow.	
		9pm	Bn marched out to 'D' huts west of VLAMERTINGHE.	
	20.6.15	10am	Bn marched into A + B huts at VLAMERTINGHE, accommodation scarce in huts, 50 extra shelters issued and 10 blankets per coy for shelters. Camp very dirty, [illegible].	
			Parade Service under Bde chaplain 2.45 pm.	
			Whizz bangs over camp in afternoon, pitched very near 8th K.R.R. huts without hitting.	
			Bn digging shelter trenches in case of fire. Found water 3ft from surface.	
	21.6.15		Quiet day. Improving shelter trenches. Whizz bangs over in afternoon. No damage	

Instructions regarding War Diaries and Intelligence Summaries are contained in F. S. Regs., Part II. and the Staff Manual respectively. Title pages will be prepared in manuscript.

WAR DIARY
or
INTELLIGENCE SUMMARY.
(Erase heading not required.)

Army Form C. 2118.

Place	Date	Hour	Summary of Events and Information	Remarks and references to Appendices
	22.6.15		150 men per coy given baths at RHENINGHELST. Water supply to the drum before 3rd & 4th coys came up. Improving shelter trenches.	
	23.6.15		Bn. Route march under Major Tod via OUDERDOM. – RHENINGHELST. No men out. Dress skeleton marching order. Shelled in camp in the afternoon.	
	24.6.15		Companies at disposal of OC coys in camp.	
	25.6.15		Companies at disposal of OC coys all day. Bn. under Major Tod detailed by RE for digging in G H 2 line east of YPRES in the evening. Owing to vague orders 1½ coys did not commence digging before daylight when they had to come home. Camp shelled at midnight. CO. Adjt. 3 OC coys went up into trenches by HOOGE to inspect with a view to taking over.	
	26.6.15		Route march by coys. Remaining officers commanding coys 2nd in command, signalling officer went up to trenches north of HOOGE held by Somerset Bn and DCLI Bn of 14th Brigade. Trenches very wet and some dangerous points.	
	27.6.15		Bn. Church Parade under Bde Chaplain. Digging communication trench from G H 2 line to support trenches at night. Got in 3 hours work before dawn, but it took 2 hours to get them actually starting, distance about ¾ mile from MENIN Gate in YPRES.	
	28.6.15		Companies using bayonet fighting equipment, sand bags in trenches. 3 casualties from H.E. shells in camp through men sitting on parapet instead of dug out.	
	29.6.15		Bn. moved up into trenches ½ mile N of HOOGE village and took over from 2 coys of Somerset L.I. in front line, and 2 coys of Y.L.I. in G H 2 line. Left section of 14th Brigade. Trenches dry and had a lot of work put into them by Somersets. Germans still lying about nearly a fortnight old, does not help sanitation. 7th K.R.R.C. on our right, 8th R.B. holds a left. Telephone communication very doubtful, and always being cut.	

W. M. Parker Capt Adjt
9th Bn Rifle Bde

Army Form B. 213.

FIELD RETURN.

No. of Report 1

(To be furnished by all arms, services, and departments to the A. G.'s Office at the Base in accordance with Field Service Regulations, Part II.)

23-5-15. Date.

RETURN showing numbers RATIONED by, and Transport on charge of, 8th Btn. Rifle Bde at MERCKEGHAM

Detail	Personnel: Officers	Personnel: Other ranks	Personnel: Natives	Animals: Horses: Riding	Horses: Draught	Horses: Heavy Draught	Horses: Pack	Mules: Large	Mules: Small	Camels	Oxen	Guns, carriages, and limbers and transport vehicles: ~~Guns, carriages and~~ limbers, G.S.	~~showing description~~ Tools, M.G.	Ammunition wagons and limbers	Machine guns	Aircraft, showing description	Horsed: 4 Wheeled	Horsed: 2 Wheeled	Mechanical: Motor Cars	Tractors	Lorries, showing description	Trucks, showing description	Trailers	Motor Bicycles	Bicycles	Remarks
Effective Strength of Unit	31.	919	-	14.		9.	9.	34	Nil.	Nil	Nil	2	2	7.	2.	Nil.	6. ✱	2.	Nil	Nil	Nil.	Nil.	Nil	Nil	9.	✱ 2 Water Carts limbered 4 Travelling Kitchens.
Details, *by Arms* attached to unit as in War Establishment:— (Includes Bde M.G. Officer)																										
R.A.M.C.	1.																									
A.O.C.		1.																								
Interpreter			1.																							
A.S.C.		4																								
Total	32.	925																							9.	
War Establishment	30.	991.		14.		9.	9.	34				2.	2.	7.	2.		6	2.							9.	
✱ Wanting to complete	/	61.																								
Surplus	2	✓	✓	✓		✓	✓	✓				✓	✓	✓	✓		✓	✓							✓	
*Attached (not to include the details shown above)	✓	✓	✓																							
Civilians:— Employed with the Unit																										
Accompanying the Unit	✓	✓	✓																							
TOTAL RATIONED ...	30.	921.		14	✓	9.	9.	34	✓	✓	✓															

* In the case of field ambulances, hospitals or depôts, the number of patients are to be included here, the names being shown in A.F.A. 36.

Signature of Commander.

Date of Despatch.

(K 11859) W. & Co., Ltd. Wt. w6005—894 500,000 10/14 Forms B. 213/5

✱ O.R.S. - at base. 3 - Div. Train 2 Bde Signalling } Not replaced.

For information of the A.G.'s Office at the Base.

Officers and men who have become casuals, been transferred or joined since last report.

Place ______________________ Date ______________________

Regtl. Number	Rank	Name	Corps	Nature of casualty, or name of unit from or to which transferred	Date of being struck off or coming on the ration return	Remarks*
	Lieut.	Squire	8th Btn Rifle Bde	Bde Machine Gun Officer – 41st Bde		

*State whether absence is of a permanent or temporary nature, adding, in the case of casuals from wounds or disease, any available information for communication to the relatives.

FIELD RETURN.

Army Form B. 213.

No. of Report 2.

(To be furnished by all arms, services, and departments to the A. G.'s Office at the Base in accordance with Field Service Regulations, Part II.)

30 - 5 - 15. Date.

RETURN showing numbers RATIONED by, and Transport on charge of, 8th Bn Rifle Bde. at

Detail	Personnel: Officers	Personnel: Other ranks	Personnel: Natives	Animals: Horses: Riding	Animals: Horses: Draught	Animals: Horses: Heavy Draught	Animals: Horses: Pack	Animals: Mules: Large	Animals: Mules: Small	Animals: Camels	Animals: Oxen	Guns, carriages and limbers, showing description	Ammunition wagons and limbers	Machine guns	Aircraft, showing description	Horsed: 4 Wheeled	Horsed: 2 Wheeled	Mechanical: Motor Cars	Mechanical: Tractors	Mechanical: Lorries, showing description	Mechanical: Trucks, showing description	Mechanical: Trailers	Motor Bicycles	Bicycles	Remarks
(Does not include Bde. M.G. Officer.) Effective Strength of Unit Details, *by Arms* attached to unit as in War Establishment:—	30	905		14	-	9	9	34	-	—	—	Tools. 2. M.G. 2.	7	2.	-	6 *	2.	-	-	-	-	-	-	9.	X 2 Water Carts limbered, 4 Travelling Kitchens.
R.A.M.C.	1.																								
A.O.C.		1.																							
Interpreter			1.																						
Total	31.	907.		14	-	9	9	34	-	-	-	2. 2.	7	2	-	6	2.	-	-	-	-	-	-	9.	
War Establishment	30.	991.		14	-	9.	9.	34	-	-	-	2. 2.	7.	2	-	6	2	.	.	-	-	-	-	9.	
Wanting to complete	-	84.	-	-	-	-	-	-	-	-	-	- -	-	-	-	-	-	-	-	-	-	-	-	-	
Surplus	1.	-	-	-	-	-	-	-	-	-	-	- -	-	-	-	-	-	-	-	-	-	-	-	-	
(Hospital 9. Attached 8 A.S.C. 6 / 23.) *Attached (not to include the details shown above)																									
Civilians:— Employed with the Unit																									
(not included) Accompanying the Unit																									
TOTAL RATIONED ...																									

* In the case of field ambulances, hospitals or depôts, the number of patients are to be included here, the names being shown in A.F.A. 36.

Signature of Commander.

Date of Despatch.

(K 11859) W. & Co., Ltd. Wt. w6005—894 500,000 10/14 Forms B. 213 / 5

For information of the A.G.'s Office at the Base.

Officers and men who have become casuals, been transferred or joined since last report.

Place ______________________ Date ______________________

Regtl. Number	Rank	Name	Corps	Nature of casualty, or name of unit from or to which transferred	Date of being struck off or coming on the ration return	Remarks*
S. 5273	Sergt.	Kerr.	A. Coy. 8th R.B	Hospital.	25-5-15 (rows S. 5273 to B. 3056)	
S. 1612.	Rfn.	Tunworth.	— do —	— do —		
S. 7691.	"	Killworth	"C" Coy. 8th R.B	— do —		
S. 7582.	"	Kendal.	— do —	— do —		
B. 3056.	"	Pickering	— do —	— do —		
S. 5225	"	Jenner.	"A" Coy. 8th R.B	— do —	29-5-15.	
B. 2046.	"	Jann.	"C" — " — 8th R.B.	— do —	28-5-15.	
B. 1505.	"	Adams.	— do —	— do —	— " —	
B. 2047.	"	Bannerman	— do —	— do —	— " —	

*State whether absence is of a permanent or temporary nature, adding, in the case of casuals from wounds or disease, any available information for communication to the relatives.

Army Form B. 213.

FIELD RETURN.

No. of Report 3

(To be furnished by all arms, services, and departments to the A. G.'s Office at the Base in accordance with Field Service Regulations, Part II.)

June 5th 15 Date.

RETURN showing numbers RATIONED by, and Transport on charge of, 8th Batt Rifle Brigade at Bailleul

Detail	Personnel			Animals								Guns, carriages, and limbers and transport vehicles													Remarks
				Horses				Mules								Horsed		Mechanical							
	Officers	Other ranks	Natives	Riding	Draught	Heavy Draught	Pack	Large	Small	Camels	Oxen	Guns, carriages and limbers, showing, description	Ammunition wagons and limbers	Machine guns	Aircraft, showing description	4 Wheeled	2 Wheeled	Motor Cars	Tractors	Lorries, showing description	Trucks, showing description	Trailers	Motor Bicycles	Bicycles	
Effective Strength of Unit	30	902		14		9	9	34				Tools 2 M.G. 2	7	2		6*	2							9	* 2 Water carts limbered 4 Travelling kitchens
Details, *by Arms* attached to unit as in War Establishment:—																									
R.A.M.C	1																								
A.O.C		1																							
Interpreter			1																						
Total	31	904		14		9	9	34				2 2	7	2		6	2							9	
War Establishment	30	991		14		9	9	34				2 2	7	2		6	2							9	
Wanting to complete	-	64																							
Surplus	1																								
*Attached (not to include the details shown above)																									
Civilians:—																									
Employed with the Unit																									
Accompanying the Unit																									
TOTAL RATIONED ...	31	904		14		9	9	34																	

* In the case of field ambulances, hospitals or depôts, the number of patients are to be included here, the names being shown in A.F.A. 36.

Signature of Commander.

Date of Despatch.

(K11859) W. & Co., Ltd. Wt. w6005—894 500,000 10/14 Forms B. 213 / 5

For information of the A.G.'s Office at the Base.

Officers and men who have become casuals, been transferred or joined since last report.

Place ____________________ Date ____________________

Regtl. Number	Rank	Name	Corps	Nature of casualty, or name of unit from or to which transferred	Date of being struck off or coming on the ration return	Remarks*
S. 5273	Sergt.	Kerr.	A. Coy. 8th R.B.	Hospital.	25-5-15	
S. 1612	Rfn.	Tusworth.	— do —	— do —		
S. 7691.	"	Killworth.	"C" Coy. 8th R.B.	— do —		
S. 7582.	"	Kendal.	— do —	— do —		
B. 3056	"	Pickering	— do —	— do —		
S. 5225	"	Jenner.	"A" Coy. 8th R.B.	— do —	29-5-15	
B. 2046	"	Jann.	"C" — " — 8th R.B.	— do —	28-5-15	
B. 1505	"	Adams.	— do —	— do —	— " —	
B. 2047	"	Bannerman	— do —	— do —	— " —	

*State whether absence is of a permanent or temporary nature, adding, in the case of casuals from wounds or disease, any available information for communication to the relatives.

Army Form B. 213.

FIELD RETURN.

No. of Report 4.

(To be furnished by all arms, services, and departments to the A. G.'s Office at the Base in accordance with Field Service Regulations, Part II.)

Date. June 12th 1915.

RETURN showing numbers RATIONED by, and Transport on charge of, 8th Bn. Rifle Bde. at

Detail	Personnel: Officers	Personnel: Other ranks	Personnel: Natives	Animals: Horses: Riding	Horses: Draught	Horses: Heavy Draught	Horses: Pack	Mules: Large	Mules: Small	Camels	Oxen	Guns, carriages and limbers and transport vehicles: Guns, carriages and limbers, showing, description	Ammunition wagons and limbers	Machine guns	Aircraft, showing description	Horsed: 4 Wheeled	Horsed: 2 Wheeled	Mechanical: Motor Cars	Tractors	Lorries, showing description	Trucks, showing description	Trailers	Motor Bicycles	Bicycles	Remarks
Effective Strength of Unit	28.	890	-	14	-	9.	9.	34	-	-		Tools. 2. M.G. 2.	7.	2.	-	6 *	2	-	-	-	-	-	-	9	* 2 Watercarts. Limbered. 4 Travelling Kitchens.
Details, *by Arms* attached to unit as in War Establishment:— R.A.M.C.	1.																								
A.O.C.		1.																							
Interpreter			2.																						
Total	29.	893.																							
War Establishment	30.	991.		14	-	9.	9.	34	-	-	-	2. 2.	7.	2.	-	6	2							9.	
Wanting to complete		68.																							
Surplus																									
*Attached (not to include the details shown above)																									
Civilians:— Employed with the Unit																									
Accompanying the Unit																									
TOTAL RATIONED ...	29	893.		14		9.	9.	34				2. 2.	7.	2.	-	6	2							9.	

* In the case of field ambulances, hospitals or depôts, the number of patients are to be included here, the names being shown in A.F.A. 36.

(K 11859) W. & Co., Ltd. Wt. w6005—894 500,000 10/14 Forms B. 213 / 5

Signature of Commander.

Date of Despatch.

For information of the A.G.'s Office at the Base.

Officers and men who have become casuals, been transferred or joined since last report.

Place Pioneer Farm. Date June 12th 1915.

Regtl. Number	Rank*	Name	Corps	Nature of casualty, or name of unit from or to which transferred	Date of being struck off or coming on the ration return	Remarks*
B.227	Rfn.	Lansdowne	8th Rifle Bde	G.S.W. Back	5-6-15	Serious
S.1485	"	Twigg A.	—do—	— Left Lung	8-6-15	Dangerous
S.1111	"	Symmons W.	—do—	— Right side & ribs	—do—	Serious
B.2602	"	Marshall	—do—	— Left breast	—do—	Slight
B.2531	"	Demant	—do—	Shrapnel Scalp	—do—	Dangerous
B.359	Corpl.	Richards	—do—	G.S.W. ankle & thigh	9-6-15	Serious
B.210	Rfn.	House	—do—	Killed in action	10-6-15	
B.1805	"	Morris	—do—	—do—	—do—	
B.549	"	Westall	—do—	G.S.W. Left shoulder	9-6-15	Serious
B.2978	"	Hartley E.	—do—	— Buttock	10-6-15	Serious
B.129	"	Haydon J.	—do—	— Right side	11-6-15	Serious
S.1727	L/Corpl.	Elliot G.	—do—	— Shoulder	—do—	Serious
B.3196	~~A/Corpl.~~ Sgt.	Lever	—do—	— Foot	12-6-15	Serious
	2/Lieut.	Hooker A.A.	—do—	— Left shoulder	8-6-15	Serious
	—do—	Walton Lawson	—do—	— Right Knee	12-6-15	Serious
	Captain	Cavendish A.T.C.	—do—	To Hospital	7-6-15	
				From —"—	9-6-15	
S.815	Rfn.	Hodges R.	—do—	To Hospital	7-6-15	
				From —do—	10-6-15	
B.1970	Corpl.	Hughes R.	—do—	To Hospital	6-6-15	
				From —	9-6-15	
	Pre. Sgt.	Etienne Maine			11-6-15	
B.2030	Rfn.	Windebank A.	—do—	From Hospital	12-6-15	

*State whether absence is of a permanent or temporary nature, adding, in the case of casuals from wounds or disease, any available information for communication to the relatives.

No. of Report 5.

FIELD RETURN.

Army Form B. 213.

(To be furnished by all arms, services, and departments to the A. G.'s Office at the Base in accordance with Field Service Regulations, Part II.)

19 - 6 - 15. Date.

RETURN showing numbers RATIONED by, and Transport on charge of, 8th Battalion Rifle Bde. at

Detail	Personnel: Officers	Personnel: Other ranks	Personnel: Natives	Animals: Horses: Riding	Horses: Draught	Horses: Heavy Draught	Horses: Pack	Mules: Large	Mules: Small	Camels	Oxen	Guns, carriages and limbers, showing, description	Ammunition wagons and limbers	Machine guns	Aircraft, showing description	Horsed: 4 Wheeled	Horsed: 2 Wheeled	Mechanical: Motor Cars	Mechanical: Tractors	Mechanical: Lorries, showing description	Mechanical: Trucks, showing description	Mechanical: Trailers	Motor Bicycles	Bicycles	Remarks
Effective Strength of Unit	28	880.		14.		8.	9.	34	/	/	/	Tools 2. T.A. 2.	7.	2.	/	6*	4	/	/	/	/	/	/	9	*4 Travelling Kitchen. 2 Baggage.
Details, *by Arms* attached to unit as in War Establishment:— R.A.M.C.	1.																								
A.O.C.		1.																							
Interpreter			1																						
A.S.C.		2				4										2.									Blanket Wagons.
Total	29.	884.																							
War Establishment	30.	991.		14		9.	9.	34				2. 2.	7.	2.		6	2							9	
Wanting to complete	-	72.																							
Surplus																									
*Attached (not to include the details shown above)																									
Civilians:— Employed with the Unit																									
Accompanying the Unit																									
TOTAL RATIONED ...																									

(Margin note beside Total / War Establishment / Wanting to complete: Does not include Wounded & sick not evacuated & attached men)

* In the case of field ambulances, hospitals or depôts, the number of patients are to be included here, the names being shown in A.F.A. 36.

Signature of Commander.

Date of Despatch.

(K 11859) W. & Co., Ltd. Wt. w6605—894 500,040 10/14 Forms B. 213 / 5

For information of the A.G.'s Office at the Base.

Officers and men who have become casuals, been transferred or joined since last report.

Place ______________________ Date 19-6-15.

Regtl. Number	Rank	Name	Corps	Nature of casualty, or name of unit from or to which transferred	Date of being struck off or coming on the ration return	Remarks*
543.	Rifleman	Kennett.	8th Rifle Bde.	Shrapnel Shoulder.	16-6-15.	Slight.
5159.	"	Britten.	-do-	— Head.	"	-do-
S.611.	S.M.	Fry W.	-do-	— Arm.	17-6-15.	Slight.
S.815.	Rifleman	Clarkson.	-do-	— Leg.	"	-do-
S.2465.	A/Cpl.	Lephard.	-do-	— Foot.	"	-do-
S.2613.	Rfn.	Cooper.	-do-	Killed in action	"	
S.1012.	Rfn.	Tunworth.	-do-	From Hospital	13.6.15	
S.9084	A/Cpl.	Biggs.	-do-	To Hospital	5.6.15	Knee trouble.
S.4628.	Corpl.	Lilly.	-do-	— do —	14.6.15.	
S.8231.	Rfn.	Hillyard.	-do-	— do —	— do —	
S.1925.	"	Hands.	-do-	— do —	15.6.15.	
		Chatel.	French Interpreter		18.6.15.	

*State whether absence is of a permanent or temporary nature, adding, in the case of casuals from wounds or disease, any available information for communication to the relatives.

Army Form B. 213.

FIELD RETURN.

No. of Report 5.

(To be furnished by all arms, services, and departments to the A. G.'s Office at the Base in accordance with Field Service Regulations, Part II.)

19. 6. 15. Date.

RETURN showing numbers RATIONED by, and Transport on charge of, 8th. Battalion Rifle Bde. at

Detail	Personnel: Officers	Personnel: Other ranks	Personnel: Natives	Animals: Horses: Riding	Horses: Draught	Horses: Heavy Draught	Horses: Pack	Mules: Large	Mules: Small	Camels	Oxen	Guns, carriages and limbers, showing, description	Ammunition wagons and limbers	Machine guns	Aircraft, showing description	Horsed: 4 Wheeled	Horsed: 2 Wheeled	Mechanical: Motor Cars	Mechanical: Tractors	Mechanical: Lorries, showing description	Mechanical: Trucks, showing description	Mechanical: Trailers	Motor Bicycles	Bicycles	Remarks
Effective Strength of Unit	28	880.		14.		8.	9.	34	/	/	/	Tools 2. M.G. 2.	7.	2.	/	6*	4	/	/	/	/	/	/	9	*4 Travelling Kitchens. 2 Baggage.
Details, *by Arms* attached to unit as in War Establishment:— R.A.M.C.	1.																								
A.O.C.		1.																							
Interpreter			1																						
A.S.C.		2				4										2.									- Blanket Wagon.
Total	29.	884.																							
War Establishment	30.	991.		14		9.	9.	34				2. 2.	7.	2.		6	2							9	
Wanting to complete	-	72.																							
Surplus																									
*Attached (not to include the details shown above)																									
Civilians:— Employed with the Unit																									
Accompanying the Unit																									
TOTAL RATIONED ...																									

(Margin note, handwritten, against Total / War Establishment / Wanting to complete: Does not include Wounded & sick not evacuated & attached men)

* In the case of field ambulances, hospitals or depôts, the number of patients are to be included here, the names being shown in A.F.A. 36.

______ Signature of Commander.

______ Date of Despatch.

(K11859) W. & Co., Ltd. Wt. w6005—894 500,040 10/14 Forms B. 213 / 5

For information of the A.G.'s Office at the Base.

Officers and men who have become casuals, been transferred or joined since last report.

Place Vlamertinghe. Date 26-6-15.

Regtl. Number	Rank	Name	Corps	Nature of casualty, or name of unit from or to which transferred	Date of being struck off or coming on the ration return	Remarks*
S.5231.	Rfn.	Hillyard.	8th Rifle Bde.	From Hospital	20-6-15	
B.1725.	-	Hards W.	— do —	— do —	— do —	
B.120.	-	Winter C.	— do —	To Hospital	19-6-15	
B.3284	-	Haynes S.	— do —	— do —	21-6-15	
B.604.	-	Bates J.	— do —	— do —	21-6-15.	Evacuated area 24-6-15.
B.2874	-	Lank W.	— do —	— do —	24-6-15.	
B.600.	A/Cpl.	Capewell E.	— do —	— do —	— do —	

*State whether absence is of a permanent or temporary nature, adding, in the case of casuals from wounds or disease, any available information for communication to the relatives.

FIELD RETURN.

Army Form B. 213.

No. of Report 4.

(To be furnished by all arms, services, and departments to the A. G.'s Office at the Base in accordance with Field Service Regulations, Part II.)

Date.

RETURN showing numbers RATIONED by, and Transport on charge of, ______ at ______

Detail	Personnel			Animals								Guns, carriages, and limbers and transport vehicles													Remarks
				Horses				Mules								Horsed		Mechanical							
	Officers	Other ranks	Natives	Riding	Draught	Heavy Draught	Pack	Large	Small	Camels	Oxen	Guns, carriages and limbers, showing, description	Ammunition wagons and limbers	Machine guns	Aircraft, showing description	4 Wheeled	2 Wheeled	Motor Cars	Tractors	Lorries, showing description	Trucks, showing description	Trailers	Motor Bicycles	Bicycles	
Effective Strength of Unit	26	913		14		8	9	34				G.S. Tools 2 MG 2	7	2	NIL	6	4							9	
Details, *by Arms* attached to unit as in War Establishment:— RAMC.	1																								
A.O.C		1																							
Interpreter			1																						
Total	27	915		14		8	9	34				2 2	7	2	-	6	4							9	
War Establishment	30	991		14		9	9	34				2 2	7	2		6	4							9	
Wanting to complete	3	53				1																			
Surplus																									
*Attached (not to include the details shown above)																									
Civilians:— Employed with the Unit																									
Accompanying the Unit																									
Total Rationed ...	27	915		14		8	9	34																	

* In the case of field ambulances, hospitals or depôts, the number of patients are to be included here, the names being shown in A.F.A. 36.

Signature of Commander.

Date of Despatch.

(K11859) W. & Co., Ltd. Wt. w6005—894 500,000 10/14 Forms B. 213 / 5

Draft on strength
as per attached roll

For information of the A.G.'s Office at the Base.

Officers and men who have become casuals, been transferred or joined since last report.

Place Vlamertinghe   Date 30/5/15

Regtl. Number	Rank	Name	Corps	Nature of casualty, or name of unit from or to which transferred	Date of being struck off or coming on the ration return	Remarks*
B3284	Rfmn	Hughes S	8th R B	From Hospital	26 6. 15	
B2874	-	Lank W	-	To Hospital	24. 6 15	
B 600	A/Cpl	Capwell E	-	-	-	
S3125	Rfm	Atkinson T	-	-	28-6-15	
B 2137	-	Dudley E	-	-	1. 7 15	
B 226	-	Stevens A	-	-	-	
S 302	A/Cpl	Champion R	-	Shrapnel Head	28-6-15	Dangerous
S 2103	-	Bradley S	-	- Neck	-	-
B 2301	Rfm	Waxman J	-	Trench Mortar Rlys	30/6/15	-
B 1348	-	Scarratt S	-	Died of wounds	-	
S 36	-	Warren G	-	G.S. R fingers	-	Slight
B 658	Sgt	Chapman S	-	Shell L hand	-	-
B 278	Rfm	Burgess J W	-	- Head	-	-
B 1426	-	Piercy A	-	Shrapnel R thigh	-	-
	Lieut	Kusly G E T	-	Shell R arm	-	-
S 917	Rfm	Morris E	-	- R leg	-	serious
B 1049	-	Knose A	-	- Head	-	-
S 7273	-	James P	-	- Face	-	slight
S 7675	-	Day P	-	G.S back	-	serious
S 3061	-	Wilcox A	-	Shell buttock	-	-
S 1361	-	Gibbons J	-	G.S. head	-	
B 2533	-	Green J T	-	Shell. head face, back	1/7/15	V. dangerous
S 5188	-	Cline E	-	- R arm off	-	dangerous
S 602	-	Knowles A	-	G.S. R foot	-	Slight
B 3253	Cpl.	Hayes J	-	Died of wounds	2. 7. 15	
B 319	Sgt	Rowbottom A	-	Shell, Head	-	Dangerous
B 581	Cpl	Duncan C	-	- -	-	Very —
S 2368	A/Cpl	Tillett C	-	Died of wounds		
S 5213	Rfm	Wade F	-	Shell Head, arm	-	Dangerous
	CAPT	Balleine C F	-	Killed in Action		

*State whether absence is of a permanent or temporary nature, adding, in the case of casuals from wounds or disease, any available information for communication to the relatives.

4/
14th Division

8th Rifle Brigade.

Vol: ~~I~~ II

1 — 29.7.15.

121/6179

23/10/17

Instructions regarding War Diaries and Intelligence Summaries are contained in F. S. Regs., Part II. and the Staff Manual respectively. Title pages will be prepared in manuscript.

WAR DIARY 8th Bn Rifle Brigade.

or

~~INTELLIGENCE SUMMARY.~~

(Erase heading not required.)

Army Form C. 2118.

Place	Date	Hour	Summary of Events and Information	Remarks and references to Appendices
In trenches East of YPRES round RAILWAY WOOD.	1.7.15		Quiet day. A troublesome sniper opposite north end of 10 trench was bombed without any apparent result. Trench mortar active in the afternoon opposite barrier at South end of 10 trench, resulting in Rfn Keeley being wounded in shoulder.	
	2.7.15		Quiet day. N. Midland Howitzer Batty sent up observing officer to observe guns firing on the strong point by enemy's barrier on railway. First two shells very short just cleared our parapet, in north end of trench 10. Capt McMichael, sent orders for guns to raise, but next shot pitched on our parapet, killing one of his observers, wounding himself and another observer very badly and 5 of our men. Gas shells in afternoon on G.H.Q line where Acy[?] were, no damage, but strong smell of gas.	
	3.7.15		8 or 11" Howitzer firing from direction of WYTSCHAETE bursting shells on 4th K.R.R. trenches on our right, but did not reach us. 3 Germans observed in old German trench opposite N end of 10, bombed by us, and not seen again. Specimen of German loopholes sent to Bde H.Q. Mutual bombardment took place at about 3 pm, resulting in heavy shelling of Acy[?] trench in G.H.Q line with gas shells. Capt Ballaine and 2 men killed, 5 others badly wounded.	
	3.7.15.		Capt Ballaine buried in ECOLE at noon. German aeroplane flying slowly up and down line all day without any offensive being taken against him by big guns. We opened rifle and machine gun fire on it, without any apparent result. Acy[?] were brought up from G.H.Q line in the early morning, and distributed round Bn. H.Q.	
	4.7.15		Anti aircraft officer selected position for his gun just behind 7 [illegible], but this was vetoed by G.O.C. Quiet day up to 9 pm, when a burst of rapid rifle fire opened on the	

Army Form C. 2118.

Instructions regarding War Diaries and Intelligence Summaries are contained in F. S. Regs., Part II. and the Staff Manual respectively. Title pages will be prepared in manuscript.

WAR DIARY
or
INTELLIGENCE SUMMARY.

(Erase heading not required.)

Place	Date	Hour	Summary of Events and Information	Remarks and references to Appendices
			right of 7th RB line, gradually taken up by line except ourselves. This drew very heavy bombardment from enemy big guns especially big Howitzer from WYTSCHAETE, they put 60 shells in 25 minutes into Railway Wood. All telephone lines cut back to Bde and guns. 8th KRR carrying party who arrived in the middle suffered some casualties. Mining reported under north end of our trench, but not confirmed by mining officer.	
	5th	9 am.	After 2 hours bombardment Germans blew in our advanced barrier by Trench 12, and buried 2Lt Backus and both platoon Sergeants. In the ensuing confusion about 20 German bombers rushed the trench ~~[illegible]~~ coming up from strong point just S.E. of barrier. North Stafford bombing officer from trenches on our left came up and organised a counter attack with our men whilst 2Lt Backus was being dug out. When 2Lt Backus was dug out they counter attacked Germans and drove them out. N Stafford bombing officer being killed. Capt Cavendish had in the meanwhile organised a counter attack up both sides of railway from trench 11 under himself and Capt Boulby, but arrived just in time to see the last German go over the barrier. Rfn Stevens did very well indeed during this action. He first collected men to dig out platoon officer and Sergeant, and then joined the attacking bombing party, though not himself a bomber. Captured a German rifle from one of the attackers. 3 men killed, 2Lt Backus and 17 wounded. ~~Strongpoint and advanced trench between 10 and 12 during night with 2Lt [illegible] platoon. Evacuated during the day, platoon going into communication trench between 11 and 12.~~	
	6th		Quiet day ~~[illegible]~~ after bombardment in morning. About 3 am our guns started a heavy bombardment into German works by BELLEWARDE F.M. in order to deceive the enemy about an attack which was being carried out by 7th RB's on left on 4th Div line.	

1577 Wt. W10791/1773 500,000 1/15 D. D. & L. A.D.S.S./Forms/C. 2118.

Instructions regarding War Diaries and Intelligence Summaries are contained in F. S. Regs., Part II. and the Staff Manual respectively. Title pages will be prepared in manuscript.

WAR DIARY
or
INTELLIGENCE SUMMARY.
(Erase heading not required.)

Army Form C. 2118.

Place	Date	Hour	Summary of Events and Information	Remarks and references to Appendices
			Drew heavy retaliation. Intermittent shelling all day. Heavy shelling started again about 9 pm and continued till about 1 am. Warned by Brigade to stand to in case of attack. No signs of attack, but a good deal of rapid fire along the line.	
	7th		One of our shells dropped behind and one on the parapet of our trench. No trace could be found of gun who fired it. 6th Division sent up an officer to reconnoitre ground about our trench with a view to opening fire, probably one of their guns. Quiet night. Capt Bodley wounded whilst looking at wire he had put out in front of our trench. Shot in right arm and left wrist.	
	8th		Trench mortar active in German strong point opposite south end of our trench. Located by 7th K.R.R., but guns could not deal with it. No shelling till about 1.30 pm when advanced parties of 8th and Bucks, relieving us, attracted attention in communication trench by G.H.Q. line, and caused intermittent shelling during the afternoon. One of the Bde Signallers was killed and one hit badly whilst going out. Also one of our Machine Gun Sergeants. Relief was completed without mishap by 1 am amidst great quiet. Bn stopped for tea about 1 mile W of VLAMERTINGHE.	
	9th		Arrived in rest camp 2 miles SW of POPERINGHE about 8 am. Remainder of day spent resting. Draft of 4 NCOs and 34 men arrived from 5th Rs SHEERNESS.	

1577 Wt. W10791/1773 500,000 1/15 D. D. & L. A.D.S.S./Forms/C. 2118.

Instructions regarding War Diaries and Intelligence Summaries are contained in F. S. Regs., Part II. and the Staff Manual respectively. Title pages will be prepared in manuscript.

WAR DIARY
or
INTELLIGENCE SUMMARY.
(Erase heading not required.)

Army Form C. 2118.

Place	Date	Hour	Summary of Events and Information	Remarks and references to Appendices
In billets 2 miles S. L. of POPERINGHE	10th		Companies at disposal of O.C. Coys. Refitting and clothing.	
	11th		Church parade by Bde Chaplain in H Q field at 12 noon.	
	12th		G.O.C. Bde inspected sanitary arrangements of billets, and with one or two exceptions expressed himself satisfied. Men allowed baths in POPERINGHE. Digging party at night on support points by G.H.Q. line at night, conveyed by motor bus.	
	13th		G.O.C. inspected boots and bathing arrangements.	
	14th		Quiet day. Very heavy shelling heard last night from direction north of YPRES. Heard later that Germans attacked trenches lately taken from them by VI Div on 6th and had been repulsed. Started sniperscope range in field near C & D Coys billets. Work in charge of Lt Hudson. Digging party on supporting points at night. Conveyed by motor bus.	
	15th		G.O.C. came and opened sniperscope range by firing first shot. Range not properly completed owing to lack of sandbags.	
	16th		Companies route marching under O.C. Coys. Sniperscope range completed. Proved of immense value to snipers, also for getting men used to telescopic sights. 3 machine guns fired on it however [illegible], distance was about 150 yards.	
	17th		Companies route marching under O.C. Coys.	

1577 Wt. W10791/1773 500,000 1/15 D. D. & L. A.D.S.S./Forms/C. 2118.

Instructions regarding War Diaries and Intelligence Summaries are contained in F. S. Regs., Part II. and the Staff Manual respectively. Title pages will be prepared in manuscript.

WAR DIARY

or

INTELLIGENCE SUMMARY.

(Erase heading not required.)

Army Form C. 2118.

Place	Date	Hour	Summary of Events and Information	Remarks and references to Appendices
	18th		Church Parade by Bde Chaplain in H.Q. field at 12 noon. Digging party at night on communication trench and supporting points by G H Q line.	
	19th		Companies at disposal of OC Coys. Rumour that Bde had to take up a new line round HOOGE.	
	20th		Bn route march via WATOU – HAUTKERQUE – STEENVOORDE about 14 miles. No men fell out mostly new draft. Passed 1st RB in billets near WATOU but did not actually see them. Also passed passed 17th Div (part of K2) in STEENVOORDE. Very hot walking. On arrival back in camp found that Bn was warned for digging at night. But GOC excused us. Warned to move next day move put off.	
	21st		Spent in packing up and getting ready to move.	
	22nd		Bn moved off at 2 pm to march into Brigade Reserve billets, via POPERINGHE. Halted 1 mile W of POPERINGHE for tea. Rain began to fall. 2 Coys A+B in ramparts C+D in dug outs North and South of YPRES – POPERINGHE road about 1 mile from YPRES.	
	23rd		Both companies settling down into their billets. A+B Coys found carrying party for 8th KRR. Had 1 Sjt killed and 1 man wounded along way behind firing line.	
	24th		CO and Adjutant went up to inspect new trenches at HOOGE with a view to taking over from 7th RB. A+B found working party.	

1577 Wt. W10791/1773 500,000 1/15 D. D. & L. A.D.S.S./Forms/C. 2118.

Army Form C. 2118.

WAR DIARY
or
INTELLIGENCE SUMMARY.
(Erase heading not required.)

Instructions regarding War Diaries and Intelligence Summaries are contained in F. S. Regs., Part II. and the Staff Manual respectively. Title pages will be prepared in manuscript.

Place	Date	Hour	Summary of Events and Information	Remarks and references to Appendices
Bde Reserve Dugouts 1 mile W of YPRES.	25.7.15		2nd in command. Capt Prior Lt & Adjt went up to inspect the new trenches to be taken over held by 7th RB.	
			Quiet day. Working party of 50 men from A & B coys to carry [illegible] to transport at night.	
			Division transferred from V to VI Corps.	
	26.7.15		Capts Cavendish, Sheepshanks, Parke went up to inspect trenches.	
			German aircraft brought down by one of our aeroplanes by a bomb which set the petrol tank on fire. Observer fell out about 1000 ft up. Driver remained in car and was burnt to death. Machine fell just behind 7th RB H.Q.	
	27.7.15		CO and Adjutant went up to trenches to inspect crater and German trenches opposite. Quiet day. Working party of 400 required to carry and dig in 7th RB trenches. Misunderstanding with [illegible] RE officer and Bde resulted in not much work.	
	28.7.15		Quiet day except for aircraft battle. German driven off but not brought down.	
	29.7.		Bn moved up by coys starting at 9pm to take over trenches held by 7th RB at HOOGE. 2 coys in firing line, 2 in support. Bn H.Q. just behind supporting coys. Strength 26 officers 758 going into trenches.	

W M Parker
Capt Adjt.
8th Bn Rifle Bde.

1577 Wt. W10791/1773 500,000 1/15 D. D. & L. A.D.S.S./Forms/C. 2118.

For information of the A.G.'s Office at the Base.

Officers and men who have become casuals, been transferred or joined since last report.

Place Poperinghe. Date 10.7.15.

Regtl. Number	Rank	Name	Corps	Nature of casualty, or name of unit from or to which transferred	Date of being struck off or coming on the ration return	Remarks*
		Draft on strength as per attached roll.				
S3188	RFM.	Daley G.	8th.Rifle Bde.	Wounded	3.7.15.	
S1031	SGT.	Wills A.	'	G.S.R. hand	3.7.15.	serious
B 42	RFM.	Simmons F.	'	shpnl. r. leg	3.7.15.	slight
B 370	'	Kite T.	'	shpnl.numers.	4.7.15.	danger
B1577	'	Baggott C.	'	Injuries from collapse of dugout	4.7.15.	serious
B1408	'	Williams F.	'	wounded	3.7.15.	
S1653	'	Jennison C.	'	shpnl. head	3.7.15	slight
B 722	A/Cpl	Surridge L.	'	shpnl. shoulder	5.7.15.	slight
B 284	RFM.	Shimmonds W.	'	shell shoulder	5.7.15.	slight
B1383	'	Dunn J.	'	shell hand	5.7.15.	slught
B1407	A/Cpl	Entwistle	'	died of wounds	5.7.15.	
B3199	RFM.	Simmons V.	'	shell chest	5.7.15.	slight
B3195	A/Cpl.	Millington W.	'	killed in act.	5.7.15.	
	LIEUT.	BACKUS A.R.	'	G.S. neck	5.7.15.	slight
4488	RFM.	Grimshaw W.	'	shpnl. head	5.7.15.	slight
			--	returnedbto duty 8.7.15.		
S3135	'	Wood W.	'	Bayonet head	5.7.15.	st
B3411	'	Higgs J.	'	G.S. elbow	5.7.15.	slight
S3190	'	Carden R.	'	shpnl. head & buttock	5.7.15.	slight
S2831	'	Williams G.	'	shell stomach	5.7.15.	
				died of wounds	7.7.15.	
S 105	A/Cpl	Wood J.	'	shell head	5.7.15.	dahgers
B 420	SGT.	Day J.	'	Fracture & Dislocation.	5.7.15.	dangers
B3402	RFM.	Richens A.	'	shpnl. head	5.7.15.	serious
B3192	SGT.	Handley J.	'	shpnl. head	5.7.15.	dangers
B3289	RFM.	Sankey T.	'	G.S. neck & fingers.	5.7.15.	slight
B 721	'	Lewendon C.	'	G.S. head	5.7.15.	slight
B3288	'	Kelly J.	'	G.S. Chest	5.7.15.	v.dangs.
S 688	'	Bennett J.	'	G.S. Foot	5.7.15.	slight
S6231	'	Trevatt E.J.	'	shell back & legs	5.7.15.	dangers
B 775	'	Travers E.	'	killed in act.	5.7.15.	
S7715	'	James A.	'	Wounded		
B3260	'	Chadwick J.	'	stomach	5.7.15.	dangers
B 422	'	Cannard T.	'	shpnl. thigh	6.7.15.	serious
S 390	'	Dixon J.	'	shpnl. head & shoulder	6.7.15.	serious
S7667	'	Leach W.	'	shpnl. head	6.7.15.	serious
B1644	'	Guant A.	'	shpl.head,leg	6.7.15.	serious
S 900	'	Grimley A.	'	shpnl. leg	6.7.15.	slight
B1560	'	Hopkins W.	'	shpnl. leg	6.7.15.	slight
B2521	'	Naylor H.	'	shpnl. leg	6.7.15.	slight Rtd duty 10/7/15
B3189	'	Downey W.	'	shpnl. back	6.7.15.	slight
S3194	A/Cpl.	Hollingworth J.	'	shpnl. head & leg.	6.7.15.	serious
B2232	RFM	Davis H.	'	shpnl. arm	6.7.15.	slight.

*State whether absence is of a permanent or temporary nature, adding, in the case of casuals from wounds or disease, any available information for communication to the relatives.

Army Form B. 213.

FIELD RETURN.

No. of Report__________

(To be furnished by all arms, services, and departments to the A. G.'s Office at the Base in accordance with Field Service Regulations, Part II.)

____________________ Date.

RETURN showing numbers RATIONED by, and Transport on charge of, ____________________ at ____________________

Detail	Personnel			Animals								Guns, carriages, and limbers and transport vehicles													Remarks
				Horses				Mules								Horsed		Mechanical							
	Officers	Other ranks	Natives	Riding	Draught	Heavy Draught	Pack	Large	Small	Camels	Oxen	Guns, carriages and limbers, showing, description	Ammunition wagons and limbers	Machine guns	Aircraft, showing description	4 Wheeled	2 Wheeled	Motor Cars	Tractors	Lorries, showing description	Trucks, showing description	Trailers	Motor Bicycles	Bicycles	
Effective Strength of Unit																									
Details, *by Arms* attached to unit as in War Establishment:—																									
Total																									
War Establishment																									
Wanting to complete																									
Surplus																									
*Attached (not to include the details shown above)																									
Civilians:—																									
Employed with the Unit																									
Accompanying the Unit																									
Total Rationed ...																									

* In the case of field ambulances, hospitals or depôts, the number of patients are to be included here, the names being shown in A.F.A. 36.

____________________ Signature of Commander.

____________________ Date of Despatch.

(K11859) W. & Co., Ltd. Wt. w6005—894 500,000 10/14 Forms B. 213 / 5

Army Form B. 213.

FIELD RETURN.

No. of Report 8

(To be furnished by all arms, services, and departments to the A. G.'s Office at the Base in accordance with Field Service Regulations, Part II.)

10. 7. 15 Date.

RETURN showing numbers RATIONED by, and Transport on charge of, 8th Batt. Rifle Brigade at Poperinghe

Detail	Personnel: Officers	Personnel: Other ranks	Personnel: Natives	Animals: Horses: Riding	Horses: Draught	Horses: Heavy Draught	Horses: Pack	Mules: Large	Mules: Small	Camels	Oxen	Guns, carriages and limbers, showing description	Ammunition wagons and limbers	Machine guns	Aircraft, showing description	Horsed: 4 Wheeled	Horsed: 2 Wheeled	Mechanical: Motor Cars	Mechanical: Tractors	Mechanical: Lorries, showing description	Mechanical: Trucks, showing description	Mechanical: Trailers	Motor Bicycles	Bicycles	Remarks
Effective Strength of Unit	23	909		14		9	9	34				G.S. Tools 2, M.G. 2	7	2	–	6	4							9	
Details, *by Arms* attached to unit as in War Establishment:— R.A.M.C.	1																								
A.O.C.		1																							
Interpreter			1																						
Total	24	911		14		9	9	34				2 2	7	2	–	6	4							9	
War Establishment	30	991		14		9	9	34				2 2	7	2		6	4							9	
Wanting to complete (Not including 18 sick or attached for duty)	6	62																							
Surplus																									
*Attached (not to include the details shown above)																									
Civilians:— Employed with the Unit																									
Accompanying the Unit																									
TOTAL RATIONED ...	24	911		14		9	9	34																	

* In the case of field ambulances, hospitals or depôts, the number of patients are to be included here, the names being shown in A.F.A. 36.

Signature of Commander.

Date of Despatch.

(K11859) W. & Co., Ltd. Wt. w6095—894 500,000 10/14 Forms B. 213 / 5

For information of the A.G.'s Office at the Base.

Officers and men who have become casuals, been transferred or joined since last report.

Place Poperinghe Date 10.7.15.

Regtl. Number	Rank	Name	Corps	Nature of casualty, or name of unit from or to which transferred	Date of being struck off or coming on the ration return	Remarks*
B 146	Rfm.	Searle H.	8th.Rif. Bde.	shpnl, back	6.7.15.	slight.
S6092	'	Gomm J.	'	' arm & leg	'	'
B1663	'	Horton T.	'	' '	'	'
B 768	'	Webster R.	'	' head	'	
B1875	A/Cpl	Gillett J.	'	' shoulder & arm		serious.
S 295	Rfm.	Cook S.	'		6.7.15.	serious.
B 803	'	Wiltshire J.	'	glass R.eye	6.7.15.	slight.
S7220	'	Cooke G.	'	glass R.eye	6.7.15.	slight.
S3200	'	Storer H.	'	G.S. R. eye	6.7.15.	dangeros
B3128	'	Dove A.	'	shpnl.head	6.7.15.	slight.
S 180	A/CPL	O'Calaghan	'	shpnl.head	6.7.15.	serious.
~~B2298~~	Rfm.	Robinson E.	'	shell head	6.7.15.	serious.
S7275				killed in act.	6.7.15.	
B2298	Rfm.	Gore T.	'	shpnl, L. eye	6.7.15.	slight
B2785	'	Grainger F.	'	returned to duty 10.7.15.		
B1970	CPL.	Hughes R.	'	shpnl. L. arm	7.7.15.	serious.
B2225	Rfm.	Leadbeatter J.	'	shpnl. L. leg	7.7.15.	slight.
B1566	'	Seerey C.	'	shpnl.	7.7.15.	v. slight
S1653	'	Jenkinson W.	'	shpnl.	7.7.15.	v. slight
B2531	'	Rowell F.	'	shpnl.	7.7.15.	v. slight
S1029	SGT	Teague W.	'	killed in act.	7.7.15.	
	CAPT.	BOWLBY H.R.	'	shpnl. R.hand	7.7.15.	serious.
6700	C.S.M.	Goode W.	'	shpnl. R.arm	7.7.15.	serious.
B3282	Rfm.	Collinge M.	'	shpnl. back	8.7.15.	serious.
S 985	'	Oddy A.	'	G.S.R.knee	8.7.15.	serious.
B1573	'	Halley F.	'	G.S. head	8.7.15.	serious.
B 845	SGT.	Browning J.	'	shpnl.	7.7.15.	slight.
B 369	Rfm.	Stillwell H.	'	shpnl. face	8.7.15.	slight.
S 914	'	Adams C.	'	shpnl. back	8.7.15.	slight.
S7704	'	Ibbotson W.	'	shpnl. ankle	8.7.15.	slight.
B 600	A/Cpl	Capewell E.	'	shpnl. foot	8.7.15.	slight.
S7691	Rfm.	Killworth D.	'	Sick Evacuated	1.7.15.	
S4628	CPL.	Lilley A.	'	'	28.5.15.	
B3284	Rfm.	Haynes S.	'	From Hospital.	26.6.15.	
B 130	'	Winter C.	'	' '	26.6.15.	
B2874	'	Lank W.	'	' '	27.6.15.	
B 600	A/CPL	Capewell E.	'	To Hospital.	24.6.15.	
S3128	RFm.	Atkinson T.	'	' '	24.6.15.	
B2137	'	Dudley E.	'	' '	28.6.15.	
				' '	1. 7.15.	
B 426	'	Stevens A.	'	From	10.7.15.	
B3030	'	Windebank A.	'	To '	1.7.15.	
				To '	1.7.15.	
B2308	'	Lake F.	'	From	10.7.15.	
	LIEUT.	SCOTT C.F.	'	To '	8.7.15.	
				To '	4.7.15.	

*State whether absence is of a permanent or temporary nature, adding, in the case of casuals from wounds or disease, any available information for communication to the relatives.

Army Form B. 213.

FIELD RETURN.

No. of Report 9

(To be furnished by all arms, services, and departments to the A. G.'s Office at the Base in accordance with Field Service Regulations, Part II.)

14/4/15 Date.

RETURN showing numbers RATIONED by, and Transport on charge of, 8th Batt Rifle Brigade at Poperinghe

Detail	Personnel: Officers	Personnel: Other ranks	Personnel: Natives	Animals: Horses: Riding	Animals: Horses: Draught	Animals: Horses: Heavy Draught	Animals: Horses: Pack	Animals: Mules: Large	Animals: Mules: Small	Camels	Oxen	Guns, carriages and limbers, showing description	Ammunition wagons and limbers	Machine guns	Aircraft, showing description	Horsed: 4 Wheeled	Horsed: 2 Wheeled	Mechanical: Motor Cars	Mechanical: Tractors	Mechanical: Lorries, showing description	Mechanical: Trucks, showing description	Mechanical: Trailers	Motor Bicycles	Bicycles	Remarks
Effective Strength of Unit	23	910		14		9	9	34				G.S. limbers 2, M.G. 2	7	2		6	4							9	
Details, *by Arms* attached to unit as in War Establishment:—																									
R.A.M.C.	1																								
A.O.C.		1																							
Interpreter			1																						
Total	24	912		14		9	9	34				2 2	7	2		6	4							9	
War Establishment	30	991		14		9	9	34				2 2	7	2		6	4							9	
Wanting to complete	6	85																							
Surplus																									
*Attached (not to include the details shown above)																									
Civilians:— Employed with the Unit																									
Accompanying the Unit																									
TOTAL RATIONED ...	24	912		14		9	9	34				2 2	7	2		6	4							9	

Not including 24 OR sick & attached for duty

* In the case of field ambulances, hospitals or depôts, the number of patients are to be included here, the names being shown in A.F.A. 36.

Signature of Commander.

18/4/15 Date of Despatch.

(K11859) W. & Co., Ltd. Wt. w6005—894 500,000 10/14 Forms B. 213 / 5

For information of the A.G.'s Office at the Base.

Officers and men who have become casuals, been transferred or joined since last report.

Place Poperinghe. Date 17.7.15.

Regtl. Number	Rank	Name	Corps	Nature of casualty, or name of unit from or to which transferred	Date of being struck off or coming on the ration return	Remarks*
	TO HOSPITAL.					
B3273	RFM.	Clancey W.	8th.Rifle Bde.		11.7.15	
B1564	"	White G.	"		8.7.15	
B1413	"	Grimshaw J.W.	"		14.7.15	
B2223	"	Arnold w.	"	From	17.7.15	
B3137	"	Gill J.	"	To	14.7.15.	
S 619	"	Hanmore J.	"		12.7.15	
B 566	"	Pinchin W.	"		16.7.15	
B3189	"	Downey W.	"		16.7.15	
					17.7.15	
	The following wounded men have returned to duty from hospital-					
B 284	RFM.	Shimmons W.	8th.Rifle Bde.		10.7.15	
4488	"	Grimshaw W.	"		8.7.15	
S3135	"	Wood W.	"		10.7.15	
S7667	"	Leech W.	"		15.8.15	
B2521	"	Naylor H.	"		10.7.15	
B3189	"	Downey W.	"		12.7.15	
S 295	"	Cook S.	"		17.7.15.	
B2298	"	Gore T.	"		10.7.15	
B1970	Cpl.	Hughes R.	"		13.7.15	
B2225	RFM.	Leadbeatter	"		11.7.15	
B1566	"	Seerey C.	"		17.7.15	
B3040	"	Jenkinson W.	"		12.7.15	
B1570	"	Halley F.	"		13.7.15	
B 362	"	Stilwell H.	"		12.7.15	

*State whether absence is of a permanent or temporary nature, adding, in the case of casuals from wounds or disease, any available information for communication to the relatives.

FIELD RETURN.

Army Form B. 213.

No. of Report 10

(To be furnished by all arms, services, and departments to the A. G.'s Office at the Base in accordance with Field Service Regulations, Part II.)

24/7/15 Date.

RETURN showing numbers RATIONED by, and Transport on charge of, 8th Batt. Rifle Brigade at Ypres

Detail	Personnel			Animals								Guns, carriages, and limbers and transport vehicles													Remarks
				Horses			Mules									Horsed		Mechanical							
	Officers	Other ranks	Natives	Riding	Draught	Heavy Draught	Pack	Large	Small	Camels	Oxen	Guns, carriages and limbers, showing, description	Ammunition wagons and limbers	Machine guns	Aircraft, showing description	4 Wheeled	2 Wheeled	Motor Cars	Tractors	Lorries, showing description	Trucks, showing description	Trailers	Motor Bicycles	Bicycles	
Effective Strength of Unit	25	900		14		9	9	34				G.S. Tools 2, M.G. 2	7	2		6	4							9	
Details, *by Arms* attached to unit as in War Establishment:—																									
R.A.M.C.	1																								
A.O.C.		1																							
Interpreter			1																						
Total (Not including sick)	26	902		14		9	9	34				2 2	7	2		6	4							9	
War Establishment (not wounded or attached for duty)	30	991		14		9	9	34				2 2	7	2		6	4							9	
Wanting to complete (1 officer 31 O.R.)	3	58																							
Surplus																									
*Attached (not to include the details shown above)																									
Civilians:— Employed with the Unit																									
Accompanying the Unit																									
TOTAL RATIONED ...	26	902		14		9	9	34				2 2	7	2		6	4							9	

* In the case of field ambulances, hospitals or depôts, the number of patients are to be included here, the names being shown in A.F.A. 36.

Signature of Commander.

Date of Despatch.

(K 11859) W. & Co., Ltd. Wt. w6005—894 500,000 10/14 Forms B. 213 / 5

For information of the A.G.'s Office at the Base.

Officers and men who have become casuals, been transferred or joined since last report.

Place YPRES. Date 24.7.15.

Regtl. Number	Rank	Name	Corps	Nature of casualty, or name of unit from or to which transferred	Date of being struck off or coming on the ration return	Remarks*
	LIEUT.	Purden S.F.	8th.Rifle Bde.	From 14th.R.B.	23.7.15	Gazetted 31.12.14
	"	Fraser W.N.	"	15th.R.B.	"	29.1.15.
	"	Pope E.	"	15th.R.B.	"	3.2.15.
	2ndLIEUT.	Coles A.N.	"			
B2870	A/Cpl.	O'Hara R.	"	To Hospital	23.7.15.	
B2854	"	Binks H.	"	"	18.7.15.	
8441	RFM.	Tickner W.	"	"	19.7.15.	
S 915	RFM.	Embury G.	"	"	21.7.15.	
B3040	"	Jenkinson C.	"	"	22.7.15.	
B3187	"	Brown G.	"	"	"	
10664	"	Holland A.	"	"	"	
B 419	"	Haddin W.	"	"	"	
S5225	"	Jenner J.	"	"	24.7.15.	
B2874	"	Lank W.	"	"	"	
B2308	"	Lake F.	"	From Hospital	19.7.15.	
S1724	"	Taylor A.	"	"	15.7.15	
S5156	"	Davis R.	"	G.S. arm	19.7.15.	
5781	A/Cpl.	Head W.	"	G.S. R.knee	23.7.15.	
				killed in act.	23.7.15.	

*State whether absence is of a permanent or temporary nature, adding, in the case of casuals from wounds or disease, any available information for communication to the relatives.

Army Form B. 213.

FIELD RETURN.

No. of Report ________

(To be furnished by all arms, services, and departments to the A. G.'s Office at the Base in accordance with Field Service Regulations, Part II.)

________ Date.

RETURN showing numbers RATIONED by, and Transport on charge of, ________ at ________

Detail	Personnel			Animals.								Guns, carriages, and limbers and transport vehicles											Motor Bicycles	Bicycles	Remarks
				Horses				Mules								Horsed		Mechanical							
	Officers	Other ranks	Natives	Riding	Draught	Heavy Draught	Pack	Large	Small	Camels	Oxen	Guns, carriages and limbers, showing, description	Ammunition wagons and limbers	Machine guns	Aircraft, showing description	4 Wheeled	2 Wheeled	Motor Cars	Tractors	Lorries, showing description	Trucks, showing description	Trailers			
Effective Strength of Unit Details, *by Arms* attached to unit as in War Establishment:—																									
Total																									
War Establishment																									
Wanting to complete																									
Surplus																									
*Attached (not to include the details shown above)																									
Civilians:— Employed with the Unit																									
Accompanying the Unit																									
TOTAL RATIONED ...																									

* In the case of field ambulances, hospitals or depôts, the number of patients are to be included here, the names being shown in A.F.A. 36.

________ Signature of Commander.

________ Date of Despatch.

(K 11859) W. & Co., Ltd. Wt. w6005—894 500,000 10/14 Forms B. 213 / 5

Sheet 2.

For information of the A.G.'s Office at the Base.

Officers and men who have become casuals, been transferred or joined since last report.

Place YPRES Date 31.7.15.

Regtl. Number	Rank	Name	Corps	Nature of casualty, or name of unit from or to which transferred	Date of being struck off or coming on the ration return	Remarks*
8313	Rifm.	Compton P.	8th. Rifle Bde.	Killed in act.	30.7.15	
S 295	"	Cook G.	"	Wounded	"	
S7216	"	Crooks S.	"	"	"	
S 292	"	Davis W.	"	"	"	
8330	"	Doyle M.	"	"	"	
B3261	"	Evans G.	"	Killed in act.	"	
S7708	"	Fisher H.	"	Wounded	"	
B1339	"	Garland G.	"	"	"	
9932	"	Gatehouse J.	"	"	"	
B1348	"	Gilbert B.	"	"	"	
S5237	"	Goodwright W.	"	"	"	
B 769	"	Graves A.	"	"	"	
S9160	"	Gregory S.	"	"	"	
B1265	"	Gresty A.	"	"	"	
B1413	"	Grimshaw J.	"	"	"	
4488	"	Grimshaw W.	"	"	"	
B 682	"	Hale E.	"	"	"	
10345	"	Hazell P.	"	"	"	
B 733	"	Harrison A.	"	"	"	
B1333	"	Horton W.	"	"	"	
S 687	"	Hunt R.	"	"	"	
B1335	"	Jones A.	"	"	"	
S6871	"	Jones W.A.	"	"	"	
B 729	"	Jones W.	"	"	"	
B3283	"	Johnson D.	"	Killed in act.	"	
5744	A/Cpl	Lawrence W.	"	Wounded	"	
S 233	"	Lee F.	"	"	"	
B3257	Rifm.	Lawton A.	"	"	"	
B1345	"	Lewis H.	"	Killed in act.	"	
B 846	"	Lockett S.	"	Wounded	"	
B3045	"	Loftus A.	"	"	"	
S7667	"	Leach W.	"	Killed in act.	"	
8381	"	Mann E.	"	Wounded	"	
S7217	"	Midgeley J.	"	"	"	
S8912	"	Moore R.	"	"	"	
S9617	"	Neale F.	"	"	"	
9177	"	Ogden J.	"	"	"	
B3186	"	Onn F.	"	"	"	
B812	"	Orme C.	"	"	"	
B 765	"	Page G.	"	"	"	
S6412	"	Pitwell E.	"	Killed in act.	"	
B 601	"	Prady C.	"	Wounded	"	(died2.8.15)
B1422	"	Price W.	"	"	"	
B 425	"	Purton H.	"	"	"	(died 2.8.15)
9710	"	Raymond B.	"	Killed in act.	"	
2307	"	Ridout W.	"	Wounded	"	
S7707	"	Ritson A.	"	"	"	
B1341	"	Rogers J.	"	"	"	
S 927	"	Rushbrook T.	"	Killed in act.	"	
B1332	"	Saunders W.	"	Wounded	"	
S 738	"	Shea R.	"	Killed in act.	"	
S 10337	"	Spalding H.	"	Wounded	"	
8926	"	Steggall A.	"	"	"	
B1638	"	Stevens A.	"	"	"	

*State whether absence is of a permanent or temporary nature, adding, in the case of casuals from wounds or disease, any available information for communication to the relatives.

For information of the A.G.'s Office at the Base.

Officers and men who have become casuals, been transferred or joined since last report.

Place YPRES. Date 31.7.15.

Regtl. Number	Rank	Name	Corps	Nature of casualty, or name of unit from or to which transferred	Date of being struck off or coming on the ration return	Remarks*
B3279	Rifm.	Stokes A.	8th.Rifle Bde.	Wounded	30.7.15.	
3281	'	Stokes T.	'	'		
B 223	'	Tubb F.	'	Kille d in act.	'	
S 186	'	Twigg R.	'	Wounded	'	
S7294	'	Turner W.	'	'	'	
S6091	'	West F.	'	'	'	
S7716	'	Willott F.	'	'	'	
B 808	'	Wingrove H.	'	'	'	
B 429	'	Withers F.	'	'	'	
S 46	'	Woods P.	'	'	'	
S7978	Sergt.	Ponsonby H.	'	'	'	
	All the above N.C.Os. and Riflemen are of 'B' Company.					
12798	C.S.M.	Onslow H.	8th.Rifle Bde.	Wounded	30.7.15.	
964	Sergt.	Portt V.	'	Killed in Act.	'	
8879	'	Taylor F.	'	Wnd. & Miss.	'	
S 978	'	Davis H.	'	Died of Wnds.	'	
B1949	'	Sandall F.	'	Wounded	'	
1134	'	Heath A.	'	Killed in Act.	'	
B 673	'	Gregory G.	'	'	'	
S2617	'	Belding R.	'	Wounded	'	
S3196	Cpl.	Clarke C.	'	Killed in Act.	'	
S2611	V	Clinch W.	'	Wounded	'	
B 475	'	George E.	'	Killed in Act.	'	
B1970	'	Hughes R.	'	Wounded	'	
S3195	'	Beal W.	'	Missing	'	
S3062	'	Band C.	'	Shock	'	
S3198	'	Belbin C.	'	Killed in Act.	'	
S3056	'	Berry F.	'	Wounded & Prisoner		
S 968	'	Hill W.	'	Wounded	'	
B1962	'	Fletcher J.	'	Killed in Act.	'	
B1948	'	Saxby C.	'	Wounded	'	
3071	A/Cpl.	Mulvaney R.	'	Missing	'	
S 490	'	Reeve S.	'	Missing	'	
S3060	'	Barton H.	'	Killed in Act.	'	
S3048	'	Buer V.	'	Missing	'	
B1563	'	Street Wm	'	Missing	'	
B3174	'	Lodge A.	'	Wounded	'	
S2614	'	Turner J.	'	Wnd. & Miss.	'	
4851	'	Heath W.	'	Missing	'	
B1950	'	Coare R.	'	Missing	'	
S 382	'	Potts S.	'	Missing	'	
B1961	'	Stocking C.	'	Wnd. & Miss.	'	
9165	Rflm.	Abell W.	'	Missing	'	
B1807	'	Bannerman A.	'	Missing	'	
S1910	'	Bell J.	'	Wounded	'	
S1790	'	Blake C.	'	Killed in Act.	'	
B1808	'	Boden T.	'	Missing	'	
B2675	'	Braund V.	'	Killed in Act.	'	
B1640	'	Brooks H.	'	Wounded	'	
S7532	'	Britland B.	'	Missing	'	
S10046	'	Bedwell F.	'	Wounded	'	

*State whether absence is of a permanent or temporary nature, adding, in the case of casuals from wounds or disease, any available information for communication to the relatives.

FIELD RETURN.

Army Form B. 213.

No. of Report ____________

(To be furnished by all arms, services, and departments to the A. G.'s Office at the Base in accordance with Field Service Regulations, Part II.)

____________ Date.

RETURN showing numbers RATIONED by, and Transport on charge of, ____________ at ____________

Detail	Personnel			Animals								Guns, carriages, and limbers and transport vehicles													Remarks
				Horses				Mules								Horsed		Mechanical							
	Officers	Other ranks	Natives	Riding	Draught	Heavy Draught	Pack	Large	Small	Camels	Oxen	Guns, carriages and limbers, showing, description	Ammunition wagons and limbers	Machine guns	Aircraft, showing description	4 Wheeled	2 Wheeled	Motor Cars	Tractors	Lorries, showing description	Trucks, showing description	Trailers	Motor Bicycles	Bicycles	
Effective Strength of Unit Details, *by Arms* attached to unit as in War Establishment:—																									
Total																									
War Establishment																									
Wanting to complete																									
Surplus																									
*Attached (not to include the details shown above)																									
Civilians:— Employed with the Unit																									
Accompanying the Unit																									
Total Rationed ...																									

* In the case of field ambulances, hospitals or depôts, the number of patients are to be included here, the names being shown in A.F.A. 36.

____________ Signature of Commander.

____________ Date of Despatch.

(K 11859) W. & Co., Ltd. Wt. w6005—894 500,000 10/14 Forms B. 213 / 5

For information of the A.G.'s Office at the Base.

Officers and men who have become casuals, been transferred or joined since last report.

Place YPRES. Date 31.7.15.

Regtl. Number	Rank	Name	Corps	Nature of casualty, or name of unit from or to which transferred	Date of being struck off or coming on the ration return	Remarks*
B1872	Rifm.	Carter F.	8th. Rifle Bde.	Wounded	30.7.15.	
B1800	"	Clardige J.	"	"	"	
B1275	"	Coley G.	"	"	"	
B3124	"	Crane H.	"	"	"	
B3064	"	Custance W.	"	Missing	"	
6138	"	Chance W.	"	"	"	
S3165	"	Davenport S.	"	Killed in Act.	"	
S 480	"	Debney C.	"	Wounded	"	
B1794	"	Deighton C.	"	"	"	
S1569	"	Dodd W.	"	Missing	"	
B 760	"	Dove H.	"	Missing	"	
S7298	"	Dowdall A.	"	Wounded	"	
S 491	"	Donkin W.	"	Missing	"	
S9042	"	Donegan J.	"	Wounded	"	
S7317	"	Edwards C.	"	Killed in Act.	V	
B1871	"	Eggington H.	"	"	"	
S6235	"	Earley J.	"	Missing	"	
1801	"	Fairhurst J.	"	Prisoner	"	
1713	"	Findon W.	"	Missing	"	
S 613	V	Fisher E.	V	Wounded	"	
B1884	"	Foden E.	"	Missing	"	
S2615	"	Freeman G.	"	Wounded	"	
S 182	"	Gaisford A.	"	Missing	"	
B2044	"	Goddard J.	"	"	"	
S1596	"	Griffiths W.	"	"	"	
B1417	"	Griffiths E.	V	Wounded	"	
B3037	"	Grinstead E.	"	"	"	
B2041	"	Harding W.	"	Missing	"	
B3039	"	Harris G.	"	Wounded	"	
B3499	"	Henshaw T.	"	Missing	"	
B1573	"	Haley F.	"	"	"	
S2620	"	Harrow W.	"	Wounded	"	
B3048	"	Heald W.	"	Killed in Act.	"	
B1880	"	Howell S.	"	Wounded	"	
B3061	"	Hovell H.	"	"	"	
B1574	"	Howarth A.	"	Wnd. & Miss.	"	
S5[illegible]	"	Hughes T.	"	Wounded	"	
S5914	"	Hurst R.	"	Missing	"	
S7297	"	Hale S.	"	"	"	
S7531	"	Hyatt E.	"	Wounded	"	
S7698	"	Hayes C.	"	Missing	"	
S7439	"	Hazeldean A.	"	"	"	
B2046	"	Jenn P.	"	Wounded	"	
S 977	"	Jeffrey H.	"	Killed in Act.	"	
S2155	"	Jones F.	"	Missing	"	
S 971	"	Joslyn A.	"	"	"	
S1156	"	Kebby W.	"	Wounded	"	
B1803	"	Knight A.	"	"	"	
S6135	"	Knibbs A.	"	Missing	"	
S8706	"	Kimber J.	"	Killed in Act.	"	
B3059	"	Lee S.	"	Missing	"	
S2151	"	Lee F.	"	Killed in Act.	"	
B1734	"	Lloyd J.	"	Missing	"	
B 726	"	Lloyd H.	"	"	"	
S1718	"	Loomes H.	"	"	"	

*State whether absence is of a permanent or temporary nature, adding, in the case of casuals from wounds or disease, any available information for communication to the relatives.

FIELD RETURN.

Army Form B. 213.

No. of Report__________

(To be furnished by all arms, services, and departments to the A. G.'s Office at the Base in accordance with Field Service Regulations, Part II.)

____________________ Date.

RETURN showing numbers RATIONED by, and Transport on charge of, ____________________ at ____________________

Detail	Personnel			Animals								Guns, carriages, and limbers and transport vehicles											Motor Bicycles	Bicycles	Remarks
	Officers	Other ranks	Natives	Horses				Mules		Camels	Oxen	Guns, carriages and limbers, showing, description	Ammunition wagons and limbers	Machine guns	Aircraft, showing description	Horsed		Mechanical							
				Riding	Draught	Heavy Draught	Pack	Large	Small							4 Wheeled	2 Wheeled	Motor Cars	Tractors	Lorries, showing description	Trucks, showing description	Trailers			
Effective Strength of Unit Details, *by Arms* attached to unit as in War Establishment:—																									
Total																									
War Establishment																									
Wanting to complete																									
Surplus																									
*Attached (not to include the details shown above)																									
Civilians:— Employed with the Unit																									
Accompanying the Unit																									
TOTAL RATIONED ...																									

* In the case of field ambulances, hospitals or depôts, the number of patients are to be included here, the names being shown in A.F.A. 36.

____________________ Signature of Commander.

____________________ Date of Despatch.

(K 11859) W. & Co., Ltd. Wt. w6005—894 500,000 10/14 Forms B. 213 / 5

Sheet 5.

For information of the A.G.'s Office at the Base.

Officers and men who have become casuals, been transferred or joined since last report.

Place YPRES. Date 31.7.15.

Regtl. Number	Rank	Name	Corps	Nature of casualty, or name of unit from or to which transferred	Date of being struck off or coming on the ration return	Remarks*
B1642	Rifm.	Lowell C.	8th.Rifle Bde.	Wounded	30.7.15.	
S 980	"	Martin G.	"	"	"	
S9303	"	McIlroy R.	"	Missing	"	
B3177	"	McManus J.	"	Killed in Act.	"	
B1503	"	McGuire J.	"	Wounded	"	
B1578	"	Middleton S.	"	Missing	"	
S3168	"	Middleton F.	"		"	
S3206	"	Morgan J.	"	"	"	
B1817	"	Moss H.	"	"	"	
B1823	"	Payne A.	"	Wounded	"	
S2152	"	Pee F.	"	Missing	"	
B1654	"	Penson J.	"	"	"	
B3056	"	Pickering F.	"	"	"	
S3171	"	Pratt A.	"	Wounded	"	
B2031	"	Raynor G.	"	Missing	"	
B1720	"	Robinson G.	"	Wounded	"	
B1646	"	Rolston A.	"	"	"	
S3189	"	Rogers H.	"	Missing	"	
B3049	"	Royle J.	"	Wounddd	"	
S7309	"	Redfearn A.	"	Missing	"	
S 402	"	Scott W.	"	"	"	
B1582	"	Sewell J.	"	"	"	
B1566	"	SEEREY E.	"	"	"	
S1716	"	Soden J.	"	"	"	
S3207	"	Smount T.	"	"	"	
B2043	"	Smith J.	"	"	"	
B3038	"	Starke W.	"	Wounded	"	
S2105	"	Stewart G.	"	"	"	
S7315	"	Spurr E.	"	Missing	"	
B1722	"	Taylor H.	"	Wounded	"	(died 31.7.15
S1723	"	Taylor E.	"	Killed in Act.	"	
B3060	"	Taylor ~~E~~ J.	"	Missing	"	
B3404	"	Thompson B.	"	Wounded	"	
B1731	"	Timms J.	"	"	"	
B1799	"	Timmins J.	"	Missing	"	
B3143	"	Turner R.	"	Wounded	"	
B2026	"	Vince N.	"	Missing	"	
S6542	"	Veevers H.	"	Wounded	"	
S6332	"	Veneer C.	"	Shock	"	
S 384	"	Walker E.	"	Missing	"	
S 974	"	Wackett J.	"	"	"	
B1632	"	Watson J.	"	"	"	
B1810	"	Webb J.	"	Wounded	"	
S1509	"	Weal H.	"	"	"	
B1966	"	Wells A.	"	"	"	
B1599	"	Whittaker R.	"	Missing	"	
8618	"	Williams S.	"	"	"	
B3054	"	Wilson J.	"	Shock	"	
B1741	"	Witts J.	"	Wounded	"	
B30[illegible]0	"	Williamson A.	"	"	"	
S2649	"	Workman C.	"	"	"	
S6245	"	Winslade W.	"	"	"	
S8772	"	Wilkinson A.	"	Missing	"	
	All	the above N.C.Os. and Riflemen are of 'C' Company.				

*State whether absence is of a permanent or temporary nature, adding, in the case of casuals from wounds or disease, any available information for communication to the relatives.

Army Form B. 213.

FIELD RETURN.

No. of Report ____________

(To be furnished by all arms, services, and departments to the A. G.'s Office at the Base in accordance with Field Service Regulations, Part II.)

____________________ Date.

RETURN showing numbers RATIONED by, and Transport on charge of, ____________________ at ____________

DETAIL	Personnel			Animals								Guns, carriages, and limbers and transport vehicles											Motor Bicycles	Bicycles	REMARKS
				Horses				Mules								Horsed		Mechanical							
	Officers	Other ranks	Natives	Riding	Draught	Heavy Draught	Pack	Large	Small	Camels	Oxen	Guns, carriages and limbers, showing description	Ammunition wagons and limbers	Machine guns	Aircraft, showing description	4 Wheeled	2 Wheeled	Motor Cars	Tractors	Lorries, showing description	Trucks, showing description	Trailers			
Effective Strength of Unit Details, *by Arms* attached to unit as in War Establishment :—																									
Total																									
War Establishment																									
Wanting to complete																									
Surplus																									
*Attached (not to include the details shown above)																									
Civilians :— Employed with the Unit Accompanying the Unit																									
TOTAL RATIONED ...																									

* In the case of field ambulances, hospitals or depôts, the number of patients are to be included here, the names being shown in A.F.A. 36.

____________________ Signature of Commander.

____________________ Date of Despatch.

(K 11859) W. & Co., Ltd. Wt. w6095—894 500,000 10/14 Forms B. 213/5

For information of the A.G.'s Office at the Base.

Officers and men who have become casuals, been transferred or joined since last report.

Place YPRES. Date 31.7.15.

Regtl. Number	Rank	Name	Corps	Nature of casualty, or name of unit from or to which transferred	Date of being struck off or coming on the ration return	Remarks*
S2249	Srgt.	Smith E.	8th.Rifle Bde.	Killed in A.	30.7.15.	
B 35	"	Roddy S.	"	"	"	
1025	"	Highland J.	"	Wounded	"	
B 418	"	Harris C.	"	Killed in A.	"	
S5223	"	Kerr F.	"	Wounded	"	
3069	"	Watkins T.	"	Killed in A.	"	
B3493	Cpl.	McCrcery W.	"	Wounded	"	
S1209	"	Mason W.	"	"	"	
S 821	"	Phillps A.	"	Killed in A.	"	
S5216	"	Parfitt H.	"	Wounded	"	
B 98	"	Spiers S	"	"	"	
B 367	"	Wright R.	"	"	"	(died3.8.15.)
B 47	"	Wheeler S.	"	"	"	
B1487	A/Cpl.	Cooksey J.	"	Killed in A.	"	
B2783	"	Hampson J.	"	Missing	"	
B 411	"	Dunn J.	"	Wounded	"	
B 409	"	Hollobone V.	"	"	"	
S1424	"	Grass W.	"	Missing	"	
S 817	"	Krajicek J.	"	Killed in A.	"	
B3155	"	Leech C.	"	Wounded	"	
S 272	"	Shaw W.	"	Killed in A.	"	
B 145	Rfmn.	Wright A.	"	Wnd & Miss.	"	
B 146	"	Abbott C.	"	Wounded	"	
B2609	"	Barnett C.	"	"	"	
B3490	"	Baizley J.	"	"	"	(died 11.8.15)
S1032	"	Bonney H.	"	Killed in A.	"	
S 838	"	Buckley J.	"	Wounded	"	
B3489	"	Cheney L.	"	Killed in A.	"	
B 48	"	Chick A.	"	Wounded	"	
S1334	"	Clements A.	"	"	"	
S2980	"	Crook J.	"	"	"	
B 470	"	Cubbit A.	"	Missing	"	
S5158	"	Casson R.	"	"	"	
S5917	"	Curtis W.	"	Wounded	"	
B 428	"	Dinmore W.	"	"	"	
B 274	"	Edge A.	"	Missing	"	
B3487	"	Godfrey W.	"	Wounded	"	
B1494	"	Green H.	"	"	"	
B2614	"	Garratt W.	"	"	"	
B 582	"	Gates E.	"	Missing	"	
B 509	"	Gooden H.	"	Wounded	"	
S7284	"	Grebham R.	"	"	"	
B 226	"	Gribben R.	"	Killed in A.	"	
B 174	"	Gittens W.	"	Wounded	"	
S6134	"	Govey W.	"	"	"	
S1285	"	Hirons S.	"	"	"	
S7350	"	Harris A.	"	"	"	
S7280	"	Hind J.	"	Missing	"	
S1038	"	Hartrey T.	"	"	"	
B1405	"	Haddock J.	"	"	"	
B1354	"	Higgings W.	"	Killed in A.	"	
S5231	"	Hillyard G.	"	Died of Wnds.	"	
B 286	"	Jessop A	"	Wounded	"	
S 820	"	Jenkins P.	"	"	"	
B 225	"	Johnson C.	"	"	"	

*State whether absence is of a permanent or temporary nature, adding, in the case of casuals from wounds or disease, any available information for communication to the relatives.

Army Form B. 213.

FIELD RETURN.

No. of Report ____________

(To be furnished by all arms, services, and departments to the A. G.'s Office at the Base in accordance with Field Service Regulations, Part II.)

____________________ Date.

RETURN showing numbers RATIONED by, and Transport on charge of, ____________________ at ____________________

Detail	Personnel			Animals								Guns, carriages, and limbers and transport vehicles													Remarks
				Horses				Mules								Horsed		Mechanical							
	Officers	Other ranks	Natives	Riding	Draught	Heavy Draught	Pack	Large	Small	Camels	Oxen	Guns, carriages and limbers, showing, description	Ammunition wagons and limbers	Machine guns	Aircraft, showing description	4 Wheeled	2 Wheeled	Motor Cars	Tractors	Lorries, showing description	Trucks, showing description	Trailers	Motor Bicycles	Bicycles	
Effective Strength of Unit																									
Details, *by Arms* attached to unit as in War Establishment:—																									
Total																									
War Establishment																									
Wanting to complete																									
Surplus																									
*Attached (not to include the details shown above)																									
Civilians:—																									
Employed with the Unit																									
Accompanying the Unit																									
TOTAL RATIONED ...																									

* In the case of field ambulances, hospitals or depôts, the number of patients are to be included here, the names being shown in A.F.A. 36.

(K 11859) W. & Co., Ltd. Wt. w6005—894 500,000 10/14 Forms B. 213 / 5

____________________ Signature of Commander.

____________________ Date of Despatch.

Sheet 7.

For information of the A.G.'s Office at the Base.

Officers and men who have become casuals, been transferred or joined since last report.

Place YPRES. Date 317.15.

Regtl. Number	Rank	Name	Corps	Nature of casualty, or name of unit from or to which transferred	Date of being struck off or coming on the ration return	Remarks*
B 126	Rfn.	Jones H.	8th.Rifle Bde.	Killed in A.	30.7.15.	
B 337	"	Jones W.	"	Wnd. & Miss.	"	
B2600	"	Jones W.	"	Wounded	"	
S1099	"	Kilborn A.	"	"	"	
S1498	"	Kenny C.	"	Wnd. & Miss.	"	
B 481	"	Kemp C.	"	Wounded	"	
S5910	"	Lemon H.	"	"	"	
S5187	"	Ludgate A	"	"	"	(died 2.8.15)
B1489	"	Law F.	"	Killed in A,	"	
B 69	"	Lewis J.	"	"	"	
B2603	"	Lye G.	"	Wounded	"	
B 734	"	Mack T.	"	Missing	"	
B 334	"	Maloney C	"	Wounded	"	
B 64	"	Morgan R.	"	Wnd. & Miss.	"	
S1499	"	Mitchell A.	"	Wounded	"	
S6747	"	Marshall H.	"	Killed in A.	"	
S2566	"	Minnins J.	"	Wounded	"	
B2785	"	Nixon H.	"	"	"	
S5204	"	Parker E.	"	Killed in A.	"	
B 221	"	Peacefell G.	"	Wounded	"	
B 208	"	Pellett E.	"		"	
B 413	"	Pennell G.	"	"	"	
B 423	"	Pickburn J.	"	"	"	
S3377	"	Pye G.	"	Killed in A.	"	
S2533	"	Parrott H.	"	Wounded	"	
S7353	"	Parkinson G.	"	"	"	(died 25.8.15)
B 335	"	Richards J.	"	Wnd. & Miss.	"	
S1495	"	Richardson J.	"	Wounded	"	
S1056	"	Rosser F.	"	"	"	
S1339	"	Rugg T.	"	Missing	"	
B 482	"	Simmonds J.	"	Wounded	"	
B 543	"	Stafford W.	"	"	"	
S1016	"	Sinfield W.	"	Missing	"	
B 47	"	Boston-Strange	"	Wounded	"	
S7669	"	Stevenson G.	V	"	"	
S7281	"	Thorogood R.	"	Wnd. & Miss.	"	
S5157	"	Turner W.	"	Wounded	"	
B 363	"	Turner A.	"	"	"	
B3494	"	Toovey A.	"	Killed in A.	"	
B 228	"	Walker C.	"	c Wounded	"	
B 416	"	Walker H.	"	"	"	
B 325	"	Walsh E.	"	Missing	"	
B 320	"	White H.	"	"	"	
S5284	"	White C.	"	"	"	
S8657	"	Wright H.	"	Wounded	"	
B1989	"	Wood T.	"	Killed in A.	"	
S1414	Sgt.	White A.	"	Wounded	"	
S6800	Rfmn.	Strawson R.	"	Missing	"	
S8267	"	Sayers F.	"	Wounded	"	
S8486	"	Wade C.	"	"	"	
S8425	"	PrescottWw	"	"	"	
S8479	"	Avais W.	"	"	"	
S8620	"	Meadows W.	"	"	"	
S8794	"	Troutbeck A.	"	"	"	

*State whether absence is of a permanent or temporary nature, adding, in the case of casuals from wounds or disease, any available information for communication to the relatives.

FIELD RETURN.

Army Form B. 213.

No. of Report__________

(To be furnished by all arms, services, and departments to the A. G.'s Office at the Base in accordance with Field Service Regulations, Part II.)

__________Date.

RETURN showing numbers RATIONED by, and Transport on charge of,__________at__________

Detail	Personnel			Animals								Guns, carriages, and limbers and transport vehicles													Remarks
				Horses				Mules								Horsed		Mechanical							
	Officers	Other ranks	Natives	Riding	Draught	Heavy Draught	Pack	Large	Small	Camels	Oxen	Guns, carriages and limbers, showing, description	Ammunition wagons and limbers	Machine guns	Aircraft, showing description	4 Wheeled	2 Wheeled	Motor Cars	Tractors	Lorries, showing description	Trucks, showing description	Trailers	Motor Bicycles	Bicycles	
Effective Strength of Unit																									
Details, *by Arms* attached to unit as in War Establishment :—																									
Total																									
War Establishment																									
Wanting to complete																									
Surplus																									
*Attached (not to include the details shown above)																									
Civilians :—																									
Employed with the Unit																									
Accompanying the Unit																									
TOTAL RATIONED ...																									

* In the case of field ambulances, hospitals or depôts, the number of patients are to be included here, the names being shown in A.F.A. 36.

__________Signature of Commander.

__________Date of Despatch.

(K 11859) W. & Co., Ltd. Wt. w6005—894 500,000 10/14 Forms B. 213 / 5

Sheet 8.

For information of the A.G.'s Office at the Base.

Officers and men who have become casuals, been transferred or joined since last report.

Place YPRES. Date Bn.H.Q. 31.7.15.

Regtl. Number	Rank	Name	Corps	Nature of casualty, or name of unit from or to which transferred	Date of being struck off or coming on the ration return	Remarks*
B1441	Rfnm.	Holt W.	8th. Rifle Bde.	Wounded	30.7.15.	
B 364	"	Dewar W.	"	Missing	"	
S6096	"	Attewell G.	"	"	"	
B 223	"	Tubb F.	"	Killed in Act.	"	
	All	the above N.C.Os. and Riflemen are of 'A' Company.				
B2855	Sgt.	Dempster R.	8th. Rifle Bde.	Wnd. & Miss.	30.7.15.	
B2856	"	Hartley H.	"	Wounded	"	
B1957	"	Pitt L	"	Wnd. & Miss.	"	
B2866	"	Evans S.R.	"	Wounded	"	
B2800	"	Sutton F.	"	Killed in Act.	"	
S2875	Corpl.	Frame J.	"	Wounded	"	
B2459	"	Humphreys E.	"	"	"	
B2524	"	McDonald D.	"	Killed	"	
B2037	"	Stevens J.	"	"	"	
Z2668	"	Sandalls E.	"	Wnd.& Mis.	"	
B 973	"	Tennant D.	"	Killed	"	
S 483	a/Corpl.	Boswell G	"	"	"	
B2860	"	Brian H.	"	"	"	
S1783	"	Carson C.	"	Wounded	"	
B2516	"	Humphreys H.	"	"	"	
B2520	"	Naylor R.	"	"	"	
B 689	"	Peak W.	"	Missing	"	
S 695	"	Alderwick A.	"	"	"	
B2801	"	Basnett J.	"	"	"	
B2954	"	Binks H.	"	Wnd. & Mis	"	
S6258	"	Borthefck J.	"	Killed	"	
S 676	Rfn.	Admitt W.	"	"	"	
S9762	"	Austing J.	"	Wounded	"	
S8469	"	Admitt E.	"	Missing	"	
S 611	"	Baker J.	"	Killed	"	
S7622	"	Baker A.	"	"	"	
B1279	"	Blake M.	"	"	"	
S6137	"	Burgess R.	"	Wounded	"	
S8481	"	BartlettR.	"	Missing	"	
B2158	"	Carter W"	"	Wounded	"	
B2228	"	Coley F.	"	"	"	
B2522	"	Cockerton F.	"	Killed	"	
S 677	"	Colebourne J.	"	Missing	"	
B2445	"	Connor J.	"	Killed	"	
S 393	"	Cousill S.	"	"	"	
S 698	"	Crotty B.	"	"	"	
S 498	"	Callaghlan F.	"	Wounded	"	
S9799	"	Dale F.	"	"	"	
S 621	"	Dallas F.	"	Wnd.& Mis.	"	
B2455	"	Davies H.	"	Wounded	"	
B 688	a/Corpl.	Davidson J.	"	"	"	
S7386	Rfn.	Davis W.	"	"	"	
B2385	"	Davies J.	"	"	"	
B2235	"	Downey A	"	"	"	
B2797	"	Dawson J.	"	"	"	
B2377	"	Emmens H	"	"	"	

*State whether absence is of a permanent or temporary nature, adding, in the case of casuals from wounds or disease, any available information for communication to the relatives.

FIELD RETURN.

Army Form B. 213.

No. of Report ____________

(To be furnished by all arms, services, and departments to the A. G.'s Office at the Base in accordance with Field Service Regulations, Part II.)

____________ Date.

RETURN showing numbers RATIONED by, and Transport on charge of, ____________ at ____________

Detail	Personnel			Animals								Guns, carriages, and limbers and transport vehicles											Motor Bicycles	Bicycles	Remarks
				Horses				Mules								Horsed		Mechanical							
	Officers	Other ranks	Natives	Riding	Draught	Heavy Draught	Pack	Large	Small	Camels	Oxen	Guns, carriages and limbers, showing, description	Ammunition wagons and limbers	Machine guns	Aircraft, showing description	4 Wheeled	2 Wheeled	Motor Cars	Tractors	Lorries, showing description	Tracks, showing description	Trailers			
Effective Strength of Unit																									
Details, *by Arms* attached to unit as in War Establishment:—																									
Total																									
War Establishment																									
Wanting to complete																									
Surplus																									
*Attached (not to include the details shown above)																									
Civilians:—																									
Employed with the Unit																									
Accompanying the Unit																									
TOTAL RATIONED ...																									

* In the case of field ambulances, hospitals or depôts, the number of patients are to be included here, the names being shown in A.F.A. 36.

(K 11859) W. & Co., Ltd. Wt. w6005—894 500,000 10/14 Forms B. 213 / 5

____________ Signature of Commander.

____________ Date of Despatch.

Sheet 9.

For information of the A.G.'s Office at the Base.

Officers and men who have become casuals, been transferred or joined since last report.

Place YPRES. Date 31.7.15.

Regtl. Number	Rank	Name	Corps	Nature of casualty, or name of unit from or to which transferred	Date of being struck off or coming on the ration return	Remarks*
B2377	Rifm.	Fay W.	8th. Rifle Bde.	Wounded	30.7.15.	
B2231	'	Geen F.	'	Died of Wnds.	'	
B2529	'	Gladman G.	'	Wounded	'	
S7381	'	Goodchild J.	'	Killed in Act.	'	
B2388	'	Groom J.	'	'	'	
S7638	'	Hall E.	'	Wounded	'	
S 678	'	Hall R.	'	'	'	
S5246	A/Cpl	Harkness W.	'	'	'	
B2234	Rfmn.	Harrison W.	'	'	'	
S7712	'	Holmes H.	'	'	'	
S 394	'	Houlston D.	'	'	'	
8312	'	Jordan J.	'	'	'	
5808	'	Joslyn C.	'	'	'	
S 681	'	Keeling G.	'	'	'	
B2308	'	Lake F.	'	'	'	
S7269	'	Lamb P.	'	'	'	
B2233	'	Littlewood H.	'	'	'	
B2136	'	Luce L.	'	'	'	
S7303	'	Machin J.	'	Killed in Act.	'	
B2602	'	Marshall R.	'	'	'	
S 479	'	Martin G.	'	'	'	
S 399	'	Metcalf F.	'	'	'	
B2858	'	Nixon D.	'	'	'	
B2374	'	North W.	'	'	'	
B2802	'	O'Brien M.	'	Wounded	'	
S 535	'	Perkins T.	'	'	'	
B2794	'	Powell A.	'	'	'	
S6240	'	Powell F.	'	'	'	
B2448	'	Preston W.	'	Missing	'	
S 697	'	Ransford W.	'	Wnd. & Miss.	'	
S6144	'	Rouse H.	'	Killed in Act.	'	
B2539	'	Smith G.	'	Wounded	'	
S5325	'	Staniford J.	'	Missing	'	
B2236	'	Stripe A.	'	Wounded	'	
B2381	A/Cpl.	Stubbs C.	'	Killed in Act.	'	
B2229	Rfmn.	Taylor E.	'	Wounded	'	
S8316	'	Thomas H.	'	'	'	
B2300	'	THRESher L.	'	'	'	
B2387	'	Wadham W.	'	Killed in Act.	'	
B2941	'	Walmsley T.	'	Wounded	'	
B2790	'	Ward G.	'	'	'	
B2379	'	White W.	'	'	'	
B2947	'	Wilson G.	'	Killed in Act.	'	
S8523	'	Walker J.	'	Wounded	'	
B2396	'	Yirrell W.	'	'	'	
B1953	'	Godwin L.	'	'	'	
B2864	'	Ball B.	'	'	'	
S8609	'	Barker A.	'	Wnd. & Miss.	'	
S7677	'	Boon A.	'	Wounded	'	
B2868	CPL.	Gordon L.D.	'	'	'	
B2521	Rfmn.	Naylor H.	'	'	'	(died 15.8.15)
B2796	'	Rimmer H.	'	'	'	
B2386	'	Worstencroft J.	'	'	'	

All the above N.C.Os. and Riflemen are of 'D' Company.

*State whether absence is of a permanent or temporary nature, adding, in the case of casuals from wounds or disease, any available information for communication to the relatives.

FIELD RETURN.

Army Form B. 213.

No. of Report ____________

(To be furnished by all arms, services, and departments to the A. G.'s Office at the Base in accordance with Field Service Regulations, Part II.)

______________ Date.

RETURN showing numbers RATIONED by, and Transport on charge of, ______________ at ______________

Detail	Personnel			Animals								Guns, carriages, and limbers and transport vehicles											Motor Bicycles	Bicycles	Remarks
				Horses				Mules								Horsed		Mechanical							
	Officers	Other ranks	Natives	Riding	Draught	Heavy Draught	Pack	Large	Small	Camels	Oxen	Guns, carriages and limbers, showing, description	Ammunition wagons and limbers	Machine guns	Aircraft, showing description	4 Wheeled	2 Wheeled	Motor Cars	Tractors	Lorries, showing description	Trucks, showing description	Trailers			
Effective Strength of Unit																									
Details, *by Arms* attached to unit as in War Establishment:—																									
Total																									
War Establishment																									
Wanting to complete																									
Surplus																									
*Attached (not to include the details shown above)																									
Civilians:—																									
Employed with the Unit																									
Accompanying the Unit																									
Total Rationed ...																									

* In the case of field ambulances, hospitals or depôts, the number of patients are to be included here, the names being shown in A.F.A. 36.

______________ Signature of Commander.

______________ Date of Despatch.

(K11859) W. & Co., Ltd. Wt. w6005—894 500,000 10/14 Forms B. 213 / 5

Sheet 10.

For information of the A.G.'s Office at the Base.

Officers and men who have become casuals, been transferred or joined since last report.

Place YPRES. Date 31.7.15.

Regtl. Number	Rank	Name	Corps	Nature of casualty, or name of unit from or to which transferred	Date of being struck off or coming on the ration return	Remarks*
S 180	A/Cpl.	O'Callaghan F.	8th.RifleBde.	From Hospital (wounds)	1.8.15.	'A'
S 985	Rfmn.	Oddy A.	'	'	'	'
B 227	'	Lansdown R.	'	'	'	'
B1408	'	Williams T.	'	'	'	'B'
S3190	'	Carden R.	'	'	'	'
B 768	'	Webster R.	'	'	'	'
B1633	'	Horton E.	'	'	'	'C'
S 688	'	Bennett J.	'	'	'	'D'
B 604	'	Bates J.	'	From Hptl.Sick	'	'B'
9725	Sgt.	May W.	'	Shell hand	27.7.15.	'D'
S6190	Rfn.	White S.	'	G.S. leg.	28.7.15.	'B'
B 66	'	Knight C.	'	Bomb practice head cut accl.	28.7.15.	'A'
B 719	Rfn.	Redman C.	'	To Hospital	27.7.15.	'D'
8439	'	Barber C.	'	'	'	'C'
B 597	'	Wilkinson A.	'	'	'	'
B3120	C.S.M.	Holt J.	'	'	'	'A'
B 121	Rfn.	Wells J.	'	'	28.7.15.	'
B1995	A/Cpl.	Carttling L.	'	'	29.7.15	'D'
B2298	Rfn.	Gore T.	'	'	'	'
S7582	'	Kendall F.	'	'	'	'C'
S3198	Cpl.	Belbin C.	'	From Hospital	19.7.15.	'C'
10664	Rfn.	Holland R.	'	'	25.7.15.	'B'
B 362	'	Stillwell H.	'	To Hospital	20.7.15.	'A'
S5156	'	Davies R.	'	'	'	'
B 362	'	Stillwell H.	'	From Hospital	2.8.15.	'
S7657	'	Morrell H.	'	Wounded	30.7.15.	'C'
9829	'	Wordhaugh F.	'	'	'	'
8515	'	Wilson W.	'	'	'	'
8783	'	Turner W.	'	'	'	'
S 719	'	Redman C.	'	From Hospital	'	'D'
B 121	'	Wells J.	'	'	'	'A'
S 526	'	Parsons J.	'	To Hospital	28.7.15.	'C'
				From Hospital	3.8.15.	'
B2854	A/Cpl	Binks H.	'	'	19.7.15.	'D'
B3137	Rfn.	Gill J.	'	'	27.7.15	'C'
B3040	'	Jenkinson C.	'	'	25.7.15.	'

*State whether absence is of a permanent or temporary nature, adding, in the case of casuals from wounds or disease, any available information for communication to the relatives.

Army Form B. 213.

FIELD RETURN.

No. of Report 11

(To be furnished by all arms, services, and departments to the A. G.'s Office at the Base in accordance with Field Service Regulations, Part II.)

3. 8. 15 Date.

RETURN showing numbers RATIONED by, and Transport on charge of, 8th Batt. Rifle Brigade at Ypres.

Detail	Personnel: Officers	Personnel: Other ranks	Personnel: Natives	Animals: Horses: Riding	Animals: Horses: Draught	Animals: Horses: Heavy Draught	Animals: Horses: Pack	Animals: Mules: Large *	Animals: Mules: Small	Animals: Camels	Animals: Oxen	Guns, carriages and limbers, showing, description	Ammunition wagons and limbers	Machine guns	Aircraft, showing description	Horsed: 4 Wheeled	Horsed: 2 Wheeled	Mechanical: Motor Cars	Mechanical: Tractors	Mechanical: Lorries, showing description	Mechanical: Trucks, showing description	Mechanical: Trailers	Motor Bicycles	Bicycles	Remarks
Effective Strength of Unit	8	398	–	14		9	9	34				G.S. Tools 2. M.G. 2	7	2		6	4							9	
Details, *by Arms* attached to unit as in War Establishment:—																									
R.A.M.C	1																								
A.O.C		1																							
Intrepeter			1																						
Total	9	399	1	14		9	9	34				2 2	7	2		6	4							9	
War Establishment	30	991	1	14		9	9	34				2 2	7	2		6	4							9	
Wanting to complete	21	560																							
Surplus																									
*Attached (not to include the details shown above)																									
Civilians:— Employed with the Unit																									
Accompanying the Unit																									
TOTAL RATIONED ...	9	399	1	14		9	9	34																	

* In the case of field ambulances, hospitals or depôts, the number of patients are to be included here, the names being shown in A.F.A. 36.

Signature of Commander.

Date of Despatch.

(K 11859) W. & Co., Ltd. Wt. w6005—894 500,000 10/14 Forms B. 213 / 5

II

14th Division

121/6753

8th Bn Rifle Brigade

Vol: III

From 28th July to 8 Sept 15

Instructions regarding War Diaries and Intelligence Summaries are contained in F. S. Regs., Part II. and the Staff Manual respectively. Title pages will be prepared in manuscript.

WAR DIARY
or
INTELLIGENCE SUMMARY.
(Erase heading not required.)

Army Form C. 2118.

Place	Date	Hour	Summary of Events and Information	Remarks and references to Appendices
Gingerbread Chateau, + YPRES.	28-7-15		On this day, the Battalion distributed as follows:— A + B Coys in the RAMPARTS at YPRES; Headquarters with C + D coys at Gingerbread Chateau. Transport &c at Vlamertinghe.	
—	29-7-15		The Battalion took over the trenches at HOOGE known as G10. G5 + G4. from 7th Btn. Rifle Bde. All O.C Coys. went up early in the day to reconnoitre the line. Owing to the ZILLEBEEKE communication trench being reserved for the 5th Corps the	
HOOGE.			original plan of sending up one Company, Machine Guns and Bombers was cancelled. Consequently all ranks were quite strange to the trenches. Relief carried out quietly. Instead of issuing rations to the men they were carried by Transport as the dumping ground was quite close to Headquarters. The strength of the Battalion taking over was 24 officers and 745 other ranks. Four machine guns were taken over from the 7th Rifle Bde and one of our own was also taken up. A dark night with moon in the third quarter.	

1577 Wt. W10791/1773 500,000 1/15 D. D. & L. A.D.S.S./Forms/C. 2118.

Instructions regarding War Diaries and Intelligence Summaries are contained in F. S. Regs., Part II. and the Staff Manual respectively. Title pages will be prepared in manuscript.

WAR DIARY
or
INTELLIGENCE SUMMARY.
(Erase heading not required.)

Army Form C. 2118.

Place	Date	Hour	Summary of Events and Information	Remarks and references to Appendices
HOOGE	30/7/15		By 2 A.M. the relief was complete except for some bombers left behind by the 7th Rifle Bde. under orders G.O.C. Distribution of the Battalion was as follows: — Front Line in G10 on left Lt. Woodroffe and one platoon "A" Coy — — on right Lt. Carey and one platoon — In support in F2. Two platoons of "A" Coy. Lt. McAfee the O.C. of "A" Coy in command of the whole. A large crater divided "A" Coy. from "C" Coy which held the remainder of the front line with three platoons in G4 + G5. The left of this Coy. rested on the crater, the right on the MENIN ROAD where it joined the 7th Btn. K.R.R.C also in the front line. One platoon of "C" Coy was in support in G.7., Capt. Prior commanding the Coy. The two other Companies were in ZOUAVE WOOD. "B" Coy. on the left in dugouts near the N.W. corner. "D" Coy. on the right in S3. ~~One platoon of "B" Coy~~ "D" Coy under Capt. Sheepshanks and "B" Coy. under Capt. Cavendish.	

1577 Wt. W10791/1773 500,000 1/15 D. D. & L. A.D.S.S./Forms/C. 2118.

Army Form C. 2118.

WAR DIARY
or
INTELLIGENCE SUMMARY.
(Erase heading not required.)

Instructions regarding War Diaries and Intelligence Summaries are contained in F. S. Regs., Part II. and the Staff Manual respectively. Title pages will be prepared in manuscript.

Place	Date	Hour	Summary of Events and Information	Remarks and references to Appendices
HOOGE	30/7/15. contd.		One platoon of "B" Coy. was in a supporting point 100 yards due S. of ZOUAVE WOOD, Headquarters, Southern edge of ZOUAVE WOOD. Four machine guns were in the front line; one in supporting point. "A" + "C" Coys both connected with Hd Qrs. by telephone. The weak points of the position were as follows:— (1) There was no wire to speak of in front. (2) The front line trenches deep + narrow and communication ~~communication~~ along them very difficult. (3) The communications to the rear also difficult and inadequate. (4) Trench howitzers of the enemy daily blew in parts of the support trenches and although these trenches are shewn on the map, hardly any of them were habitable consequently too many men were crammed into the front line and there was not enough depth. (5) The crater divided the front line as the part blown up there was not held though bomber's posts were established on each side At about 3-15 AM. the Germans attacked. It had already been reported that they were very active in front and the whole front line was "standing to" as usual at that hour.	

1577 Wt. W10791/1773 500,000 1/15 D. D. & L. A.D.S.S./Forms/C. 2118.

Instructions regarding War Diaries and Intelligence Summaries are contained in F. S. Regs., Part II. and the Staff Manual respectively. Title pages will be prepared in manuscript.

WAR DIARY
or
INTELLIGENCE SUMMARY.
(Erase heading not required.)

Army Form C. 2118.

Place	Date	Hour	Summary of Events and Information	Remarks and references to Appendices
HOOGE	30/7/15 contd		Part of the front trenches was subjected to an intense bombardment which lasted only about two or three minutes, then suddenly sheets of flame broke out all along the front and clouds of thick, black smoke. The Germans had turned on liquid fire, from hoses apparently, which had been established just in front during the night. Under cover of the flames, swarms of bombers appeared on the parapet and in rear of the line. The mass of them had broken through at the crater and then swung left and right. The fighting became very confused and the machine guns were soon all out of action. The extreme right and left hand platoons of the front line of the Battalion repulsed all attempts to bomb them out as they had not been affected by the flames; however the Germans had pushed through the whole centre in spite of most gallant fighting by officers and men and they (the Germans) were established with machine guns in the ruins of HOOGE on the S. of the MENIN ROAD commanding all the ground between there and ZOUAVE WOOD. At about between 4 AM and 5 AM B Coy counter-attacked	

1577 Wt. W10791/1773 500,000 1/15 D. D. & L. A.D.S.S./Forms/C. 2118.

Instructions regarding War Diaries and Intelligence Summaries are contained in F. S. Regs., Part II. and the Staff Manual respectively. Title pages will be prepared in manuscript.

WAR DIARY
or
INTELLIGENCE SUMMARY.
(Erase heading not required.)

Army Form C. 2118.

Place	Date	Hour	Summary of Events and Information	Remarks and references to Appendices
HOOGE	30/7/15 contd		but were beaten back by machine gun fire but established itself temporarily half-way along Old Bond Street and covered the withdrawal of Lt. McAfee and a few remnants left of two platoons of A Coy. When this counter-attack failed, the officer commanding in G10. who was then almost surrounded, fought his way back due W. along the road to the CULVERT. ~~The~~ Nearly all the platoon in G4 on the right were overwhelmed and the Germans established themselves along the whole of my front and were at once strongly reinforced ~~the~~ by the machine guns + rifles. They then attempted to bomb down the two communication trenches Old Bond Street + the Strand but these were blocked about halfway up and held throughout the day. From the beginning of the action, ZOUAVE WOOD had been subjected to violent artillery bombardment and all communication was difficult and telephones were cut. Reinforcements meanwhile had arrived from the Brigade in the shape of one Coy. of the K.R.R.C. which got up about 9 A.M. The remains of the Battalion held the	

1577 Wt. W10791/1773 500,000 1/15 D. D. & L. A.D.S.S./Forms/C. 2118.

Army Form C. 2118.

Instructions regarding War Diaries and Intelligence Summaries are contained in F. S. Regs., Part II. and the Staff Manual respectively. Title pages will be prepared in manuscript.

WAR DIARY
or
INTELLIGENCE SUMMARY.
(Erase heading not required.)

Place	Date	Hour	Summary of Events and Information	Remarks and references to Appendices
HOOGE	30/7/15 contd.		Northern edge of the ZOUAVE WOOD. about 12 (noon) the order was received from the G.O.C for a counter-attack to take place at 2-45 P.M. after the artillery had bombarded for 3/4 hour. The Battalion was to lead the attack on the left with its right on the STRAND and left on BOND STREET. The objective of the attack were G 8. and G 9. on the MENIN ROAD. Only one organised Coy. remained in hand i.e., "D" Coy. "C" Coy was non-existent, "B" + "A" Coys. had suffered heavy losses. The O.C Battn. gave the following verbal orders to Capt. Sheepshanks firstly that he was to attack on a front of two platoons, with two platoons in support. His right was to rest on the Strand; that a bombing attack was to be made by him up the Strand at the same time. That he was to move into his position during the bombardment and get beyond our own wire which protected the Northern edge of ZOUAVE WOOD. He was to hope to get touch with the Coy. on his left as the frontage allotted was too big, but he was to keep touch with the 7th Bn. K.R.R.C. on his right. The remains of "A" + "B" Coys were given practically the same verbal orders	

1577 Wt. W10791/1773 500,000 1/15 D. D. & L. A.D.S.S./Forms/C. 2118.

Instructions regarding War Diaries and Intelligence Summaries are contained in F. S. Regs., Part II. and the Staff Manual respectively. Title pages will be prepared in manuscript.

WAR DIARY
or
INTELLIGENCE SUMMARY.
(Erase heading not required.)

Army Form C. 2118.

Place	Date	Hour	Summary of Events and Information	Remarks and references to Appendices
HOOGE	30/7/15		and told to attack G9. with their centre on Old Bond Street and bombers up the communication trench itself. At 2-45 P.M. exactly the counter attack started. D Coy. on the right advance as if on parade. The enemy's machine guns & rifle fire had apparently not been in any way silenced by the bombardment. The whole ground was absolutely swept by bullets The attack was brought to a complete standstill halfway towards its objective and no reinforcements could reach it. The same thing happened on the left up Old Bond Street. The second counter-attack had failed. The remnants of the Battalion held on to the communication trench till dark & the front line of ZOUAVE WOOD was gradually taken over, first by the 7th Rifle Bde and then by the D.C.L.I. At 2 AM that morning the Battalion was taken out of action and had suffered the following casualties:— 6 officers killed, 3 officers missing almost certainly killed, 10 officers wounded most of whom were believed to be killed – Other ranks 80 killed, 267 wounded and 132 missing, in addition to five O.R. suffering from shock.	

Instructions regarding War Diaries and Intelligence Summaries are contained in F. S. Regs., Part II. and the Staff Manual respectively. Title pages will be prepared in manuscript.

WAR DIARY
or
INTELLIGENCE SUMMARY.
(Erase heading not required.)

Army Form C. 2118.

Place	Date	Hour	Summary of Events and Information	Remarks and references to Appendices
HOOGE	30/7/15		Four machine guns out of five were lost (disabled by the enemy's fire) The men fought without rations or water throughout the day I attach a Trench Map to amplify this report.	

1577 Wt. W10791/1773 500,000 1/15 D. D. & L. A.D.S.S./Forms/C. 2118.

Instructions regarding War Diaries and Intelligence Summaries are contained in F. S. Regs., Part II. and the Staff Manual respectively. Title pages will be prepared in manuscript.

WAR DIARY
or
INTELLIGENCE SUMMARY.
(*Erase heading not required.*)

Army Form C. 2118.

Place	Date	Hour	Summary of Events and Information	Remarks and references to Appendices
Bivouac. 1 mile E of Poperinghe	31st		Arrived from Hooge (Zouave Wood) in two parties at 6 a.m.	
"	1st		Battalion resting & refitting. Nine Riflemen, who had been wounded rejoined from Hospital	
	2nd		Inspected by Lt.Gen. Sir John Keir K.C.B. who specially thanked the telephone section for its work in recent action. Lieut Gladstone & 6 men rejoined from a course of instruction in the Trench Mortar.	
Ypres	3rd		Battalion marched to cellars in Ypres - Dug that night on G.H.Q. 2nd line	
"	4th		Digging at night on G.H.Q. line. 2/Lt Bevis sick (from wound) & evacuated	
	5th		Vicinity of Battalion Billets very heavily shelled 2.30 a.m & again 3.30 a.m. Whole Battalion mustering 200 digging night 5/6 on Menin Road near Ecole. Major Tod & 2/Lt Foxwell evacuated suffering from exhaustion result of recent fighting - Draft of 50 arrived. H.Q. (Transport	

Army Form C. 2118.

WAR DIARY
or
INTELLIGENCE SUMMARY.
(Erase heading not required.)

Instructions regarding War Diaries and Intelligence Summaries are contained in F. S. Regs., Part II. and the Staff Manual respectively. Title pages will be prepared in manuscript.

Place	Date	Hour	Summary of Events and Information	Remarks and references to Appendices
Ypres	6th Aug.		Battalion digging on night 6/7th on Menin Road – Billets shelled that night – Eight men wounded by shrapnel in billets 11 a.m.	
	7th		Unusually heavy shelling round billets about 3.30 a.m. Battalion put at disposal of 42nd Brigade – Digging by White Chateau Menin Road night 7/8 – a draft of 150 arrived at HQrs (transport)	
	8th		Usual shelling – one man wounded	
	9th		Battalion took no part in attack made by 6th Division on lost trenches at Hooge. a draft of 110 arrived – Battalion carried rations up this night for 42nd Brigade	
	10		Quitted the cellars Ypres 7.45 pm – Marched to bivouacs 1½ miles East of Poperinghe a Guard of 1 NCO 30 Riflemen left to guard trenches at Vlamertinghe	
Rest Bivouac G.H.	11		14 officers arrived – Reorganisation of Battalion begun	
	12th		NCOs promoted, & drafts posted	

1577 Wt. W10791/1773 500,000 1/15 D. D. & L. A.D.S.S./Forms/C. 2118.

Instructions regarding War Diaries and Intelligence Summaries are contained in F. S. Regs., Part II. and the Staff Manual respectively. Title pages will be prepared in manuscript.

WAR DIARY
or
INTELLIGENCE SUMMARY.
(*Erase heading not required.*)

Army Form C. 2118.

Place	Date	Hour	Summary of Events and Information	Remarks and references to Appendices
Canal Bank North Ypres	13th		Heavy Rains all day. Moved here after dark in relief of Royal Scot. Fusiliers. The Battalion on this day was split up as follows; (a) Watou 1 Off. 25 O.R. (Telephone & Bombing class) (b) 1 N.C.O. & 4 Riflemen to Ypres (police) (c) 105 left at Transport H.Q's (d) 4 Officers 326 O.R. to Trenches with 7 Bn. R.B. (e) 3 Officers 90 O.R. to garrison Potijze Defences under Lt Squire (f) 11 Officers 155 O.R. with H.Q. to Canal Bank.	
"	14th		All quiet a draft of 50 arrived at Transport H.Q. One Rifleman wounded in trenches. 1 Rifleman wounded. T/Lt.Col R.C. Maclachlan gazetted to permanent Rank d. 1st June. Lt E.A. McAfee (since killed in action) to be Captain d. 3 July. 2 Lt C. Le Blanc Smith to be Lieutenant d. 3rd July	
	15th		A Test of the new tube smoke helmet carried out at H.Q's of Div. A court of enquiry on loss of all telescopic rifles belonging to Brigade on 30/7/	
	16th		1 Rifleman died of wounds in the Trenches - Heavy Shelling along Menin Gate 9 p.m. Draft of 11 wounded returned to duty Transport H.Q's	
	17th		Heavy Rains all day. Following return of casualties among full rank NCOs submitted - 1 Sgt. Major w. 3 C.S.M's wounded & sick - 10 Sgts killed 20 w. 3 wounded (duty) 2 missing 11 Cpls k. 20 w. 1 w (duty) 3 missing. 1 Sergeant killed this day.	

1577 Wt. W10791/1773 500,000 1/15 D. D. & L. A.D.S.S./Forms/C. 2118.

Instructions regarding War Diaries and Intelligence Summaries are contained in F. S. Regs., Part II. and the Staff Manual respectively. Title pages will be prepared in manuscript.

WAR DIARY
or
INTELLIGENCE SUMMARY.
(Erase heading not required.)

Army Form C. 2118.

Place	Date	Hour	Summary of Events and Information	Remarks and references to Appendices
Canal Bank I.1.b.	18th		Nothing of importance - German aeroplanes very active & the shelling on both sides still heavier than usual.	
"	19th		2 Lt Crichton wounded at Potijze. 1 Rifleman killed 1 wounded in trenches. 1 Rifleman wounded H.Q.	
"	20th		1 Rifleman wounded in trenches. Very quiet.	
"	21st		2 Lt Atkinson wounded & two Riflemen. 98 Riflemen sent back to me from 7th R.B. - They had been lent to strengthen the 7th Bn.	
	22nd		O.C. & Adjutant visited trenches which were to be taken over. Draft of 67 Riflemen arrived at Transport Camp, & also 21 old hands returned from being sick or wounded. Two Riflemen wounded. Heavy shelling on main road in rear, & transport much delayed. Four machine guns to trenches	
I.4.a+c.	23rd		To trenches - Relieved 8th K.R.R. in A 5 & took over a part of A4 from 7th K.R.R. - The left of 8th K.R.R. in A.6 was taken over by Sherwood Foresters 6th Division - Battalion reassembled from all points - 225 of my men from 7th R.B. - the Company (D) from Potijze Defences - a draft of 40 men, which had been left at Transport Camp - Companies therefore made up afresh - Relief quiet. A & D Companies in front line - B & C in support	

Instructions regarding War Diaries and Intelligence Summaries are contained in F. S. Regs., Part II. and the Staff Manual respectively. Title pages will be prepared in manuscript.

WAR DIARY
or
INTELLIGENCE SUMMARY.
(Erase heading not required.)

Army Form C. 2118.

Place	Date	Hour	Summary of Events and Information	Remarks and references to Appendices
I.4.a+c.	23/8/15		a quiet part of line, very little sniping. A battery, 48th Bde. support us. I find great improvement in the co-ordination of Infantry + Artillery + the Engineers. a representative of each reported himself to me. The Battalion Hd. Qrs. in I.4.a.7.2. Trenches in I.5.a+c.	
	24th		Three Machine Guns withdrawn from front line + put in G.H.Q. Line with supports (Trenches X2, X3) Trenches shelled by Crumps + Whizz-bangs during day. No damage. 2/Lt. Newton to hospital. Find wire in front very feeble – wiring parties out all night.	
	25th		2/Lt. Le Blanc Smith, M.G. Officer (wounded) returned to duty. a party of 6 R.E attached for technical advice in wiring the front. Rations sent direct to front line in handcarts, rubber wheeled. Front quiet. Enemy busy digging + improving their parapets.	
	26th.		G.O.C. round trenches. Patrols this night report (a) that they were in touch with German covering party on our right + reached within listening distance of their parapet on left. We had large working parties out in front improving parapet + wiring. Capt. Sheepshanks returned from leave. Trenches shelled during day but our battery retaliated on enemy's trenches at once. One enemy	

Instructions regarding War Diaries and Intelligence Summaries are contained in F. S. Regs., Part II. and the Staff Manual respectively. Title pages will be prepared in manuscript.

WAR DIARY
or
INTELLIGENCE SUMMARY.
(Erase heading not required.)

Army Form C. 2118.

Place	Date	Hour	Summary of Events and Information	Remarks and references to Appendices
I.4.a+c.	26/8/15		sniper killed. a message received from His Majesty the King through Lord Stamfordham condoling with the Brigade on its losses &c. 1 O.R. wounded. Lt. Wenham + 9 bombers rejoined from bombing course.	
	27/8/15		a new pattern tube helmet issued to certain specialists i.e. Machine Gunners as a precaution against poison gas.	
	28/8/15		2/Lt. S.C. Garrard killed by a sniper. 3 O.R. wounded. Shrapnel shell burst near ration dump about 9 P.M. No casualties.	
	29/8/15		a representative from the Munitions Board visited the trenches. a streaming wet day + so he heard few shells + saw much mud.	
	30/8/15		2 O.R. wounded. [illegible] iron sniperscope taken into use.	

1577 Wt. W10791/1773 500,000 1/15 D

Army Form C. 2118.

Instructions regarding War Diaries and Intelligence Summaries are contained in F. S. Regs., Part II. and the Staff Manual respectively. Title pages will be prepared in manuscript.

WAR DIARY
or
INTELLIGENCE SUMMARY.
(*Erase heading not required.*)

Place	Date	Hour	Summary of Events and Information	Remarks and references to Appendices
I.4.a + c.	31/8/15		7th Rifle Bde. relieved 7th K.R.R. on our right on night of 30th/31st. Enemy's aeroplanes dropped two bombs on our lines, which has never been done before. 3rd Divn. artillery heavily bombarded BELLEWARDE FARM, HOOGE position at 4 AM on the morning of 1-9-15. All available men working at full pressure preparing present trenches for Winter Campaign. The strength of the officers in the trenches on the last day of the month. One Lieut. Colonel, one captain + 12 subalterns.	
	1/9/15		The usual German artillery retaliation for the bombardment by the 3rd Divn. We have now heavily wired our front + strengthened the parapet to an average of 10 ft. Tactical employment of machine guns + bombers rather changed + few of either are kept in the front line. It is recognised that given sufficient bombardment a front line becomes untenable as it is practically blown to pieces. 1 O.R. wounded	

1577 Wt. W10791/1773 500,000 1/15 D. D. & L. A.D.S.S./Forms/C. 2118.

Army Form C. 2118.

WAR DIARY
or
INTELLIGENCE SUMMARY.
(*Erase heading not required.*)

Instructions regarding War Diaries and Intelligence Summaries are contained in F. S. Regs., Part II. and the Staff Manual respectively. Title pages will be prepared in manuscript.

Place	Date	Hour	Summary of Events and Information	Remarks and references to Appendices
I 4 a + c	2/9/15		Enemy still quiet on the front but reports indicate that he is busily engaged mining + entrenching himself. I think any small enterprise that he next undertakes will probably be against ODER HOUSES or RAILWAY WOOD. A pouring wet night and the trenches almost impossible. At 5 P.M. a very heavy artillery bombardment from either side commenced on the line of RAILWAY WOOD + HOOGE. A mine is reported to have been exploded in that vicinity. Our Hd. Qrs. carefully registered by German Artillery yesterday for the first time.	
	3/9/15.		Heavy rain throughout the day. Trenches flooded. Work at a standstill. 1 O.R. Killed.	
	4/9/15		Nothing to report. 2 O.R. wounded.	
	5/9/15		One of our aeroplanes brought down apparently behind the German lines. The weather has cleared but the trenches are a sea of mud + water. Enemy's aeroplanes very active all day. Our artillery were bombarding the DELLEWARDE FARM, HOOGE position during the morning. A draft of 57 O.R. including 27 N.C.O's arrived at Transport Camp.	

1577 Wt. W10791/1773 500,000 1/15 D. D. & L. A.D.S.S./Forms/C. 2118.

Instructions regarding War Diaries and Intelligence Summaries are contained in F. S. Regs., Part II. and the Staff Manual respectively. Title pages will be prepared in manuscript.

WAR DIARY
or
INTELLIGENCE SUMMARY.
(Erase heading not required.)

Army Form C. 2118.

Place	Date	Hour	Summary of Events and Information	Remarks and references to Appendices
I.4.a+c.	6/9/15.		Weather fine + trenches drying. A whizzbang shell caused 5 casualties. The total casualties in the trenches for the 14 days were 1 officer killed + 25 O.R. killed + wounded. Battalion relieved this night by 8th Bn. K.R.R. Corps. Marched out to GINGERBREAD CHATEAU, picked up by busses + taken to the Rest area at WATOU.	
WATOU	7/9/15		Resting. Three cases of accidental shooting a comrade had occurred in the trenches + one case of self inflicted wounding. A large number of men arrive from England in drafts untrained in safely handling their arms. Two officers and 7 O.R. leave for England (Leave). The days paper officially announces a V.C. to 2/Lt. G.C. Woodroffe, killed in action, a D.S.O. to Capt. A.C. Sheepshanks and a D.C.M. to No. 57625 Rfn. Hamilton J. Unofficially announced that G.O.C., Brigade appointed to command Ulster Division.	
	8/9/15		A party of 300 digging on defences at P1 + P2 L4 just W. of YPRES. Remainder of Battalion to bathes where a complete change of linen was obtainable.	

1577 Wt. W10791/1773 500,000 1/15 D. D. & L. A.D.S.S./Forms/C. 2118.

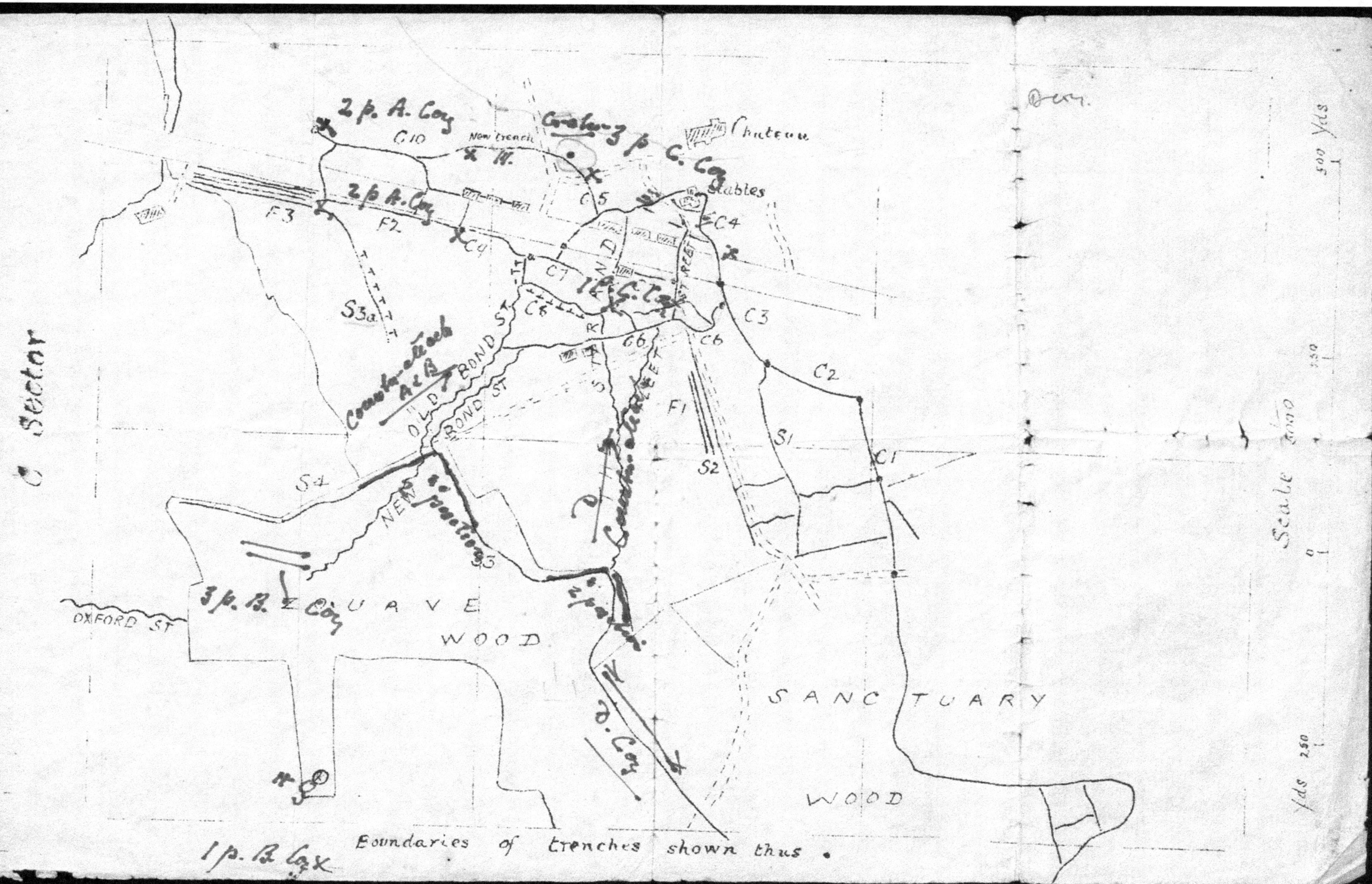
C Sector
2 p. A. Coy
C10
New trench
3 p. C. Coy
Chateau
Stables
C5
C4
2 p A. Coy
F3
F2
C4
C7
C3
C6
C6
C6
S3a
OLD BOND ST
BOND ST
F1
S1
C2
C1
S2
S4
NEW
S3
3 p. B. Coy
ZOUAVE
WOOD
OXFORD ST
SANCTUARY
WOOD
D. Coy
1 p. B Coy
Boundaries of trenches shown thus
Scale
500 Yds
250
0
Yds 250

For information of the A.G.'s Office at the Base.

Officers and men who have become casuals, been transferred or joined since last report.

Place YPRES. Date 7.8.15.

Regtl. Number	Rank	Name	Corps	Nature of casualty, or name of unit from or to which transferred	Date of being struck off or coming on the ration return	Remarks*
S 985	Rfn.	Oddy A.	8th.Rifle Bde.	Shpnl. foot	4.8.15.	slight
B 365	'	Davey J.	'	' arm	6.8.15.	
S 836	'	Dagnan J.	'	' leg	'	
B 849	'	Rawles A.	'	' face	'	
S7414	'	Cade J.	'	' elbow	'	
S5835	'	Walden T.	'	' back&foot	'	
B 507	'	Cording G.	'	' foot & thigh	'	
S8342	'	Coles C.	'	' thigh	'	
S7656	'	Green A.	'	' foot	'	
S 835	'	Sharratt A.	'	' slight	'	at duty
Draft of 50 N.C.Os. & men (as per attached list) on strength 5.8.15.						
8441	Rfn.	Tickner W.	8th.Rifle Bde.	From Hospital	4.8.15.	
B 419	'	Haddon W.	'	'	5.8.15.	
B1995	A/Cpl.	Carttling L.	'	'	4.8.15.	
B1849	RFn.	George E.	'	To Hospital	2.8.15.	
B2051	'	Thomas W.	'	'	3.8.15.	
S5835	'	Wilkinson H.	'	'	'	
S1798	'	Churchill J.	'	'	'	
B 312	'	Riggs E.	'	'	5.8.15.	
B 655	'	Henry C.	'	'	'	
B3131	'	Churn J.	'	'	'	
	MAJOR	Tod A.	'	'	'	
	2/Lt.	Beves D.H.	'	'	'	
	'	Foxwell D.F.	'	'	'	
S6084	Rfn.	Wier W.	'	'	'	
S5203	A/Cpl.	Ward W.	'	'	7.8.15.	
9725	Sgt.	May W.	'	From Wounds	4.8.15.	
B1652	Cpl.	Hobday W.	'	'	'	
S7699	Rfn.	Wood S.	'	'	'	
S2618	'	Workman W.	'	'	'	
Draft of ~~1~~ 150 N.C.Os. and men (as per attached list) on strength 7.8.15.						

*State whether absence is of a permanent or temporary nature, adding, in the case of casuals from wounds or disease, any available information for communication to the relatives.

Army Form B. 213.

FIELD RETURN.

No. of Report 12.

(To be furnished by all arms, services, and departments to the A. G.'s Office at the Base in accordance with Field Service Regulations, Part II.)

7. 8. 15 Date.

RETURN showing numbers RATIONED by, and Transport on charge of, 8th Batt. Rifle Bde. at Ypres.

Detail	Personnel: Officers	Personnel: Other ranks	Personnel: Natives	Animals: Horses: Riding	Animals: Horses: Draught	Animals: Horses: Heavy Draught	Animals: Horses: Pack	Animals: Mules: Large	Animals: Mules: Small	Camels	Oxen	Guns, carriages and limbers, showing, description	Ammunition wagons and limbers	Machine guns	Aircraft, showing description	Horsed: 4 Wheeled	Horsed: 2 Wheeled	Mechanical: Motor Cars	Mechanical: Tractors	Mechanical: Lorries, showing description	Mechanical: Trucks, showing description	Mechanical: Trailers	Motor Bicycles	Bicycles	Remarks
Effective Strength of Unit	6	618		14		9	9	34				Tools MG 2 2	7	4		6	4							9	
Details, *by Arms* attached to unit as in War Establishment:—																									
RAMC.	1																								
A.O.C.		1																							
Interpreter			1																						
Total	7	619	1	14		9	9	34				2. 2	7	4		6	4							9	
War Establishment	30	991	1	14		9	9	34				2 2	7	4		6	4							9	
Wanting to complete	23	334																							
Surplus																									
*Attached (not to include the details shown above)																									
Civilians:— Employed with the Unit																									
Accompanying the Unit																									
Total Rationed ...	7	619	1	14		9	9	34																	

* In the case of field ambulances, hospitals or depôts, the number of patients are to be included here, the names being shown in A.F.A. 36.

Signature of Commander.

Date of Despatch.

(K 11859) W. & Co., Ltd. Wt. w6005—894 500,000 10/14 Forms B. 213 / 5

For information of the A.G.'s Office at the Base.

Officers and men who have become casuals, been transferred or joined since last report.

Place YPRES. Date 15.8.15.

Regtl. Number	Rank	Name	Corps	Nature of casualty, or name of unit from or to which transferred	Date of being struck off or coming on the ration return	Remarks*
Drafts of ~~QQ~~ 110 N.C.Os. and men, and 50 N.C.Os. and men on strength as per attached lists 1 & 3.						
14 Officers on strength as per attached list 2.						
S7582	Rfn.	Kendall F.	8th.Rifle Bde.	From Hospital	8.8.15.	
B2051	"	Thomas W.	"	"	"	
S1798	"	Churchill J.	"	"	10.8.15.	
B 653	"	Henry G.	"	"	"	
S1347	"	Dobson J.	"	"	9.8.15.	
S5203	A/Cpl.	Ward W.	"	"	14.8.15.	
B3136	Rfn.	Emmett W.	"	"	13.8.15.	
B 603	"	Snow G.	"	"	"	
B2942	A/Cpl.	Crisp F.	"	"	14.8.15.	
B 315	Rfn.	King A.	"	"	15.8.15.	
B 121	"	Wells J.	"	"	"	
9938	"	Gold E.	"	"	"	
7276	"	Robinson A.	"	"	"	
S5203	A/Cpl.	Ward W.	"	To Hospital	7.8.15.	
B2140	RFn.	Fisher R.	"	"	6.8.15.	
S1347	"	Dobson J.	"	"	7.8.15.	
B2364	"	Robinson W.	"	"	"	
B 723	"	Hickton F.	"	"	"	
S7541	"	Southall T.	"	"	8.8.15.	
B3136	"	Emmett W.	"	"	"	
B 603	"	Snow G.	"	"	"	
S5205	"	Dyer G.A.	"	"	"	
B 315	"	King A.	"	"	"	
B 121	"	Wells J.	"	"	"	
B2942	A/Cpl.	Crisp S.	"	"	9.8.15.	
10021	Rfm.	Hill J.	"	"	"	
9938	"	Gold E.	"	"	10.8.15.	
7276	"	Robinson A.	"	"	"	
604	"	Bates J.	"	"	"	
664	"	Gregory A.	"	"	"	
B3175	A/Cpl.	Waldron C.	"	"	"	
7710	Rfn.	Cherritt R.	"	"	"	
8702	"	Pringle J.	"	"	9.8.15.	
S8881	"	Richards S.	"	"	"	
B3167	"	Gill R.	"	"	11.8.15.	
S6141	"	EllottA.	"	"	12.8.15.	
Z1671	"	Finch J.C.	"	"	"	
S7784	"	Terry A.	"	"	13.8.15.	
8487	"	Norris C.	"	"	"	
B 721	"	Lewendon C.	"	From Wounds	11.8.15	
B 663	"	Hopkins F.	"	"	15.8.15.	
B 224	"	Kerr N.	"	"	13.8.15.	
S1346	"	Llloyd F.	"	"	11.8.15.	
S 625	"	Rogers P.	"	"	"	

*State whether absence is of a permanent or temporary nature, adding, in the case of casuals from wounds or disease, any available information for communication to the relatives.

Army Form B. 213.

FIELD RETURN.

No. of Report 13.

(To be furnished by all arms, services, and departments to the A. G.'s Office at the Base in accordance with Field Service Regulations, Part II.)

15. 8. 15 Date.

RETURN showing numbers RATIONED by, and Transport on charge of, 8th Batt. Rifle Brigade at Ypres

Detail	Personnel: Officers	Personnel: Other ranks	Personnel: Natives	Animals: Horses: Riding	Animals: Horses: Draught	Animals: Horses: Heavy Draught	Animals: Horses: Pack	Animals: Mules: Large	Animals: Mules: Small	Animals: Camels	Animals: Oxen	Guns, carriages and limbers, showing, description	Ammunition wagons and limbers	Machine guns	Aircraft, showing description	Horsed: 4 Wheeled	Horsed: 2 Wheeled	Mechanical: Motor Cars	Mechanical: Tractors	Mechanical: Lorries, showing description	Mechanical: Trucks, showing description	Mechanical: Trailers	Motor Bicycles	Bicycles	Remarks
Effective Strength of Unit	20	760		14		9	9	34				Tools 2 M.G. 2	7	4		6	4							9	
Details, *by Arms* attached to unit as in War Establishment:—																									
R.A.M.C.	1																								
A.O.C.	*	1																							
Intrepeter			1																						Sick not evac^d att. for duty
	1	24																							Sick not evacuated
Total	22	815	1	14		9	9	34				2 2	7	4		6	4							9	
War Establishment	30	991	1	14		9	9	34				2 2	7	4		6	4							9	
Wanting to complete	8	176																							
Surplus																									
*Attached (not to include the details shown above)																									
Civilians:—																									
Employed with the Unit																									
Accompanying the Unit																									
Total Rationed ...	21	762		14		9	9	34																	

* In the case of field ambulances, hospitals or depôts, the number of patients are to be included here, the names being shown in A.F.A. 36.

Signature of Commander.

Date of Despatch.

(K11859) W. & Co., Ltd. Wt. w6005—894 500,000 10/14 Forms B. 213 / 5

For information of the A.G.'s Office at the Base.

Officers and men who have become casuals, been transferred or joined since last report.

Place YPRES. Date 21.8.15.

Regtl. Number	Rank	Name	Corps	Nature of casualty, or name of unit from or to which transferred	Date of being struck off or coming on the ration return	Remarks*
S3335	Rfn.	Foxlee A.	8th.Rifle Bde.	Shpnl. foot	7.8.15.	
B3498	"	Holloway H.	"	Killed in Act.	9.8.15.	
S5245	Cpl.	Leftwich W.	"	Bullet foot	14.8.15.	
S9191	Rfn.	Bonehill A.	"	Shell legs	16.8.15.	
495	"	Valinia B.	"	Died of Wnds.	"	
B3285	Sgt.	Smith G.	"	"	17.8.15.	
Z 822	Rfm.	Hughes F.	"	Shpnl. leg	19.8.15.	
Z1828	"	Savage J.	"	Killed in Act.	"	
8980	"	Hume J.	"	Hand	"	
	2/Lt.	Grebbin W.A.	"	Bullet Ribs	20.8.15.	Accidental
Z1902	Rfn.	Moore T.	"	Shrapnel	"	
S6141	"	Ellott A.	"	To Hospital	12.8.15.	
Z1671	"	Finch J.C.	"	"	"	
S7784	"	Terry A.	"	"	13.8.15.	
8487	"	Norris C.	"	"	"	
	"	George	"	From Hospital	17.8.15.	
324	"	Feullade G.	"	To Hospital	16.8.15.	
B3273	"	Clancey W.	"	"	19.8.15.	
B2298	"	Gore T.	"	From Hospital	16.8.15.	
5835	"	Wilkinson H.	"	"	17.8.15;	
S6084	"	Wier W.	"	"	18.8.15.	
604	"	Bates J.	"	"	15.8.15	
B 664	"	Gregory A.	"	"	17.8.15.	
7710	"	Cherrett R.	"	"	"	
3175	A/Cpl.	Waldron C.	"	"	"	
8708	Rfn.	Pringle J.	"	"	16 8.15;	
S5881	"	Richards S.	"	"	"	
B 130	"	Winter C.	"	From Evacuatn.	"	
S7273	"	James P.	"	From Wounds	"	
B1577	"	Baggott C.	"	"	"	
S6090	"	White P.	"	"	"	
B 817	"	Archer J.	"	"	18.8.15.	
8991	"	Cafferty T.	"	"	16.8.15.	
S9618	"	Everett W.	"	"	"	
B3065	"	Brome C.	"	"	"	
B1576	"	Hoban T.	"	"	"	
B 324	"	Feullade G.	"	"	"	
B 66	"	Knight C.	"	"	"	
B 318	"	Wells G.	"	"	"	
S6239	"	Bowers W.	"	"	"	
B2385	"	Davies J.	"	"	"	

*State whether absence is of a permanent or temporary nature, adding, in the case of casuals from wounds or disease, any available information for communication to the relatives.

FIELD RETURN.

Army Form B. 213.

No. of Report 14

(To be furnished by all arms, services, and departments to the A. G.'s Office at the Base in accordance with Field Service Regulations, Part II.)

Aug 21st 15 Date.

RETURN showing numbers RATIONED by, and Transport on charge of, 8th Batt. Rifle Bde at Ypres

Detail	Personnel			Animals								Guns, carriages, and limbers and transport vehicles													Remarks
				Horses				Mules								Horsed		Mechanical							
	Officers	Other ranks	Natives	Riding	Draught	Heavy Draught	Pack	Large	Small	Camels	Oxen	Guns, carriages and limbers, showing, description	Ammunition wagons and limbers	Machine guns	Aircraft, showing description	4 Wheeled	2 Wheeled	Motor Cars	Tractors	Lorries, showing description	Trucks, showing description	Trailers	Motor Bicycles	Bicycles	
Effective Strength of Unit	19	801		13		9	9	34				Toto M.G 2 2	7	4		2	4							9	
Details, *by Arms* attached to unit as in War Establishment:— R.A.M.C	1																								
A.V.C		1																							
Interpreter			1																						
Sick not Evacuated		20																							
Total	20	822	1	13		9	9	34				2 2	7	4		2	4							9	
War Establishment	30	991	1	13		9	9	34				2 2	7	4		2	4							9	
Wanting to complete	10	169																							
Surplus																									
*Attached (not to include the details shown above)																									
Civilians:— Employed with the Unit																									
Accompanying the Unit																									
Total Rationed ...	19	802	1	13		9	9	34																	

* In the case of field ambulances, hospitals or depôts, the number of patients are to be included here, the names being shown in A.F.A. 36.

Signature of Commander.

Date of Despatch.

(K 11859) W. & Co., Ltd. Wt. w6005-894 500,000 10/14 Forms B. 213 / 5

For information of the A.G.'s Office at the Base.

Officers and men who have become casuals, been transferred or joined since last report.

Place YPRES Date ~~WI.I.QT~~ 28.8.15.

Regtl. Number	Rank	Name	Corps	Nature of casualty, or name of unit from or to which transferred	Date of being struck off or coming on the ration return	Remarks*
2/LIEUT.		ATKINSON A.	8th.Rifle Bde.	Bullet Ribs	21.8.15.	
5279	Rfm.	Melpass A.	"	Shell	"	
S9472	"	DriscollW.	"		"	
S6133	"	Vincent C.	"	Wounded	30.7.15.	
S8783	"	Farmer W.	"	Missing	"	
B2501	"	Norman J.	"	shell wound	22.8.15.	
S6155	"	Peat W.	"	Bullet wound	"	
B3043	"	Macdonald W.	"	Bullet buttock	26.8.15.	
S7273	"	James P.	"	To Hospital	22.8.15.	
2018	"	Dennis A.	"	"	23.8.15.	
B1505	"	Adams L.	"	"	"	
3164	"	Scholfield L.	"	"	24.8.15.	
10295	"	Cottrell G.	"	"	"	
B2877	a/Cpl.	Osbaldeston G.	"	"	26.8.15	
S9005	Rfn.	Dean D.	"	"	27.8.15	
2145	Cpl.	Pendlington G.	"	"	"	
S7218	Rfn.	Whitehead E.	"	"	"	
2nd.Lt.		NEWTON A.M.	"	"	24.8.15	
LIEUT.		TRYON H.	"	"	27.8.15	
B 2870	a/Cpl.	O'Hara R.	"	From Hospital	22.8.15	
B 3167	Rfn.	Gill R.	"	"	27.8.15	
S6141	"	Ellot A.	"	"	22.8.15	
B 324	"	Feullade G.	"	"	21.8.15	
S10017	"	Spreadbury S.	"	"	27.8.15	
B 663	"	Hopkins F.	"	"	28.8.15	
S2483	"	Fabray C.	"	"	"	
S10017	"	Spreadbury S.	"	To Hospital	22.8.15	
B 663	"	Hopkins F.	"	"	24.8.15	
2483	"	Fabray C.	"	"	"	

*State whether absence is of a permanent or temporary nature, adding, in the case of casuals from wounds or disease, any available information for communication to the relatives.

FIELD RETURN.

Army Form B. 213.

No. of Report 15

(To be furnished by all arms, services, and departments to the A. G.'s Office at the Base in accordance with Field Service Regulations, Part II.)

28. 8. 15. Date.

RETURN showing numbers RATIONED by, and Transport on charge of, 8th Batt. Rifle Brigade at Ypres

Detail	Personnel			Animals								Guns, carriages, and limbers and transport vehicles													Remarks
				Horses				Mules								Horsed		Mechanical							
	Officers	Other ranks	Natives	Riding	Draught	Heavy Draught	Pack	Large	Small	Camels	Oxen	Guns, carriages and limbers, showing description	Ammunition wagons and limbers	Machine guns	Aircraft, showing description	4 Wheeled	2 Wheeled	Motor Cars	Tractors	Lorries, showing description	Trucks, showing description	Trailers	Motor Bicycles	Bicycles	
Effective Strength of Unit Details, *by Arms* attached to unit as in War Establishment:—	17	859		13		9	9	34				Tools 2 MG 2	7	4		2	4							9	
RAMC	1																								
AVC		1																							
Interpreter			1																						
Sick not evacuated	2	25																							
Details		22																							
Total	20	907	1	13		9	9	34				2 2	7	4		2	4							9	
War Establishment	30	991	1	13		9	9	34				2 2	7	4		2	4							9	
Wanting to complete	10	84																							
Surplus		-																							
*Attached (not to include the details shown above)																									
Civilians:— Employed with the Unit																									
Accompanying the Unit																									
Total Rationed ...	18	861		13		9	9	34																	

* In the case of field ambulances, hospitals or depôts, the number of patients are to be included here, the names being shown in A.F.A. 36.

Signature of Commander.

Date of Despatch.

(K 11859) W. & Co., Ltd. Wt. w6005—894 500,000 10/14 Forms B. 213 / 5

For information of the A.G.'s Office at the Base.

Officers and men who have become casuals, been transferred or joined since last report.

Place Ypres Date 4.9.15

Regtl. Number	Rank	Name	Corps	Nature of casualty, or name of unit from or to which transferred	Date of being struck off or coming on the ration return	Remarks*
9158	Rfn.	Bacon N.	8th. Rifle Bde	G.S.Thigh	27.8.15	'B'
7051	'	Thomas W.	'	G.S.Shoulder	'	'C'
2/LIEUT.		GARRARD E.C.	'	Killed in action	28.8.15	
3306	Rfn.	Donaldson G.	'	Wounded since rejoined in draft 25.8.15	30.7.15	'A'
852	'	Cook H.	'	Wounded	30.7.15	'B'
1791	'	Sands F.	'	Head.Bomb	29.8.15	'D'
7380	Cpl.	Rich W.	'	G.S.Leg	30.8.15	'D'
497	Rfn.	Hall J.	'	G.S.Shoulder accidental	30.8.15	'D'
1874	'	Riley R.		G.S.L.Head accidental	1.9.15	'B'
3842	'	Hughes J.	'	G.S.head	4.9.15	'C'
S6143	Rfn.	Urry R.	'	To hospital	28.8.15	'A'
S8559	a/Cpl.	Cane C.	'	'	'	'
S10240	Rfn.	Clifton J.	'	'	'	'B'
S2197	'	Brooks G.	'	'	'	'
S2708	'	Gore T.	'	'	'	'D'
S 224	'	Kerr N.	'	'	'	'A'
S5783	'	White D.	'	'	'	'D'
S9725	Sgt.	May W.	'	'	'	'D'
S8013	Rfn.	Hogan M.	'	'	'	'A'
S3072	'	Peat A.	'	'	'	'C'
B 130	'	Winter C.	'	'	29.8.15	'A'
S10887	'	Sullivan D.	'	'	'	'C'
S7215	a/Cpl.	Cavanagh H.	'	'	'	'B'
S8796	Rfn.	Wood W.	'	'	'	'B'
S8306	'	Donaldson G.	'	'	30.8.15	'A'
B3486	'	Daggleby F.	'	'	'	'A'
S5528	'	Colter C.	'	'	'	'A'
B2619	'	Workman W.	'	'	'	'C'
B2483	'	Fabrey C.	'	'	'	'D'
S8387	'	Hamilton F.	'	'	'	'C'
S5835	'	Wilkinson H.	'			'B'
B3437	'	Godfrey W.	'	'	'	'A'
B3067	'	Grinstead C.	'	'	'	'C'
S6034	'	Weir W.	'	'	1.9.15	'D'
B3391	'	Rocke A.	'	'	2.9.15	'D'
S7207	'	Aspden J.	'	'	'	'A'
S3175	a/Cpl.	Waldron C.	'	'	'	'C'
2161	Rfn.	West T.	'	'	'	'C'
B1344	'	Allins T.	'	'	3.9.15	'B'
S9281	'	Day J.	'	'	'	'B'
B 685	'	Wardon A.	'	'	'	'B'
S9641	'	Hay T.	'	'	'	'B'

*State whether absence is of a permanent or temporary nature, adding, in the case of casuals from wounds or disease, any available information for communication to the relatives.

Army Form B. 213.

FIELD RETURN.

No. of Report 6.

(To be furnished by all arms, services, and departments to the A. G.'s Office at the Base in accordance with Field Service Regulations, Part II.)

4th Sept. 1915 Date.

RETURN showing numbers RATIONED by, and Transport on charge of, 8th Batt. Rifle Brigade at Ypres

Detail	Personnel: Officers	Personnel: Other ranks	Personnel: Natives	Animals: Horses: Riding	Horses: Draught	Horses: Heavy Draught	Horses: Pack	Mules: Large	Mules: Small	Camels	Oxen	Guns, carriages and limbers, showing description (G.S.)	Ammunition wagons and limbers	Machine guns	Aircraft, showing description	Horsed: 4 Wheeled	Horsed: 2 Wheeled	Mechanical: Motor Cars	Tractors	Lorries, showing description	Trucks, showing description	Trailers	Motor Bicycles	Bicycles	Remarks
Effective Strength of Unit	18	830		13		9	9	34				Tools 2, M.G. 2	7	4		2	4							9	
Details, *by Arms* attached to unit as in War Establishment:— R.A.M.C.	1																								
Interpreter & A.O.C.		1	1																						
		22																							Details { 41st Bde 4, 14th Div. 8, Town Guard Ypres 6, Miners 3 M.M.G. L. 1 }
		43																							Sick not evacuated
Total	19	896	1	13		9	9	34				2 2	7	4		2	4							9	
War Establishment	30	991	1	13		9	9	34				2 2	7	4		2	4							9	
Wanting to complete	11	95																							
Surplus																									
*Attached (not to include the details shown above)																									
Civilians:— Employed with the Unit																									
Accompanying the Unit																									
Total Rationed ...	19	831	1	13		9	9	34																	

* In the case of field ambulances, hospitals or depôts, the number of patients are to be included here, the names being shown in A.F.A. 36.

Signature of Commander.

Date of Despatch.

(K 11859) W. & Co., Ltd. Wt. w6005—894 500,000 10/14 Forms B. 213 / 5

For information of the A.G.'s Office at the Base.

Officers and men who have become casuals, been transferred or joined since last report.

Place Ypres | Date 4.9.15

Regtl. Number	Rank	Name	Corps	Nature of casualty, or name of unit from or to which transferred	Date of being struck off or coming on the ration return	Remarks*
B1506	Rfn.	Adams L.	8th. Rifle Bde	From Hospital	30.8.15	'C'
	2/LIEUT	NEWTON A.M.	'	'	3.9.15	
	LIEUT.	TRYON H.	'	'	2.9.15	
B3164	Rfn.	Scholfield L.	'	'	31.8.15	'C'
S10295	'	Cottrell G.	'	'	30.8.15	'D'
2143	Cpl.	Pendlington G	'	'	3.9.15	'C'
S7216	Rfn.	Whitehead E.	'	'	31.8.15	'B'
S2197	'	Brooks G.	'	'	2.9.15	'B'
B2798	'	Gore T.	'	'	1.9.15	'D'
S5783	'	White D.	'	'	31.8.15	'D'
B 234	'	Kerr N.	'	'	2.9.15	'A'
B 130	'	Winter C.	'	'	'	'
S8796	'	Wood W.	'	'	'	'B'
S7316	a/Cpl.	Cavanagh H.	'	'	1.9.15	'D'
S5835	Rfn.	Wilkinson H.	'	'	4.9.15	'B'
B3487	'	Godfrey W.	'	'	'	'A'
B3037	'	Grinstead C.	'	'	'	'C'
B3121	'	Beaxley J.	'			
S8960	'	Perkins E.	'	To hospital	4.9.15	'B'
				'	'	'C'
5/9540	a/Cpl.	Smith J.	'			
Z1519	Rfn.	Parker A.	'	G.S.Elbow	3.9.15	'C'
				Killed in action	'	'
S7359	'	Hackett L.	'	G.S.Hand accidental	'	'B'

*State whether absence is of a permanent or temporary nature, adding, in the case of casuals from wounds or disease, any available information for communication to the relatives.

Army Form B. 213.

FIELD RETURN.

No. of Report ____________

(To be furnished by all arms, services, and departments to the A. G.'s Office at the Base in accordance with Field Service Regulations, Part II.)

____________ Date.

RETURN showing numbers RATIONED by, and Transport on charge of ____________ at ____________

Detail	Personnel			Animals								Guns, carriages, and limbers and transport vehicles													Remarks
				Horses				Mules								Horsed		Mechanical							
	Officers	Other ranks	Natives	Riding	Draught	Heavy Draught	Pack	Large	Small	Camels	Oxen	Guns, carriages and limbers, showing description*	Ammunition wagons and limbers	Machine guns	Aircraft, showing description	4 Wheeled	2 Wheeled	Motor Cars	Tractors	Lorries, showing description	Trucks, showing description	Trailers	Motor Bicycles	Bicycles	
Effective Strength of Unit																									
Details, *by Arms* attached to unit as in War Establishment:—																									
Total																									
War Establishment																									
Wanting to complete																									
Surplus																									
*Attached (not to include the details shown above)																									
Civilians:—																									
Employed with the Unit																									
Accompanying the Unit																									
TOTAL RATIONED ...																									

* In the case of field ambulances, hospitals or depôts, the number of patients are to be included here, the names being shown in A.F.A. 36.

____________ Signature of Commander.

____________ Date of Despatch.

(K11859) W. & Co., Ltd. Wt. w6005—894 500,000 10/14 Forms B. 213 / 5

"C" Form (Duplicate). Army Form C. 2123.

MESSAGES AND SIGNALS.

No. of Message

Charges to Pay. £ s. d.

Office Stamp.

Service Instructions.

Handed in at RRH Office 12 35p m. Received 1 P m.

TO Adam 14 Divn

Sender's Number	Day of Month	In reply to Number	AAA
CBA4	21	—	

Reference nominal roll please substitute Capt S. MILLER for Lieut J E OLOGHLEN

✓

1/10pm

FROM
PLACE & TIME Comdg 8 KRR

(6900) W.9668—1672. 50,000 Pads—12/14. F. T. & Co., Ltd.—Forms/C.2123.

14th Division

121/7198

8th Rifle Brigade.

Vol. IV

Sep 1 & Oct 15.

Hooge
Notification

Instructions regarding War Diaries and Intelligence Summaries are contained in F. S. Regs., Part II. and the Staff Manual respectively. Title pages will be prepared in manuscript.

WAR DIARY
or
INTELLIGENCE SUMMARY.
(Erase heading not required.)

Army Form C. 2118.

Place	Date	Hour	Summary of Events and Information	Remarks and references to Appendices
WATOU	9/9/15		another hot day. 300 men digging at P1 & P2 going by bus. The baths at POPERINGHE available for the rest of the Battalion. An excellent cinematograph show goes on here run by the enterprise of the officers of the 14th Divl. ammunition column. A careful inspection of the Battalion resulted as follows:— 35 obviously unfit ~~for~~ on medical grounds, 10 others under 18 years of age. 15 found to be suffering from nervous breakdown & recommended for a month's rest.	
	10/9/15.		Still fine & warm. 300 men digging as usual.	
	11/9/15		Weather continues brilliant. Digging party as usual. Lt. Fraser returned from Hospital. The strength of the Btn. is now 18 officers (including Transport Officer & Qr. Mr).	
	12/9/15		Weather still fine. 1 O.R. died of natural causes. Buried at WATOU. Lt. Col. R.C. Maclachlan proceeding on leave. Capt. A.C. Sheepshanks assumed command. 13/9/15.	
	13/9/15		The Battalion moved up into Brigade Reserve. Marched to POPERINGHE & entrained there. Marched from H 11. Central. Hd. Qrs. & "A" & "C" Coys billeted in houses on BRIELEN ROAD. "B" & "D" Coys. garrisoned ~~in~~ KAAIE defences. Previous to leaving WATOU the Battalion was inspected ~~B~~ by the Army Commander. Some shelling on the line of march from H. 11. Central to YPRES. 2 O.R. slightly wounded. Temp/Lts. C.E. Squire and K.S. Gladstone promoted Temp. Captains to date from 1-8-15.	

1577 Wt. W10791/1773 500,000 1/15 D. D. & L. A.D.S.S./Forms/C. 2118.

Army Form C. 2118.

Instructions regarding War Diaries and Intelligence Summaries are contained in F. S. Regs., Part II. and the Staff Manual respectively. Title pages will be prepared in manuscript.

WAR DIARY
or
INTELLIGENCE SUMMARY.
(Erase heading not required.)

Place	Date	Hour	Summary of Events and Information	Remarks and references to Appendices
YPRES.	14/9/15.		Weather fair. Slight rain. Heavy shelling during afternoon. Enemy apparently trying to locate battery behind us. 30 men working on new Battalion dugouts all day. 10 men carrying timber at Brigade Workshops all day. 50 men working on PICCADILLY and 50 men on PICCADILLY Switch. Working from 6-45 P.M. to 1 A.M. 50 men working on trench from HAYMARKET to Dressing Station. 50 men working on HAYMARKET. Returned at 2 AM. Two officers sent on the one-day bombing course.	
	15/9/15.		Weather still fair. Working parties out continuing work of yesterday. Two officers returned from one day bombing course.	
	16/9/15		Lt. Gen. J. L. Keir K.C.B. Comdg. 6th Corps. inspected the Transport. Work of yesterday continued. Fine day. Informed that the Artillery would fire 1000 rounds 18 pndr. practice ammunition. Temp. Lts. G. E. H. Keesey and A. Carey promoted Temp. Captains + 2/Lt. C. R. Gnell Barnes promoted Temp. Lt. in Gazette.	
	17/9/15		Working parties continuing work of yesterday. In addition 1 N.C.O. and 10 men on a small work behind Brigade Hd. Qrs. during the day. One O.R. wounded. Informed that Port of BOULOGNE closed.	
	18/9/15.		Artillery bombarded enemy's trenches at 5 AM. Enemy aeroplane dropped two bombs in this vicinity but no damage reported. One O.R. wounded. Usual working parties out digging. In addition 100 men were burying cable. 50 rendezvous at POTIJZE X Roads for 48th F.A. Bde and 50 at road junction I. 9. a. 2. 9. for 46th F.A.	

Instructions regarding War Diaries and Intelligence Summaries are contained in F. S. Regs., Part II. and the Staff Manual respectively. Title pages will be prepared in manuscript.

WAR DIARY
or
INTELLIGENCE SUMMARY.
(Erase heading not required.)

Army Form C. 2118.

Place	Date	Hour	Summary of Events and Information	Remarks and references to Appendices
YPRES	19/9/15.		Lt. Col R. C. Maclachlan in Command of Battalion on return from leave. Our guns again heavily bombarded enemy's trenches at 3-30 A.M. Rather heavier shelling by enemy on guns in our vicinity at 5 P.M. Transport camp again moved to A. 28. d. 4. 8. Aeroplanes very active.	
	20/9/15		Still fine and warm. Situation normal. Our guns shelled heavily from 3-45 A.M. to 4-15 A.M. Germans replied in the evening at 6 P.M.	
	21/9/15		Vicinity of billets shelled during the morning & Battalion put into dugouts. Total casualties – 5 O.R. wounded. 300 men detailed as working party to the front line. Battalion moved back to A.28.d.9.9. where it bivouacked.	
A.28. d.9.9.	22/9/15.		Battalion bivouacked. Refitting and reorganizing. Authy. received to send back to England men under 17 years of age.	
	23/9/15		Continued reorganizing. Fine day.	
	24/9/15		A.D.M.S inspected Battalion & weeded out 10 O.R. First information given to the troops of a general advance to take place all along the line. Capt. Keesey, 2/Lt. Sword, 2/Lt. Hughes & 2/Lt Adair joined from 14th Btn. Rifle Bde.	
	25/9/15.		Suddenly ordered at 10 A.M. to move forward to H.11.d.9.9. Packed & off within the hour. Btn. accomodated in dugouts at H.11.d.9.9. The attack of the 42nd Bde. which had been successful had been driven back	

577 Wt. W10791/1773 500,000 1/15 D. D. & L. A.D.S.S./Forms/C. 2118.

Instructions regarding War Diaries and Intelligence Summaries are contained in F. S. Regs., Part II. and the Staff Manual respectively. Title pages will be prepared in manuscript.

WAR DIARY
or
INTELLIGENCE SUMMARY.
(Erase heading not required.)

Army Form C. 2118.

Place	Date	Hour	Summary of Events and Information	Remarks and references to Appendices
H.11.d.9.9.	25/9/15	2.	to original line by enemy's counter attack.	
	26/9/15		One of our aeroplanes seen brought down by enemy's 'planes near PILKEM. Heavy bombardment started about 10 P.M. Battalion ordered to stand-to as enemy reported to be attacking at HOOGE + BELLEWARDE turned out a false alarm. 2/Lts. Farmiloe, Matthews, Meredith + Seward from Artists Rifles joined the Battalion.	
	27/9/15		C.O., Adjt. and Company Officers reconnoitred trenches of D.L.I. found them battered + flattened + many dead lying on the front. Lt. Backus rejoined the Btn. from 4th Bn. Rifle Bde. Heavy rain in evening.	
	28/9/15.		Dry but much colder. Enemy's aeroplanes active about 10 a.m. Machine Guns, Bombers + Signallers moved at 9 a.m. to relief of D.L.I. in trenches opposite BELLEWARDE FARM. Battalion moved from MENIN GATE at 7 P.M. to take over from same Battalion. Strength in trenches:— 25 officers and 726 O.R. A heavy shell burst in 43rd Bde. Hd. Qrs. which was to be taken over by our Brigade this evening. Genl. Jeudwine in command of 41st Inf. Bde. vice Lt-Col. Maitland in Temp. Command.	

1577 Wt. W10791/1773 500,000 1/15 D. D. & L. A.D.S.S./Forms/C. 2118.

Army Form C. 2118.

Instructions regarding War Diaries and Intelligence Summaries are contained in F. S. Regs., Part II. and the Staff Manual respectively. Title pages will be prepared in manuscript.

WAR DIARY
or
INTELLIGENCE SUMMARY.
(Erase heading not required.)

Place	Date	Hour	Summary of Events and Information	Remarks and references to Appendices
Trenches	29/9/15		Pouring wet day. Trenches water-logged. Remnants of the recent fighting seen everywhere. Our own dead lying in scores in front of the parapet. The parapets + communications themselves much blown about. Btn. Hd. Qrs. right up in the front line + far too forward for control. Heavy fighting heard on our right at HOOGE.	
	30/9/15	—	Heavy rain. A heavy bombardment going on at HOOGHE where we have apparently lost + gained some trenches. Our own front very weak from lack of wire which had all been cleared preparatory to the attack.	
	1/10/15	—	Trenches drying up. About 20 cases of "feet" due to the wet weather. An intensely painful ailment. Gumboots issued to the men and an issue of rum sanctioned.	
	2/10/15	—	Quiet day.	
	3/10/15		Battalion Hd. Qrs. heavily crumped and the Artillery officer attached severely wounded.	
	4/10/15		Heavy rain again.	
	5/10/15		A heavy enemy bombardment on the ODER house sector on our left. Our own line bombarded in the afternoon. 20 O.R. arrived in a draft	

Instructions regarding War Diaries and Intelligence Summaries are contained in F. S. Regs., Part II. and the Staff Manual respectively. Title pages will be prepared in manuscript.

WAR DIARY
or
INTELLIGENCE SUMMARY.
(Erase heading not required.)

Army Form C. 2118.

Place	Date	Hour	Summary of Events and Information	Remarks and references to Appendices
Trenches	6/10/15		Our front line heavily crumped for two hours in the morning. Wires all cut and the parapet badly knocked about. Germans evidently looking for trench mortars situated in our line. Sniping heavier than usual. Relieved at night by 7th Btn. K.R.R.C. A general feeling throughout the Battalion that the 14th Division has had more than its share of this unpleasant salient. Men have lost confidence and do not show themselves at their best.	
	7/10/15		Relieved the 7th Bn. K.R.R.C. in support trenches X1, X1a + F13 with one Coy. at Hd. Qrs. in I.10.c.1.1. G.O.C. Division backed by G.O.C. Brigade sent a complimentary order to the Battalion congratulating them on the work done + their cheeriness under discomfort in the last trenches.	
	8/10/15		Heavy fatigue parties for work on the front line. Very little shelling of our line. Casualties in the last trenches 5 Killed + 17 O.R. wounded. 2 O.R. wounded by shellfire. 34 evacuated sick from last trenches.	
	9/10/15		Fine + quiet all day. The Germans heavily shelled the transport + approaches at 7 P.M. A good many casualties on the roads. 2/Lt. Marriott + 2 O.R. killed. Reported that a red rocket was put up within our lines just before the shelling. Heavy fatigue parties as usual.	

Instructions regarding War Diaries and Intelligence Summaries are contained in F. S. Regs., Part II. and the Staff Manual respectively. Title pages will be prepared in manuscript.

WAR DIARY
or
INTELLIGENCE SUMMARY.
(Erase heading not required.)

Army Form C. 2118.

Place	Date	Hour	Summary of Events and Information	Remarks and references to Appendices
Trenches	11/10/15		Quiet day. Nothing to report.	
	12/10/15		Casualties 3 O.R. killed 6 O.R. wounded. An enemy's aeroplane stopped by anti-aircraft guns above us. Managed to land in enemy's lines. Btn relieved by 7th Btn. R. Dub. Heavy fatigues of over 300 men before relief. Marched to huts H.1.c. 9.7. The problem has arisen as how to deal with many men whose nerves become broken in the trenches. Marched out of trenches Strength - 603 showing total wastage of 85 since 26th September.	
	13/10/15		In huts H.1.c.9.9. Btn. bathing. Fine + warm. The issue of rum in the trenches proved to have a doubtful advantage. Up-to-date the following numbers have been granted leave to England :— 7 officers + 51 rank + file.	

For information of the A.G.'s Office at the Base.

Officers and men who have become casuals, been transferred or joined since last report.

Place YPRES Date 8th.October 1915.

Regtl. Number	Rank	Name	Corps	Nature of casualty, or name of unit from or to which transferred	Date of being struck off or coming on the ration return	Remarks*
B3164	Rfn.	Scholfield L		Shell, Shoulder	8-10-15	"C"
Z1340	Rfn.	Thomas R.	8th. Rifle Bde.	Died of Wounds	2-10-15.	'D'
Z279	"	Shaw W.	"	G.S.W.Knee.	2-10-15.	'A'
S7745	"	Howcroft W.	"	Grenade, legs.	"	'D'
S6000	"	Coxon H.	"	"	"	'D'
6/461	"	Bartholemeu A.	"			'D'
S8013	"	Hogan M.	"	Shpnl, head.	3-10-15.	'C'
B3139	"	Roberts B.	"	G.S.W. Head.	3-10-15.	'A'
3065	"	Brome C.	"	Shell buttock	"	'C'
S6301	"	Adger E.	"	" Face.	"	'C'
B2030	"	Windebank A.	"	" (Arm, leg)	"	'C'
Z940	"	Cross J.	"	" Arm.	"	'C'
Z592	' ~~Rarry~~	Perry J.	"	Grenade	"	'C'
B802	"	Howard J.	"	"	"	'C'
				G.S.W. Leg.	4-10-15.	'B'
Z2047	"	Chamberlain H.	"	Returned to duty 6-10-15.		
S6084	"	Weir W.	"	G.S.W.	4-10-15.	'D'
B3133	"	Mallinson D.	"	Killed in action	4-10-15.	'D'
Z1568	"	Haddoe F.	"	G.S.W. Ankle.	5-10-15.	'B'
S2619	"	Workman C.	"	Killed in action	6-10-15.	'A'
9008	"	Wiseman A.	"	G.S"W. R.Arm.	6-10-15.	'C'
S6010	A/Cpl.	Knoght R.	"	Shock and loss of speech.	6-10-15.	'D'
S5452	Rfn.	Marshall S.	"	Killed in action	7-10-15.	'D'
				Shell, Leg.	7-10-15.	'C'
B1409	Sgt.	Marshall C.	"	From wounds	1-10-15.	'B'
S3135	Rfn.	Wood W.	"	To hospital	3-10-15,	'B'
S7075	"	Smith A.	"	" "	2-10-15.	'B'
1348	"	Gilbert A.	"	" "	"	'B'
8193	"	Williamson J.	"	" "	"	'D'
9641	"	Modder V.	"	" "	"	'B'
B341	"	Tompsett E.	"	" "	"	'C'
B3127	"	Croxford A.	"	" "	"	'C'
1411	"	Holt W.	"	" "	"	'A'
1691	Sgt.	Crispen J	"	" "	"	'B'
5744	Rfn.	Lawrence W.	"	" "	"	'B'
B1737	"	McCaffrey J.	"	" "	"	'C'
S815	"	Hodges R.	"	" "	3-10-15.	'A'
Z1108	"	Baker J.	"	" "	"	'A'
B143	"	Connell J.	"	" "	"	'A'
2609	"	Barnett C.	"	" "	"	'A'
Z1155	"	Leech W.	"	" "	"	'A'
S6154	"	Steers E.	"	" "	"	'A'
S1356	"	Buttress G.	"	" "	"	'A'
B1442	Sgt.	Cooper H.	"	" "	"	'C'
11032	Rfn.	Boulton W.	"	" "	"	'D'
324	"	Feuillade G.	"	" "	"	'A'
B196	"	Abbott C.	"	" "	4-10-15.	'A'
B762	"	Holt J.	"	" "	5-10-15.	'B'
11754	"	Risby E.	"	" "	"	'B'
10033	"	Holmes A.	"	" "	"	'C'
3027	"	Axtell E.	"	" "	"	'C'
B2302	A/Cpl.	Turney A.	"	" "	6-10-15.	'D'
Z2011	Rfn.	Howe J.	"	" "	"	'D'

*State whether absence is of a permanent or temporary nature, adding, in the case of casuals from wounds or disease, any available information for communication to the relatives.

FIELD RETURN.

Army Form B. 213.

No. of Report 21.

(To be furnished by all arms, services, and departments to the A. G.'s Office at the Base in accordance with Field Service Regulations, Part II.)

8. 10. 15. Date.

RETURN showing numbers RATIONED by, and Transport on charge of, 8th R. B. at Ypres.

Detail	Personnel			Animals								Guns, carriages, and limbers and transport vehicles													Remarks
				Horses				Mules								Horsed		Mechanical							
	Officers	Other ranks	Natives	Riding	Draught	Heavy Draught	Pack	Large	Small	Camels	Oxen	Guns, carriages and limbers, showing, description	Ammunition wagons and limbers	Machine guns	Aircraft, showing description	4 Wheeled	2 Wheeled	Motor Cars	Tractors	Lorries, showing description	Trucks, showing description	Trailers	Motor Bicycles	Bicycles	
Effective Strength of Unit	24	798 ~~[illegible]~~		13		9	9	34				Tools 2 M.G. 2	7	4		2	4							4	
Details, *by Arms* attached to unit as in War Establishment:— R.A.M.C.	1																								
A.O.C.		1																							
Interpreters			1																						
	2	48 ~~48~~ 50																							Details Sick not evac.
Total	27	897 ~~[illegible]~~	1	13		9	9	34				2 2	7	4		2	4							4	
War Establishment	30	991	1	13	–	9	9	34				2 2	7	4		2	4							9	
Wanting to complete	3	94																							
Surplus																									
*Attached (not to include the details shown above)																									
Civilians:— Employed with the Unit																									
Accompanying the Unit																									
Total Rationed ...	25	779 ~~[illegible]~~	1	13		9	9	34																	

* In the case of field ambulances, hospitals or depots, the number of patients are to be included here, the names being shown in A.F.A. 36.

Signature of Commander.

Date of Despatch.

(K11859) W. & Co., Ltd. Wt. w6005—894 500,000 10/14 Forms B. 213 / 5

For information of the A.G.'s Office at the Base.

Officers and men who have become casuals, been transferred or joined since last report.

Place YPRES Date 8-10-15.

Regtl. Number	Rank	Name	Corps	Nature of casualty, or name of unit from or to which transferred	Date of being struck off or coming on the ration return	Remarks*
10582	Rfn.	Smith S.	8th. Rifle Bde.	To hospital	7-10-15.	'B'
20512	"	Harper W.	"	"	6-10-15.	'C'
3197	"	Axford G.	"	"	"	'A'
35442	"	Haydock J.	"	"	"	'A'
S11257	"	Thursfield A.	"	"	"	'A'
B2862	Sgt.	Westcott K	"	"	8-10-15	D
Z 1038	Rfn.	Beeson E	"	"	" " "	D
Z1155	"	Leech W.	"	From hospital	8-10-15.	'A'
B143	"	Connell J.	"	"	8-10-15.	'A'
5744	"	Lawrence W.	"	"	5-10-15.	'B'
1411	"	Holt W.	"	"	7-10-15.	'A'
S7075	"	Smith A.	"	"	8-10-15.	'B'
B3398	"	Gore T.	"	"	4-10-15.	'D'
S9803	"	Braham J.	"	"	8-10-15.	'B'
5806	"	Martin W.	"	"	7-10-15.	'C'
S7639	"	Missen H.	"	"	5-10-15.	'D'
22	"	Harrison H.	"	"	8-10-15.	'D'

*State whether absence is of a permanent or temporary nature, adding, in the case of casuals from wounds or disease, any available information for communication to the relatives.

Army Form B. 213.

FIELD RETURN.

No. of Report ________

(To be furnished by all arms, services, and departments to the A. G.'s Office at the Base in accordance with Field Service Regulations, Part II.)

________ Date.

RETURN showing numbers RATIONED by, and Transport on charge of, ________ at ________

Detail	Personnel			Animals								Guns, carriages, and limbers and transport vehicles											Motor Bicycles	Bicycles	Remarks
				Horses				Mules								Horsed		Mechanical							
	Officers	Other ranks	Natives	Riding	Draught	Heavy Draught	Pack	Large	Small	Camels	Oxen	Guns, carriages and limbers, showing, description	Ammunition wagons and limbers	Machine guns	Aircraft, showing description	4 Wheeled	2 Wheeled	Motor Cars	Tractors	Lorries, showing description	Trucks, showing description	Trailers			
Effective Strength of Unit Details, *by Arms* attached to unit as in War Establishment:—																									
Total																									
War Establishment																									
Wanting to complete																									
Surplus																									
*Attached (not to include the details shown above)																									
Civilians:— Employed with the Unit																									
Accompanying the Unit																									
TOTAL RATIONED ...																									

* In the case of field ambulances, hospitals or depôts, the number of patients are to be included here, the names being shown in A.F.A. 36.

________ Signature of Commander.

________ Date of Despatch.

(K 11859) W. & Co., Ltd. Wt. w6005—894 500,000 10/14 Forms B. 213 / 5

For information of the A.G.'s Office at the Base.

Officers and men who have become casuals, been transferred or joined since last report.

Place W A T O U. Date 11-9-15.

Regtl. Number	Rank	Name	Corps	Nature of casualty, or name of unit from or to which transferred	Date of being struck off or coming on the ration return	Remarks*
5/9540	A/Cpl.	Smith J.	6th.Rifle Bde.	G.S.Elbow.	3-9-15.	'C'Coy.
Z1819	Rfn.	Parker A.	"	KILLED IN ACTION	3-9-15.	
7559	"	Hackett L.	"	G.S.Hand (Accidental)	3-9-15.	'B'
S572	A/Cpl.	Burke W.	"	G.S.L.Arm.	6-9-15.	'C'
S5312	Rfn.	Monk E.	"	Shell R.Hand.	6-9-15.	'A'Coy.
B628	Cpl.	Forton E.	"	Shell shoulder	6-9-15.	'B'
B3262	A/Cpl.	Collier J.	"	" Arm & shoulder	6-9-15	'B'
S10015	Rfn.	Hannant H.	"	" Skull & leg.	6-9-15	'B'
B2853	Cpl.	Davies S.	"	" Forearm.	6-9-15	'D'
B2863	A/Cpl.	Leyshon S.	"	Bullet Neck.	6-9-15.	'D'
S7671	Rfn.	Adams J.	"	Bullet shoulder & hand (Accidental)	7-9-15.	'B'
S9962	Rfn.	Perkins E.	"	To hospital	4-9-15.	'C'
B3181	Rfn.	Beasley J.	"	" "	"	'B'
S668	Rfn.	Mills D.	"	" "	5-9-15.	'A'
B719	Rfn.	Redman C.	"	" "	6-9-15.	'D'
S7478	Rfn.	Taylor G.	"	" "	"	'C'
S9621	Rfn.	Iredale W.	"	" "	"	'B'
B2274	Rfn.	[illegible] W.	"	" "	"	'D'
B685	Rfn.	Waldron H.	"	" "	"	'B'
6/522	Rfn.	[illegible] E.	"	" " (Venereal)	10-9-15.	'C'
B3107	Rfn.	Brown J.	"	From hospital	5-9-15.	'C'
S52[illegible]	Rfn.	Jenner J.	"	" "	5-9-15.	'A'
B2877	A/Cpl.	Osbaldeston C.	"	" "	5-9-15.	'D'
S9728	Sgt.	Day W.	"	" "	10-9-15	'D'
B3072	Rfn.	Pett A.	"	" "	10-9-15.	'C'
S10067	Rfn.	Sullivan D.	"	" "	5-9-15.	'C'
S8306	Rfn.	Donaldson C.	"	" "	5-9-15.	'A'
B3436	Rfn.	Duggleby F.	"	" "	5-9-15.	'A'
B2612	Rfn.	Wormen W.	"	" "	5-9-15	'C'
B2459	Rfn.	Fabray C.	"	" "	6-9-15.	'D'
[illegible] 7625	Rfn.	Hamilton F.	"	" "	5-9-15	'C'
S3391	Rfn.	Rooke A.	"	" "	9-9-15.	'B'
S7287	Rfn.	Aspden J.	"	" "	6-9-15.	'A'
S3175	A/Cpl.	Waldron C.	"	" "	8-9-15.	'C'
S9201	Rfn.	Day J.	"	" "	10-9-15.	'D'
B3181	Rfn.	Beasley J.	"	" "	8-9-15.	'B'
S668	Rfn.	Mills D.	"	" "	10-9-15.	'A'
B719	Rfn.	Redman C.	"	" "	8-9-15.	'D'
S7478	Rfn.	Taylor G.	"	" "	9-9-15.	'C'
	Draft of 55 N.C.O's and men on strength as per attached list from 5-9-15.					
B2289	Corpl	Heighway B.	"	To England - Commission Authy. BM 354 41st Bde. d/- 7-9-15.	8-9-15	'D'
	2/LIEUT.	FRASER H.J.	"	To hospital	1-9-15	

*State whether absence is of a permanent or temporary nature, adding, in the case of casuals from wounds or disease, any available information for communication to the relatives.

FIELD RETURN.

Army Form B. 213.

No. of Report 17

(To be furnished by all arms, services, and departments to the A. G.'s Office at the Base in accordance with Field Service Regulations, Part II.)

11. 9. 15. Date.

RETURN showing numbers RATIONED by, and Transport on charge of, 8th Batt. Rifle Brigade at Waton.

Detail	Personnel			Animals								Guns, carriages, and limbers and transport vehicles														Remarks
				Horses				Mules									Horsed		Mechanical							
	Officers	Other ranks	Natives	Riding	Draught	Heavy Draught	Pack	Large	Small	Camels	Oxen	Guns, carriages and limbers, showing, description (Tools)	(MG)	Ammunition wagons and limbers	Machine guns	Aircraft, showing description	4 Wheeled	2 Wheeled	Motor Cars	Tractors	Lorries, showing description	Trucks, showing description	Trailers	Motor Bicycles	Bicycles	
Effective Strength of Unit	16	875		13		9	9	34				2	2	7	4		2	4							8	
Details, *by Arms* attached to unit as in War Establishment:— R.A.M.C	1																									
A.O.C		1																								
Interpreter			1																							
	1	31																								Sick not evacuated
	2																									On leave
	1	29																								Details {14th Div. 41st Bde (6 Corps Ypres [illegible])
Total	19	943	1	13		9	9	34				2	2	7	4		2	4							8	
War Establishment	30	991	1	13		9	9	34				2	2	7	4		2	4							9	
Wanting to complete	11	48																							1	
Surplus																										
*Attached (not to include the details shown above)																										
Civilians:— Employed with the Unit																										
Accompanying the Unit																										
TOTAL RATIONED ...	17	876	1	13		9	9	34																		

* In the case of field ambulances, hospitals or depôts, the number of patients are to be included here, the names being shown in A.F.A. 36.

[illegible] Lt. Col. Signature of Commander.

11. 9. 15. Date of Despatch.

(K11859) W. & Co., Ltd. Wt. w6005—894 500,000 10,14 Forms B. 213 / 5

For information of the A.G.'s Office at the Base.

Officers and men who have become casuals, been transferred or joined since last report.

Place Ypres. Date 18.9.15.

Regtl. Number	Rank	Name	Corps	Nature of casualty, or name of unit from or to which transferred	Date of being struck off or coming on the ration return	Remarks*
S9469	A/Cpl.	Norman G.	8th.Batt.R.B.	To Hospital	3.9.15.	'D'
S1267	Rfn.	Roberts R.	"	"	"	
S4992	"	Butterfield J.	"	"	11.9.15	'A'
S 299	"	Mead W.	"	"	13.9.15.	'D'
S8336	"	Salmon W.	"	"	"	'A'
S7273	"	Janes P.	"	"	14.9.15.	'A'
B2465	A/Cpl.	Leppard F.	"	"		'D'
B 605	Rfn.	D'Arcy G.	"	"	"	'B'
S8430	"	Kay E.	"	"	"	'D'
B2618	"	Workman W.	"	"	15.9.15.	'C'
B 172	Sgt.	Quince W.	"	"	"	'A'
9725	"	May W.	"	"	"	'D'
10064	Rfn.	Holland R.	"	"	"	'B'
B 116	"	Head A.	"	"	"	'C'
B2302	"	Brown L.	"	"	"	'D'
S8268	A/Cpl.	Cork C.	"	"	"	'A'
S5245	Rfn.	Palmer H.	"	"	"	'B'
B 423	"	Pickburn J.	"	"	16.9.15.	'A'
B2384	"	Haynes H.	"	"	"	'B'
B2042	"	Thornhill J.	"	"	"	'C'
2/Lieut.		FRASER H.J.	"	"	1.9.15.	'C'
1341	A/Cpl.	Dunne J.	"	"	18.9.15	'A'
Z1734	Rfmn.	McCoy L.	"	"	"	'B'
S6191	Rfn.	George D.	"	From Hospital	16.8.15.	'B'
S7273	"	Janes P.	"	"	13.9.15.	'A'
S8013	"	Hogan M.	"	"	12.9.15.	'A'
S6084	"	Weir W.	"	"	5.9.15.	'D'
S3391	"	Rooke A.	"	"	9.9.15.	'B'
2161	"	West T.	"	"	17.9.15.	'C'
B1344	"	Alliss T.	"	"	7.9.15.	'B'
S9469	A/Cpl.	Norman G.	"	"	12.9.15.	'D'
S8336	Rfn.	Salmon W.	"	"	16.9.15.	'A'
S7273	"	Janes P.	"	"	17.9.15.	'A'
S8430	"	Kay E.	"	"	17.9.15.	'D'
B2618	"	Workman W.	"	"	18.9.15.	'C'
2/Lieut.		FRASER H.J.	"	"	11.9.15.	
S9005	Rfn.	Dean D.	"	"	12.9.15	'B'
B2874	"	Lank W.	"	"	18.9.15	'D'
S299		Mead W.				
S8495	Rfn.	Harvey W.J.	"	Death from natural causes	12.9.15.	'A'
S5484	"	Shepherd S.D.	"	Shell Head	13.9.15.	'A'
S7358	"	Whiley A.	"	Shpnl. Thigh	14.9.15.	'A'
S 855	Cpl.	Barrett T.	"	Wound Bomb accidental.	17.9.15.	'A'
				Died	do	
S7358	Rfn.	Whilay A.	"	From Wounds	18.9.15.	'A'

*State whether absence is of a permanent or temporary nature, adding, in the case of casuals from wounds or disease, any available information for communication to the relatives.

FIELD RETURN.

Army Form B. 213.

No. of Report 18

(To be furnished by all arms, services, and departments to the A. G.'s Office at the Base in accordance with Field Service Regulations, Part II.)

Sept. 18th 15. Date.

RETURN showing numbers RATIONED by, and Transport on charge of, 8th Batt. The Rifle Brigade at Ypres

Detail	Personnel: Officers*	Personnel: Other ranks*	Personnel: Natives	Animals: Horses*: Riding	Horses*: Draught	Horses*: Heavy Draught	Horses*: Pack	Mules*: Large	Mules*: Small	Camels	Oxen	Guns, carriages and limbers and transport vehicles: Guns, carriages and limbers, showing description	Ammunition wagons and limbers	Machine guns	Aircraft, showing description	Horsed: 4 Wheeled	Horsed: 2 Wheeled	Mechanical: Motor Cars	Tractors	Lorries, showing description	Trucks, showing description	Trailers	Motor Bicycles	Bicycles	Remarks
Effective Strength of Unit	17	865		13		9	9	34				Dob. MG 2 2	7	4		2	4							8	
Details, by Arms attached to unit as in War Establishment:— R.A.M.C.	1																								
A.O.C.		1																							
Interpreter			1																						
		30																							Sick not evacuated
	1	37																							{14th Div. 41st Bde 6th Corps. {Ypres Guard On leave
Total	19	933	1	13		9	9	34				2 2	7	4		2	4							8	
War Establishment	30	991	1	13		9	9	34				2 2	7	4		2	4							9	
Wanting to complete	11	58																						1	
Surplus																									
*Attached (not to include the details shown above)																									
Civilians:— Employed with the Unit																									
Accompanying the Unit																									
Total Rationed ...	18	866		13		9	9	34																	

* In the case of field ambulances, hospitals or depots, the number of patients are to be included here, the names being shown in A.F.A. 36.

Lt. QM for O.C. 8th R.B. Signature of Commander.

18/9/15. Date of Despatch.

(K 11859) W. & Co., Ltd. Wt. w6095—894 500,000 10/14 Forms B. 213 / 5

Instructions regarding War Diaries and Intelligence Summaries are contained in F. S. Regs., Part II. and the Staff Manual respectively. Title pages will be prepared in manuscript.

WAR DIARY
or
~~INTELLIGENCE SUMMARY.~~
(*Erase heading not required.*)

Army Form C. 2118.

8th (S) Bn Rifle Brigade

Place	Date	Hour	Summary of Events and Information	Remarks and references to Appendices
	1916			
ARRAS	April		In reserve billets in ARRAS. Fine weather	CRWB
reserve billets	7th		Working parties up to 200 every night	
	8th	→	Lecture by Brigadier to all officers	CRWB
	9th		Two companies and HQ bathed.	CRWB
	10th		Fine weather. Usual working parties	acs
	11th		Weather breaks. Very heavy storm in afternoon. Remainder of Battalion bathed. Usual working-parties.	acs
Trenches 749 - I 60.	12th		Stormy day. Relieved 7th R.B in trenches. Quiet relief. C Company on left A in Centre B on right D in Reserve.	acs
	13th		Enemy quiet with exception of a few whizz-bangs. Showery day. Communication Trenches in poor state.	acs
	14th		Very heavy showers of rain and hail. Enemy very quiet. Work confined to Communication Trenches and Dug-outs.	acs
	15th		Showery morning. Weather clears later. Very little activity on either side.	acs

2353 Wt. W2544/1454 700,000 5/15 D. D. & L. A.D.S.S./Forms/C. 2118.

Instructions regarding War Diaries and Intelligence Summaries are contained in F. S. Regs., Part II. and the Staff Manual respectively. Title pages will be prepared in manuscript.

WAR DIARY
or
~~INTELLIGENCE SUMMARY.~~
(Erase heading not required.)

8th Bn Rifle Brigade

Army Form C. 2118.

Place	Date	Hour	Summary of Events and Information	Remarks and references to Appendices
ARRAS Trenches 249 - I.60	16th		A fine day, and much aeroplane activity. A shoot in the afternoon by Divisional and Corps Artillery opposite ACHICOURT and opposite 8 KRRC front.	ACS
	17th		Weather again bad. Quiet day. Commanding Officer returns from leave.	ACS
	18th		Bad day again. Relieved by 7th R.B. at night. Battalion goes out to rest to WANQUETIN, 9 miles.	
WANQUETIN	19th		Battalion resting, and cleaning up. Capt A L C CAVENDISH appointed 2nd in command and Temporary Major: to date 13.4.16	ACS
	20th		Wet. Companies training	[illegible]
	21st		Wet. Companies training	[illegible]
	22nd		Wet. Companies training	[illegible]
	23rd		Fine. Easter Sunday. Parade service. Brigadier Genl Lord BINNING hands over command of the Brigade to Brigadier Genl P.S. SKINNER.	[illegible]
	24th		Fine. Battalion relieves 7th RB in trenches. 'D', 'A', 'B' Companies in front line. 'C' Coy in Bn Reserve.	[illegible]

2353 Wt. W2544/1454 700,000 5/15 D. D. & L. A.D.S.S./Forms/C. 2118.

Instructions regarding War Diaries and Intelligence Summaries are contained in F. S. Regs., Part II. and the Staff Manual respectively. Title pages will be prepared in manuscript.

WAR DIARY
or
~~INTELLIGENCE SUMMARY.~~
(*Erase heading not required.*)

8th Bn Rifle Brigade

Army Form C. 2118.

Place	Date	Hour	Summary of Events and Information	Remarks and references to Appendices
ARRAS	1916 April			
Trenches	25th		Wet. Conference of commanding officers at Brigade H^d. Qrs at 3 p.m.	[illegible]
I 49 - I 60	26th		Wet. Lt Genl Sir J [illegible] Comd XI Corps visited trenches	[illegible]
	27th		Wet. Brigadier Genl P.S. SKINNER visits trenches. Trenches quite dry owing to hot weather. Work continued on construction of Support Line & dug outs for the men. Enemy very quiet.	[illegible]
	26th		2nd Lt F. P. MATTHEWS rejoined & 2nd Lt A. D. MACNAGHTEN joined the battalion.	
	28th		Wet. Enemy [illegible] up in I [illegible] at 8 a.m. for third day in succession & about 100 shells over trenches I 55 - I 56 in morning. Fighting Strength of Battalion 23 officers 848 O.R.	[illegible]
	29th		Wet; very quiet day	[illegible]
	30th		Wet: our trench mortars shell enemy's saps in front of I.60 & I.52 in afternoon very slight retaliation on trenches: a few shells near RUE St QUENTIN. Relieved by 7th Bn Rifle Brigade & go into billets in ARRAS. Relief completed at 11.15 p.m.	[illegible]
			List of casualties attached	
			H. L. [illegible] Lt Col Cmdg 8th Bn Rifle Brigade	

2353 Wt. W2544/1454 700,000 5/15 D. D. & L. A.D.S.S./Forms/C. 2118.

8th Bn Rifle Brigade
Casualties April 1916

No	Rank & Name	Coy	Date	Nature	Remarks
S8669	Rfn. O'Brien W	A	2. 4. 16	G.S.W. arm	fracture
S13704	- Towersey T	C	4. 4. 16	- neck	(at duty)
S14469	- Wood J	D	5. 4. 16	Shpnl. neck	rejoined 12/4/16
1086	- Ladd T	B	6. 4. 16	G.S.W. arm	
Z 209	- Rose W	D	9. 4. 16	- leg	at duty
S12779	A/Cpl. Snowden F	D	11. 4. 16	- face	To England 15/4/16
B 2942	Rfn. Crisp S	D	11. 4. 16	- arm	
S 6770	- Miller JH	C	13. 4. 16	- buttock	rejoined 20/4/16
S10110	- Waugh F	A	15. 4. 16	- neck	rejoined 23/4/16
S 7668	A/Cpl Bastow J	A	16. 4. 16	died of wounds	
5886	Rfn. Ward J	A	17. 4. 16	G.S.W. Head	
S7121	- Tench W	D	26. 4. 16	Shprl. Thorax	died 28/4/16
S12788	- Topping T	C	26. 4. 16	G.S.W. Leg	
B 563	- Wells P	A	27. 4. 16	- head	died 28/4/16
S12780	- Ettery T	C	27. 4. 16	- shoulder	
S7445	A/Cpl. Jarvis J	D	27. 4. 16	Wounded	While attached New Zealand Tunnelling Coy.

8th. BATTALION THE RIFLE BRIGADE.

Roll of Officers.

Lieut.Col.H.D.Ross

Major A.L.C.Cavendish

Major A.C.Sheepshanks D.S.O.	
Capt. E.F.Prior	
Capt. M.E.Yorke Eliot	41st. Brigade Transport Officer
Capt. G.E.H.Keesey	Third Army School of Instruction.
Capt. K.S.M.Gladstone	42nd. Brigade Headquarters.
Capt. A.R.Backus	
Capt. W.C.F.V.Barker-Mill	
Lieut. C.N.Thompson	
Lieut. A.N.Coles	
Lieut. C.H.Wenham	Batt. Bombing Officer.
Lieut. W.A.Crebbin	Batt. Signalling Officer.
2/Lt. J.R.Abbey	
" D.H.Beves	Batt. Lewis Gun Officer
" H.R.Adair	
" D.F.Foxwell	
~~" A.F.Atkinson~~	~~Divisional Anti-Gas Officer.~~
" A.D.Macnaghten	
" K.M.Farmiloe	In Hospital.
" E.P.Matthews	
" R.H.F.Devereux	
" E.Poole	Batt. Transport Officer.
" E.L.Vickers	
" D.S.Ashforth	Batt. Intelligence Officer.
" G.R.Sayer	
" W.R.H.Merriman	

Lieut. & Adjt. C.R.Gorell Barnes D.S.O.

Lieut. & Quartermaster F.H.Pryor

Lieut. F.J.Strachan R.A.M.C.

H.D. Ross Lt Col
Comdg 8th Bn Rifle Bde

Instructions regarding War Diaries and Intelligence Summaries are contained in F. S. Regs., Part II. and the Staff Manual respectively. Title pages will be prepared in manuscript.

WAR DIARY
or
~~INTELLIGENCE SUMMARY.~~
(Erase heading not required.)

XIV

Army Form C. 2118.

Vol 12

8th (S) Battalion Rifle Brigade

Place	Date 1916	Hour	Summary of Events and Information	Remarks and references to Appendices
	MAY			
ARRAS	1st		A Coy in HOTEL de L'UNIVERS. B Coy in GRANDE PLACE. C Coy in defence of St SAUVEUR. D Coy in defence of the CEMETERY. Hd Qrs just off GRANDE PLACE	[illegible]
	2nd		Thunder showers. O.C. 1st Bn DEVONSHIRE REGt comes to inspect billets previous to taking over.	[illegible]
			2nd Lt C. D. H. VANSTONE joined the battalion.	[illegible]
	3rd		Orders received that the Brigade will be relieved on night of 4th-5th by 95th Brigade: 5th Division. Billeting parties take over new billets in ARRAS in & around RUE de CHATEAUDUN	[illegible]
	4th		Hot: Battalion relieved by 1st Bn DEVON REGt: relief completed 10.45 p.m. One casualty during tour. Battalion proceeds to billets around RUE de CHATEAUDUN. 41st Bde Hd Qrs at AGNEZ les DUISANS. Battalion is under orders of 42nd Brigade while in ARRAS.	[illegible]
	5th		Hot. Clean up billets. Hd Qrs, 'A' & 'B' Companies to baths.	
	6th		Battalion in billets resting. C & D Coys to baths	[illegible]
	7th		Commanding officer to conference at 2nd Army School. Major A.F.C. Cavendish in command. A considerable amount of shelling in the morning and afternoon near Bn HQ.	

2353 Wt W2544/1454 700,000 5/15 D. D. & L. A.D.S.S./Forms/C. 2118.

Instructions regarding War Diaries and Intelligence Summaries are contained in F. S. Regs., Part II. and the Staff Manual respectively. Title pages will be prepared in manuscript.

WAR DIARY
or
~~INTELLIGENCE SUMMARY.~~
(Erase heading not required.)

Army Form C. 2118.

8th Bn Rifle Brigade

Place	Date 1916	Hour	Summary of Events and Information	Remarks and references to Appendices
	May 7th		Order received that 41st INF BDE would be attached to XVII Corps for work in connection with mining shifts from 9th inst. Two battalions working and 2 resting. Bde HQ would be at SAVY. BN HQ to be at MAROEUIL NW of ARRAS 2 Coys at MAROEUIL and 2 COYS at ANZIN. Advance parties went and reconnoitred the area	
	8th		Battalion moved at 8 p.m. as follows. HQ & A COY to MAROEUIL. B and C COYS to LOUEZ where they were billeted for the night in the SUCHERIE. D COY to ANZIN. 1/4th LINCOLNSHIRE REGT were not to move out until 3 PM 9th inst, in order that the fatigues should be continuous.	CRWB
	9th		Rain. Fatigues consist of long shifts 6 to 8 hours carrying filled sandbags from	CRWB

Instructions regarding War Diaries and Intelligence Summaries are contained in F. S. Regs., Part II. and the Staff Manual respectively. Title pages will be prepared in manuscript.

WAR DIARY
or
~~INTELLIGENCE SUMMARY.~~
(Erase heading not required.)

Army Form C. 2118.

8th Bn Rifle Brigade

Place	Date	Hour	Summary of Events and Information	Remarks and references to Appendices
	MAY 1916			
	9th		the mine shafts and emptying them behind the line. There is a three mile march to get to the work from both MAROEUIL and ANZIN.	
			After dinners B Coy moved to MAROEUIL, and C Coy moved to ANZIN. 2/Lt W.R. MERRIMAN joined the Battalion from Cadet School and posted to C Coy.	CRLHB
	10th		Battalion at MAROEUIL and ANZIN. In certain eventualities the Corps reserve line running approximately NORTH from a point 400 yds East of St AUBIN is to be manned. This line reconnoitred	CRLHB
	11th		Battalion at MAROEUIL and ANZIN.	CRLHB.
	12th		Battalion at MAROEUIL and ANZIN. B.G.C visited HQ and discussed the occupation of the Corps line. ANZIN heavily shelled during	

2353 Wt. W2544/1454 700,000 5/15 D. D. & L. A.D.S.S./Forms/C. 2118.

Instructions regarding War Diaries and Intelligence Summaries are contained in F. S. Regs., Part II. and the Staff Manual respectively. Title pages will be prepared in manuscript.

WAR DIARY
or
~~INTELLIGENCE SUMMARY.~~
(Erase heading not required.)

Army Form C. 2118.

8th Bn Rifle Brigade

Place	Date	Hour	Summary of Events and Information	Remarks and references to Appendices
	MAY 1916			
MAROEUIL	12th		during the afternoon. Not much damage done	CRNB.
	13th		Commanding Officer returned from Third Army conference.	CRNB.
	14th		Sunday. Working parties as usual.	[illegible]
	15th		Working parties as usual. Advance party sent to SAVY to take over billets from 7th Bn K.R.R.C. Advance parties of 7th Bn K.R.R.C came to take over our billets. 2nd Lt I.C. MONTFORD & 2nd Lt O.B. TABOR joined the battalion	[illegible]
	16th		March to SAVY by companies: last working parties brought by lorries & arrive at 1.30 a.m.	[illegible]
SAVY	17th		Hot. Visit Major CRUM, 8th Bn K.R.R.C at ACQ & arrange to send 1 officer & 12 O.R. for a short course of sniping.	[illegible]
	18th		Hot. C & D companies have baths in SAVY. Company parades	[illegible]
	19th		Hot. A & B companies have baths in SAVY. All companies route marches	[illegible]
	20th		Battalion route march of just over 9 miles through PENIN & TINCQUES. Strength of battalion 34 officers & 960 O.R.	[illegible]
	21st		Sunday. Church parade in morning. Orders received at 11.15 p.m. to move to BOIS des ALLEUX N.W of MONT St ELOY via AUBIGNY & ACQ: packs to be carried on motor lorries. The	
MONT St ELOY	22nd		battalion moves off with transport at 1.15 a.m. & arrives at BOIS des ALLEUX at 3.45 a.m.	

2353 Wt. W2344/1454 700,000 5/15 D. D. & L. A.D.S.S./Forms/C. 2118.

Instructions regarding War Diaries and Intelligence Summaries are contained in F. S. Regs., Part II. and the Staff Manual respectively. Title pages will be prepared in manuscript.

WAR DIARY
or
~~INTELLIGENCE SUMMARY.~~
(Erase heading not required.)

8th Bn Rifle Brigade

Army Form C. 2118.

Place	Date	Hour	Summary of Events and Information	Remarks and references to Appendices
	MAY 1916			
MONT St ELOY	22nd		The battalion is quartered, 3 companies in 3 huts in the wood, A Coy & HdQrs in 2 huts outside wood: transport animals in wood. The battalion remains in readiness to move at short notice owing to the enemy having driven back the 47th Division out of two lines of trenches half a mile north of NEUVILLE St VAAST.	[initials]
	23rd		Remain in wood	[initials]
	24th		Relieve 7th Bn Rifle Brigade at LA TARGETTE: all 4 companies in large cave with 67 steps leading down to it. HdQrs are half a mile north of LA TARGETTE in dug-outs east of BETHUNE-ARRAS road: in rear of 7th Brigade.	[initials]
~~LA TARGETTE~~ LA TARGETTE	25th		All battalion employed under 172nd & 175th mining companies Royal Engineers, carrying earth from their saps in the area of the 25th Division.	[initials]
	26th		Quiet day. All battalion on working parties.	[initials]
	27th		" " " "	[initials]
	28th		Sunday " " Chaplain holds service in the cave	[initials]
	29th		Battalion on working parties	[initials]
	30th		" "	[initials]
	31st		Battalion on working parties. Captain L. WOODROFFE joins from 14th Bn Rifle Brigade. Appendix: casualties for the month.	[initials]

H. D. R[illegible] Lt Col
Comdg 8th Bn Rifle Brigade

2353 Wt. W2544/1454 700,000 5/15 D. D. & L. A.D.S.S./Forms/C. 2118.

8th. Batt. Rifle Brigade.

Casualties. May 1916.

No.	Rank & Name.	Coy.	Date.	Remarks.
S11050	Rfn. Jones P.	C	1st.	G.S.W. leg
S9231	A/Cpl.Gilbert H.	B	11th.	Shell foot (at duty)
S8581	Rfn. Whawell W.	B	11th.	Shell head
S11049	Rfn. Goodman S.	C	12th.	Shell arm (at duty)
12860	Rfn. Wakeford W.	B	12th.	Shell head (at duty)
3014	Rfn. Clegg T.	B	15th.	G.S.W. arm
S3199	Sgt. Kimberley A.	B	25th.	Killed in Action.
S10945	Rfn. Molyneaux G.	B	24th.	Killed in Action.
S9541	Rfn. Hay T.	B	24th.	Wounded, aeropalne sharpnel.
S11032	Rfn. Boulton W.	D	31st.	Killed in Action.

XIV

Instructions regarding War Diaries and Intelligence Summaries are contained in F. S. Regs., Part II. and the Staff Manual respectively. Title pages will be prepared in manuscript.

WAR DIARY
or
~~INTELLIGENCE SUMMARY.~~
(Erase heading not required.)

Army Form C. 2118.

8th Bn Rifle Brigade VOL 13

June

Place	Date 1916	Hour	Summary of Events and Information	Remarks and references to Appendices
LA TARGETTE	June 1st		Capt L. WOODROFFE wounded severely in thigh. About 4.30 p.m. heavy bombardment opened on front of 2nd Division, 4th Corps immediately to south of sector in which the battalion is working: this continues intermittently till midnight. The enemy reply on left of our sector, working parties unable to go up at night.	HMR
	2nd		Quiet day: battalion relieved after dark by 7th Bn K.R.R.C.: relief completed about midnight. The Battalion goes into huts at ECOIVRES: Hd Qrs in the same chateau as 41st Brigade Hd Qrs. LA TARGETTE is part of NEUVILLE St VAAST: while there accommodation only available for 3 officers per company & 3 at Hd Qrs: remainder stay with transport in BOIS des ALLEUX	HMR
ECOIVRES	3rd		Battalion cleaning up & resting. Weather dull & cold.	HMR
	4th		Sunday. Church parade. Conference of Commanding Officers at Brigade Headquarters	HMR
	5th		Capt L. WOODROFFE dies at Casualty Clearing Station at BARLIN. Working party of 5 officers & 150 men to put up wire for 51st Division in new line: they parade at 7.15 p.m. & return about 4 a.m.: very wet	HMR
	6th		Wet. Leave vacancies cut down by one half. C.S.M. KENWARD granted a commission in the 16th Bn RIFLE BRIGADE. Working party reduced to 3 officers & 100 men, divided into 5 gangs. Demonstration of wiring as approved by Major Genl HARPER: Comdg 51st Division	HMR
	7th		Fine. Working party as before. O.C. Battn visits 7th Bn RIFLE BRIGADE at MAROEUIL to	

2353 Wt. W2544/1454 700,000 5/15 D. D. & L. A.D.S.S./Forms/C. 2118.

Instructions regarding War Diaries and Intelligence Summaries are contained in F. S. Regs., Part II. and the Staff Manual respectively. Title pages will be prepared in manuscript.

WAR DIARY
or
~~INTELLIGENCE SUMMARY.~~
(*Erase heading not required.*)

8th Bn Rifle Brigade

Army Form C. 2118.

Place	Date	Hour	Summary of Events and Information	Remarks and references to Appendices
	1916 June			
ECOIVRES	7th		Find out distribution of battalion.	HRC
	8th		Fine. Company commanders visit companies of 7th Bn RIFLE BRIGADE at MAROEUIL. The Chestnut Troop (A Battery) R.H.A. is billetted in ACQ. Working parties	HRC
	9th		Working parties.	HRC
MAROEUIL	10th		Relieve 7th Bn Rifle Brigade in afternoon & evening. H^d Qrs & 'D' Company at MAROEUIL, 'C' Coy in ELBE Trench, 'B' Coy at ANZIN & ROCLINCOURT, 'A' Coy at ANZIN	HRC
	11th		Sunday. Working parties for mining companies. Weather wet & unsettled	HRC
	12th		Working parties as usual. Weather very cold & wet. Conference of C.Os at Brigade Head-quarters.	HRC
	13th		" " " Weather wet. Slight bombardment on M sector: one corporal of 'B' Coy wounded	HRC
	14th		Working parties. Time advanced one hour at 11 p.m.	HRC
	15th		" "	HRC
	16th		" " ~~Lt Col H.D. Ross Capt~~ Lt Col H.D. ROSS, Capt E.F. PRIOR & Lt I.C. MONTFORD reconnoitre K.1 sector of trenches.	HRC
	17th		Orders received for relief on 18th to be carried out by 7th Bn RIFLE BRIGADE. Working parties	HRC
	18th		Above order cancelled & relief to be carried out by 3 regiments of 1st Indian Cavalry Division.	

2353 Wt. W2544/1454 700,000 5/15 D. D. & L. A.D.S.S./Forms/C. 2118.

WAR DIARY
or
~~INTELLIGENCE SUMMARY.~~
(Erase heading not required.)

Army Form C. 2118.

Instructions regarding War Diaries and Intelligence Summaries are contained in F. S. Regs., Part II. and the Staff Manual respectively. Title pages will be prepared in manuscript.

8th Bn Rifle Brigade

Place	Date	Hour	Summary of Events and Information	Remarks and references to Appendices
	1916 JUNE			
MAROEUIL	18th		Lt Col Beran: Central India Horse arrives with advance party about midday: remainder of troops arrive about 6 p.m.: 300 men & 6 British officers from 3 regiments Ind.	HRR
	19th		Fire. 2 squadrons 29th Lancers relieve 'A' Coy at ANZIN	
			1 " Central India Horse " 'B' " " ANZIN	
			2 " 29th Lancers " 'B' " " L'ABRI CENTRALE	
			A Detachment Central India Horse " 'C' " " ELBE TRENCH	
			" 2nd Lancers " 'D' " " MAROEUIL	
			The remainder C.I.H & 2nd Lancers remain in billets in MAROEUIL	
			2 Lewis guns & teams from each of 'A' & 'D' Coys join 7th Bn R. Bde for attachment in trenches of K.1 sector just north of ARRAS.	
			Battalion returns to billets at ECOIVRES on relief	HRR
ECOIVRES	20th		Battalion rests in billets. 4 officers & 120 O.R. march at 7.30 p.m. to St NICHOLAS to Hd Qrs 15th Bn ROYAL WARWICKSHIRE REGt to take over billets for Battalion & working parties on 21st	HRR
	21st		Reinforcement of 102 O.R. join from base having been sent from 6th (Reserve) Bn RIFLE BRIGADE. The Bn marks off at 8 p.m. into BRIGADE RESERVE at St NICHOLAS: transport	

2353 Wt. W2544/1454 700,000 5/15 D. D. & L. A.D.S.S./Forms/C. 2118.

Instructions regarding War Diaries and Intelligence Summaries are contained in F. S. Regs., Part II. and the Staff Manual respectively. Title pages will be prepared in manuscript.

WAR DIARY
or
~~INTELLIGENCE SUMMARY.~~
(Erase heading not required.)

8th Bn Rifle Brigade

Army Form C. 2118.

Place	Date	Hour	Summary of Events and Information	Remarks and references to Appendices
	1916 ~~MAY~~ JUNE			
ECOIVRES	21st		to DUISANS: 'A' Co moved to St NICOLAS	
			'D' " ROCLINCOURT	
			'C' " ARRAS	
			'B' " ARRAS (2 platoons): THELUS REDOUBT (1 platoon): OBSERVATORY (1 platoon)	
			H.Qrs St NICHOLAS	
St NICHOLAS	22nd		Relief of 15th Bn WARWICKSHIRE REGt. 13th Bde: 5th Division completed at 2.15 a.m.	[initials]
	22nd		Battn furnished working parties: Officers reconnoitre approaches to front line. Weather fine	[initials]
	23rd		" " " " Thunderstorm in afternoon.	
			Advanced quarter-master's store established in ARRAS under Regt Qr Mr Sgt JACKSON	[initials]
	24th		2nd Lt O.B. TABOR struck off strength (sick). Duty state of Battalion 21 Officers: 848 O.R. Working parties. Continuous fire by our artillery nearly all day.	[initials]
	25th		Working parties: intermittent fire by our artillery all day. Enemy sends two patrols in early morning right up to K.1. sector: driven off by 7th Bn Rifle Brigade	[initials]
	26th		Lewis guns & bombers of Battalion relieve those of 7th Bn Rifle Brigade. Baths in ARRAS for the companies. Working parties as usual. Weather showery.	[initials]
	27th		Battalion relieves 7th Bn Rifle Brigade in K.1. Sector of trenches: EAST of ROCLINCOURT. 'A' Co in	

Instructions regarding War Diaries and Intelligence Summaries are contained in F. S. Regs., Part II. and the Staff Manual respectively. Title pages will be prepared in manuscript.

WAR DIARY

or

~~INTELLIGENCE SUMMARY.~~

(*Erase heading not required.*)

8th Bn Rifle Brigade

Army Form C. 2118.

Place	Date	Hour	Summary of Events and Information	Remarks and references to Appendices
	1916 JUNE			
TRENCHES K.1. 102–111	27th		trenches 102–104 with one crater: 'C' Co in trenches 105–107 with two craters: 'D' Co in trenches 108–111 with one crater: 'B' Co in support at trench 40: Hd Quarters in SUNDAY AVENUE.	
			Front line platoons, signallers & snipers relieved in afternoon. 'C' Co had 2 platoons in front line & A & D had 3 each.	HBR
	28th		Relief completed at 12.10 a.m. Demonstration against enemy's second line by artillery & trench mortars of the brigade from 5 p.m to 5.30 p.m: retaliation feeble. ~~Weather showery~~	HBR
			Standing patrols from each company go out at 11 p.m & stay out till 2 a.m. Weather showery.	HBR
	29th		A fine day: trenches drying up. About 3.20 a.m enemy opened fire on right company 'A' & the fire gradually spread north to the VIMY RIDGE: At 3.45 a.m the enemy's artillery and trench mortars ceased fire on the battalion front, even after our artillery had opened fire. There were no casualties from this fire.	
			Good work was done in improving fire trenches & communication trenches.	HBR
	30th		A fine day. Trenches much improved. A few high explosive & trench mortars sent over about 8 p.m by enemy: no damage. A few rifle grenades earlier in the day.	
			Strength in the trenches: 19 Officers & 720 other ranks.	HBR
Appendices			{ List of casualties ~~attached~~. List of officers strength on 30.6.16.	

H.B. Ripp Lt Col
Comdg 8th Bn Rifle Brigade

2353 Wt W2544/1454 700,000 5/15 D. D. & L. A.D.S.S./Forms/C. 2118.

8th. BATTALION THE RIFLE BRIGADE.

List of Casualties for June 1916.

Capt.L.Woodroffe	Wounded 1/6/16. Died of wounds 4/6/16.
2/Lt.Hartley H.R.	Wounded Accidentally 26/6/16.

Z	1160	Serjt.	Abdurehman	B.	"A" Coy.	Killed in Action 28/6/16.			
B	3046	A/Corpl.	Jenn	P.	"C" Coy.	Killed in Action 29/6/16.			
B	2069	Corpl.	Rogers	P.	"B" Coy.	Wounded in Action		13/6/16.	(Rejoined)
B	3037	A/Corpl.	Grinstead	C.	"C" Coy.	do.	do.	14/6/16	(Rejoined)
S	13750	Rfn.	Carratt	G.	"C" Coy.	do.	do.	16/6/16	(Rejoined)
S	3167	A/Serjt.	Gill	R.	"C" Coy.	do.	do.	25/6/16.	-
S	15588	Rfn.	Golden	A.	"B" Coy.	do.	do.	25/6/16	(Gas)
	1021	"	Kay	C.	"D" Coy.	do.	do.	26/6/16	-
S	1503	A/Corpl.	Maguire	J.	"C" Coy.	do.	do.	27/6/16	(Gas)
B	308	"	Stone	J.	"C" Coy.	do.	do.	do.	(Gas)
S	13865	Rfn.	Gibbs	A.	"C" Coy.	do.	do.	do.	(Gas)
S	11363	"	Elvin	G.	"C" Coy.	do.	do.	do.	(Gas)
S	11263	"	Winfield	A.	"C" Coy.	do.	do.	do.	(Gas)
S	13276	"	Foster	H.	"A" Coy.	do.	do.	do.	(Gas)
	3668	"	Heritage	J.	"D" Coy.	do.	do.	29/6/16	
Z	8958	"	McCarthy	J.	"D" Coy.	do.	do.	30/6/16	
	2493	"	Todd	C.	"D" Coy.	do.	do.	do.	
B	2456	"	Bettington	P.	"D" Coy.	do.	do.	do.	
B	3335	"	Wain	A.	"A" Coy.	do.	do.	do.	
S	9473	"	Driscoll	W.	"A" Coy.	do.	do.	do.	
B	50	"	Blunden	B.	"A" Coy.	do.	do.	do.	

JUNE 30 1916.

8th. BATTALION THE RIFLE BRIGADE.

ROLL OF OFFICERS.

Lieut.Col.H.D.Ross.	
Major A.L.C.Cavendish.	
Major A.C.Sheepshanks D.S.O.	
Capt. E.F.Prior.	
Capt. M.E.Yorke Eliot	41st. Brigade Transport Officer
Capt. G.E.H.Keesey.	
Capt. K.S.M.Gladstone	42nd. Inf.Bde. Headquarters.
Capt. A.R.Backus.	
Capt. W.C.F.V.Barker-Mill	Third Army School of Instrn.
Lieut. I.C.Montford.	
Lieut. C.N.Thompson.	
Lieut. A.N.Coles.	
Lieut. C.H.Wenham.	14th. Div. Grenade School.
Lieut. W.A.Crebbin	14th. Div. Signal Course.
2/Lt. D.H. Beves.	
2/Lt. H.R.Adair.	
2/Lt. D.F.Foxwell	~~Temp.A.D.C.~~ 14th. Division. Grenade School
2/Lt. A.F.Atkinson	14th. Div. Anti-Gas School.
2/Lt. A.D.Macnaghten.	
2/Lt. K.M.Farmiloe.	
2/Lt. E.P.Matthews.	
2/Lt. R.H.F.Devereux	14th. Div. School (Course)
2/Lt. N.F.H.Mather.	
2/Lt. E.Poole	Transport Officer.
2/Lt. E.L.Vickers	
2/Lt. D.S.Ashforth	Intelligence Officer.
2/Lt. W.R.H.Merriman.	
Lieut. & Adjt.C.R.Gorell Barnes D.S.O.	
Lieut. & Q.M. F.H.Pryor.	
Lieut. F.J.Strachan R.A.M.C. (attd.)	

C O N F I D E N T I A L.

W A R D I A R Y

- of -

8th Bn., THE RIFLE BRIGADE.

From: 1st July, 1916.
To: 31st " 1916.

Volume. 15.

Instructions regarding War Diaries and Intelligence Summaries are contained in F. S. Regs., Part II. and the Staff Manual respectively. Title pages will be prepared in manuscript.

WAR DIARY
or
~~INTELLIGENCE SUMMARY.~~
(Erase heading not required.)

Army Form C. 2118.

8th/Bn Rifle Brigade

Place	Date 1916	Hour	Summary of Events and Information	Remarks and references to Appendices
Trenches E of ROCLINCOURT K.1. 102 – 111	JULY 1st		Brigade Machine Gun Company fires intermittently from midnight till 3 a.m. on enemy's dumps and strong points: our working parties not disturbed. Enemy's patrol met just N of crater 106: no one captured. 8th/Bn K.R.R.C held K.2 sector on our left: 6th/Bn D.C.L.I (43rd Infantry Brigade) held J2 sector on our right. News received of advance of 4th Army B.E.F. in the south.	
		10.45 p.m.	Enemy blows up mine in trench 112–113 in K.2 sector immediately north of battalion sector & in sector of 8th/Bn K.R.R.C. "D" Co under command of Capt. KRESEY help to consolidate crater by [illegible] rifle fire & sending bombers to support 8th/Bn K.R.R.C. Heavy bombardment & news received of successful advance of 4th Army B.E.F. Weather fine.	[illegible]
	2nd		Weather fine. Bombardment to south continues. 2nd Lt. A. R. SAYER joins the battalion from ENGLAND. Quiet day on battalion front.	[illegible]
	3rd	2.30 p.m.	Battery near TILLOY shell our right trenches with 5.9" shells	
		5 p.m.	Centre company shelled with heavy trench mortars. In both cases shelling stopped on retaliation by our artillery. [illegible] Signallers & snipers relieved by 7th/Bn Rifle Brigade in afternoon: remainder of battalion relieved after dark	[illegible]
DUISANS	4th		Relief completed at 2 a.m.: companies march to DUISANS and go into billets there. The last company arrived about 4 a.m.: heavy showers during relief. Lewis guns of B & C companies left in the trenches	

Instructions regarding War Diaries and Intelligence Summaries are contained in F. S. Regs., Part II. and the Staff Manual respectively. Title pages will be prepared in manuscript.

WAR DIARY
or
~~INTELLIGENCE SUMMARY.~~
(Erase heading not required.)

(2)

Army Form C. 2118.

8th Bn Rifle Brigade

Place	Date 1916	Hour	Summary of Events and Information	Remarks and references to Appendices
	JULY			
DUISANS	4th		and attached to 7th Bn RIFLE BRIGADE.	HRC
	5th		Fine. 'A & B' companies bathe in River SCARPE. Kit inspections of kit. Working party of 1 Officer & 50 O.R. to DAINVILLE.	HRC
	6th		Fine. 'C & D' companies bathe. Working party as before. Musketry parades.	HRC
	7th		Officers & N.C.Os to WARLUS to demonstration of methods of communication between aircraft & infantry in battle given by No 12 Squadron Royal Flying Corps under command of Major HALAHAN. A good demonstration but spoilt by the heavy rain. Heavy showers all day. Working party to DAINVILLE.	HRC
	8th		Fine. No working party	HRC
	9th		Sunday. Church parade at 9.30 a.m. Relieve 7th Bn Rifle Brigade in trenches. 'B' Coy in right sector, 'C' Coy in centre, 'D' Coy in left sector: 'A' Coy in support at trench 40.	HRC
Trenches E of ROCLINCOURT	10th	2 a.m.	Relief completed. Trenches still rather wet. Weather fine & day quiet. Work on clearing up trenches & improving communications.	HRC
	11th	2.30 p.m.	Howitzers fire with new experimental shell	
		6 p.m.	Enemy retaliate with heavy trench mortar for about one hour, our artillery of all calibres fire but trench mortar takes no notice. 3 men killed & 1 severely wounded by one shell from trench mortar: otherwise no damage.	HRC

2353 Wt. W2544/1454 700,000 5/15 D. D. & L. A.D.S.S./Forms/C. 2118.

Instructions regarding War Diaries and Intelligence Summaries are contained in F. S. Regs., Part II. and the Staff Manual respectively. Title pages will be prepared in manuscript.

(3)

WAR DIARY
or
~~INTELLIGENCE SUMMARY.~~
(*Erase heading not required.*)

Army Form C. 2118.

8th Bn Rifle Brigade

Place	Date	Hour	Summary of Events and Information	Remarks and references to Appendices
	1916 JULY			
Trenches E of ROCLINCOURT.	12th contd		Fine. A quiet day. Work continued of improving trenches & communications. 2nd Lt J. R. ABBEY rejoined the battalion from sick leave.	HMC
	13th		Fine. Trenches dry: good progress made in repair of trenches & opening communication trenches.	
		3 p.m.	Howitzer battery shelled enemy's front line opposite left half of sector held by battalion.	HMC
	14th		Showers in morning. Demonstrations by right of division against enemy's front in conjunction with operations further south. Quiet on battalion front.	HMC
	15th		Fine. Battalion relieved by 7th Bn RIFLE BRIGADE: relief completed at 11.30 p.m. Hd Qrs & 'C' Coy to ST. NICHOLAS: 'A' Coy to ROCLINCOURT: 'D' Coy to ARRAS: 'B' Coy, 2 platoons to ARRAS 1 platoon to FORT THELUS, 1 platoon to OBSERVATORY REDOUBT.	HMC
St NICHOLAS	16th		Sunday. Rain in afternoon. Working parties for front line.	HMC
	17th		A wet night. Working parties. A few shells near Battalion Hd Quarters about 9 p.m.	HMC
	18th		Fine. Working parties.	HMC
	19th		Fine. Working parties. Baths in ARRAS available for battalion.	HMC
	20th		Fine. Working parties. St NICHOLAS slightly shelled about 8 p.m.	HMC
	21st		Fine. 2nd Lt A. F. ATKINSON transferred to the General List as anti-gas instructor to the division, dated 26/6/16 & to be temporary Lt: 2nd Lt K. M. FARMILOE sent sick with appendicitis. The Battalion relieves 7th Bn Rifle Bde	

2353 Wt. W2544/1454 700,000 5/15 D. D. & L. A.D.S.S./Forms/C. 2118.

Instructions regarding War Diaries and Intelligence Summaries are contained in F. S. Regs., Part II. and the Staff Manual respectively. Title pages will be prepared in manuscript.

(4)

Army Form C. 2118.

WAR DIARY
or
~~INTELLIGENCE SUMMARY.~~
(Erase heading not required.)

8th Bn Rifle Brigade

Place	Date 1916	Hour	Summary of Events and Information	Remarks and references to Appendices
	JULY			
St NICHOLAS	21st		In the trenches: companies in same positions as before: relief starts at 4.30 p.m.: relief completed 2.35 a.m.	HMC
Trenches E of	22nd		Fine. A quiet day.	HMC
ROCLINCOURT	23rd		Fine. A quiet day on battalion front. Work on trenches & communications continued. Enemy opens a heavy fire at 9.30 p.m. on J.1 sector of 43rd Infantry Brigade & attempts a raid, which is driven back. fire ceases about 10.30 p.m.	HMC
102 - 111 MAP REF. 51B. 1/40,000	24th		Fine. From 3.30 p.m. to 4.30 p.m. the artillery & trench-mortars of the 41st Infantry Brigade fire at selected points on brigade front: viz suspected gun emplacements etc: apparently a successful bombardment. No retaliation by enemy. 'A' Co in support, relieved 'C' Co in centre sector: relief completed 12.30 a.m.: 25th	HMC
From G.6.c.1½.4 to A.30.c.4.3	25th		Fine. Major-General D. CAMPBELL. C.B. Comdg 21st Division visits the sector. The enemy shell 'D' Co Hdqrs & get a direct hit on the Co Sgt Major's dug-out, which is knocked in: no one in it at the time.	HMC
	26th		Fine. A quiet day. Officers of the 15th Bn DURHAM LIGHT INFANTRY: 64th Brigade: come to reconnoitre the Battn sector	HMC
	27th		Fine. About 6 p.m. enemy sweeps left sector from south to north with trench mortars & also fires some 5.9" shells on 'F' work. 2nd Lt N.F.H. MATHER wounded & 4 O.R.: also 2 O.R. of 7th Bn RIFLE BRIGADE belonging to Lewis gun section in 'F' work. All officers & O.R. on courses of instruction	HMC
	~~28th~~		~~Fine~~. rejoin transport.	

2353 Wt. W2544/1454 700,000 5/15 D. D. & L. A.D.S.S./Forms/C. 2118.

Instructions regarding War Diaries and Intelligence Summaries are contained in F. S. Regs., Part II. and the Staff Manual respectively. Title pages will be prepared in manuscript.

WAR DIARY
or
~~INTELLIGENCE SUMMARY.~~
(Erase heading not required.)

(5) Army Form C. 2118.

8th Bn Rifle Brigade

Place	Date 1916	Hour	Summary of Events and Information	Remarks and references to Appendices
Trenches E of ROCLINCOURT 102 – 111.	JULY 28th		A quiet day. ~~Battalion rest~~ till about 6 p.m. when enemy again traversed up & down battalion sector with trench mortar & artillery: this ceased about 8.30 p.m.	HWR
		6.30 p.m.	A flight of 16 of our aeroplanes going east was fired on by the enemy: one was hit, caught fire & was steered down by the pilot to about 200 yards from battalion H^d Q^rs: the enemy fired two heavy shells at it at half hour intervals during the night. The machine was destroyed but the pilot, though scorched, was taken to the dressing station at ROCLINCOURT. The pilot was Lt E.S. HAWKINS. 12th Squadron, ROYAL FLYING CORPS	HWR
	29th		A quiet day. Battn relieved by 15th Bn DURHAM. Lt INFANTRY in afternoon: relief completed at 4.30 p.m. Platoons as they are relieved proceed to billets in AGNEZ les DUISANS.	
On the march	30th		The battalion starts at 10.30 a.m. & proceeds via HABARCQ & AVESNES-le-COMTE to billets at GRAND RULLECOURT. Strength on parade 23 officers & 804 O.R. March only about 10 miles but weather very hot & a lot of men fell out. 41st Bde HdQrs, 8th Bn K.R.R.C & Bde MACHINE GUN Co also in the village: 7th Bn K.R.R.C at SUS St LEGER: 7th Bn RIFLE BRIGADE at BEAUDICOURT.	HWR
	31st		The Battalion moves off at 8.30 a.m. & marches as the last battalion of the brigade to BARLY, arriving at 4.30 p.m. The Brigade marches via IVERGNY-LE SOUICH-BOUQUELMAISON-NEVELLETTE: halting for 2 hours from 12-2 p.m. The Bn halts in LE SOUICH & the companies have tea in the orchards of the village, in which the	

Instructions regarding War Diaries and Intelligence Summaries are contained in F. S. Regs., Part II. and the Staff Manual respectively. Title pages will be prepared in manuscript.

(6.)

Army Form C. 2118.

WAR DIARY
or
~~INTELLIGENCE SUMMARY.~~
(Erase heading not required.)

8th Bn Rifle Brigade

Place	Date 1916	Hour	Summary of Events and Information	Remarks and references to Appendices
	JULY			
On the march	31st		3rd Bn GRENADIER GUARDS are billetted. Weather very hot & the men's packs are carried by motor lorry as on the previous day. Lt A. N. COLES & 5 N.C.Os go on ahead, as usual, as a billetting party. Also billetted in BARLY are 8th Bn K.R.R.C.: 44th Field Ambulance: & No 2 Co A.S.C.: all part of the 41st Infantry Brigade.	
			Numbers present with the battalion 25 officers: 826 other ranks: out of a total strength 29 officers: 959 other ranks.	HRR
			Appendix 1. List of casualties during month	
			2. " " officers serving on 31.7.16.	
			31.7.16.	
			H.L. Rifs Lt Col	
			Comd 8th Bn Rifle Brigade	

2353 Wt. W2544/1454 700,000 5/15 D. D. & L. A.D.S.S./Forms/C. 2118.

8th. Battalion Rifle Brigade.

Casualties July 1916.

S 3335	A/Cpl.	Foxlee	F.	"C" Coy.	1/7/16	G.S.W.Elbow.
6/8638	Rfn.	Norton	F.	"C" Coy.	do.	Wounded accidentally.
Z 632	"	Dyde	A.	"A" Coy.	2/7/16	Shell wound
1315	"	Lacey	C.	"D" Coy.	do.	- (died of wounds)
S 13870	"	Thornley	T.	"D" Coy.	do.	- Back. (at duty)
S 8857	"	Bettis	A.	"C" Coy.	do.	- Hand.(rejoined 8/7/16)
S 9265	"	Ablett	J.	"C" Coy.	9/7/16	- Hand.
S 2414	"	Kendal	E.	"C" Coy.	6/7/16.	G.S.W. Arm.
S 2154	"	Quick	F.	"C" Coy.	11/7/16.	Killed inAction
S10796	"	Perry	J.	"C" Coy.	do.	do.
S11933	"	Mawdett	A.	"C" Coy.	do.	do.
S12792	"	Hardcastle	E.	"C" Coy.	do.	Shell - Leg.
S14077	Cpl.	Robinson	S.	"A" Coy.	13/7/16	G.S.W. Thigh
S15679	Rfn.	Terry	J.	"A" Coy.	do.	- Head.
S16985	"	Willis	E.	"A" Coy.	do.	Gas - Mine.
S14126	"	Molden	A.	"A" Coy.	do.	do.
S 5642	"	Haydock	J.	"A" Coy.	17/7/16.	Wounded (attd. T.M.B.)
S10916	"	Bracher	T.	"B" Coy.	20/7/16.	Shrapnel - Arm.
S10933	A/Cpl.	Hunt	W.	"C" Coy.	24/7/16.	- Hand.
Z 2283	Rfn.	Cook	H.	"C" Coy.	do.	T.M.Foot.
B 724	Serjt.	Driver	F.	"B" Coy.	26/7/16.	Killed in Action
S 8761	Rfn.	Hammond	H.	"A" Coy.	26/7/16.	T.M.Head
B 143	"	Connell	J.	"A" Coy.	do.	- Shoulder
S10925	"	Edge	G.	"A" Coy.	do.	- Neck.
S15044	"	Fowler	A.	"D" Coy.	27/7/16.	Killed in Action.
S12905	A/Cpl.	Sharples	F.	"D" Coy.	do.	T.M.
S 7678	Rfn.	Kilroy	J.	"D" Coy.	do.	T.M.
S 8438	"	Annison	A.	"D" Coy.	do.	T.M.
B 767	Serjt.	Hockley	L.	"B" Coy.	do.	Killed Accidentally at Grenade School.
S 8487	Rfn.	Norris	F.	"A" Coy.	do.	Wounded do. (died 30/7/16)
S14477	A/Cpl.	Cragg	F.	"A" Coy.	28/7/16.	Killed in Action
S 9225	Rfn.	Langley	H.	"A" Coy.	do.	do.
S 3516	A/Cpl.	Newton	F.	"A" Coy.	do.	Wounded.
	2/Lt.	N.F.H.Mather			27/7/16	Shell - Head and shock.

H.B. [illegible] Lt Col

Comdg 8th Bn Rifle Bde.

41st Brigade.
14th Division.

1/8th BATTALION

THE RIFLE BRIGADE.

AUGUST 1 9 1 6

C O N F I D E N T I A L.

W A R   D I A R Y

- of -

8th (S) Bn.,   THE   RIFLE   BRIGADE.

From: 1st August, 1916 - To: 31st August, 1916.

Volume XVI.

Vol 15

(1)

Army Form C. 2118.

WAR DIARY
or
~~INTELLIGENCE SUMMARY.~~

(Erase heading not required.)

Instructions regarding War Diaries and Intelligence Summaries are contained in F. S. Regs., Part II. and the Staff Manual respectively. Title pages will be prepared in manuscript.

August 1916. 8th Bn Rifle Brigade

Place	Date	Hour	Summary of Events and Information	Remarks and references to Appendices
On the march	1st		Battalion leaves BARLY at 8.30 a.m. & marches to LONGUEVILLETTE independently via OCCOCHES & MONPLAISIR arriving at 11.45 a.m. Weather very hot & the men wear their packs. Billeting party under Lt A.N. COLES. A very clean village & no other troops in it. Brigade Hd Qrs at BEZANCOURT. 2nd Lt V.R.G. BIDDULPH joins the battalion & is posted to 'A' Coy.	HRC
LONGUEVILLETTE	2nd		Weather very hot. Hd Qrs Company organised consisting of transport, scouts, signallers, 4 Lewis guns under the administrative command of Major A.L.C. CAVENDISH. Receive information that Battn will halt for several days. The C.O. addresses the officers & N.C.Os on the new conditions under which they will be required to fight: viz offensive action instead of defensive trench action.	HRC
	3rd		Weather very hot. Companies training.	HRC
	4th		Weather hot. Companies training.	HRC
	5th		Cooler. Companies training. Orders received for move of brigade by road & rail to CORBIE on the R. SOMME. Conference of C.Os at Bde Hd Qrs at 5 p.m.	HRC
	6th		Sunday. Church parade at 12.10 p.m. At 11.30 a.m. transport, the 8 Bn hand-carts, & nine Bn bicycles move off under 2nd Lt E. POOLE, & march to VIGNACOURT, via CANDAS, & VICOGNE: joining the transport of the Division, which all moves under command of Colonel RICHARDS: A.S.C. the O.C. Divl Train.	HRC
	7th		Hot. Transport moves on again & Battn transport marches to DERNANCOURT. The Battn parades at 3.30 p.m. &	

Instructions regarding War Diaries and Intelligence Summaries are contained in F. S. Regs., Part II. and the Staff Manual respectively. Title pages will be prepared in manuscript.

WAR DIARY
or
~~INTELLIGENCE SUMMARY.~~
(Erase heading not required.)

August 1916 (2) 8th Bn Rifle Brigade

Army Form C. 2118.

Place	Date	Hour	Summary of Events and Information	Remarks and references to Appendices
LONGUEVILLETTE	7th		marches to CANDAS to entrain. Train is late & does not leave till 11 p.m. Also on the train are Bde H.Qrs: 9th Bn RIFLE BRIGADE; 89th Field Coy, R.E.: 42nd Field Ambulance.	WBC
DERNANCOURT.	8th		Train arrives at MERICOURT at 4.15 a.m. & Bn detrains, marches to DERNANCOURT, arriving at 6.15 a.m. Bn goes into billets there. Men rather crowded & officers in tents.	WBC
	9th		H.Q. Bathing parades in R. ANCRE & inspections. The division now forms part of the XVth Corps & of the IVth Army.	WBC
			One officer per company goes to a demonstration of new flammen-werfer.	
	10th		Slight rain. The C.O.: Adjt: & 4 Company Commanders go to reconnoitre trenches occupied by 50th Brigade, which the 41st Brigade are going to relieve. 2nd Lt. K.M. FARMILOE is struck off the strength of the battalion on proceeding to England sick. H.M. King GEORGE accompanied by H.R.H. The Prince of Wales & General Sir D. HAIG pass through the village in the morning.	
			1 officer & 50 men start on ammunition fatigue	WBC
	11th		The Brigade is inspected at 11.30 a.m. by Lt Genl HORNE: Commanding XVth Corps: present on parade 23 officers: 663 other ranks. In afternoon 7th Bn RIFLE BRIGADE march to take over trenches from 58th Brigade. Transport officers of the brigade go to inspect transport camps.	WBC
	12th		Orders received for completion of relief of 51st Brigade, immediately to the north of DELVILLE WOOD. 2nd Lt. D.J. ASHFORTH joins 41st Bde Hd Qrs as Bde Intelligence Officer. Great coats & packs will	

WAR DIARY
or
INTELLIGENCE SUMMARY.
(Erase heading not required.)

Instructions regarding War Diaries and Intelligence Summaries are contained in F. S. Regs., Part II. and the Staff Manual respectively. Title pages will be prepared in manuscript.

(3)

Army Form C. 2118.

August 1916 — 8th/Bn Rifle Brigade

Place	Date	Hour	Summary of Events and Information	Remarks and references to Appendices
	12th		Caps inside them left in store: men march up in fighting order with water proof sheets.	HWC
	13th	4 a.m.	Battalion marches with 5 minutes intervals between companies to MONTAUBAN ALLEY, via FRICOURT & MAMETZ, about 1 mile EAST of MAMETZ & goes into support: the brigade occupying trenches in N E corner of DELVILLE WOOD & to the NORTH of the wood.	HWC
	14th		The 8th/Bn relieves 7th/Bn RIFLE BRIGADE in front line DORSET TRENCH & PEAR St (S.11.C.8.6 to S.11.C.0.8: sheet FRANCE 57.C: S.W.): 'A & C' companies in front line, 'B & D' companies in support & Hd Qrs in CARLTON TRENCH (S.16.b.5.3): the 8th/Bn K.R.R.C is on the right of the battalion: the SUFFOLK REGt in the 33rd Division on the left.	
			Task of the battalion is to improve the approaches to DORSET TRENCH so that an attack can be made on WOOD LANE & ORCHARD TRENCHES	HWC
	15th	10 a.m.	2nd Lt W. R. H. MERRIMAN killed while going out with a covering party from DORSET TRENCH.	
			Work of previous night continued: assisted by working parties of 7th/Bn RIFLE BRIGADE.	
			Enemy's fire on trenches behind the front trench is very continuous.	HWC
	16th		Work continued	HWC
	17th		In the evening the battalion is relieved by 7th/Bn RIFLE BRIGADE. 'B' Coy remain in CARLTON TRENCH & 'D' Coy in YORK TRENCH: rest of battalion move back to MONTAUBAN ALLEY.	HWC

2353 Wt. W2544/1454 700,000 5/15 D. D. & L. A.D.S.S./Forms/C. 2118.

Instructions regarding War Diaries and Intelligence Summaries are contained in F. S. Regs., Part II. and the Staff Manual respectively. Title pages will be prepared in manuscript.

WAR DIARY
or
INTELLIGENCE SUMMARY.
(Erase heading not required.)

Army Form C. 2118.

(4)

August 1916. 8th Bn Rifle Brigade

Place	Date	Hour	Summary of Events and Information	Remarks and references to Appendices
TRENCHES	18th		Relief completed at 2 a.m. Orders received for the attack by the 4th Army. The 7th Bn RIFLE BRIGADE to attack ORCHARD TRENCH & WOOD LANE from S.11.c.8½.8½ to S.11.d.3.2 (Ref 1/10,000 Trench Maps 12a, 12b & 13). The 33rd Division to attack on left	
		3 p.m.	Attack takes place: 7th Bn R. Bde reaches objective but division on left fail to do so, thus leaving left flank exposed. 'B' Coy (Capt. E.F. PRIOR) is ordered to support left flank of 7th Bn.	
		8 p.m.	Hd Qrs & 2 companies ordered up to immediate support in CARLTON TRENCH & YORK ALLEY. The position is consolidated during night.	[initials]
	19th	2.15 p.m.	C.O & 2 Coy Commanders ordered to proceed to DELVILLE WOOD & take over trenches from the 43rd Bde. 'A & C' companies in front line 'B' Coy in support about 100 yards in rear, 'D' Coy in ANGLE TRENCH to south of wood. Hd Qrs in old dug-out in S.18.b.6.2: at Hd Qrs only the C.O & adjutant: no room for more.	[initials]
	20th		Relief completed at 5 a.m. Enemy's fire in wood is very heavy, especially near the edge of the wood: it mostly goes over the trenches in the wood: a number of dead & some wounded still in trenches. During night dead buried & trenches improved. 8th Bn K.R.R.C. on left of battalion, 9th Bn RIFLE BRIGADE on right.	[initials]
	21st		Heavy fire on Battn Hd Qrs. R.S.M. STAINES killed & others buried. Hd Qrs moved to ANGLE TRENCH (S.18.c.6.6). Took over HOP ALLEY & trenches to south from 9th Bn R.B.: our trenches taken over by 9th Bn K.R.R.C. Hd Qrs	

Instructions regarding War Diaries and Intelligence Summaries are contained in F. S. Regs., Part II. and the Staff Manual respectively. Title pages will be prepared in manuscript.

WAR DIARY
or
INTELLIGENCE SUMMARY.
(Erase heading not required.)

Army Form C. 2118.

(5)

August 1916. 8th Bn Rifle Brigade

Place	Date	Hour	Summary of Events and Information	Remarks and references to Appendices
TRENCHES	21st		Still in ANGLE TRENCH. 'D' Coy in HOP ALLEY: 'B' Coy on right, 'A' in support, 'C' in ANGLE TRENCH. 2nd Lt G.R. SAYER wounded.	[illegible]
	22nd		Relief completed about 6.30 a.m. At night improvement of communications & a new line started by working party of 7th Bn RB to join up with 61st Brigade on our right	[illegible]
	23rd		'D' Coy relieved by a company of 7th Bn K.R.R.C. & proceeds to YORK ALLEY. Heavy shelling of battalion area during the day & of working parties during night. 2nd Lt A.N. COLES killed	[illegible]
	24th		'D' Coy moved up to front line to make strong points on left flank of 61st Bde. Operation counter-ordered about 1 p.m. Capt G.E.H. KEESEY killed: 2nd Lt H.R. ADAIR wounded; Lt C.N. THOMPSON & 2nd Lt D.H. SYKES	[illegible]
	25th		Battalion relieved by 7th Bn RIFLE BRIGADE & returns to POMMIER REDOUBT. Relief completed (shell shock) about 6 a.m. Major A.L.C. CAVENDISH to hospital.	[illegible]
	26th		Battalion moves off at 8.10 p.m. & marches back to DERNANCOURT. Strength 16 officers. 615 O.R.	[illegible]
DERNANCOURT	27th		Battalion resting. 2nd Lt H. TRYON rejoins the battalion & is posted to 'C' Coy.	[illegible]
	28th		Usual inspections	[illegible]
	29th		Battalion at rest.	W.R.S.
	30th		Lt Col. A.D. Ross to hospital. Capt W.R. STEWART assumes temporary command of battalion. Battalion moves by train to AIRAINES, thence by march route to LALEU.	W.R.S.
LALEU	31st		Battalion at rest. Billets good.	W.R.S.

W.R. Stewart Capt.
Comdg. 8th Batt. R. Bde.

2353 Wt. W2544/1454 700,000 5/15 D. D. & L. A.D.S.S./Forms/C. 2118.

8th. BATTALION THE RIFLE BRIGADE.

ROLL OF OFFICERS.

Capt. W.R. Stewart	Commanding Officer.
Major A.L.C. Cavendish	Hospital.
Major A.C. Sheepshanks D.S.O.	Second in Command.
Capt. E.F. Prior	Commanding "B" Coy.
Capt. M.E. Yorke Eliot	Attd. 55th. Division.
Capt. K.S.M. Gladstone	Attd. 42nd. Brigade.
Capt. A.R. Backus	Commanding "A" Coy.
Capt. W.C.F.V. Barker-Mill	Commanding "D" Coy.
Lieut. H. Tryon	Commanding "C" Coy.
Lieut. C.H. Wenham	Bombing Officer.
Lieut. W.A. Crebbin	A/Adjutant. (Signalling Officer)
2/Lt. J.R. Abbey	Lewis Gun Officer.
" D.F. Foxwell	
" V.R.G. Biddulph.	
" A.D. Macnaghten.	
" E.P. Matthews	
" R.H.F. Devereux.	
" E. Poole	Transport Officer.
" E.L. Vickers	
" D.S. Ashforth	41st. Brigade Intelligence Officer.
Lieut. & Adjt. C.R. Gorell Barnes D.S.O.	Hospital.
Lieut. & Quartermaster F.H. Pryor	
Lieut. F.J. Strachan R.A.M.C. (Attd.)	

8th.Batt. Rifle Brigade.

Casualties August 1916.

2/Lieut. W.R.H. Merriman	Died of wounds	15.8.16.
2/Lieut. G.R. Sayer	Wounded	21.8.16.
Lieut. A.N. Coles	Killed in Action	23.8.16.
Capt. G.E.H. Keesey	Killed in Action	24.8.16.
Lieut. C.N. Thompson	Shell Shock	24.8.16.
2/Lieut. H.R. Adair	Wounded	24.8.16.
2/Lieut. D.H. Beves	Shell Shock	24.8.16.

S7205	Cpl.	Aspden C.	Wounded	14.8.16.	Rejoined 27.8.16.
B3308	Rfn.	Wood N.	"	"	
S14480	"	Pitfield A.	"	"	
6820	"	Hudspith J.	"	"	
S9584	"	Bragg C.	"	"	
S8293	A/C.	Clompass J.	"	"	
B2449	Sgt.	Sheppard A.	Shell Shock	"	
4558	Cpl.	Foreman C.	" "	"	
S11451	Rfn.	Ridley E.	Killed	"	
S1067	"	Savage J.	Wounded	15.8.16.	
Z1937	"	Hall J.	"	"	
S8835	"	White H.	"	16.8.16.	
S10484	Sgt.	Higginbottom J.	Shell Shock	16.8.16.	Rejoined 18.8.16.
S15617	Rfn.	Aust R	Wounded	16.8.16.	
S13704	"	Towersey T.	"	"	
S5974	Sgt.	Badham C.	Killed	"	
S12913	Rfn.	Hughes J.	"	"	
S10175	"	Mahon T.	Wounded	"	
Z 966	"	Bruce E.	Shell Shock	"	
S10596	"	Smith R.	" "	"	
B 176	Sgt.	Cowan C.	Wounded	18.8.16.	
S10991	Rfn.	Clough D.	"	17.8.16.	
S5065	"	Croft T.	"	"	
B1294	"	Jackson N.	"	"	
S4448	"	Head W.	"	"	
S7346	"	Campbell A.	"	"	
B2788	"	Gumbley W.	"	"	
5372	"	Marsh W.	"	"	
S8125	"	Cripps G.	"	"	
1051	Sgt.	Watson M.	"	"	
S2785	Rfn.	Lead L.	"	"	Died of wounds 18.8.16.
2662	Cpl.	Gore E.	Killed	"	
~~Z497~~	~~A/C.~~	~~Murphy T.~~			
Z497	A/C.	Martin R.	"	"	
S8369	Rfn.	Pearce R.	"	"	
S13738	"	Barker H.	"	"	
S10552	"	West C.	Wounded	18.8.16.	
S5277	"	Chambers H.	"	17.8.16.	
S4059	Sgt.	Hume F.	Shell Shock	14.8.16.	
4637	A/C.	Hoath A.	Wounded	18.8.16.	
S7712	Rfn.	Holmes H.	"	19.8.16.	
S8892	"	Medcroft W.	"	18.8.16.	(Attached 41/1 T.M.B.)
S7215	"	Cavanagh M.	"	18.8.16.	
B2051	"	Thomas W.	"	19.8.16.	
B 190	"	Brown T.	"	20.8.16.	
S8170	"	Ridley G.	"	"	
S9581	"	Whawell W.	"	"	
B 800	Sgt.	Slade A.	Shell Shock	"	
S11602	Rfn.	Adams G.	Wounded	"	
S9818	"	Hunt W.	"	"	
S13109	"	Janes W.	Killed	"	
S10614	"	Buswell S.	Wounded	18.8.16.	
S1809	R.S.M.	Staines J.M.	Killed	21.8.16.	
S8317	Rfn.	Hayes D.	Killed	" x	
B1507	"	Bliss J.	Wounded		
S6837	A/C.	Bateman	"	18.8.16.	

No.2.

S3057	Sgt.	Buck J.	Wounded	21.8.16.	
8551	"	Leppard J.	"	19.8.16.	
B2297	A/C.	Green G.	"	"	
S13668	Rfn.	Chapman G.	"	"	
S5998	"	Brennan J.	"	18.8.16.	
S13559	"	Town J.	"	20.8.16.	
Z 961	"	Elliott R.	"	"	
S 688	"	Bennett J.	S Shock	"	Rejoined 21.8.16.
S2849	"	Farrell S.	"	"	Rejoined 25.8.16.
Z 822	R"	Hughes F.	Wounded	21.8.16.	Rejoined 25.8.16.
S13406	"	Collepy J.	S Shock	"	Rejoined 26.8.26.
S7445	A/C.	Jarvis J.	Wounded	"	Rejoined 23.8.16.
S11552	Rfn.	Parsons J.	Killed	19.8.16.	
S6193	"	Newton J.	Wounded	"	
S14116	"	Volke F.	"	"	
S3186	A/C.	Onn F.	"	"	
S 186	Rfn.	Twigg R.	"	"	
Z1087	"	Ladd T.	"	"	
6/377	"	Wa rd W.	"	22.8.16.	
S15664	"	Shott G.	"	"	
5928	"	Ellis A,	"	20.8.16.	
Z 752	"	Hemstock C.	"	18.8.16.	
B1800	"	Claridge J.	"	17.8.16.	
S12799	"	Hill W.	S Shock	22.8.16.	
S12781	"	Howes A.	"	"	Rejoined 26.8.16.
S5215	"	Lovatt J.	"	"	
B1498	"	Kenny C.	"	"	Rejoined 24.8.16.
S10925	"	Edge G.	"	"	Rejoined 25.8.16.
S9268	"	Bayliss F.	"	"	
S6154	S	Stears H.	"	"	Rejoined 25.8.16.
B3037	A/C.	Grinstead C.	Wounded	"	
S8820	Rfn.	Bell A.	"	"	
S9867	"	Stocks A.	Killed	"	
Z 219	Cpl.	Carnell F.	Wounded	"	
B 128	A/C.	Danton G.	"	"	
Z1098	Rfn.	RobinsonT.	S. Shock	"	Rejoined 24.8.16.
S1306	"	Atkins F.	Wounded	23.8.16.	
S7382	A/C.	Hammond H.	"	22.8.16.	Rejoined 25.8.16.
S6046	Rfn.	Mills A.	"	"	
Z2012	"	Moss P.	"	23.8.16.	
S10453	"	Wickens W.	"	"	Rejoined 26.8.16.
S9693	"	Rooney J.	Killed	18.8.16.	
B1816	Sgt.	Bond P.	Wounded	24.8.16.	
S5472	A/C.	Murphy T.	"	"	
S10953	"	Hunt J.	"	"	Died of wounds 26.8.16.
S8697	Rfn.	Chandler H.	Killed	"	
S9938	"	Raven W.	Wounded	""	
6/424	"	Pain R.	S. Shock	"	
S15673	"	Worboys C.	Wounded	"	
Z1530	"	Saw F.	"	"	
5/265	"	Mayhew P.	Killed	"	
S15460	"	Stead J.	Wounded	"	Died of wounds 25.8.16.
2827	Sgt.	Mortimore H.	Killed	"	
B1373	Rfn.	Simpson W.	Killed	"	
S 36	A/C.	Warreh G.	Wounded	"	
S7581	"	Backinsell F.	Wounded	"	
S3100	Rfn.	Carden R.	"	"	
S14228	"	Wiltshire H.	"	"	Died of wounds 25.8.16.
5156	A/C.	Bright A.	"	"	
S14471	Rfn.	Dickinson J.	"	"	
B 720	"	Fitzgerald G.	"	"	
S8993	"	Gray S.	"	"	
S14782	"	Hassell E.	"	"	
S14107	"	Carter L.	"	"	Died of wounds 24.8.16.
S9888	"	Jelly R.	"	"	
S9427	"	Round A.	"	"	
S15467	"	Shambrook J.	"	"	
S9871	"	Williams F.	"	"	
2780	"	Wright G.	"	"	
S14476	"	Holland C.	Killed	"	

No. 3.

B 332	Rfn.	Connelly R.	Killed	24.8.16.	
S9189	"	Smith P.	"	"	
S13394	"	Carter A.	"	"	
B3280	"	Gardner E.	"	"	
Z1772	"	Webb F.	"	"	
S5866	"	Nicholls G.	Wounded	"	
580	C.S.M.	Hayward W.	"	"	
B1477	Rfn.	Salt H.	"	"	
S13532	"	Hudson J.	"	"	
S8442	"	Payne G.	Killed	"	
S11903	"	Jenkinson G.	"	22.8.16.	
Z 38	"	Brookfield R.	"	23.8.16.	
B 850	"	Neale E.	Wounded	"	
B2540	"	Bond F.	"	19.8.16.	(Att. Bde.M.G.Coy.)
4736	"	Sweet W.	"	23.8.16.	(Att. 41/1 T.M.B.)
5767	"	Tucker A.	"	24.8.16.	(Att. 41/1 T.M.B.)

4/14

C O N F I D E N T I A L.

W A R D I A R Y

-of-

8th Bn., T H E R I F L E B R I G A D E.

From: 1st September, 1916.
To: 30th September, 1916.

Volume XVII.

Vol 16

Instructions regarding War Diaries and Intelligence Summaries are contained in F. S. Regs., Part II. and the Staff Manual respectively. Title pages will be prepared in manuscript.

WAR DIARY
or
INTELLIGENCE SUMMARY.
(Erase heading not required.)

Army Form C. 2118.

Vol. XVII

Place	Date	Hour	Summary of Events and Information	Remarks and references to Appendices
LALEU				
[redacted].	1.9.16	–	Bn resting, party of 32 granted 48 hours leave for AULT.	RdeL
–	2 –	–	Bn training, free afternoon –	RdeL
–	3 –		do.	RdeL
–	4 –		do	RdeL
–	5 –		do. draft of 50 men arrived, inspected by Brigadier General	RdeL
–	6 –		do draft inspected by Medical officer –	RdeL
–	7 –		C.O proceeded on 48 hrs leave to England — draft 100 arrived & inspected.	RdeL
–	8 –		Party of 17 proceeded to AULT on 48 hrs leave –	RdeL
–	9 –		Major X R A de La Chapelle, & 2/Lt Gould, Groom & Ward joined the Bn	RdeL.
–	–		Warning order received re move to DORNANCOURT. transport proceeds	
–	–		to AILLY SUR SOMME – Party of 17 returned from leave	
–	10		Bn embus at 3 pm 43 Lorries available for Bn arrive DORNANCOURT	RdeL
–	–		at 6.30 and occupy billets – Receive warning order to proceed to FRICOURT	
–	–		camp. F13.B	
DORNANC-OURT	11		Major Sheepshanks & Coy officers report to Brig General & reconnoitre	RdeL
			position T.13 A. PILSNER LANE E of DELVILLE Wood. Bn moves at 2.30 pm	
			to FRICOURT camp. C O Lt Col Stewart returns from leave – Major X R A de	
			La Chapelle takes over duties of 2d in Command –	

2353 Wt. W2544/1454 700,000 5/15 D. D. & L. A.D.S.S./Forms/C. 2118.

Instructions regarding War Diaries and Intelligence Summaries are contained in F. S. Regs., Part II. and the Staff Manual respectively. Title pages will be prepared in manuscript.

WAR DIARY
or
INTELLIGENCE SUMMARY.
(Erase heading not required.)

Army Form C. 2118.

Place	Date	Hour	Summary of Events and Information	Remarks and references to Appendices
	Sept 16			
FRICOURT Camp.	12.	2.30pm	Bn march off to take over line E of DELVILLE WOOD from 2/5 Lancs Fusiliers. Transport remains at FRICOURT with details. Total at	Adel
		5pm	Transport Camp. 6 officers. 229 O.R. Bn halts for tea at 5 pm between POMMIERES REDOUBT & MONTAUBAN. Bn moves off	
		8.30pm	at 8.30 pm met by guides at the quarry S 22 D 9.4. relief	
DELVILLE WOOD.	13	1.30 AM	completed at 1.30 am. Intermittent shelling of front line trenches of PILSNER LANE by 5.9. Six killed and 16 wounded O.R. Captain A R Baden wounded in face not serious – usual patrols sent out, report HOR ALLEY TRENCH demolished – Coys A & C occupy 3 posts average 80 yds in front of PILSNER LANE. T 13 A.	Adel
	14.	8.30pm	2 Coys K.O.Y.L.I relieve Bn in Sector from T 13 A. central to junction of JAMES street with EDGE STREET.	Adel
	"	11pm	Relief completed at 11 pm. B & D Coys occupy trench dug by pioneers in front of BROWN TRENCH. D on right B on left. C Coy in Brown trench supporting B. A Coy in JAMES STREET supporting D.	Adel
	15.	1.30am	Battn H.Q. moved to BROWN TRENCH. A Coy suffer some casualties	

Instructions regarding War Diaries and Intelligence Summaries are contained in F. S. Regs., Part II. and the Staff Manual respectively. Title pages will be prepared in manuscript.

WAR DIARY
or
INTELLIGENCE SUMMARY.
(Erase heading not required.)

Army Form C. 2118.

Place	Date	Hour	Summary of Events and Information	Remarks and references to Appendices
DELVILLE WOOD	15 (cont)		from our own gas shells. Fairly quiet night. Intense Bombardment at zero 6.20 A.M. Battn moves forward under barrage. V. few casualties for 150 yards. Heavy losses in next 200 yards. Many Germans in PINT TRENCH. PINT TRENCH captured. Battn reaches its objective SWITCH TRENCH with no officers. Dug-outs bombed. Some prisoners taken. 2 M. G's captured 1 blown up – C.O. Lt Col STEWART and Adjutant Lt W.A. CREBBIN move up to SWITCH TRENCH. Consolidation started. Connection established with 8th KRR on left and Guards on right. Remainder of Brigade and whole of 42nd Brigade pass over SWITCH TRENCH and take their objectives further forward. 10.30 AM C.O. wounded by Shrapnel. 1. P.M. MAJOR SHEEPSHANKS Lt WENHAM 2/Lt ABBEY reach SWITCH TRENCH. C.O. leaves. MAJOR SHEEPSHANKS takes over temporary command. 2.30 PM. 2/Lt BALDOCK arrives. Consolidation and resorting of units. 8.30 PM MAJOR X R.A. DE LA CHAPELLE arrives and takes over command. Strength of Battalion in Trench 6 officers and M.O. and 160 O.R. A great shortage of Stretchers and Bearers.	

2353 Wt. W2544/1454 700,000 5/15 D. D. & L. A.D.S.S./Forms/C. 2118.

Instructions regarding War Diaries and Intelligence Summaries are contained in F. S. Regs., Part II. and the Staff Manual respectively. Title Pages will be prepared in manuscript.

WAR DIARY
or
INTELLIGENCE SUMMARY
(Erase heading not required.)

Army Form C. 2118

Place	Date	Hour	Summary of Events and Information	Remarks and references to Appendices
SWITCH TRENCH	16th		43rd Brigade in front of SWITCH TRENCH make an attack on GEUDUECOURT at 9. A.M. Enemy put barrage on SWITCH TRENCH. Heavy shelling at intervals during the day. Relieved at 7 P.M. by 5th Oxford and Bucks. Battalion march back to advanced Transport Camp near FRICOURT. Bivouac in the open.	aes
FRICOURT	17th		Battalion move back in morning to permanent Transport Camp near MEAULTE. Move again in afternoon to old billets in DERNANCOURT	aes
DERNANCOURT	18th		Battalion resting - Very wet day.	aes
"	19th		Companies under O.C. Coys for inspections and drill.	aes
"	20th		Brigadier inspects the Brigade and presents medals won for gallantry on 18th August. He congratulates ~~and thanks~~ the Brigade and thanks them for what they have done.	aes
	21st		Transport leaves at Midday and billets at TALMAS. Major XRA de la CHAPELLE evacuated sick. Major A.C. SHEEPSHANKS takes over temporary command of Battalion	aes

1875 Wt. W593/826 1,000,000 4/15 J.B.C. & A. A.D.S.S./Forms/C. 2118.

Army Form C. 2118

Instructions regarding War Diaries and Intelligence Summaries are contained in F. S. Regs., Part II. and the Staff Manual respectively. Title Pages will be prepared in manuscript.

WAR DIARY
or
INTELLIGENCE SUMMARY
(Erase heading not required.)

Place	Date	Hour	Summary of Events and Information	Remarks and references to Appendices
DERNANCOURT	22nd		Battalion leave DERNANCOURT 6 30 AM. and after a long delay embus on ALBERT – AMIENS road at midday – Proceed via AMIENS and DOULLENS to LUCHEOX – arrive 5 P.M. Transport already there. All 4 Battalions and Brigade H.Q. in billets in the village.	aes
LUCHEOX	23rd		Battalion passes at midnight 22/23 from 4th Army to 3rd Army and from 15th Corps to 6th Corps. Specialists team under Lt WENHAM and 2/Lt ABBEY. Lt Col. R.C. MACLACHLAN D.S.O. returns to Battalion and takes over command.	
–	24th		Battalion at rest	
–	25th		Battalion still at rest	
–	26th		Battalion moves to WANQUETIN – Transport by route, battalion by lorries, arriving at 4.10pm Battalion in large huts. R.S.M. Fry & 11 other ranks join.	

1875 Wt. W593/826 1,000,000 4/15 J.B.C. & A. A.D.S.S./Forms/C. 2118.

Instructions regarding War Diaries and Intelligence Summaries are contained in F. S. Regs., Part II. and the Staff Manual respectively. Title Pages will be prepared in manuscript.

WAR DIARY
or
INTELLIGENCE SUMMARY
(Erase heading not required.)

Army Form C. 2118

Place	Date	Hour	Summary of Events and Information	Remarks and references to Appendices
WANQUETIN	27th		Battalion moves into support of Brigade at RIVIERE. Other three battalions in Front Line. Battalion mostly billeted in houses, although only 1200 yards from enemy. Transport Lines at BEAUMETZ.	
RIVIERE	28		In support. Quiet line. Battery of 6" guns behind us fire a couple of salvoes after dark before leaving the area. CAPT K.S.M. GLADSTONE rejoins from 42nd Bde Staff & takes over command of 'A' Cy	
–	29		Quiet day. O.C. Cys reconnoitre front line.	
–	30		A ruling received from W.O. that the term "Acting" used in the Rifle Bde since its formation is to be discontinued. A raid on sap heads on our right made by Sherwood Foresters.	

Strength.

	Officers	O.R.
With battalion	11	447
Command	1	88
Courses	–	19
Hospital	1	10
Leave		4
	13	568

R.M. Maclachlan Lt Col
Comdg 8th Bn Rifle Bde

1875 Wt. W593/826 1,000,000 4/15 J.B.C. & A. A.D.S.S./Forms/C. 2118.

Army Form C. 2118

Instructions regarding War Diaries and Intelligence Summaries are contained in F. S. Regs., Part II. and the Staff Manual respectively. Title Pages will be prepared in manuscript.

WAR DIARY
or
INTELLIGENCE SUMMARY
(Erase heading not required.)

Place	Date	Hour	Summary of Events and Information	Remarks and references to Appendices
GRAND RULLECOURT	30		Still wet. Training continues as far as weather permits	
			2/Lt A A Hooker & 2/Lt D E H Skuse struck off establishment of battalion.	WO 1221773 (M.S.4)
	31.		Still wet - very heavy storms. The allotment of leave during the month has been very limited, averaging a little more than 2 a week.	
			Total Strength 17 Officers, 838 O.R. - actually available 12 Officers 750 O.R.	
			Casualties for month as per attached list	
			Roll of officers attached.	

R Maclachlan
Lt Col
Comdg 8th Bn Rifle Bde

For information of the A.G.'s Office at the Base.

Officers and men who have become casuals, been transferred or joined since last report.

Place In the Field. Date

Regtl. Number	Rank	Name		Corps	Nature of casualty, or name of unit from or to which transferred	Date of being struck off or coming on the ration return	Remarks*
B 2045	Rfn.	Stainton	W.	8th.Bn. Rifle Brigade.	~~Missing.~~ Wounded	1[illegible].9.16.	"D" Coy.
S 1079	"	Thornley	J.	"	Missing	"	"C"
S17961	"	Turley	C.	"	"	"	
S13323	"	Wadhams	J.	"	"	"	
S18043	"	Walters	C.	"	"	"	
~~S20540~~	~~"~~	~~Read~~	~~A.~~	~~"~~	~~"~~	~~"~~	
835	Cpl.	Stanley	T.	"	Wounded	"	
S 7963	A/Cpl.	Rushmore	R.	"	"	"	"D" Coy.
S 304	"	Sopp	G.	"	"	"	
S18636	"	Savidge	P.	"	"	"	
S 8603	Rfn.	Adams	C.	"	Missing	"	
S 620	"	Bell	R.	"	"	"	
Z 1869	"	Barnes	J.	"	Wounded	"	
S13492	"	Cooke	S.	"	Wounded	"	
S 1142	"	Cresshull	F.	"	Missing	"	
B 2170	"	Edwards	R.	"	"	"	
S17803	"	Elliott	C.	"	"	"	
6022	"	Edwards	W.	"	"	"	
~~S17803~~ S17953	"	Eagleton	F.	"	"	"	
Z 1395	"	Crain	A.	"	"	"	
6/9859	"	Hayes	H.	"	Wounded	"	
S17980	"	Hoborough	H.	"	Missing	"	
S 9607	"	James	J.	"	Wounded	"	
B 2136	"	Luce	L.	"	Died of Wounds	" [illegible].9.16	
S14317	"	Masters	A.	"	Missing	"	
S17491	"	Mason	H.	"	"	"	
S17478	"	Oatley	J.	"	"	"	
S17462	"	Phillips	J.	"	"	"	
S 8892	"	Medcroft	W.	"	Wounded	"	
S10589	"	Mundy	W.	"	Missing	"	
S 6716	"	Richings	A.	"	Wounded	"	
S17442	"	Ramsey	S.	"	" believed killed	"	
S17413	"	Rowe	J.	"	Missing	"	
Z 1663	"	Skinner	G.	"	Wounded	"	
S17423	"	Swanwick	L.	"	Missing	"	
S 586	"	Smith	H.	"	"	"	
S17444	"	Scott	J.	"	"	"	
S14463	"	Skelton	H.	"	"	"	
S14170	"	Timberlake	H.	"	"	"	
S15220	"	Tindell	J.	"	"	"	
S 1931	"	Wordsworth	W.	"	"	"	
S11169	"	Watson	A.	"	"	"	
S 8671	"	Wood	R.	"	"	"	
Z 984	"	Coleman	E.	"	Missing bel. Killed	"	"C" Coy.
S17474	A/C.	Hammond	W.	"	"	"	"D" Coy.
S 24114	Rfn	Kendall	E.	"	Missing	"	"C"

*State whether absence is of a permanent or temporary nature, adding, in the case of casuals from wounds or disease, any available information for communication to the relatives.

Army Form B. 213.

FIELD RETURN.

No. of Report ____________

(To be furnished by all arms, services, and departments to the A. G.'s Office at the Base in accordance with Field Service Regulations, Part II.)

____________________ Date.

RETURN showing numbers RATIONED by, and Transport on charge of, ____________________ at ____________________

Detail	Personnel			Animals.								Guns, carriages, and limbers and transport vehicles											Motor Bicycles	Bicycles	Remarks
				Horses				Mules								Horsed		Mechanical							
	Officers	Other ranks	Natives	Riding	Draught	Heavy Draught	Pack	Large	Small	Camels	Oxen	Guns, carriages and limbers, showing, description	Ammunition wagons and limbers	Machine guns	Aircraft, showing description	4 Wheeled	2 Wheeled	Motor Cars	Tractors	Lorries, showing description	Trucks, showing description	Trailers			
Effective Strength of Unit Details, *by Arms* attached to unit as in War Establishment:—																									
Total																									
War Establishment																									
Wanting to complete																									
Surplus																									
*Attached (not to include the details shown above)																									
Civilians:— Employed with the Unit Accompanying the Unit																									
Total Rationed ...																									

* In the case of field ambulances, hospitals or depôts, the number of patients are to be included here, the names being shown in A.F.A. 36.

____________________ Signature of Commander.

____________________ Date of Despatch.

(K 11859) W. & Co., Ltd. Wt. w6095—894 500,000 10/14 Forms B. 213 / 5

For information of the A.G.'s Office at the Base.

Officers and men who have become casuals, been transferred or joined since last report.

Place ______________________ Date ______________________

Regtl. Number	Rank	Name		Corps	Nature of casualty, or name of unit from or to which transferred	Date of being struck off or coming on the ration return	Remarks*
S13406	Rfn.	Collepy	J.	8th. R.B.	W in A	15.9.16	'C' Coy. Died 17-9-16
S 5745	'	Crompton	J.	'	'	'	
S 5277	'	Chambers	H.	'	'	'	
B 3034	'	Didcock	R.	'	'	'	
Z 3109	'	Dixon	E.	'	'	'	
S13365	'	Dixon	H.	'	'	'	
5928	'	Ellis	A.	'	'	'	
S11949	'	Goodman	H.	'	'	'	
S 8191	'	Greenwood	J.J.	'	'	'	
S 8541	'	Greenwood	J.	'	'	'	
S17809	'	Groves	J.	'	'	'	
S 8387	'	Hambledon	T.	'	'	'	
S13786	'	Haycock	H.	'	'	'	
S 8540	'	Hurling	J.	'	'	'	
B 3346	'	Jeffreys	A.	'	'	'	
S 9695	'	Jukes	W.	'	'	'	
S 1156	'	Kebby	W.	'	'	'	
S 9260	'	Levy	D.	'	'	'	
S 8005	'	Lewis	G.	'	'	'	
S 9083	'	Lyons	W.	'	'	'	
S 7726	'	Mann	E.	'	'	'	
S 7129	'	Margerison	R.	'	'	'	
S10850	'	Middlemiss	W.	'	'	'	
S18040	'	Mason	H.	'	'	'	
G/424	'	Pain	R.	'	'	'	
S 6279	'	Palmer	J.	'	'	'	
S10259	'	Peasley	F.	'	'	'	
B 1958	'	Pursley	V.	'	'	'	
S 9283	'	Redman	A.	'	'	'	
S18009	'	Smart	R.	'	'	'	
9723	'	Sibthorpe	A.	'	'	'	
S 7103	'	Swarbrick	J.	'	'	'	
S18038	'	Simpson	A.	'	'	'	
S17942	'	Scott	A.	'	'	'	
S10200	'	Taylor	N.	'	'	'	
S 6542	'	Veevers	H.	'	'	'	
S 6196	'	Williams	G.	'	'	'	
S10613	'	Willis	F.	'	'	'	
S10640	'	Read	A.	'	'	'	
S 6279	'	Palmer	J.	'	Rejoined	18.9.16	
S17366	a/Cpl.	Kerswell	G.	'	Missing	15.9.16	'A' Coy
S16517	'	Stevens	J.	'	'	'	
S11109	Rfn.	Boden	J.	'	'	'	
S14467	'	Baker	P.	'	' believed Killed	'	
B 565	'	Boughton	G.	'	'	'	
S18006	'	Berryman	A.	'	'	'	
S18553	'	Chipp	G.	'	'	'	
S17947	'	Clarke	J.	'	'	'	
S 5205	'	Dyer	G.A.	'	'	'	
S18003	'	Dale	B.	'	'	'	
S1[illegible]	'	Ellis	W.	'	'	'	

* State whether absence is of a permanent or temporary nature, adding, in the case of casuals from wounds or disease, any available information for communication to the relatives.

To be made up to and for Sunday in each week.

No. of Report__________

FIELD RETURN.

Army Form B. 213.

(To be furnished by all arms, services, and departments (except A.S.C. units) to the A. G.'s Office at the Base in accordance with Field Service Regulations, Part II.)

RETURN showing numbers (*a*) Effective strength of Unit. (*b*) Rationed by Unit. ____________________ at ____________________ ____________ Date.

Detail	Personnel			Animals.								Guns, carriages, and limbers and transport vehicles											Motor Bicycles	Bicycles	Remarks
				Horses				Mules								Horsed		Mechanical							
	Officers	Other ranks	Natives	Riding	Draught	Heavy Draught	Pack	Large	Small	Camels	Oxen	Guns, carriages and limbers, showing description	Ammunition wagons and limbers	Machine guns	Aircraft, showing description	4 wheeled	2 wheeled	Motor Cars.	Tractors	Lorries, showing description	Trucks, showing description	Trailers			
Effective Strength of Unit																									
Details, *by Arms* attached to unit as in War Establishment:—																									
Total																									
War Establishment																									
Wanting to complete (Detail of Personnel and Horses below)																									
Surplus																									
*Attached (not to include the details shown above)																									
Civilians:— Employed with the Unit																									
Accompanying the Unit																									
Total Rationed...																									

* In the case of field ambulances, hospitals or depots, the number of patients are to be included here, the names being shown in A. F. A. 36.

____________________ Signature of Commander.

____________________ Date of Despatch.

For information of the A.G.'s Office at the Base.

Officers and men who have become casuals, been transferred or joined since last report.

Place __________ Date __________

Regtl. Number	Rank	Name		Corps	Nature of casualty, or name of unit from or to which transferred	Date of being struck off or coming on the ration return	Remarks*
S18075	Rfn.	Eversheed	A.	8th. R.B.	~~Missing~~ W.	15.9.16	'A' Coy Rejoined [illegible]/16
S16491	"	Fritz	A.	"	Missing	"	Rejoined 26-9-16
S11336	"	George	P.	"	Wounded	"	
S17986	"	Grovery	W.	"	M. believed killed	"	
S13739	"	Hawkins	H.	"	died of wounds	17/9/16	
S17975	"	Higham	W.	"	Missing	"	
S18590	"	Heard	A.	"	"	"	
S15687	"	Jones	T.	"	" believed Killed	"	
S18568	"	Kersch	H.	"	"	"	
B 66	"	Knight	C.	"	"	"	
S10256	"	Lee	T.	"	"	"	
S 2354	"	Muddell	C.	"	"	"	
B 3186	"	McKen	A.	"	"	"	
S 5212	"	Monk	E.	"	"	"	
S 7927	"	Palmer	F.	"	"	"	
S11454	"	Ray	J.	"	"	"	
S14754	"	Simpson	F.	"	"	"	
3359	"	Taplin	W.	"	"	"	
S15691	"	Williamson	W.	"	" believed Killed	"	
S17481	a/Cpl.	Attwood	L.	"	Wounded	"	'B' Coy
S17380	Rfn.	Bartrop	J.	"	Missing	"	
S 9913	"	Bayes	A.	"	"	"	
S17377	"	Butcher	W.	"	"	"	
S17449	"	Brown	R.	"	"	"	
S 9991	"	Cafferty	T.	"	"	"	
S16872	"	Davies	F.	"	"	"	
S18074	"	Eldridge	G.	"	"	"	
S15595	"	Mills	J.	"	"	"	
S16591	"	Murray	S.	"	"	"	
Z 2489	"	Perkins	A.	"	"	"	
S 5084	"	Spellman	F.	"	"	"	
B 840	"	Smyth	J.	"	"	"	
S18503	"	Woolf	L.	"	"	"	
S 3138	"	Wood	W.	"	"	"	
				"	"	"	'C' Coy.
B 1580	Rfn.	Bird	A.	"	"	"	
B 3187	"	Brown	J.	"	"	"	
S13750	"	Carrott	G.	"	"	"	
S18515	"	Chapleman	W.	"	"	"	
Z 2018	"	Dennis	A.	"	"	"	
S1373	"	Drury	D.	"	"	"	
S17167	"	Elvery	J.	"	"	"	
Z 2094	"	Griffen	L.	"	"	"	
S18047	"	Gregg	J.	"	"	"	
S17611	"	Hilton	J.	"	"	"	
B 1561	"	Hopkins	W.	"	"	"	
S 8879	"	Ince	G.	"	"	"	
S10707	"	Zackson	S.	"	"	"	
S10513	"	Lane	J.	"	"	"	
S18449	"	Monks	A.J.	"	"	"	
S18523	"	Morton	W.	"	"	"	
S 8192	"	Neale	H.	"	"	"	
S16001	"	Rothwell	G.				

* State whether absence is of a permanent or temporary nature, adding, in the case of casuals from wounds or disease, any available information for communication to the relatives.

To be made up to and for Sunday in each week.

No. of Report________

FIELD RETURN.

Army Form B. 213.

(To be furnished by all arms, services, and departments (except A.S.C. units) to the A. G.'s Office at the Base in accordance with Field Service Regulations, Part II.)

RETURN showing numbers (*a*) Effective strength of Unit. (*b*) Rationed by Unit. ________ at ________ ________ Date.

DETAIL	Personnel			Animals.								Guns, carriages, and limbers and transport vehicles												Motor Bicycles	Bicycles	REMARKS
				Horses				Mules		Camels	Oxen	Guns, carriages and limbers, showing description	Ammunition wagons and limbers	Machine guns	Aircraft, showing description	Horsed		Mechanical								
	Officers	Other ranks	Natives	Riding	Draught	Heavy Draught	Pack	Large	Small							4 wheeled	2 wheeled	Motor Cars.	Tractors	Lorries, showing description	Trucks, showing description	Trailers				
Effective Strength of Unit																										
Details, *by Arms* attached to unit as in War Establishment :—																										
Total																										
War Establishment																										
Wanting to complete (Detail of Personnel and Horses below)																										
Surplus																										
*Attached (not to include the details shown above)																										
Civilians :— Employed with the Unit																										
Accompanying the Unit																										
TOTAL RATIONED...																										

* In the case of field ambulances, hospitals or depots, the number of patients are to be included here, the names being shown in A. F. A. 36.

________ Signature of Commander.

________ Date of Despatch.

<u>8th. BATTALION THE RIFLE BRIGADE.</u>

<u>Casualties Sept.1916.</u>

						(rejoined 15th.)
S 17956	Rfn.	Ellams	W.	"C" Coy.	13-9-16	Wounded in Action.
S 18554	"	Chapman	W.	"C" Coy.	do.	do. (at duty)
S 9952	"	Ede	L.	"A" Coy.	do.	do.
S 18536	A/Cpl.	Rushmore	W.G.	"A" Coy.	do.	do. (at duty)
S 18534	Rfn.	West	W.C.	"B" Coy.	do.	do.
B 121	"	Wells	J.	"A" Coy.	do.	do.
S 10513	"	White	E.	do.	do.	Killed in Action.
S 17958	"	Lucas	W.	do.	do.	do.
S 17981	"	Myers	J.	do.	do.	do.
	Capt.	A.R.BACKUS			do.	Wounded in Action.
B 1477	Rfn.	Salt	H.	"D" Coy.	do.	do.
5377	Serjt.	Champ	W.G.	"A" Coy.	do.	do.
S 12715	Rfn.	Talkington	A.M.	do.	do.	do.
S 1406	A/Cpl.	Parkes	G.	do.	do.	do. (rejoined
S 8949	Rfn.	Collinson	F.	"B" Coy.	do.	do. 18-9-16)
3726	"	Davis	W.	do.	do.	do.
B 2787	"	Knibbs	W.	"A" Coy.	do.	Killed in Action.
2487	A/Cpl.	Irving	S.	"C" Coy.	do.	Wounded in Action.
Z 1688	Rfn.	Pitman	F.	do.	do.	do.
S 18469	"	Bones	G.E.	do.	do.	do.
6/377	"	Ward	W.	"A" Coy.	do.	do.
S 2619	"	Workman	C.	"C" Coy.	do.	Killed in Action.
S 14219	"	Murray	A.G.	do.	do.	do.
S 18460	"	Baldrati	F.	do.	14-9-16	Wounded in Action.
S 18525	A/Cpl.	Loughlin	F.C.	"D" Coy.	do.	do.
S 17498	Rfn.	Strangwick	E.	do.	do.	do.
1196	A/Serjt.	Miller	R.	do.	do.	do.
S 14464	Rfn.	Ansell	P.	"A" Coy.	do.	do.
S 18014	"	Brooks	W.	"B" Coy.	do.	do.
S 17394	"	Scott	F.R.	"D" Coy.	do.	do.
S 625	"	Rogers	P.	"D" Coy.	do.	do. (at duty)

Contd

For information of the A.G.'s Office at the Base.

Officers and men who have become casuals, been transferred or joined since last report.

Place In the Field. Date

Regtl. Number	Rank	Name		Corps	Nature of casualty, or name of unit from or to which transferred	Date of being struck off or coming on the ration return	Remarks*
	CAPT.	R.F. PRIOR		8th.Bn. Rifle Brigade.	Killed in Action.	15.9.16.	
	CAPT.	W.C.F.V. BARKER-MILL		"	"	"	
	CAPT.	H. TRYON		"	"	"	
	2/LIEUT.	A.D. MACNACHTEN		"	"	"	
	2/LIEUT.	D.S. ASHFORTH		"	"	"	
	2/LIEUT.	V.R.G. BIDDULPH		"	"	"	
	LIEUT.	E.F. MATTHEWS		"	Died of Wnds.	"	
	LT.COL.	W.R. STEWART		"	Wounded	"	
	2/LIEUT.	R.H.F. DEVEREUX		"	"	"	
	2/LIEUT.	E.L. VICKERS		"	"	"	
	2/LIEUT.	W.J. WARD		"	Wounded ~~Missing believed Killed~~	"	
	2/LIEUT.	S.H. GROOM		"	Wounded ~~Missing.~~	"	
	Lieut	F.J. STRACHAN RAME		"	Wounded	"	at duty
S 901	A/Cpl.	Coombes	A.	"	Killed in Action.	"	"A" Coy.
B 780	Rfn.	Blunden	B.	"	"	"	
S14700	"	Cook	W.	"	"	"	
S 6194	"	Channing	A.	"	"	"	
S14484	"	Midgley	L.	"	"	"	
S 6153	"	Regan	S.	"	"	"	
S 8336	"	Salmon	W.	"	"	"	
S13116	"	Woodward	J.	"	"	"	
6/9603	"	Farmey	G.	"	"	"	
B 600	A/Sgt.	Capewell	E.	"	"	"	
S 7417	Rfn.	Cade	J.	"	"	"	"B" Coy.
S18589	"	Dimsey	S.	"	"	"	
Z 1927	"	Eustace	F.	"	"	"	
Z 798	"	Mucklow	W.	"	"	"	
S 6601	Sgt.	Marshall	G.	"	"	"	"C" Coy.
B 1442	"	Cooper	H.	"	"	"	
S13563	Cpl.	Higgins	J.	"	"	"	
S18522	Rfn.	Butler	J.	"	"	"	
Z 631	"	Bailey	E.	"	"	"	
S13380	"	Bateman	T.	"	"	"	
S15478	"	Brunton	G.	"	"	"	
7976	"	Dalton	S.	"	"	"	
S14610	"	Ede	H.	"	"	"	
B 3040	"	Jenkinson	C.	"	"	"	
Z 1237	"	Robinson	A.	"	"	"	
S15649	"	Smith	R.	"	"	"	
S 8335	"	Spurrwick	T.	"	"	"	
S13895	A/Cpl.	Drew	H.	"	"	"	"D" Coy.
S15185	"	Hunt	W.	"	"	"	
S15952	Rfn.	Blackman	H.	"	"	"	
S 8646	"	Cater	F.	"	"	"	
S 2159	"	Debney	S.	"	"	"	
B 2140	"	Fisher	R.	"	"	"	

* State whether absence is of a permanent or temporary nature, adding, in the case of casuals from wounds or disease, any available information for communication to the relatives.

To be made up to and for Sunday in each week.

No. of Report ____________

FIELD RETURN.

Army Form B. 213.

(To be furnished by all arms, services, and departments (except A.S.C. units) to the A. G.'s Office at the Base in accordance with Field Service Regulations, Part II.)

RETURN showing numbers (*a*) Effective strength of Unit. (*b*) Rationed by Unit. ____________ at ____________ ____________ Date.

Detail	Personnel			Animals.								Guns, carriages, and limbers and transport vehicles											Motor Bicycles	Bicycles	Remarks
				Horses				Mules								Horsed		Mechanical							
	Officers	Other ranks	Natives	Riding	Draught	Heavy Draught	Pack	Large	Small	Camels	Oxen	Guns, carriages and limbers, showing description	Ammunition wagons and limbers	Machine guns	Aircraft, showing description	4 wheeled	2 wheeled	Motor Cars.	Tractors	Lorries, showing description	Trucks, showing description	Trailers			
Effective Strength of Unit																									
Details, *by Arms* attached to unit as in War Establishment:—																									
Total																									
War Establishment																									
Wanting to complete (Detail of Personnel and Horses below)																									
Surplus																									
*Attached (not to include the details shown above)																									
Civilians:— Employed with the Unit																									
Accompanying the Unit																									
Total Rationed...																									

* In the case of field ambulances, hospitals or depots, the number of patients are to be included here, the names being shown in A. F. A. 36.

____________ Signature of Commander.

____________ Date of Despatch.

For information of the A.G.'s Office at the Base.

Officers and men who have become casuals, been transferred or joined since last report.

Place ____________________ Date ____________________

Regtl. Number	Rank	Name		Corps	Nature of casualty, or name of unit from or to which transferred	Date of being struck off or coming on the ration return	Remarks*
Z 3047	Rfn.	Chamberlain	H.	8th. R.B.	W in A	15.9.16	'D' Coy
S 806	"	Drake	C.	"	"	"	
B 2377	"	Emmens	H.	"	"	"	
433	"	Edmunds	A.	"	"	"	
S 8979	"	Franklin	W.	"	"	"	
S 8858	"	Green	G.	"	"	"	
S18325	"	High	W.	"	"	"	
S13639	"	Hudson	J.	"	"	"	
S 8598	"	Linstead	T.	"	"	"	
S 7639	"	Missen	H.	"	"	"	
					rejoined	18.9.16	
Z 8858	"	McCarthy	J.	"	W in A	15.9.16	
S10648	"	Murphy	D.	"	"	"	
S 625	"	Rogers	P.	"	"	"	
2687	"	Steed	C.	"	"	"	
B 2541	"	Thorne	A.	"	"	"	
S13870	a/C	Thornley	T.	"	"	"	
1915	Rfn.	Tapner	B.	"	"	"	
S10960	"	Tomkinson	G.	"	"	"	
S13609	"	Tarkenter	J.	"	"	"	
S12032	"	Wright	T.	"	"	"	
[illegible]	"	Wainwright	J.	"	"	"	
S 8140	a/C	Selser	C	"	"	"	at duty
S 5986	Rfn.	Brennan	J.	"	"	"	at duty
B 2204	Sgt.	Lee	A.	"	"	"	'C' Coy
B 1658	a/Sgt.	Hobday	W.	"	"	"	
S 8791	"	Newby	A.	"	"	"	
9782	Cpl.	McGinley	J.	"	"	"	
S 4220	"	Rice	A.	"	"	"	
Z 404	"	Heeson	F.	"	"	"	
S16552	"	Shurry	B.	"	"	"	
Z 106	"	Dennis	E.	"	"	"	
S17138	a/C	Knowlden	A.	"	"	"	
S12866	"	Hancock	A.	"	"	"	
B 1678	"	Hoban	T.	"	"	"	
5507	"	Holloway	E.	"	"	"	
Z 3193	"	Machin	C.	"	"	"	
S11053	"	Yardley	S.	"	"	"	
S 978	"	Skevington	F.	"	"	"	
S18556	"	Bexley	J.	"	"	"	
S18539	"	Bye	F.	"	"	"	
S18528	"	Denyer	W.	"	"	"	
S10907	Rfn.	Ayres	E.	"	"	"	
S18397	"	Alldis	H.	"	"	"	
S18448	"	Ashington	A.J.	"	"	"	
S18504	"	Asser	G.	"	"	"	
S18445	"	Bridgeden	H.	"	"	"	
S18547	"	Bennett	H.	"	"	"	
Z 302	"	Barber	E.	"	"	"	
S 5857	"	Bettis	A.	"	"	"	
Z 329	"	Bowker	E.	"	"	"	

* State whether absence is of a permanent or temporary nature, adding, in the case of casuals from wounds or disease, any available information for communication to the relatives.

To be made up to and for Sunday in each week.

No. of Report__________

FIELD RETURN.

Army Form B. 213.

(To be furnished by all arms, services, and departments (except A.S.C. units) to the A. G.'s Office at the Base in accordance with Field Service Regulations, Part II.)

RETURN showing numbers (*a*) Effective strength of Unit. (*b*) Rationed by Unit. ____________________at____________________ ____________Date.

Detail	Personnel			Animals								Guns, carriages, and limbers and transport vehicles												Motor Bicycles	Bicycles	Remarks
				Horses				Mules								Horsed		Mechanical							
	Officers	Other ranks	Natives	Riding	Draught	Heavy Draught	Pack	Large	Small	Camels	Oxen	Guns, carriages and limbers, showing description	Ammunition wagons and limbers	Machine guns	Aircraft, showing description	4 wheeled	2 wheeled	Motor Cars.	Tractors	Lorries, showing description	Trucks, showing description	Trailers			
Effective Strength of Unit																									
Details, *by Arms* attached to unit as in War Establishment :—																									
Total																									
War Establishment																									
Wanting to complete (Detail of Personnel and Horses below)																									
Surplus																									
*Attached (not to include the details shown above)																									
Civilians :— Employed with the Unit																									
Accompanying the Unit																									
Total Rationed...																									

* In the case of field ambulances, hospitals or depots, the number of patients are to be included here, the names being shown in A. F. A. 36.

____________________Signature of Commander.

____________________Date of Despatch.

For information of the A.G.'s Office at the Base.

Officers and men who have become casuals, been transferred or joined since last report.

Place In the Field. Date

Regtl. Number	Rank	Name	Corps	Nature of casualty, or name of unit from or to which transferred	Date of being struck off or coming on the ration return	Remarks*
3065	Rfn.	Janes A.	8th.Bn.R.B.	Wounded in A.	15/9/16.	"B"Coy.
4099	"	Jobson H.	"	"	"	
7416	"	Jones H.	"	"	"	
5060	"	Kelly J.	"	"	"	
901	"	Knott W.	"	"	"	
0083	"	Lane W.	"	"	"	
0960	"	Murrell F.	"	"	"	
5246	"	Nash J.	"	"	"	
7361	"	Newman A.	"	"	"	
2697	"	Newman C.	"	"	"	
2131	"	Nixon R.	"	"	"	
5401	"	Nutley R.	"	"	"	
5491	"	Oldring A.	"	"	"	
5433	"	Owen F.	"	"	"	
7580	"	Peachey C.	"	"	"	
6109	"	Pears E.	"	"	"	
6115	A/Cpl.	Peat W.	"	"	"	
0475	Rfn.	Pinchin A.	"	"	"	
1493	"	Potter A.	"	"	"	
7771	"	Rogers L.	"	"	"	
3269	"	Sankey T.	"	"	"	
10870	"	Scott H.	"	"	"	
13492	"	Scott D.	"	"	"	
18540	"	Sealey J.	"	"	"	
15238	"	Smith C.	"	"	"	
19865	"	Smith F.	"	"	"	
3166	"	Smith G.	"	"	"	
2579	"	Smith H.	"	"	"	
1290	"	XXXXX Stevens T.	"	"	"	
14118	"	Tadd J.	"	"	"	
10543	"	Trendall A.	"	"	"	
15494	"	Turner H.	"	"	"	
0477	"	Warden H.	"	"	"	
768	"	Webster J.	"	"	"	
7716	"	Willett F.	"	"	"	
19610	"	Winlow J.	"	"	"	
12944	"	Yates A.	"	"	"	
2465	A/Sgt.	Leppard F.	"	"	"	"D"Coy.
2870	Sgt.	O'Hara R.P.	"	"	"	
16861	Cpl.	Field A.	"	"	"	
759	"	Harris A.	"	"	"	
5799	"	Horton A.	"	"	"	
65	"	Owen H.	"	"	"	
17479	a/Cpl.	Corri H.	"	"	"	
682	"	France E.	"	"	"	
6655	"	Fowell J.	"	"	"	
1409	"	Fryer A.	"	"	"	
7446	"	Jarvis J.	"	"	"	
6123	"	King E.	"	"	"	
14400	"	Mason F.	"	"	"	
981	"	Phillips B.	"	"	"	
13922	Rfn.	Brown A.	"	"	"	
2456	"	Bettington P.	"	"	"	

*State whether absence is of a permanent or temporary nature, adding, in the case of casuals from wounds or disease, any available information for communication to the relatives.

FIELD RETURN.

Army Form B. 213.

No. of Report__________

(To be furnished by all arms, services, and departments to the A. G.'s Office at the Base in accordance with Field Service Regulations, Part II.)

____________________Date.

RETURN showing numbers RATIONED by, and Transport on charge of,____________________ at ________________

DETAIL	Personnel			Animals								Guns, carriages, and limbers and transport vehicles											Motor Bicycles	Bicycles	REMARKS
				Horses				Mules		Camels	Oxen	Guns, carriages and limbers, showing, description	Ammunition wagons and limbers	Machine guns	Aircraft, showing description	Horsed		Mechanical							
	Officers	Other ranks	Natives	Riding	Draught	Heavy Draught	Pack	Large	Small							4 Wheeled	2 Wheeled	Motor Cars	Tractors	Lorries, showing description	Trucks, showing description	Trailers			
Effective Strength of Unit																									
Details, *by Arms* attached to unit as in War Establishment :—																									
Total																									
War Establishment																									
Wanting to complete																									
Surplus																									
*Attached (not to include the details shown above)																									
Civilians :—																									
Employed with the Unit																									
Accompanying the Unit																									
TOTAL RATIONED ...																									

* In the case of field ambulances, hospitals or depôts, the number of patients are to be included here, the names being shown in A.F.A. 36.

____________________Signature of Commander.

____________________Date of Despatch.

(K11859) W. & Co., Ltd. Wt. w6005—894 500,000 10/14 Forms B. 213 / 5

For information of the A.G.'s Office at the Base.

Officers and men who have become casuals, been transferred or joined since last report.

Place In the Field. Date

Regtl. Number	Rank	Name		Corps	Nature of casualty, or name of unit from or to which transferred	Date of being struck off or coming on the ration return	Remarks*
B 3308	Sgt.	Walker	W.	8th.Bn.R.B.	Wounded in A.	15/9/16	"B" Coy.
S 9015	"	Knight	W.	"	"	"	
B 2069	A/"	Rogers	F.	"	"	"	
S 1314	Cpl.	Bryant	S.	"	"	"	
S 6233	"	Bowers	F.	"	"	"	
S18367	"	Dowdell	J.	"	"	"	
3303	"	Fairbell	A.	"	"	"	
B 3307	"	Reid	W.	"	"	"	
S14387	A/Cpl.	Barnett	S.	"	"	"	
B 384	"	Chambers	E.	"	"	"	
6231	"	Gilbert	H.	"	"	"	
S13237	"	Gent	H.	"	"	"	
B10602	"	Golden	F.	"	"	"	
1668	"	King	G.	"	"	"	
4907	"	Lindfield	W.	"	"	"	
Z 204	"	Oliver	C.	"	"	"	
S 36	"	Warren	G.	"	"	"	
S 6321	"	Pratt	J.	"	"	"	
S11762	"	Strudwick	H.	"	"	"	
S18618	Rfn.	Aust	J.	"	"	"	
S 3043	"	Allen	E.	"	"	"	
S15895	"	Bailey	A.	"	"	"	
[illegible]	"	Block	P.	"	"	"	
S 6217	"	Bridge	A.	"	"	"	
S13697	"	Bridgeman	H.	"	"	"	
S17798	"	Bynon	H.	"	"	"	
S15460	"	Carter	C.	"	"	"	
S16668	"	Carter	C.	"	"	"	
S14135	"	Chalkley	E.	"	"	"	
S14117	"	Clark	J.	"	"	"	
B 3037	"	Collins	G.	"	"	"	
S 3324	"	Cutbill	A.	"	"	"	
S18646	A/Cpl.	Collins	C.	"	"	"	
1961	Rfn.	Day	W.	"	"	"	
S 6381	"	Day	J.	"	"	"	
R 1731	"	Davis	D.	"	"	"	
S 8483	"	Dean	R.	"	"	"	
S17487	A/Cpl.	Dove	W.	"	"	"	
S 6330	Rfn.	Doyle	J.	"	"	"	
6/8999	"	Foggerty	J.	"	"	"	
S14481	"	Gibson	F.	"	"	"	(died 17/9/16)
S15615	"	Graham	A.	"	"	"	
S13856	"	Guppy	D.	"	"	"	
7613	"	Hall	J.	"	"	"	
B 1760	"	Halliday	T.	"	"	"	
S10537	"	Highley	J.	"	"	"	
S 7960	"	Holding	F.	"	"	"	
S14692	"	Holland	W.	"	"	"	
B 1343	"	Holton	H.	"	"	"	
3843	"	Hughes	J.	"	"	"	
S 8971	"	Hunt	C.	"	"	"	
S 9621	"	Iredale	W.	"	"	"	
Z 2374	"	Isherwood	C.	"	"	"	
S 1177	"	Jackson	T.				

*State whether absence is of a permanent or temporary nature, adding, in the case of casuals from wounds or disease, any available information for communication to the relatives.

No. of Report ________

FIELD RETURN.

Army Form B. 213.

(To be furnished by all arms, services, and departments to the A. G.'s Office at the Base in accordance with Field Service Regulations, Part II.)

________ Date.

RETURN showing numbers RATIONED by, and Transport on charge of, ________ at ________

Detail	Personnel			Animals								Guns, carriages, and limbers and transport vehicles											Motor Bicycles	Bicycles	Remarks
				Horses				Mules								Horsed		Mechanical							
	Officers	Other ranks	Natives	Riding	Draught	Heavy Draught	Pack	Large	Small	Camels	Oxen	Guns, carriages and limbers, showing, description	Ammunition wagons and limbers	Machine guns	Aircraft, showing description	4 Wheeled	2 Wheeled	Motor Cars	Tractors	Lorries, showing description	Trucks, showing description	Trailers			
Effective Strength of Unit Details, *by Arms* attached to unit as in War Establishment:—																									
Total																									
War Establishment																									
Wanting to complete																									
Surplus																									
*Attached (not to include the details shown above)																									
Civilians:—																									
Employed with the Unit																									
Accompanying the Unit																									
Total Rationed ...																									

* In the case of field ambulances, hospitals or depôts, the number of patients are to be included here, the names being shown in A.F.A. 36.

________ Signature of Commander.

________ Date of Despatch.

(K 11859) W. & Co., Ltd. Wt. w6005—894 500,000 10/14 Forms B. 213 / 5

For information of the A.G.'s Office at the Base.

Officers and men who have become casuals, been transferred or joined since last report.

Place In the Field. Date

Regtl. Number	Rank	Name		Corps	Nature of casualty, or name of unit from or to which transferred	Date of being struck off or coming on the ration return	Remarks*
82	Rfn.	Harrison	H.	8th.Bn.Rifle Brigade.	Killed in Action.	16.9.16	"D" Coy.
Z 2168	"	Hingley	A.	"	"	"	
S 1612	"	Mercer	T.	"	"	"	
S10558	"	Turney	A.	"	"	"	
S17468	"	Collins	W.	"	"	"	
2341	C.S.M.	Holden	J.	"	"	"	
2053	Cpl	Emms	J	7th Dragoon G.	"	"	C. Coy.
B 24	Sgt.	Clarke	G.	"	Wounded	"	"A" Coy.
B 127	"	Chipps	H.	"	"	"	
S10484	"	Higginbottom	J.	"	"	"	
913	"	Ridout	G.	"	"	"	
S 7277	Cpl.	Halliwell	M.E.	"	"	"	
S14478	"	Clarke	H.	"	"	"	
6/4868	"	Blacksley	G.	"	"	"	
B 48	A/Cpl.	Chick	A.	"	"	"	
S 7164	"	Skelton	W.	"	"	"	
S 1906	"	Yardley	S.	"	"	"	
Z 2179	"	Carson	J.	"	"	"	
S 5884	"	Coules	B.	"	"	"	
9841	"	Owen	J.	"	"	"	
S18500	"	Flack	J.	"	"	"	
S10037	Rfn.	Blackwell	A.	"	"	"	
S 1109	"	Cole	H.	"	"	"	
S 9376	"	Chase	W.	"	"	"	
S13544	"	Crook	A.	"	"	"	
S 1334	"	Clements	A.	"	"	"	
B 3496	"	Duggleby	F.	"	"	"	
S13287	"	Davison	J.	"	"	"	
S17984	"	Dyson	S.	"	"	"	
S18535	"	Foulsham	J.	"	"	"	
B 384	"	Feuillade	G.	"	"	"	
8568	"	Fricker	W.	"	"	"	
S18207	"	Haven	L.	"	"	"	
S15563	"	Harmer	W.	"	"	"	
S18542	"	Hewey	R.	"	"	"	
B 328	"	Irwin	H.	"	"	"	
S 7273	"	Janes	P.	"	"	"	
S18544	"	Jones	H.C.	"	"	"	
S14298	"	Pullen	R.	"	"	"	
S14473	"	Rimmer	J.	"	"	"	
S 6164	"	Stears	T.	"	"	"	
S 835	"	Sharratt	A.	"	"	"	
S13061	"	Sweeney	A.	"	"	"	
B 371	"	Turner	T.	"	"	"	
6196	"	Taylor	F.	"	"	"	
S10110	"	Waugh	F.	"	"	"	
B 758	A/C.S.M.	Morris	J.	"	"	"	"B" Coy.
S 6254	Sgt.	Burgess	H.	"	"	"	
Z 409	"	Hollibone	J.	"	"	"	
1400	"	Marshall	G.	"	(Died 17/9/16) Wounded	"	
[illegible]	"	Scotman	A.	"	"	"	

*State whether absence is of a permanent or temporary nature, adding, in the case of casuals from wounds or disease, any available information for communication to the relatives.

Army Form B. 213.

FIELD RETURN.

No. of Report ______

(To be furnished by all arms, services, and departments to the A. G.'s Office at the Base in accordance with Field Service Regulations, Part II.)

______ Date.

RETURN showing numbers RATIONED by, and Transport on charge of, ______ at ______

Detail	Personnel			Animals.								Guns, carriages, and limbers and transport vehicles											Motor Bicycles	Bicycles	Remarks
				Horses				Mules								Horsed		Mechanical							
	Officers	Other ranks	Natives	Riding	Draught	Heavy Draught	Pack	Large	Small	Camels	Oxen	Guns, carriages and limbers, showing, description	Ammunition wagons and limbers	Machine guns	Aircraft, showing description	4 Wheeled	2 Wheeled	Motor Cars	Tractors	Lorries, showing description	Trucks, showing description	Trailers			
Effective Strength of Unit																									
Details, *by Arms* attached to unit as in War Establishment:—																									
Total																									
War Establishment																									
Wanting to complete																									
Surplus																									
*Attached (not to include the details shown above)																									
Civilians:—																									
Employed with the Unit																									
Accompanying the Unit																									
TOTAL RATIONED ...																									

* In the case of field ambulances, hospitals or depôts, the number of patients are to be included here, the names being shown in A.F.A. 36.

______ Signature of Commander.

______ Date of Despatch.

(K 11859) W. & Co., Ltd. Wt. w6005—894 500,000 10/14 Forms B. 213 / 5

8th. BATTALION THE RIFLE BRIGADE.

ROLL OF OFFICERS.

Lieut.Col.R.C.Maclachlan,D.S.O.	Commanding Officer.
Major A.C.Sheepshanks,D.S.O.	Second in Command.
Major X.R.A.de La Chapelle	Hospital.
Capt.K.S.M.Gladstone	Commanding "A" Coy.
Lieut.C.H.Wenham	Commanding "B" Coy.
Lieut.W.A.Crebbin	Acting Adjutant.
2/Lt.J.R.Abbey	Lewis Gun Officer.
" D.F.Foxwell	41st. Brigade I.O.
" T.A.Baldock	Commanding "C" Coy.
" E.Poole	Transport Officer
" B.Franklin	
" J.A.Gould	Commanding "D" Coy.

Lieut. & Quartermaster F.H.Pryor -

CAPT BUNT
R.A.M.C.

R.C.Maclachlan

Lieut.Col.
Comdg. 8th. Batt. The Rifle Brigade.

30/9/16.

8th. Battalion THE RIFLE BRIGADE.

Roll of Officers.

Lieut.Col.R.C.Maclachlan,D.S.O.	Commanding Officer.
Major A.C.Sheepshanks,D.S.O.	Second in Command.
Major A.L.C.Cavendish	O.C.Divisional Musketry School.
Capt.G.V.Carey	Third Army School.
Capt.K.S.M.Gladstone	Commanding "A" Coy.
Capt.B.H.Bennett	Commanding "C" Coy.
Capt.C.N.Thompson	Commanding "B" Coy.
Lieut.C.H.Wenham	Tour of duty - England.
Lieut.W.A.Crebbin	Acting Adjutant.
2/Lieut.J.R.Abbey	Lewis gun Officer.
" D.F.Foxwell	Brigade Intelligence Officer.
" T.A.Baldock	Divisional Bombing Course.
" W.A.Teakle	Commanding "D" Coy.
" E.Poole	Transport Officer.
" B.Franklin	
" J.A.Gould	Bombing Officer.
" H.R.Hartley	
" E.A.F.Batty	
" W.W.Wines	
" F.A.Newell	
" P.H.Wooding	Leave to England.

Lieut.F.J.Strachan M.C. (R.A.M.C.) Attached.

WO217

C O N F I D E N T I A L.

W A R   D I A R Y.

- of -

8th Bn., T H E   R I F L E   B R I G A D E.

From: 1st October, 1916.
To: 31st October, 1916.

Volume XVIII.

Instructions regarding War Diaries and Intelligence Summaries are contained in F. S. Regs., Part II. and the Staff Manual respectively. Title Pages will be prepared in manuscript.

WAR DIARY
or
INTELLIGENCE SUMMARY
(Erase heading not required.)

Army Form C. 2118

Volume 18.

Place	Date	Hour	Summary of Events and Information	Remarks and references to Appendices
RIVIERE	1st		Billets in Brigade Reserve. A deserter came over from enemy to 8th 60th front line.	
	2nd		Quiet Day.	
	3rd		Relieve 8th Bn KRRC in F3 sector. Only 9 Officers & 326 O.R to take over the whole sector! A & D Coys in front line, B & C in support. Trenches excellent. 2 Sgts, 4 Riflemen Killed, 12 O.R wounded, by one shell during relief. Draft of 10 O.R arrived. 1 Officer, servant & 2 N.C.O's attached from the Yeomanry for instruction.	
Trenches R.33.b.7.5	4th		60 pounders Trench Mortars, supported by B62 battery, blew in G1 sap.	
	5th		2/Lt. W.A. TEAKLE joined & takes over command of D Coy.	
	6th		A few 77 mm shells on Support Company. Otherwise quiet.	
	7th		A few whizz-bangs on Communication Trenches.	

1875 Wt. W593/826 1,000,000 4/15 J.B.C. & A. A.D.S.S./Forms/C. 2118.

Army Form C. 2118

Instructions regarding War Diaries and Intelligence Summaries are contained in F. S. Regs., Part II. and the Staff Manual respectively. Title Pages will be prepared in manuscript.

WAR DIARY
or
INTELLIGENCE SUMMARY
(Erase heading not required.)

Place	Date	Hour	Summary of Events and Information	Remarks and references to Appendices
Trenches. R.23.b 7.5.	8th		Lt.Col. R.C. MACLACHLAN goes to Brigade H.Q. to command the Brigade in temporary absence of the Brigadier-General. Major A.C. SHEEPSHANKS assumes command. Lt Col E.T. SAINT attached to Battalion from Cambridgeshire Regiment for 1 month's instruction. 2/Lt A.F. NEWELL and 2/Lt W.W. WINES posted to Battalion. 2/Lt STOPS and 2/Lt HOMPHRIES of Northamptonshire Yeomanry with 5 NCO's attached to Battalion for one week.	
	9th		Very quiet day.	
	10th		Following NCO's and Riflemen awarded Military Medals for gallantry on Sept. 15th. S.7205 Cpl ASPDEN J. 6/621 Rfn SMITH F. S 11346 Rfn MEECH H. B 1113 a/cpl MATHER S. 6600 Rfn PARKER C. B 623 Rfn WARDEN H. S 9482 Rfn ECKMAN F. S 688 Rfn BENNETT J. S 526 Rfn PARSONS G.	
	11th		Quiet day.	

1875 Wt. W593/826 1,000,000 4/15 J.B.C. & A. A.D.S.S./Forms/C. 2118.

Instructions regarding War Diaries and Intelligence Summaries are contained in F. S. Regs., Part II. and the Staff Manual respectively. Title Pages will be prepared in manuscript.

WAR DIARY
or
INTELLIGENCE SUMMARY

(Erase heading not required.)

Army Form C. 2118

Place	Date	Hour	Summary of Events and Information	Remarks and references to Appendices
Trenches R.23.6.7.5.	12th		Inter-relief of Companies. Another uneventful day-	
	13th		Quiet day- A few shells 77 mm on Communication Trenches-	
	14th		Draft of 14 O.R.s arrived. Capt. K.S.M. GLADSTONE to Bde H.Q. to act as Staff-Captain in temporary absence of Staff-Captain-	
	15th		Quiet day-	
	16th		Draft of 1 officer 52 O.R. arrived at Transport Camp-	
	17th		Divisional Commander visits the trenches with acting Brigadier. Draft arrived from Transport, officer being 2/Lt HARTLEY, O.R. including 7 old Battalion men. 2 officers and 3 OR attached from 6th Corps Mounted Troops- Two shells near Battalion H.Q. one a blind. Enemy showing greater activity by day, and being quieter at night- Relief probable-	

1875 Wt. W593/826 1,000,000 4/15 J.B.C. & A. A.D.S.S./Forms/C. 2118.

Instructions regarding War Diaries and Intelligence Summaries are contained in F. S. Regs., Part II. and the Staff Manual respectively. Title Pages will be prepared in manuscript.

WAR DIARY
or
INTELLIGENCE SUMMARY
(Erase heading not required.)

Army Form C. 2118

Place	Date	Hour	Summary of Events and Information	Remarks and references to Appendices
TRENCHES R.23 b 7 5	18.		Lt. Strachan J.J. R.A.M.C., 7603 CSM Baldock A.T. 3469 C.S.M. Jackson G. awarded The Military Cross B683 Rfn. Warden H. awarded a bar to Military Medal.	
	19.		Very wet day – trenches beginning to slip in. Col Maclachlan returns from Brigade & assumes command of the Btn.	
	20.		Gas alert. Very quiet in the line.	
	21.		Relieved by 7th Btn K.R.R.C. Marching out strength 8 Officers 405 O.R. Casualties during tour O.R. 7 Killed 1 Missing, believed killed, 14 wounded. Gas alert on. Much aerial activity – one of our machines down in F2 sector.	
RIVIERE	22		Good deal of aerial activity. Warning order to move at short notice	
	23		Received orders of move to BERNEVILLE 25th. All spare Officers & N.C.O's attend demonstration of liason action between aircraft & infantry at BERNEVILLE – lecture was the only result as it was too foggy to fly.	
	24		Demonstration to Officers & N.C.O's on the care of pigeons & their use – all displayed the greatest ignorance of their handling. Heavy fatigue parties continue to carry accessories to the front line. Kits all packed and sent back for the move next day. Billetting party under Col. Saint moves out.	

1875 Wt. W593/826 1,000,000 4/15 J.B.C. & A. A.D.S.S./Forms/C. 2118.

Army Form C. 2118

Instructions regarding War Diaries and Intelligence Summaries are contained in F. S. Regs., Part II. and the Staff Manual respectively. Title Pages will be prepared in manuscript.

WAR DIARY
or
INTELLIGENCE SUMMARY
(Erase heading not required.)

Place	Date	Hour	Summary of Events and Information	Remarks and references to Appendices
RIVIERE	25		Relieved by 6th Bn Queens Regt. Relief complete by 12 noon – very quiet but wet. Marched to BERNEVILLE by Companies – arrived 2.0 pm. Billets poor, place all mud & slush. Orders received re move to GRAND RULLECOURT on 26th. Lieut. C. H. WENHAM. to ENGLAND.	
BERNEVILLE	26		Battalion moves by route march to GRAND RULLECOURT. Route – SIMENCOURT, GOUY, FOSSEUX, BARLY. March discipline very poor owing to confusion caused by dragging Lewis Gun carts. Battalion arrived at 2.30 pm. & occupied the same billets as when here in July last.	
GRAND RULLECOURT	27.		Commanding Officer inspects Coys. Arrangements made for training & reorganisation of Specialists etc. Lt. F. J. STRACHAN RAMC returns from leave. Draft of 97 O.R. arrives. B2384 Sgt. DAWES J. awarded the Military Medal.	
	28		Issue of Jerkins to all the troops. 125 draft arrives – also 2/Lt E. A. F. BATTY. Draft mostly from 17th Bn K.R.R.C., a fine stamp of men, between 35 and 40 years of age.	
	29		Church Services. Military Medals awarded to B2870 Sgt. O'HARA R.P. B2859 Sgt. AUSTIN T. J. 33067 Sgt. BUCK J. B. H. 37277 Cpl HALLIWELL M. E. 580 Sgt. HAYWARD N. 2841 C.Q.M.S. HOLDEN J. F. 31783 Sgt CARSON C. H. B724 Sgt. DRIVER F. Constant rain for the last few days has made the place a sea of mud. 6.	London Gazette 27.10.16.

1875 Wt. W593/826 1,000,000 4/15 J.B.C. & A. A.D.S.S./Forms/C. 2118.

8th. Batt. Rifle Brigade.

List of Officers serving October 31st.1916.

Lt.Col. R.C. Maclachlan D.S.O.	
Major A.C. Sheepshanks D.S.O.	(On leave)
Capt. K.S.M. Gladstone	(On leave)
2/Lieut. J.R. Abbey	Lewis Gun Officer
2/Lieut. D.F. Foxwell	Bde. Intelligence Officer
2/Lieut. T.A. Baldock	
2/Lieut. W.A. Teakle	
2/Lieut. B. Franklin	
2/Lieut. J.A. Gould	
2/Lieut. H.R. Hartley	
2/Lieut. E.A.F. Batty	
2/Lieut. A.F. Newell	
2/Lieut. W.W. Wines	
Lieut. & A/Adjt. W.A. Crebbin	
Lieut. & Quarter Master F.H. Pryor	(Hospital)
2/Lieut. E. Poole	Transport Officer.
Lieut. F.J. Strachan M.C. (R.A.M.C.)	

R Maclachlan

Lt.Col.

31.10.16. Cmdg. 8th.Battn. Rifle Brigade.

8th. Battn. Rifle Brigade.

Casualties - - October 1916.

S	7207	Sgt.	Aspden J.	"A" Coy.	Killed in Action	3.10.16.
S	12906	"	Cobbold J.	"	"	"
S	17797	Rfn.	Gordon B.	"	"	"
S	17988	"	Farr L.	"	"	"
B	2158	"	Kittle W.	"	"	"
S	14261	"	Turner E.	"D" Coy.	"	11.10.16.
Z	1289	"	Wilkinson W.	"C" Coy.	"	13.10.16.
S	18505	"	Grundy S.	"A" Coy.	Missing bel. K.	3.10.16.
S	8945	A/C.	Collinson F.	"B" Coy.	~~killed~~ wounded	"
S	1360	"	Beesty J.	"A" Coy	Wounded	"
S	6007	Rfn.	Bass H.	"	"	"
S	11336	"	George D.	"	"	"
S	10990	"	Kane G.	"	"	"
S	18008	"	Callard F.	"	"	"
S	18529	"	Haydon F.	"	"	"
S	9605	"	Hennessey E.	"	"	"
	5164	Sgt.	Douche R.	"	"	"
Z	1544	Rfn.	Croxton W.	"	"	"
S	15672	"	Hollick A.	"	"	"
S	18507	"	Longhurst G.	"	"	"
B	2857	Sgt.	Austin T.	"D" Coy.	"	8.10.16.
S	11323	Rfn.	Wood S.	"	"	"
S	9792	"	Idenden A.	"B" Coy.	"	21.10.16.

R M Maclachlan

Lt.Col.,
Cmdg. 8th. Battn. Rifle Brigade.

C O N F I D E N T I A L.

W A R D I A R Y

- of -

8th (S) Bn., THE RIFLE BRIGADE.

From: 1st November, 1916.
To: 30th November, 1916.

Volume XIX.

Instructions regarding War Diaries and Intelligence Summaries are contained in F. S. Regs., Part II. and the Staff Manual respectively. Title Pages will be prepared in manuscript.

WAR DIARY
or
INTELLIGENCE SUMMARY
(Erase heading not required.)

Army Form C. 2118

Volume 19

Place	Date	Hour	Summary of Events and Information	Remarks and references to Appendices
GRAND RULLECOURT	1		Still very wet. Lt. B. N. Bennett rejoins from England. A special Estaminet reserved for the comfort of N.C.O's – which later on was formed into a Sergeants Mess.	
	2.		Usual rain. General Officer Commanding inspects the three last drafts – 275 men.	
	3.		More rain. Lord Derby's band plays to the Garrison.	
	4.		Very wet. Battalion Route march – strength 8 Officers 404 O.R., all specialists & classes left off parade. Route – AVESNES & LIENCOURT.	
	5.		Rain as usual.	
	6.		Heavy rain. Capt. G. V. Carey rejoins for duty from the Cambridge University Cadet Corps – 2/Lt. P. H. Wooding from G.H.Q. Cadet Corps on first appointment.	
	7.		More heavy rain. Baths started for the men in the Chateau. Lt. C. N. Thompson rejoins from A Base, with draft of 26 O.R.	
	8		Continuous heavy rain. Training almost impossible. Boxing competition held in the evening.	

1875 Wt. W593/826 1,000,000 4/15 J.B.C. & A. A.D.S.S./Forms/C. 2118.

Instructions regarding War Diaries and Intelligence Summaries are contained in F. S. Regs., Part II. and the Staff Manual respectively. Title Pages will be prepared in manuscript.

WAR DIARY
or
INTELLIGENCE SUMMARY
(Erase heading not required.)

Army Form C. 2118

Place	Date	Hour	Summary of Events and Information	Remarks and references to Appendices
GRAND RULLECOURT	9		Fine, for the first time for many days. The whole battalion parade under the Comdg. Officer for assault practice.	
	10.		Fine. Lecture by Lt ATKINSON, DIV. GAS OFFICER, on the new box respirator. Cross country run against 8th Bn. Kings Royal Rifle Corps.	
	11.		Fine. Battalion route march – 15 Officers, 613 O.R. 'A' Coy. win inter-company Bombing Competition.	
	12.		Fine, but dull, usual church parade services.	
	13.		Fine, but damp. 'B' Coy. win inter-company shooting competition. Army Commander inspects units of the Brigade. DIV. Band from 3–4.30 p.m.	
	14.		Fine, but dull. 'A' Coy win inter-company football competition. Battalion parade under the Comdg. Officer. Capt. G.V. CAREY & two N.C.O's to THIRD ARMY SCHOOL	
	15.		Fine. 'D' Coy win inter-company Lewis Gun Competition. Military Medals awarded to S5472 A/Cpl MURPHY T. & S898 Rfn McKEOWN J.	D.R.O. 1931.

1875 Wt. W593/826 1,000,000 4/15 J.B.C. & A. A.D.S.S./Forms/C. 2118.

Army Form C. 2118

Instructions regarding War Diaries and Intelligence Summaries are contained in F. S. Regs., Part II. and the Staff Manual respectively. Title Pages will be prepared in manuscript.

WAR DIARY
or
INTELLIGENCE SUMMARY
(Erase heading not required.)

Place	Date	Hour	Summary of Events and Information	Remarks and references to Appendices
GRAND RULLECOURT	16		Fine again. Major A.L.C. CAVENDISH rejoins from sick leave. Lieuts. THOMPSON C.N. & BENNET authorised to wear badges of Captain. 'A' Coy tie with 'C' Coy 7th Bn RIFLE BRIGADE in 1st round Brigade inter-company football.	
	17		Fine, but very cold. Comdg. Officer to a lecture on artillery at HESDIN. Brigade Cross country race – 1st 'C' Coy 8th Bn Kings Royal Rifle Corps, 2nd 'A' Coy 8th Bn Rifle Bde, 3rd 'B' Coy 8th Bn Rifle Bde.	
	18		First fall of snow – later rain. Further lecture on the new box respirator by Brigade Gas N.C.O. Instructions received to clear all barns of corn etc for further accommodation for troops.	
	19		Wet. Usual church services, except C of E parade service which was cancelled.	
	20		Fine & cold. Beaten in football by 7th Bn. Rifle Bde. Great stress is being laid on raising the morale of the troops while in rest, by less work & more games.	

1875 Wt. W593/826 1,000,000 4/15 J.B.C. & A. A.D.S.S./Forms/C. 2118.

Army Form C. 2118

Instructions regarding War Diaries and Intelligence Summaries are contained in F. S. Regs., Part II. and the Staff Manual respectively. Title Pages will be prepared in manuscript.

WAR DIARY
or
INTELLIGENCE SUMMARY
(Erase heading not required.)

Place	Date	Hour	Summary of Events and Information	Remarks and references to Appendices
GRAND RULLECOURT	21st		Fine. Battalion won Brigade Bombing Competition. Second to 7th Bn Rifle Bde in competition for best "turn-out" of Transport & second to 7th Bn K.R.R.C. in Lewis-Gun competition.	
			Corps Commander visited the area	
	22nd		Fine. New Master Cook arrives. The fact is noted as of intense importance between good & bad feeding of battalions.	
			Major A.L.C Cavendish selected to start a Divisional Musketry School.	
	23rd		Very nice day. Defeated by 8th Bn K.R.R.C in battalion football, and by 7th Bn K.R.R.C in rapid shooting.	
			An effort being made to raise the standard of discipline amongst N.C.O's by forming classes under the R.S.M.	
	24th		Third in Stretcher Bearer Competition & also in Bayonet Fighting Competition.	
	25th		Route march in pouring rain. Names called for to join the "Tanks". As a new organization would probably attract the best from a battalion, the Comdg. Officer shelves the question. The new box respirator issued & fitted.	
	26th		Very wet. Voluntary Church Service.	

1875 Wt. W593/826 1,000,000 4/15 J.B.C. & A. A.D.S.S./Forms/C. 2118.

Instructions regarding War Diaries and Intelligence Summaries are contained in F. S. Regs., Part II. and the Staff Manual respectively. Title Pages will be prepared in manuscript.

Army Form C. 2118

WAR DIARY
or
INTELLIGENCE SUMMARY
(Erase heading not required.)

Place	Date	Hour	Summary of Events and Information	Remarks and references to Appendices
GRAND RULLECOURT.			Divisional Cross country race – Battalion placed 8th.	
	27th		Conference of Comdg Officers with the Corps Ordnance Officer.	
			Battalion tested in 'gas chamber' with the new box respirators.	
	28th		Brigade Runners race won by 7th Bn Rifle Bde. Very foggy. Great difficulty in getting barns in the village cleared of corn – responsibility put on Comdg Officers. The villagers strongly objected to having their crops thrown outside, and naturally so. Lecture by the Brigadier General to all officers.	
	29th		Very foggy. B.G.C. inspects the Battalion in the "attack" – the main difficulty of this practice is to imagine a moving barrage. Extraordinary progress has been made in communications by the Signal Service & Runners, who are now highly trained specialists.	
	30th		Fine but dull. Brigade Baths at SOMBRIN allotted to the battalion.	
			Strength – total 22 Officers, 850 O.R., effective 19 Officers 777 O.R.	
			List of Officers attached.	
			No casualties during the month.	

[illegible] Lt Col
Comdy 8th Bn Rifle Bde.

1875 Wt. W593/826 1,000,000 4/15 J.B.C. & A. A.D.S.S./Forms/C. 2118.

Confidential

War Diary

of

6th Bn. The Rifle Brigade

1st to 31st December 1916

Volume 20

Vol 19

Instructions regarding War Diaries and Intelligence Summaries are contained in F. S. Regs., Part II. and the Staff Manual respectively. Title Pages will be prepared in manuscript.

WAR DIARY
or
~~INTELLIGENCE SUMMARY~~
(Erase heading not required.)

8th Battn The Rifle Bde

Volume 20

Army Form C. 2118

Place	Date 1916	Hour	Summary of Events and Information	Remarks and references to Appendices
GRAND RULLECOURT	Dec. 1st		Fine. Brigade Route March. Result of Brigade Efficiency Competition. – 1. 8th K.R.R.C. 13 pts. 2. 8th Bn Rifle Bde 12 pts. 3. 7th Bn. K.R.R.C. 11 pts. 4. 7th Rifle Bde. Brigadier very satisfied & awards a second bugle to the battalion owing to the closeness of the contest.	
	2nd		Dull. Brigade Boxing Competition at SOMBRIN. 2/Lt. T.A. BALDOCK to hospital	
	3rd		Voluntary C of E. Services. Other services as usual. Brigade Observers Competition won by 8th Bn Rifle Bde section.	
	4th		Fine & frosty. Box Respirators of H.Q. Coy again tested in gas.	
	5th		Dull & wet. Capt. K.S.M. GLADSTONE goes to Division as Temp. D.A.A. & Q.M.G. Div. Gas Officer tests Companies in Box Respirator drill.	
	6th		Fine. Brigade Route March. Only 7 Officers doing duty with the battalion owing to Courses, leave etc.	
	7th		Dull. 2/Lt A.E.F. BATTY to hospital. Brigade Working party of 250 O.R. found by the Battalion – digging replica of German system of trenches.	

9875 Wt. W593/826 1,000,000 4/15 J.B.C. & A. A.D.S.S./Forms/C. 2118.

Army Form C. 2118

Instructions regarding War Diaries and Intelligence Summaries are contained in F. S. Regs., Part II. and the Staff Manual respectively. Title Pages will be prepared in manuscript.

WAR DIARY
or
INTELLIGENCE SUMMARY
(Erase heading not required.)

Place	Date	Hour	Summary of Events and Information	Remarks and references to Appendices
GRAND RULLECOURT	8th		Night Operations – Battalion in the trenches, practising gas alarms, and repelling hostile raids	
	9th		Dull & misty. Brigade working party again provided – 200 men.	
	10th		Voluntary C of E. services, others as usual. Div. Shooting Competition – 13th Platoon nominated by G.O.C. to represent the Battalion, and are placed 8th on the results. Competition won by 5th K.S.L.I.	
	11th		Fine. Draft of 86 O.R arrive. Warning order received that 41st Inf Bde will relieve the 37th Inf Bde in F Sector on the 15th.	
	12th		Snow. Comdg Officer & Medical Officer inspect the draft.	
	13th		Dull. Comdg Officer & OC Coys reconnoitre the front line. Brigade Working Party of 200 O.R again found. Draft fitted with Box Respirators & tested in gas chambers.	

1875 Wt. W593/826 1,000,000 4/15 J.B.C. & A. A.D.S.S./Forms/C. 2118.

Instructions regarding War Diaries and Intelligence Summaries are contained in F. S. Regs., Part II. and the Staff Manual respectively. Title Pages will be prepared in manuscript.

WAR DIARY
or
INTELLIGENCE SUMMARY
(Erase heading not required.)

Army Form C. 2118

8th Battn The Rifle Brigade

Place	Date 1916	Hour	Summary of Events and Information	Remarks and references to Appendices
GRAND RULLECOURT	Dec 14		2/Lt P B REID joined Battalion from Base. Draft of 16 other ranks arrived and taken on strength including a C.Q.M. Sgt.	
BEAUMETZ	15		Battalion marched to BEAUMETZ. Three men only falling out. Billeted here for the night, relieving part of the 6th Bn East Surrey Regt. Billets very poor.	
WAILLY	16		Battalion relieved the 6th Bn Royal West Kent Regt. in left sub sector of 'F' sector. Quiet relief completed by 1.20 pm. Distribution 'B' Coy on the right - 'A' Coy centre - 'D' Coy left - 'C' Coy in Reserve. 2/Lt H.K Kines returns to transport camp for course of Musketry assembling 17th inst. Very quiet day and night. Two shells near Headquarters about midnight. One Rifleman wounded	
–	17		Quiet day. One Rfn killed by comrade. Working parties supplied by Battn in Brigade Reserve (7th Bn Rifle Bde) but rather hung up owing to difficulty in obtaining R.E. material. Battn Canteen opened at 'SOMERSET HOUSE'	
–	18		Fine day - cold. Enemy artillery rather more active. Two Rfn wounded accidentally. Rum applied for in the front line, but the decision is that no rum shall	

1875 Wt. W593/826 1,000,000 4/15 J.B.C. & A. A.D.S.S./Forms/C. 2118.

Instructions regarding War Diaries and Intelligence Summaries are contained in F. S. Regs., Part II. and the Staff Manual respectively. Title Pages will be prepared in manuscript.

WAR DIARY
or
~~INTELLIGENCE~~ SUMMARY
(Erase heading not required.)

8th Bn The Rifle Brigade

Army Form C. 2118

Place	Date 1916	Hour	Summary of Events and Information	Remarks and references to Appendices
WAILLY	Dec 18th		be issued to troops except in rest. German searchlights on our front. Our first experience of them. It is unnaturally quiet in the line. Wire weak and parties out every night. We only average two officers per Company in trenches and the strain on them is very great.	
	19th		Fine-cold. Brig General visits sector. Parties from 7th Bn Rifle Brigade reconnoitre the position. Quiet day generally. At 2 pm our Trench Mortars fired on enemy emplacements hoping to draw his fire. There was no retaliation.	
	20th		Hard Frost. Aeroplanes on both sides very active. 2/LT E.A.F. BATTY rejoins from hospital. Readjustment of line, leaving two platoons of each Company in the front line and two in the support line. All dugouts in the front line are wired in. No man in the front line is allowed in any shelter during the hours of darkness.	
	21st		Fine-cold. Aeroplanes fairly active. Major JENNINGS (Fusiliers) attached for tour of instruction in trenches. Enemy fire two phosphorous bombs in front of Right Company. Usual M.G. bursts at dusk. Generally quiet.	
RIVIERE	22nd		Wet. Battn relieved by 7th Bn Rifle Bde. Three Companies proceeding to billets in RIVIERE. 'D' Coy take over the following keeps - PETIT CHATEAU - WAILLY - PETIT MOULIN - SUGAR FACTORY. Quiet relief completed 1.30 pm. Casualties for tour 1 OR killed. 3 OR wounded. Two other ranks wounded at night returning with transport to BEAUMETZ.	

1875 Wt. W593/826 1,000,000 4/15 J.B.C. & A. A.D.S.S./Forms/C. 2118.

Army Form C. 2118

Instructions regarding War Diaries and Intelligence Summaries are contained in F. S. Regs., Part II. and the Staff Manual respectively. Title Pages will be prepared in manuscript.

WAR DIARY
or
~~INTELLIGENCE SUMMARY~~
(Erase heading not required.)

8th Bn The Rifle Brigade

Place	Date 1916	Hour	Summary of Events and Information	Remarks and references to Appendices
RIVERIE	Dec 23		Wet day. Large working parties to find all men of the three available Companies fully employed. Company in the keeps making knife rests (30 daily). Leave temporarily cancelled. Half rations fuel only available	
–	24th		Bright fine day. Aeroplanes active. Enemy drop few shells near FLANK ST. 2/Lt H.H. HINES returns from Musketry Course. Every man on working parties. One Company on F1 sector was spotted by enemy aeroplane and heavily shelled. Luckily only three casualties	
–	25th		Christmas Day. Fine day. Draft of 8 other ranks arrived. Working parties as usual.	
–	26th		Commanding Officer goes on leave. Great aeroplane activity. Gas suspected on enemys front – extra precautions taken	
–	27th		Fine. Heavy bombardment of enemys front line from 2pm to 4pm. Enemy shell BEAUMETZ.	
–	28th		Battn relieved 7th Bn. Rifle Brigade in F2 sector. Quiet relief completed at 1.50pm. Further bombardment of enemy front line from 2pm to dusk by heavy guns & Field Howitzers. No retaliation. 2/Lt H.B. OAKLEY joins Battalion. Quiet night.	
F. Sector				

1875 Wt. W593/826 1,000,000 4/15 J.B.C. & A. A.D.S.S./Forms/C. 2118.

Army Form C. 2118

Instructions regarding War Diaries and Intelligence Summaries are contained in F. S. Regs., Part II. and the Staff Manual respectively. Title Pages will be prepared in manuscript.

WAR DIARY
or
~~INTELLIGENCE SUMMARY~~
(Erase heading not required.)

8th Battn. The Rifle Brigade.

Place	Date 1916	Hour	Summary of Events and Information	Remarks and references to Appendices
F. 2. Sector	Dec 29th		Wet & Our guns active in the morning. Enemy gives F1 sector a bad half hour at 1pm. 2/Lieuts. G. C. DALGOUTTE and W N SPROSTON join Battalion. Very wet night. Short barrage of our front line on left about 9 pm. The result of two red Very lights fired by us.	
–	30th		Wet day. Trenches on left impassable. Quiet night.	
–	31st		Dull - some rain. Quiet day. More rifle fire than usual at night.	

A C Sheepshanks Major
Cmdg. 8th Battn. The Rifle Brigade

1875 Wt. W593/826 1,000,000 4/15 J.B.C. & A. A.D.S.S./Forms/C. 2118.

8th Bn. THE RIFLE BRIGADE.

ROLL OF OFFICERS. **Dec.31st 1916.**

Lieut.Col.R.C.Maclachlan,D.S.O.	On leave.
Major A.C.Sheepshanks,D.S.O.	A/Commanding Officer.
Major A.L.C.Cavendish	Cmdt.14th Div.School of Musketry.
Capt. G.V.Carey	A/Second in Command.
Capt. K.S.M.Gladstone	Acting D.A.A. & Q.M.G. 14th Div.
Capt. C.N.Thompson	
Capt. C.H.Wenham	Tour of duty in England.
Capt. B.H.Bennett	
Lieut.W.A.Crebbin	Acting Adjutant.
Lieut.J.R.Abbey	L.G.O.
Lieut.D.F.Foxwell	41st Brigade Intelligence Officer.
Lieut.T.A.Baldock	Hospital.
Lieut.E.Poole	Transport Officer.
2/Lieut.W.A.Teakle	
2/Lieut.B.Franklin	
2/Lieut.J.A.Gould	Bombing Officer.
2/Lieut.P.B.Reid	
2/Lieut.H.R.Hartley	
2/Lieut.E.A.F.Batty	
2/Lieut.W.W.Wines	
2/Lieut.F.A.Newell	
2/Lieut.H.B.Oakley	
2/Lieut.P.H.Wooding	
2/Lieut.G.C.Dalgontte	
2/Lieut.W.N.Sproston	
Capt.F.J.Strachan,M.C.(R.A.M.C)	Medical Officer.

A.C.Sheepshanks. Major.
Cmdg. 8th Bn.The Rifle Brigade.

8th Battn. The Rifle Brigade

Casualties December 1916

No.	Rank	Name		Coy	Date	Casualty	Remarks
S7714	Rfn.	Rowe	R	D	16. 12. 16	Wounded	
S14305	"	Price	J	D	17. 12. 16	Killed	Buried R 22 b 9 7 Sheet 51c
S26283	"	Percival	G	C	18. 12. 16	Wounded	Self-inflicted
S11992	A/Cpl.	Shewring	E	D	18. 12. 16	Wounded	Accidentally self-inflicted by Very light
S2676	Rfn.	Price	R	C	22. 12. 16	"	
S10988	"	Baker	G	D	"	"	
S22343	"	Kopinsky	J	C	24-12-16	"	Died 27/12/16 B. Military Cem. AVESNES
S26200	"	Lamb	A	"	"	"	
S7302	"	McArthur	D	"	"	"	
S20939	"	Clench	G	"	26-12-16	"	Self-inflicted
S26509	"	Colonello	N	A	28-12-16	"	
B200682	"	Humphreys	A	D	31-12-16	"	
B200683	"	Throp	A	"	"	"	

A C Sheepshanks Major.
8th Bn. The Rifle Brigade.

4/12

Vol: 20

C O N F I D E N T I A L.

W A R D I A R Y

- of -

8th (S) Bn., THE RIFLE BRIGADE.

From: 1st January, 1917.
To: 31st January, 1917.

Volume ~~XXI~~.

Army Form C. 2118

Instructions regarding War Diaries and Intelligence Summaries are contained in F. S. Regs., Part II. and the Staff Manual respectively. Title Pages will be prepared in manuscript.

WAR DIARY
or
INTELLIGENCE SUMMARY
(Erase heading not required.)

Volume 21.
8th R.B.

Place	Date	Hour	Summary of Events and Information	Remarks and references to Appendices
Trenches. R 28 51c.	January 1		Fine but dull. Quiet day. 2/Lt. F W C REED joined.	
	2.		Fine. Conversation between two German Officers picked up "Something on tonight, are you coming up?" Due precautions taken, but nothing unusual occurred during the night.	
	3		Relieved by 7th Bn Rifle Brigade & proceed to rest in billets in BEAUMETZ. Quiet relief. 2 Officers from 9th DIV attached - Capt. J. B LORIMER & Lieut T.D.F. MacNEAL. Dull & drizzly.	
BEAUMETZ	4.		Fine. Major A.C. SHEEPSHANKS D.S.O. & servant left for Senior Officers Course in England. Capt. G V. CAREY temporarily in Command. Between 3.30 & 4.15 p.m. ~~8~~ 9 shells from what is believed to be an 11" naval gun fell in the village - all pitching within 200 yards of Bn. H.Q. - 2 casualties, one slightly scratched & one man 'shell shock'!	
	5.		Fine. Battalion contributes 38 N.C.O's & men to the Tanks. 2 Officers & 129 O.R. on working parties for 7th Bn Rifle Bde & 7th Kings R.R.C. 2/Lt S.R EVANS joined. Quiet day.	
	6.		Fine, after heavy rain during night. Another quiet day. 43rd Inf. Bde co-operated with 9th DIV. in carrying out a considerable raid on our left. 2 Officers & 108 O.R. for 7th Bn Rifle Bde & 7th Bn Kings R.R. Corps fatigues during the night.	
	7.		Fine. Voluntary Church Services. 2/Lt Evans goes to SIMENCOURT to ascertain available billeting accommodation, with a view to BEAUMETZ being evacuated by the resting battalion.	

1875 Wt. W593/826 1,000,000 4/15 J.B.C. & A. A.D.S.S./Forms/C. 2118.

Instructions regarding War Diaries and Intelligence Summaries are contained in F. S. Regs., Part II. and the Staff Manual respectively. Title Pages will be prepared in manuscript.

WAR DIARY
or
INTELLIGENCE SUMMARY
(Erase heading not required.)

Army Form C. 2118

Volume 21
8th R B

Place	Date	Hour	Summary of Events and Information	Remarks and references to Appendices
BEAUMETZ	8		Cold, some showers. Very quiet day. Transferred to VII Corps.	
	9		Wet, cold day. Relieve 7th R B in trenches – quiet relief. Disposition of Coys – right to left – B, C, D, A in reserve.	
Trenches R 23 (51c)	10.		Fine & cold. Some Lewis Gun activity during the night. German plane flew very low over the Village line & got back without being effectively fired at. Lt Col. R. C. Maclachlan returns from leave.	
	11.		Fine & cold, with some snow. 2/Lt. G. H. Murray & 2/Lt. A. F. MacGillivray attached for duty. Lt-Col. R. C. Maclachlan D.S.O. promoted Brigadier General to command 112th Inf. Brigade. Quiet day.	
	12.		Showery. Lt Col R. C. Maclachlan D.S.O. relinquishes command of the Batt. & leaves to take up command of 112th I. B. Capt. G. V. Carey assumes command of the Batt. Capt C. H. Wenham rejoins from three months tour of duty in England.	
	13.		Cold & wet. Very quiet day.	
	14.		Fine. 2/Lt. D Meacock joins.	
	15.		Dull. Relieved by 7th R B without incident. Batt goes into Brigade Reserve at RIVIERE.	
RIVIERE	16.		Dull. Large working parties supplied of about 300 men.	
	17.		Heavy fall of snow during the night. Germans drop 8 shells near Chateau Grosville – 2 duds! Large working parties again found.	

1875 Wt. W593/826 1,000,000 4/15 J.B.C. & A. A.D.S.S./Forms/C. 2118.

Instructions regarding War Diaries and Intelligence Summaries are contained in F. S. Regs., Part II. and the Staff Manual respectively. Title Pages will be prepared in manuscript.

WAR DIARY
or
INTELLIGENCE SUMMARY
(Erase heading not required.)

Army Form C. 2118

Place	Date	Hour	Summary of Events and Information	Remarks and references to Appendices
Trenches R 23 (51c)	25		Fine with continued frost. Enemy again show some T.M. activity, doing a certain amount of damage to front & support line.	
	26		Fine & very frosty. Enemy trench Mortaring began in the morning & was very active between 2 & 6 p.m. Trenches badly knocked in in places. 2/Lt M A Young, Sgt Ritson & 2 men of C Coy buried – Sgt Ritson killed, but the other three got out without injury. 13 Men of A Coy imprisoned in a dugout, but were safely got out, largely owing to fine work on the part of Bull Cpl Dunn J. Artillery retaliation was not very effective. Precautions were taken to meet a possible hostile raid, but the night passed quietly	
	27		Fine & keen frost. A few 90 pounder T.M.s fell between 9 & 10 a.m., wounding 2 men, but the relief of the Batt by the 7th R.B. passed quietly. One of our aeroplanes carried out a reconnaissance flying very low, supported by a barrage on the enemy's front line from our 18 pounders. The Batt less B Coy (who remain in Reserve to 7th R.B) proceed to billets in SIMENCOURT.	
SIMENCOURT	28		Fine with keen frost. Comdg Officer inspects the last draft.	
	29		Fine & frosty. Draft test their box respirators in gas. Warning order received of relief by 49th DIV commencing on the 1st prox, also that 'B' Coy would rejoin on the 30th.	

Instructions regarding War Diaries and Intelligence Summaries are contained in F. S. Regs., Part II. and the Staff Manual respectively. Title Pages will be prepared in manuscript.

WAR DIARY
or
INTELLIGENCE SUMMARY
(Erase heading not required.)

Army Form C. 2118

Place	Date	Hour	Summary of Events and Information	Remarks and references to Appendices
SIMENCOURT	30		Cold & dull, some snow. 'B' Coy return from Reserve Line to billets in SIMENCOURT.	
	31		Dull with some snow. Orders received that the battalion has to find a working party of 8 officers & 450 O.R. at BERNEVILLE. Capt CH WENHAM appointed to command this Detachment – A, C, D Coys & 23 new draft from B Coy. Remainder of Batt to proceed to GRAND RULLECOURT on the 1st.	

Attached –
1. List of Casualties
2. List of Officers

[signature] Capt.
Comdg. 8th Batt Rifle Bde

1875 Wt. W593/826 1,000,000 4/15 J.B.C. & A. A.D.S.S./Forms/C. 2118.

8th Battn. The Rifle Brigade

Casualties **January 1917**

No	Rank & Name		Coy	Date	Casualty
S 25592	Rfn. Skeggs	A	A	2. 1. 17	Died natural causes
S 26533	" Homden	G	B	4. 1. 17	Wounded
Z 1283	Sgt. Every	W	C	21. 1. 17	Killed in Action
S 7707	" Ritson	A	C	26. 1. 17	Killed in Action
S 28566	Rfn. Hinskill	J	C	27. 1. 17	Wounded
S 23953	" Knibbs	H	C	27. 1. 17	Wounded
S 26227	" Cose	J	B	28. 1. 17	Wounded (Self-Inf.)
S 5394	" Kemp	G	D	27. 1. 17	Wounded
	2/Lt. M.A. Young			26. 1. 17	Wounded

[illegible] Captn.
Cmdg. 8th Bn. Rifle Brigade

8th Battn. The Rifle Brigade

List of Officers Serving January 31st - 17.

Major	A. E. Sheepshanks D.S.O	Course, Aldershot
"	A. L. C Cavendish	Divnl Musketry School
Capt.	G. V. Carey	A/ Commanding Off
"	K. S. M. Gladstone	A/D.A.A. & Q.M.G. 14th DIV.
"	C. N. Thompson	A/ 2nd in Cmd.
"	C. H. Henham	O.C D. Coy
"	B. H. Bennett	O.C C. Coy
Lieut.	H. A. Crebbin	A/Adjutant
"	T. R. Abbey	Lewis Gun Officer
"	D. F. Foxwell	Bde Intelligence Off.
"	T. A. Baldock	Hospital
"	E. Poole	Transport Officer
2/Lt.	H. A. Teakle	
"	B. Franklin	O.C A. Coy
"	J. A. Gould	
"	P. B. Reid	
"	H. R. Hartley	Town Major, Riviere
"	E. A. F. Batty	
"	H. H. Hines	
"	A. F. Newell	
"	D. Meacock	
"	H. B. Oakley	
"	S. R. Evans	
"	M. H. House	

(Contd)

2/Lieut. O. F. Savege
" W. G. Stanton
" P. H. Hooding
" J. Greig
" Y. B. Nicol
" G. C. Dalgoutte
" H. N. Sproston
" F. C. H. Reed

Attached :-

Capt. F. T. Strachan M.C. — R.A.M.C.

Capt. J. B. Lorimer — 5th Camerons
(Town Major - Beaudricourt)

Lieut. T. D. F. Macneal — Gordon Highlanders
(from att. 8th Black Watch)

2/Lieut. G. H. Murray — 5th Camerons
" A. F. MacGillivray — " —

[illegible] Capt.
Cmdg 8th Bn Rifle Brigade

Vol 21

C O N F I D E N T I A L.

W A R D I A R Y

- of -

8th (S) Bn., T H E R I F L E B R I G A D E.

From: 1st February, 1917.
To: 28th February, 1917.

Volume XXII.

Instructions regarding War Diaries and Intelligence Summaries are contained in F. S. Regs., Part II. and the Staff Manual respectively. Title Pages will be prepared in manuscript.

WAR DIARY
or
INTELLIGENCE SUMMARY
(Erase heading not required.)

Volume 22

Army Form C. 2118

Place	Date	Hour	Summary of Events and Information	Remarks and references to Appendices
SIMENCOURT	Feb 1st		Fine, frosty day. The battalion, less A & D Coys & most of C Coy, move to GRAND RULLECOURT, leaving at Noon & arriving at 3.40pm. Most of our old billets having been occupied by the DIV. DEPOT BATTALION, it became clear that there would not be room for the whole battalion in the village. The detachment under Capt C.H. Wenham left SIMENCOURT for BERNEVILLE & DAINVILLE at 1.0pm. JRPB.	
GRAND RULLECOURT	2.		Fine & cold. Day spent in inspections etc. JRPB.	
	3.		Sunny & frosty. Both Battalion & Detachment parade to hear farewell message from Brig Gen. R.C. Maclachlan DSO. & to send him their reply. JRPB.	
	4.		Continued sun & frost. Notice received that the Detachments at BERNEVILLE & DAINVILLE will be relieved on the 5th & 6th insts. Decided to billet two of the Coys included in the Detachment at SOMBRIN. JRPB.	
	5.		Still cold & frosty. D Coy rejoin from BERNEVILLE & take over billets at SOMBRIN. B411 Cpl. Dunn J. awarded Military Medal for gallantry during enemy trench mortar bombardment in F Sector on Jan. 26th. B Coy inspected on parade by Comdg Officer. JRPB.	
	6		A & C Coys rejoin from DAINVILLE – A Coy taking over billets in SOMBRIN, C Coy in GRAND RULLECOURT. Details received of 2 further working parties to be supplied in neighbourhood of SAULTY. Scotch officers rejoin their Regiments. JRPB.	

1875 Wt. W593/826 1,000,000 4/15 J.B.C. & A. A.D.S.S./Forms/C. 2118.

Instructions regarding War Diaries and Intelligence Summaries are contained in F. S. Regs., Part II. and the Staff Manual respectively. Title Pages will be prepared in manuscript.

WAR DIARY
or
INTELLIGENCE SUMMARY
(Erase heading not required.)

Volume 22

Army Form C. 2118

Place	Date	Hour	Summary of Events and Information	Remarks and references to Appendices
GRAND RULLECOURT	7		Fine & frosty. Coy returned from working parties occupied by inspections etc. RPB	
	8		Fine, with continued frost. B Coy & part of C Coy proceed to GOBREMETZ & COUTURELLE on working parties, under Command of 2/Lt A F Newell. Orders received that A & D Coys are to transfer to billets in GRAND RULLECOURT vacated by 6th Batt K.R.R.C., owing to return of working parties of 7th Batt R B & 7th Batt K.R.R.C. H Q Coy & C Coy inspected by Medical Officer. RPB.	
	9		Fine & frosty. A & D take over billets in GRAND RULLECOURT. C Coy inspected on parade by Comdg Officer. RPB.	
	10		Fine & frosty. Orders received for still another working party to be provided at BERNEVILLE. D Coy inspected on parade by Comdg Officer. A & D Coys inspected by Medical Officer. RPB.	
	11.		Continued fine weather & frost. Voluntary Services for C of E, and parade services for other denominations. Further rearrangement of billets made to make room for another Coy of the Depot Battalion. D Coy, less Lewis Gun teams, proceeds to BERNEVILLE to supply working party. Disposition of Batt is now as follows – Head Quarters, A Coy, Details } GRAND RULLECOURT; C Coy – LUCHEUX, MONDICOURT, GOBREMETZ; B Coy – GOBREMETZ, COUTURELLE; D Coy – BERNEVILLE 60 O.R. attached to Depot Btn for course of instruction & 2/Lt H R Hartley, Sergts Henley & Rideout & Cpl Cook as instructors. Slight thaw during the day, followed by keen frost at night. RPB.	

1875 Wt. W593/826 1,000,000 4/15 J.B.C. & A. A.D.S.S./Forms/C. 2118.

Instructions regarding War Diaries and Intelligence Summaries are contained in F. S. Regs., Part II. and the Staff Manual respectively. Title Pages will be prepared in manuscript.

WAR DIARY
or
INTELLIGENCE SUMMARY
(Erase heading not required.)

Volume 22

Army Form C. 2118

Place	Date	Hour	Summary of Events and Information	Remarks and references to Appendices
GRAND RULLECOURT.	12.		Dull, with signs of thaw during afternoon. A Coy inspected on parade by Comdg Officer. Brigade Anti Gas N.C.O. inspects appliances of H.Q.rs. JRPB.	
	13		Dull & cold. H.Q. Coy inspected on parade by Comdg Officer. A Coys anti gas appliances inspected by Brigade Gas NCO. JRPB.	
	14		Fine & cold. 10 extra men sent to join working party at BERNEVILLE. JRPB.	
	15		Fine, with thaw during afternoon JRPB.	
	16		Dull wet afternoon. 2/Lt. W.H. BLADES joins on appointment. Draft of 10 O.R. arrive from Base – 6 old hands. Comdg Officer attends Conference at Brigade H.Q. Scheme of reorganisation of Battalions received JRPB.	
	17		Dull & misty. Brigade operations at O.5 central (51c) – A Coy represent the battalion in the attack. Comdg Officer inspects draft. JRPB.	
	18		Dull. Parade Services for C of E. Wesleyans etc & R.C. Further party of 50 O.R. sent to BERNEVILLE to join working party there – supplied by A Coy. Acting Rank authorised – Capt G.V. CAREY – Lt Col. Capt C.H. THOMPSON – Major. 2/Lt A.E. NEWELL – Captain JRPB.	

1875 Wt. W593/826 1,000,000 4/15 J.B.C. & A. A.D.S.S./Forms/C. 2118.

Instructions regarding War Diaries and Intelligence Summaries are contained in F. S. Regs., Part II. and the Staff Manual respectively. Title Pages will be prepared in manuscript.

WAR DIARY
or
INTELLIGENCE SUMMARY
(Erase heading not required.)

Army Form C. 2118

Volume 22

Place	Date	Hour	Summary of Events and Information	Remarks and references to Appendices
GRAND RULLECOURT	19		Dull Major D.E. PRIDEAUX-BRUNE assumes temp. Command of the Battalion. Warning order received of move to ARRAS on working party. JRPB.	
	20		Wet day. Move to ARRAS cancelled. Comdg Officer visits the various detachments. Adjt attends lecture at ARRAS on "Procedure at F.G.C.M" given by Third Army Court Martial Officer. 'A' Coy, Hd 2rs & Details now billets at SOMBRIN. JRPB.	
	21		Dull & damp 2/Lt. B. Franklin to be Acting Capt 20.12.16 JRPB.	
	22		Dull & wet. Quiet day JRPB.	
	23		Dull. Coy Officers come to H.Q. for conference. JRPB.	
	24		Fine. Nothing of interest to report. JRPB.	
	25		Fine Parade Services for C of E, Wesleyans & R.C. Lieut. T.A. BALDOCK rejoins from hospital, with draft of 11 O.R. Comdg Officer attends Conference at Bde. H.Q. Aeroplanes active. JRPB.	

1875 Wt. W593/826 1,000,000 4/15 J.B.C. & A. A.D.S.S./Forms/C. 2118.

Instructions regarding War Diaries and Intelligence Summaries are contained in F. S. Regs., Part II. and the Staff Manual respectively. Title Pages will be prepared in manuscript.

WAR DIARY
or
INTELLIGENCE SUMMARY
(Erase heading not required.)

Volume 22.

Army Form C. 2118

Place	Date	Hour	Summary of Events and Information	Remarks and references to Appendices
GRAND RULLECOURT	26.		Fine. Detachment at BERNEVILLE not required for work after this date, but will remain there until further orders. JEPB.	
	27		Fine. Draft inspected by Medical Officer. JEPB.	
	28		Orders received that Detachment at BERNEVILLE (D Coy & portion of A Coy) will return to GRAND RULLECOURT on March 1st.	
			Dull day. Capt B H Bennett & 2/Lt W H Teakle reconnoitre 42nd Bde Front. JEPB	
			Casualties during the month - NIL	
			List of Officers attached.	
			Strength 35 Officers 1027 O.R. JEPB	
			Owing to the fact that the battalion has been split up so during the month on working parties, practically nothing has been possible in the way of training & reorganisation on the new lines laid down. J. P. Bass-Bennett Major Comdg 8th Btn Rifle Bde	

1875 Wt. W593/826 1,000,000 4/15 J.B.C. & A. A.D.S.S./Forms/C. 2118.

Copy.

Please tell all ranks how sorry I was to have no opportunity of wishing them "Good Bye".

I am intensely proud of having commanded for so long and know that the splendid spirit and esprit de corps of the old 8th Battalion is as strong as ever in spite of constant fighting and incessant losses.

I believe the love of our Regiment & of our Battalion is the keynote of all success & nothing can ever take its place.

I wish everyone the best of luck.

8th Bn. THE RIFLE BRIGADE.

Roll of Officers.

Major D.E.Prideaux-Brune	Commanding Officer.
Major A.C.Sheepshanks D.S.O.	Senior Officers' Course, England.
Major A.L.C.Cavendish	O.C.14th Div. Musketry School
Capt. G.V.Carey	On Leave.
Capt. K.S.M.Gladstone	A/Staff Captain, 43rd Brigade
Capt. C.N.Thompson	On Leave.
Capt. C.H.Wenham	Third Army Infantry School Course
Lieut.(A/Capt.) B.H.Bennett	A/2nd in Command.
Lieut. W.A.Crebbin	Acting Adjutant.
Lieut. J.R.Abbey	Lewis Gun Officer.
Lieut. D.F.Foxwell	41st Brigade Intelligence Officer
Lieut. T.A.Baldock	
Lieut. E.Poole	Transport Officer.
2/Lieut.W.A.Teakle	
2/Lieut.(A/Capt.)B.Franklin	
2/Lieut.J.A.Gould	Battn. Bombing Officer.
2/Lieut.P.B.Reid	
2/Lieut.H.R.Hartley	14th Div. Depot Battalion.
2/Lieut.E.A.F.Batty	
2/Lieut.W.W.Wines	
2/Lieut.(A/Capt.) A.F.Newell	
2/Lieut.D.Meacock	
2/Lieut.H.B.Oakley	
2/Lieut.S.R.Evans	
2/Lieut.M.H.House	
2/Lieut.O.F.Savege	
2/Lieut.W.G.Hanton	
2/Lieut.P.H.Wooding	Battn. Signalling Officer.
2/Lieut.J.Greig	
2/Lieut.V.B.Nicol	
2/Lieut.G.C.Dalgoutte	
2/Lieut.W.N.Sproston	VII Corps Lewis Gun Course.
2/Lieut.F.W.C.Reed	
2/Lieut.W.H.Blades	

Capt. R.N.Hunter (R.A.M.C.) Attd.

W.A.Crebbin Lt & A/Adj
for Major
Comdg.8th.Btn.The Rifle Brigade.

28-2-17.

C O N F I D E N T I A L.

W A R D I A R Y

- of -

8th (S) Bn., T H E R I F L E B R I G A D E.

From: 1st March, 1917.
To: 31st March, 1917.

VOLUME XXIII.

Instructions regarding War Diaries and Intelligence Summaries are contained in F. S. Regs., Part II. and the Staff Manual respectively. Title Pages will be prepared in manuscript.

WAR DIARY
or
INTELLIGENCE SUMMARY
(Erase heading not required.)

Volume 23

Army Form C. 2118

Place	Date	Hour	Summary of Events and Information	Remarks and references to Appendices
GRAND RULLECOURT	March 1.		Fine. BERNEVILLE detachment (D Coy & portion of A Coy) rejoin & take over billets in GRAND RULLECOURT. JSPB	
	2.		Fine & cold. D Coy inspected by the Medical Officer. Party of 37, provided by A Coy, leave for SAULTY for work with 7th Bn K.R.R.C. JSPB	
	3.		Fine. Working party from COUTURELLE rejoin the battalion in GRAND RULLECOURT. Conference of OC Coys at Bn H.Q. JSPB	
	4.		Fine & cold. Parade Services for Roman Catholics & Wesleyans. No C of E service owing to medical inspection by the A.D.M.S. Working party from COUTURELLE isolated owing to a case of Mumps. JSPB	
	5.		Fall of snow during the night. Working party of 100 O.R. found by A Coy for trench digging on the AVESNES Road. JSPB	
	6.		Fine & cold. Similar working party again provided. Route march for remainder of Bn - via AVESNES, LIENCOURT. JSPB	
	7.		Fine & cold. Working party as for two previous days. Lecture by Bde Gas N.C.O. to D Coy & H.Q. JSPB	

1875 Wt. W593/826 1,000,000 4/15 J.B.C. & A. A.D.S.S./Forms/C. 2118.

Instructions regarding War Diaries and Intelligence Summaries are contained in F. S. Regs., Part II. and the Staff Manual respectively. Title Pages will be prepared in manuscript.

WAR DIARY
or
INTELLIGENCE SUMMARY
(Erase heading not required.)

Volume 23

Army Form C. 2118

Place	Date	Hour	Summary of Events and Information	Remarks and references to Appendices
GRAND RULLECOURT	8		More snow early, afterwards fine & cold. Working party as above completes work on the trench system. JRPB	
	9		Fine early, snow in the afternoon. Route march – SUS ST LEGER – ESTREE WAMIN – LE CAUROY – LIENCOURT. JRPB	
	10.		Dull & very cold. A & D Coys practise "attack" & artillery formations on the trenches between GRAND RULLECOURT & AVESNES. Brig Gen R C Maclachlan DSO pays a surprise visit to the Btn. during the afternoon. JRPB	
	11.		Fine & warm. Parade services for C of E. RCs & Wesleyans. Personnel from the Dept Btn rejoin. JRPB	
	12.		Fine after heavy downpour of rain during the night. Cmdg Officer inspects personnel from Dept Btn. JRPB	
	13.		Dull. Btn started on a short course of musketry on improvised ranges. Warning order received of possible move to FOSSEUX & BARLY en route for DAINVILLE to relieve 7th Btn R.B. at work. C Coy return to GRAND RULLECOURT from MONCHIET & LUCHEUX JRPB	

Instructions regarding War Diaries and Intelligence Summaries are contained in F. S. Regs., Part II. and the Staff Manual respectively. Title Pages will be prepared in manuscript.

WAR DIARY
or
INTELLIGENCE SUMMARY
(Erase heading not required.)

Volume 23

Army Form C. 2118

Place	Date	Hour	Summary of Events and Information	Remarks and references to Appendices
GRAND ROLLECOURT	14.		Wet. A. C & D Coys continue musketry. Notice received that Major CAVENDISH, A.L.C. is posted to 12th Bn. R.B.	
			B Coy ordered at short notice to return to GRAND RULLECOURT from GOMBREMETZ & 37 of A Coy from SAULTY – they rejoin at 12.30 am 15th. JRPB	
	15.		Dull & cold. The whole Bn is now concentrated in the same place for the first time since leaving the forward area on Feb 1st.	
			C & D Coys practice artillery formations & the assault on the AVESNES Rd trenches. A Coy at musketry.	
			Orders issued for move to GOUY on 16th. JRPB.	
	16		Fine & mild. Bn moves to GOUY, leaving GRAND RULLECOURT 9.45 am, arriving 1.45 p.m. Transport proceed to BERNEVILLE. Roads very heavy & great congestion of traffic in places.	
			One Coy & H.Q. in huts, remainder of Bn in Billets. JRPB.	
GOUY	17		Fine spring day. Telegram of sympathy sent to H.R.H. Duke of Connaught on the death of the Duchess of Connaught.	
			Coys at disposal of O.C. Coys for close order drill. JRPB.	

1875 Wt. W593/826 1,000,000 4/15 J.B.C. & A. A.D.S.S./Forms/C. 2118.

Instructions regarding War Diaries and Intelligence Summaries are contained in F. S. Regs., Part II. and the Staff Manual respectively. Title Pages will be prepared in manuscript.

WAR DIARY
or
INTELLIGENCE SUMMARY
(Erase heading not required.)

Volume 23

Army Form C. 2118

Place	Date	Hour	Summary of Events and Information	Remarks and references to Appendices
GOUY	18		Fine & warm. Bn moves to DAINVILLE via WANQUETIN & WARLUS, proceeding by Companies GOUY to WARLUS, and by platoons WARLUS to DAINVILLE. Transport remain at BERNEVILLE. Move started at 1-0pm & last party arrived at DAINVILLE at 5.30pm – thus releasing the 7th Bn R.B. who had been working at DAINVILLE for the last fortnight. During the move, news received that Germans were retiring on this front – the Bn was therefore ordered on arrival to "stand to" & be ready to move off at ½ hour's notice. Coy alarm posts & dumps arranged for emergency. 2/Lt N.F.H. Mather rejoins. JRPB.	
DAINVILLE	19		The night passed quietly, though our guns were very active. Fine morning, with wind & rain in the afternoon. Draft of 14 O.R. arrive – 12 of whom have been with the Bn before. Two working parties of 40 & 100 respectively found by D Coy for work in ARRAS from 7.0 pm. JRPB.	

1875 Wt. W593/826 1,000,000 4/15 J.B.C. & A. A.D.S.S./Forms/C. 2118.

Instructions regarding War Diaries and Intelligence Summaries are contained in F. S. Regs., Part II. and the Staff Manual respectively. Title Pages will be prepared in manuscript.

Army Form C. 2118

Volume 23

WAR DIARY
or
INTELLIGENCE SUMMARY
(Erase heading not required.)

Place	Date	Hour	Summary of Events and Information	Remarks and references to Appendices
DAINVILLE	20		Wet. Comdg Officer inspects draft. Battalion released from "Standto". JRPB.	
	21		Dull & wet. Working parties up to 260 found for unloading reserve rations at ARRAS & work on the BEAURAINS – RONVILLE Road. Lieut H.R. Adair rejoins. JRPB.	
	22		Cold with snow showers. Warning order received during the afternoon for move to ARRAS. Working parties up to 200 found for work on BEAURAINS – RONVILLE road & for burying cable. Battalion moves off from DAINVILLE to billets in ARRAS, leaving DAINVILLE by platoons commencing at 6.0 p.m. Orders received that the Brigade will relieve the 22nd & 48th Brigades in H Sector on the 24th – this battalion to take over the left sector. JRPB.	
ARRAS	23.		Fine & cold. Comdg. Officer & Second in Command reconnoitre trenches during the afternoon. Capt C.H. WENHAM takes over command of A Coy, and Lieut H.R ADAIR takes over D Coy. JRPB.	
	24		Fine clear day. Aeroplanes very active. Battalion relieves 9th Rif Bde in H2 Sector starting at 6.0 p.m. Disposition of Companies:– 'C' right front, 'D' left front, 'B' Supports, 'A' Reserve, 'C' & 'D' Coys occupying the CORDITE LINE & old German second & first lines behind it; 'B' Coy occupying old British Support & Front Line – 'A' Coy the old 'C' Line. R.S.M. with cookers etc quartered at RONVILLE. Relief passed quietly, but from about 1.0 am to dawn D Coy were shelled heavily. Summer Time adopted at 11.0 p.m. JRPB.	

1875 Wt. W593/826 1,000,000 4/15 J.B.C. & A. A.D.S.S./Forms/C. 2118.

Instructions regarding War Diaries and Intelligence Summaries are contained in F. S. Regs., Part II. and the Staff Manual respectively. Title Pages will be prepared in manuscript.

WAR DIARY
or
INTELLIGENCE SUMMARY
(Erase heading not required.)

Army Form C. 2118

Volume 23

Place	Date	Hour	Summary of Events and Information	Remarks and references to Appendices
Trenches G35.d.3.6 51b 3W1.	25.		Fine Sunny day. Intermittent shelling of the line, but without serious results. Heavy shelling of RONVILLE caused much annoyance, but no casualties in our party. After 9.0 p.m. frequent bursts of fire on SUNKEN ROAD from enemy field guns, probably in advanced night positions, hamper the work of carrying parties. D Coy on the left front also heavily shelled & prevented from working on their line. A patrol under 2/Lt S.R. EVANS which went out to investigate TELEGRAPH HILL was engaged by machine gun fire from several points — it stayed out for three hours & reported TELEGRAPH HILL occupied by the enemy. DRPB.	NEUVILLE VITASSE Map.
	26.		Dull & showery, improving later. Rain in the night & early morning reduced trenches to very bad state. Fairly quiet day. Arrangements made for cooking at RONVILLE to be done underground, and for cookers to return at night to Transport at BERNEVILLE. Intermittent shelling again after 9.0 p.m, but no casualties during the night. DRPB.	
	27		Showery. Intermittent shelling of front line Coys. which died down during the afternoon & did not reopen until about 11.0 p.m — after that hour D Coy were shelled heavily left of CORDITE TRENCH & left of GALWAY. C Coy did a good deal of work during the night, joining up with the 8th KRRC on the right of CORDITE TRENCH. DRPB.	
	28		Fine. Quieter day than usual. Battalion relieved by 7th R.B. from 7.0 p.m. onwards. Relief took some time, but there were no casualties. The whole Battalion (except part of H.Q.) proceeded to CAVES at RONVILLE — H.Q. at the FACTORY G35.a.00.70. Casualties for tour — 3 OR Killed 4 Wounded (1 at duty) DRPB.	

Instructions regarding War Diaries and Intelligence Summaries are contained in F. S. Regs., Part II. and the Staff Manual respectively. Title Pages will be prepared in manuscript.

WAR DIARY
or
INTELLIGENCE SUMMARY
(Erase heading not required.)

Volume 23

Army Form C. 2118

Place	Date	Hour	Summary of Events and Information	Remarks and references to Appendices
RONVILLE CAVES.	29.		Wet. Working parties up to 400 provided for work on various parts of the line and communications throughout the day & night. H.Q. at the FACTORY heavily shelled in the early hours of the morning, necessitating the removal of the Batt. Office to the CAVES. JSPR.	
	30		Fine. Working parties provided on a similar scale to the previous day. Signallers give a concert in the CAVES. JSPR.	
	31.		Fine. Comdg Officer attends Conference at Brigade. Working parties as for two previous days. JSPR.	
			Total Strength 37 Officers 1010 O.R.	
			Enclosed –	
			1. List of Casualties.	
			2. List of Officers	
			D. Prideaux-Brune Major Comdg 8th Battn Rifle Bde	

8th Bn The Rifle Brigade

Effective Strength, Officers — March 31st 1917

Major D. E. Prideaux-Brune	Commanding
Major A. C. Sheepshanks D.S.O.	Course, England
Capt. (A/Major) G. Y. Carey	A/Second in Command
Capt. K. S. H. Gladstone	14th Divnl Head Qrs.
Capt. C. N. Thompson	O. C. B Co.
Capt. C. H. Kenham	O. C. A Co.
Lieut. (A/Capt.) B. H. Bennett	O. C. C Co.
Lieut. W. A. Crebbin	A/Adjutant
Lieut. H. R. Adair	O. C. D. Co.
Lieut. J. R. Abbey	Lewis Gun Officer
Lieut. D. F. Foxwell	Bde. Intelligence Officer
Lieut. T. A. Baldock	
Lieut. E. Poole	Transport Officer
2/Lt. W. A. Teakle	On leave
2/Lt. N. F. H. Mather	
2/Lt. B. Franklin	
2/Lt. J. A. Gould	Bombing Officer
2/Lt. H. R. Hartley	
2/Lt. E. A. F. Batty	Bn. Intelligence Officer
2/Lt. H. W. Wines	
2/Lt. A. F. Newell	Third Army School
2/Lt. D. Meacock	
2/Lt. H B Oakley	

(contd)

2/Lieut. S. R. Evans
2/Lieut. H. H. House
2/Lieut. O. J. Savege
2/Lieut. H. G. Hanton
2/Lieut. P. H. Wooding Signal Officer
2/Lieut. G. H. Bloomer
2/Lieut. J. Greig
2/Lieut. V. B. Nicol
2/Lieut. P. B. Reid
2/Lieut. G. C. Dalgoutté
2/Lieut. H. K. Sproston Sick
2/Lieut. F. H. C. Reed
2/Lieut. H. H. Blades.

attached:- Capt. R. J. Hunter R.A.M.C.

[signature]
Lt & A/Adjt
for OC 8th Bn Rifle Brigade

8th Bn. The Rifle Brigade

Casualties for March 1917.

No	Rank & Name	Coy	Date	Casualty	Remarks.
S17435	Rfn. Holbrook	G	D	25. 3. 17	Killed	Buried at M. 4 b 5. 2 Sheet 51b SW.1 Neuville Vitasse
S 6230	" Ryan	J	D	"	"	
S 17480	" Hogan	J	D	28. 3. 17	"	
S 1888	a/Cpl. Soar	J	D	25. 3. 17	Wounded	
S 26061	Rfn. Smith	A	D	"	"	
B 2225	L/Cpl. Readbeater	J	D	"	"	
B 92	Sgt. Clark	G	A	"	"	At duty.

[illegible]
Lieut- & A/Adjt
for O.C. 8th Bn. The Rifle Brigade

31/3/17

SECRET.

Vol 23

WAR DIARY

OF

8th Bn. RIFLE BRIGADE

From April 1st, 1917 to April 30th, 1917.

VOLUME 24.

Instructions regarding War Diaries and Intelligence Summaries are contained in F. S. Regs., Part II. and the Staff Manual respectively. Title Pages will be prepared in manuscript.

WAR DIARY
or
INTELLIGENCE SUMMARY
(Erase heading not required.)

Volume 24

Army Form C. 2118

Place	Date	Hour	Summary of Events and Information	Remarks and references to Appendices
RONVILLE CAVES (ARRAS)	1		Fine. Battalion relieves 7th R.B. in H 2 Sector.	
			With a view to future operations, the following personnel are left out of the line:—	
			5 Officers 120 O.R. (as laid down in "Training of Divisions for offensive action," para XXX)	
			1 - 31 O.R. — additional men it is considered advisable to leave out. These proceed to LE SOUICH later.	
			4 - 24 O.R. remain at Rear Transport Camp, BERNEVILLE	
			1 - 65 O.R. at Advanced Transport Camp at the CITADEL, ARRAS.	
			2/Lt E.A.F. Batty & 2/Lt S.R. Evans go out on patrol & get into touch with the enemy. [initials]	
Trenches G35 d 3.6 5.1 b.	2		Fine morning, with snow in the afternoon. Very quiet day, enemy guns inactive. Two enemy balloons brought down in flames. [initials]	
	3.		Fine. Great activity by British aeroplanes. One brought down by direct hit from AA gun. Relieved by 5th Bn Oxford & Bucks L.I. Relief complete by 11.30 pm. Batt. billeted in ARRAS. [initials]	
ARRAS	4		Dull. Bombardment of enemy lines N & S of the SCARPE throughout the day. Little retaliation on ARRAS. Fatigue party of 2/Lt F.W.C. Reed & 15 men found for R.G.A. at ACHICOURT. Major A.C. Sheepshanks rejoins from England. [initials]	

1875 Wt. W593/826 1,000,000 4/15 J.B.C. & A. A.D.S.S./Forms/C. 2118.

Instructions regarding War Diaries and Intelligence Summaries are contained in F. S. Regs., Part II. and the Staff Manual respectively. Title Pages will be prepared in manuscript.

WAR DIARY
or
INTELLIGENCE SUMMARY
(Erase heading not required.)

Volume 24

Army Form C. 2118

Place	Date	Hour	Summary of Events and Information	Remarks and references to Appendices
ARRAS	5.		Fine. Bombardment of enemy trenches continues. Working party of 2 Officers & 150 O.R. & another of 1 Officer & 40 O.R. found for unloading stores, supplied by C & D Coys. Large working party of 200 O.R. found at night for trench digging. Great aerial activity. HPB.	
	6.		Shortly after midnight enemy shelled ARRAS with gas & incendiary shells for a short period. Fine day. Bombardment continues. Planes again very active. Three O.R. wounded by shell bursting on D Coy's billet. HPB.	
	7.		Fine. Heavy bombardment continues. 2 O.R. wounded. 2/Lt. J. A Gould takes over duties of A/Adjt. Slight shelling of ARRAS. HPB.	
	8		Easter Day. Fine. Increased bombardment by our artillery. Some enemy shelling. Two celebrations of Holy Communion in the cellar at Battalion Headquarters. Lieut. B. Poope in charge of the Brigades transport at the CITADEL. Battalion moved into the CHRISTCHURCH CAVES at night. HPB.	
G. 35. d. 3. 6 51b.	9		Battalion left caves at 9 am. and moved up to the reserve line (H. 2 Sector). Here Captn. C. N. THOMPSON wounded. At 2.30pm. Battalion moved forward to Old British Front Line, with Headquarters in HUNTER ST. Large number of German Prisoners marched back down SUNKEN ROAD. British Cavalry going forward in large numbers. News received that first and second objectives had been successfuly carried. Lt. D. F. Forewell (att. Brigade H.Q. as Intelligence Officer) wounded. HPB.	
HARP	10		Some Snow during night. The Brigade ordered to be ready to move forward several miles and go into action at half an hours notice. About noon orders received to move forward to Old German Front System. On arrival orders to proceed to crest of TELEGRAPH HILL. Eventually halted in Southern part of The HARP. No information as to what was going on in front. About 4.30 pm. orders received for the Battalion to advance and clear up the situation in the direction of WANCOURT and the high ground South West of that village. Battalion advance in artillery formation for half a mile, and coming under a light artillery barrage and machine gun fire, deployed. The advance was ~~carried out~~ continued in a heavy snow storm. When this lifted it was discovered that the leading Companies were in an exposed position about 800 yards West of WANCOURT, & suffered casualties	

1875 Wt. W593/826 1,000,000 4/15 J.B.C. & A. A.D.S.S./Forms/C. 2118.

Instructions regarding War Diaries and Intelligence Summaries are contained in F. S. Regs., Part II. and the Staff Manual respectively. Title Pages will be prepared in manuscript.

WAR DIARY
or
INTELLIGENCE SUMMARY
(Erase heading not required.)

Army Form C. 2118

8 ½

Place	Date APRIL	Hour	Summary of Events and Information	Remarks and references to Appendices
WEST of WANCOURT	10		from machine gun fire from direction of WANCOURT CEMETERY and HILL 90. Lieut H.R. ADAIR (O.C. D Co) and 2/Lieut N.F.H. MATHER wounded. There being no signs of any troops on our right a defensive flank was formed on the line of the WANCOURT – NEUVILLE VITASSE Road. Patrols were pushed out and touch obtained with the 56th Division about midway between WANCOURT and NEUVILLE VITASSE. HPB	
	11		Battalion in support of 7th Bn K.R.R.C in attack on WANCOURT. Attack was caught by cross machine gun fire from WANCOURT and HILL 90. The 7th Bn K.R.R.C suffered heavily and our 'A' Company lost 2/Lt B. FRANKLIN (O.C. A Co.) wounded and 20 other rank casualties. During the afternoon after sending out patrols a line was established by 'C' Co joining up the 41st Brigade with the 56th Division. At night the Battalion was relieved by the 7th Bn. Rifle Brigade, and moved back to the BROWN LINE. The weather was extremely cold and snow fell heavily during the relief, which was not completed until 3 am 12th inst. During day Rear Transport camp moved up to Arras. HPB	
	12		About 5 am a patrol from 'B' Co penetrated into WANCOURT and MARLIÈRE. Patrols were pushed out in an Easterly direction and touch was gained with the enemy, who were holding GUEMAPPE in force. After several attempts 'C' Co. on left were able to join up with 3rd Division and line was consolidated from the right of the 3rd Division to MARLIÈRE. During the action 'C' Co. captured a 77 mm. field gun. Lieut T.A. BALDOCK (O.C. C Co) wounded. At 11 am orders were issued for an attack to be launched on the high ground South East of WANCOURT; the 8th Bn K.R.R.C. on right crossing CONJEUL RIVER South of WANCOURT and the Battalion (8th Rifle Bde.) on left, crossing the river North of the village. The operation was not carried out, as it involved advancing the whole of the Battalion straight across the enemy's front, for a distance of about a mile, at GUEMAPPE. At 2.30 pm orders were again issued for an assault on the high ground S.E. of WANCOURT. The Battalion supported the 8th Bn K.R.R.C. Both Battalions were to cross the CONJEUL RIVER South of WANCOURT. The mud was very deep and sticky, and by 5 pm (half an hour before the assault was to take place) only two Companies of the leading Battn. and one Company and Headquarters of the supporting Battalion had succeeded in affecting the passage of the CONJEUL RIVER. The enemy must have seen the concentration of troops, as the moment our 18-pdr barrage started, a heavy hostile barrage (chiefly 5·9 & 4·2) was put on the valley of the CONJEUL from WANCOURT to HENINEL. Before the assault had even started, the whole area to be covered was subjected to heavy machine gun fire from North and South of the CONJEUL RIVER, and from the high ground South East of WANCOURT.	

1875 Wt. W593/826 1,000,000 4/15 J.B.C. & A. A.D.S.S./Forms/C. 2118.

Instructions regarding War Diaries and Intelligence Summaries are contained in F. S. Regs., Part II. and the Staff Manual respectively. Title pages will be prepared in manuscript.

WAR DIARY

or

~~INTELLIGENCE SUMMARY.~~

(*Erase heading not required.*) 8th Bn. The Rifle Brigade

Army Form C. 2118.

Place	Date APRIL	Hour	Summary of Events and Information	Remarks and references to Appendices
West of WANCOURT	12.		It was found impossible for the men to get forward, and the attack was abandoned; a line being consolidated from WANCOURT in a South Easterly direction, joining up with the advanced troops of the 56th Division. During the evening a continuous line was established from the right of the 3rd Division (about 1000 yards West of GUEMAPPE) to the left of the 56th Division (about HENINEL CEMETERY). The Battalion was relieved at midnight by the 9th Bn. D.L.I. (151st Bde). Casualties for tour - 5 officers wounded. 25 other ranks killed, 5 other ranks Missing and 68 other ranks wounded. JPPB	
ARRAS	13		On relief Battalion proceeded to billets in ARRAS. Headquarters established in Rue Frederic Degeorge. Battalion rested all day. JPPB	
MONCHIET	14		Fine. Battalion marched out of ARRAS at 11.am. and proceeded to MONCHIET. Billeted for night in Hut Camp. Camp in very dirty condition. JPPB	
GRAND RULLECOURT	15		Wet. Battalion marched out of MONCHIET at 10.am, and proceeded to billets at GRAND RULLECOURT, arriving at 1.15 pm. Billets very crowded. 2/Lt J.A.WEBB and 28 other ranks (including 11 signallers) joined Bn. Party from LE SOUICH rejoined. JPPB	
-	16		Fine morning, with rain later. Commanding Officer attends conference at Brigade Headquarters. JPPB	
-	17		Wet, with strong wind. ~~Conference~~ Capt. G.V. CAREY takes over command of 'B' Co. Battalion bathed from 3.30pm. to 12 midnight. JPPB	
-	18		Dull and showery. Very quiet day. JPPB	
-	19		Dull. Draft tested 'in gas' at SOMBRIN by Brigade Gas N.C.O. Medical Officer inspects Companies. JPPB	

A5834 Wt. W4973/M687 750,000 8/16 D. D. & L. Ltd. Forms/C.2118/13.

Instructions regarding War Diaries and Intelligence Summaries are contained in F. S. Regs., Part II. and the Staff Manual respectively. Title pages will be prepared in manuscript.

WAR DIARY
or
~~INTELLIGENCE~~ SUMMARY.
(*Erase heading not required.*)

8th Bn The Rifle Brigade

Army Form C. 2118.

Place	Date 1917	Hour	Summary of Events and Information	Remarks and references to Appendices
GRAND RULLECOURT	APRIL 20th		Fine morning. Party of 1 officer and 70 other ranks found to report to OC 19th C.C.S. at AGNEZ les DUISANS. A and B Companies firing practice. C and D Companies practise artillery formation etc. JRPB	
	21.		Dull. CAPT G V CAREY to 6th KSLI (42nd Inf Bde) as Temp. Second in Command. Lt W.A. CREBBIN takes over command & payment of B Coy. C & D Coys firing practice – A Coy on the DUESNES trenches. JRPB	
	22.		Fine. Parade services for all denominations. Br Major D E PRIDEAUX BRUNE to be a/Lt Col whilst comdg batt March 7th 1917. CAPT K.S.M GLADSTONE appointed Staff Capt to 42nd Inf Bde & transferred to the General List 29.3.17. JRPB	
	23		Orders received for Battalion to move to La CAUCHIE – parade at 2.0 p.m. & move at 5.15 p.m., and occupy billets, which are rather crowded. Fine warm day. JRPB	
La CAUCHIE	24		Sudden orders received at 5.35 am for the battalion to move at 7.30 am to BLAIRVILLE. Battalion paraded & marched off at 8.20 a.m. & after a trying march arrived in the ruined village at 12.30 p.m & occupy billets, such as there are. Orders received on arrival to be ready to move again at short notice, but no further move made. 2/Lt. W.W. Wines & 1 O.R. proceed at short notice on leave. JRPB	

A5834 Wt. W4973/M687 750,000 8/16 D. D. & L. Ltd. Forms/C.2118/13.

Instructions regarding War Diaries and Intelligence Summaries are contained in F. S. Regs., Part II. and the Staff Manual respectively. Title pages will be prepared in manuscript.

WAR DIARY
or
INTELLIGENCE SUMMARY.
(Erase heading not required.)

Volume 24

Army Form C. 2118.

Place	Date	Hour	Summary of Events and Information	Remarks and references to Appendices
BLAIRVILLE	25.		Fine. Btn stood to all day ready to move, but finally received orders to stay the night at BLAIRVILLE & leave early the following ~~[illegible]~~ morning. JPB.	
	26.		Fine, but dull & cold. Rose at 4.0 a.m. and Batt (less party left out under para XXX Divisional Training) marched off at 5.0 am. A Halt was made on the outskirts of the ruined village of MERCATEL for breakfast. Here the transport left the battalion & proceeded to RONVILLE. The Batt. marched to N.7.b.2.2 (Sheet 51b S.W.) & relieved the 6th Bn. D.L.I. (50th Div) at 12.30 p.m. Remainder of the day passed quietly. JPB.	
N.7.b.2.2 Sheet 51b S.W.	27		Fine. Heavy shelling heard just N of MONCHY. Working party of 50 O.R found for improving track over TELEGRAPH HILL. Quiet day. Party left out at BLAIRVILLE proceeded to MONCHIET. JPB.	
	28		Fine. Notice received from 41st Inf Bde that Capt. F.E. Young & draft of 24 O.R arrived at DIV Depot Bn on the 25th inst. Working party of 1 Officer & 25 O.R found for work under the R.E. Artillery active all day & much aerial activity in the evening. 2/Lt. G.H. BLOOMER to hospital. JPB.	
	29		Fine. Working party of 1 Officer & 100 O.R. found for work under R.E. repairing Infantry tracks. Also small party of 1 N.C.O. & 8 men for work at DIV. H.Q. JPB.	

Instructions regarding War Diaries and Intelligence Summaries are contained in F. S. Regs., Part II. and the Staff Manual respectively. Title pages will be prepared in manuscript.

WAR DIARY
or
INTELLIGENCE SUMMARY.
(Erase heading not required.)

Volume 24

Army Form C. 2118.

Place	Date	Hour	Summary of Events and Information	Remarks and references to Appendices
Trenches N 7 b 2.2 Sheet 51 b S.W.	30		June. Notice received that the following Officer reinforcements would join the detachment at MONCHIET today – 2/Lts. W.G SPENCER, G J STEPTOE, J.S SIMPSON, C.H.SLATFORD + H. CLAYTON. Also that 2/Lt E.R MAGENTY arrived at Depot Bn 29th. Quiet day. Troops working on improving tracks, accomodation etc. JPB.	
			Attached. – 1. Roll of Officers 2. List of Casualties	

J. Prideaux Brune Lt Col
Cmdg 8th Bn Rifle Bde

A5834 Wt. W4973/M687 750,000 8/16 D. D. & L. Ltd. Forms/C.2118/13.

8th Bn Rifle Bde

Casualties for Month of April 1917

Capt	C N Thompson	Wounded	9.4.17
Lieut	D F Foxwell	— do —	
–	H R Adam	Wounded	10.4.17
2/Lt	N F H Mather	— do —	
–	B Franklin	Wounded	11.4.17
Lieut	T A Baldock	–	12.4.17

Regtl. No	Rank	Name		Date	Nature of Casualty
S 20564	R/m	Horschard	A	6.4.17	Wounded (at duty)
S 5998	–	Brennan	J	–	–
S 27615	–	Howe	J	–	–
S 20761	–	Barber	R	–	–
S 26504	–	Coote	F	7.4.17	–
S 29400	–	Townsend	G	–	–
S 10832	A/Sgt	Timmons	G	11.4.17	Killed
S 29398	R/m	Arthur	J	–	–
S 26501	–	Bishop	E	–	–
S 26493	–	Banfield	J	–	–
S 27356	–	Godin	J	–	–
S 10110	–	Waugh	F	–	–
B 721	Cpl	Lewendon	C	–	–
S 6817	L/Cpl	Sparkes	H	–	–

1st Bn. Rifle Bde.

[illegible] Officers

[illegible]	D. E. [illegible]	Commanding
Major	H. C. [illegible] D.S.C.	2nd in Comd.
Captain	C. V. Craig	([illegible])
"	E. H. [illegible]	([illegible])
"	C. H. Walker	OC A Coy.
Lieut. (A/Capt.)	B. M. D[illegible]	OC C Coy.
"	W. H. Collins	OC B Coy.
"	J. R. Attley	L.G.O.
"	D. E. Fox [illegible]	(Wounded 9.4.17)
"	T. M. Baldwin	(Wounded 11.4.17)
"	E. R. [illegible]	Transport Officer
"	H. R. [illegible]	(Wounded 11.4.17)
2/Lieut.	W. H. Turnbull	OC D Coy.
"	M. H. Jury	A/Adjutant
"	B. [illegible]	(Wounded 11.4.17)
"	T. S. [illegible]	[illegible]
"	H. E. Hartley	[illegible]
"	E. A. F. [illegible]	[illegible] Officer
"	W. H. [illegible]	On Leave
"	R. F. [illegible]	[illegible] School
"	D. M[illegible]	T.M. Course
"	H. B. Oakley	
"	S. R. [illegible]	
"	D. A. [illegible]	
"	C. F. [illegible]	

[illegible]

2/Lieuts.	W G Hunter	i/c of Trench Warden Sect.
"	P H Wooding	Signalling Officer
"	J Gray	
"	V D Nicoll	
"	G C Dalgairns	
"	W N Spurden	Hospital
"	J W C Reid	
"	W H Blakes	
"	S H Bloomer	Hospital.
"	N F R Mather	(wounded 10-4-17)
"	J R Webb	Hospital

J Richardson Brown.

Lt Col.

for O C 5th [illegible] Rifle Bde

8th Btn. Rifle Bde

Roll of Officers

Bt Major (A/Lt. Col.)	D.E. Prideaux Brune	Commanding
Major	A.C. Sheepshanks. D.S.O.	2nd in Cmd.
Captain	G.V. Carey	(att 5th KSLI)
-	C.N. Thompson	(Wounded 9-4-17)
-	C.H. Wenham	OC A Coy.
Lieut. (A/Capt.)	B.H. Bennett	OC C Coy.
-	W.A. Crabben	OC B Coy.
-	J.R. Abbey	L.G.O.
-	D.F. Foxwell	(Wounded 9-4-17)
-	T.A. Baldock	(Wounded 12-4-17)
-	E. Poole	Transport Officer
-	H.R. Adair	(Wounded 10-4-17)
2/Lieut.	W.A. Tickle	OC 'D' Coy.
-	M.A. Young	a/ Adjutant
-	B. Franklin	(Wounded 11-4-17)
-	J.A. Gould	41st Bde Bombing Officer
-	H.R. Hartley	VII Corps Cage
-	E.A.F. Batty	Intelligence Officer
-	W.W. Wines	On Leave
-	A.F. Newell	Third Army School
-	D. Meacock	T.M. Course
-	H.B. Oakley	
-	S.R. Evans	
-	M.H. House	~~41st Bde~~
-	O.F. Savage	

2/Lieut.	W. G. Hanton	i/c 41st Trench Wireless Set.
-	P. H. Wooding	Signalling Officer
-	J. Greig	
-	V. B. Nicol	
-	G. C. Dalgoutte	
-	W. N. Sproston	Hospital
-	J. W. C. Reed.	
-	W. H. Blades	
-	G. H. Bloomer	Hospital ~~i/c Party att. 19 C.C.S.~~ (wounded 10.4.17)
-	N. F. H. Mather	Hospital.
-	J. A. Webb.	

[illegible]
Lt Col. ~~Major~~
for O.C. 8th ~~Bn~~ Rifle Bde

8th Btn Rifle Bde

Casualties for Month of April 1917.

Capt.	C N Thompson	Wounded	9.4.17
Lieut.	D.F. Foxwell	-do-	
-	H R. Adair	Wounded	10.4.17
2/Lt	N.F.H. Mather	-do-	
-	B. Franklin	Wounded	11.4.17
Lieut.	T.A Baldock	-	12.4.17.

Regtl. No.	Rank	Name		Date	Nature of Casualty.
S20564	Rfn	Blanchard	A	6.4.17	Wounded (at duty)
S 5998	-	Brennan	J	-	-
S 27615	-	Howe	J	-	-
S 20761	-	Barber	R	-	-
S 26504	-	Coote	F	7.4.17	-
S 29400	-	Townsend	G	-	-
S 10832	L/Sgt.	Timmons	G	11.4.17	Killed
S 29398	Rfn.	Arthur	J	-	-
S 26501	-	Bishop	E	-	-
S 26493	-	Binfield	J	-	-
S 27356	-	Gordon	J	-	-
S 10110	-	Waugh	F.	-	-
B 721	Cpl.	Lewendon	C	-	-
S 6817	L/Cpl.	Sparkes	H	-	-

Regtl. No	Rank	Name		Date	Nature of Casualty.
[illegible]	Rfn	Potter	S	11.4.17	Killed
S26843	-	Mills	G	-	-
S26548.	-	Naylor	H	-	-
S9823	-	Smith	W	-	-
S29428	-	Wright	A	-	-
S25567	-	Horsley	R	-	-
S26148	-	Capers	T	12.4.17	-
S29441	-	Shinn	E	-	-
S6253	Cpl.	Holloway	W	11.4.17	-
S26254	Rfn	Parker	A	-	-
B3072	-	Peet	A	-	-
S25998	-	Smith	S	-	-
S26165	-	Flawn	L	16.4.17	-
S26269	-	Williams	F	11.4.17	-
S26223	-	Brown	A	10.4.17	-
S4045	-	Boden	E	-	-
Z1409	L/Cpl.	Fryer	A	-	-
Z2504	Cpl.	French	F	9.4.17	-
S18003	Rfn	Dale	R	11.4.17	Missing
S16742	-	Clark	W	-	-
B1737	-	McCaffery	J	-	Wounded
S9457	-	Thompson	R	-	Missing
S28494	Rfn	Dando	W	16.4.17	Died at No. 6 Stationary Hospital from 'Peritonitis'

Regt No.	Rank	Name		Date	Nature of Casualty
B 440	Rfn	Tappen	J	11.4.17	Wounded
B 92	Sgt	Clark	G	-	-
S 12620	L/Cpl	Bates	A	-	-
S 26515	-	Dutton	F	-	-
4531	-	Pattern	A	-	-
S 29401	Rfn	Angel	W	-	-
S 26205	-	Adams	A	-	-
S 15596	-	Broughton	R	-	-
S 14468	-	Betts	H	-	-
S 27061	-	Church	H	-	-
S 18537	-	Groundsell	E	-	-
B 201	-	Johnson	J	-	-
S 26048	-	Kelman	W	-	-
				11/4/17	Died at 96th FA }
P 323	-	Lovatt	H	-	Wounded
Z 336	L/Cpl	Bibby	W	-	-
S 18623	Rfn	Meston	W.	-	W -
S 5460	-	Whatnough	F	-	-
S 27122	-	Wicks	W	-	-
S 3374	-	Tongue	D	-	-
S 29425	-	Jackson	H	-	-
S 17959	-	Golding	W	-	-
S 17456	Cpl	Charlton	W	-	-
S 1214	-	Bryant	S	-	-
S 11132	-	Porter	E	-	-
S 13300	L/Cpl	Gregg	E	-	-
B 200667	-	Krajicek	S	-	-

Regt No.	Rank	Name		Date	Nature of Casualty.
S26238	Rfn	Hillman	W	11.4.17	Wounded
S24500	-	Harvey	T	-	-
S26547	-	Nyburg	A	-	-
Z 676	-	Whitehouse	G	-	-
S 21636	-	Edwards	E	-	-
S 29432	-	Bennett	J	-	-
S 23300	-	Evans	T	-	-
S 26072	-	Whysall	H	-	-
S 26242	-	Horne	F	-	-
S 25109	-	Taylor	C	-	-
S 26009	-	Turner	P	-	-
S 2145	L/Sgt	Pendlington	G	12.4.17	-
S 26002	L/Cpl	Sullivan	J	-	-
S 26019	Rfn	Winchester	H	-	-
S 20335	-	Bishop	J	-	-
S 6188	-	Jones	E	-	-
S 26281	-	Miles	W	-	-
S 15341	-	Taylor	T	-	-
S 15479	-	Plowright	E	-	-
S 12799	-	Hill	W	-	-
S 26588	-	Ward	J	-	-
S 26249	-	Marks	W.	9.4.17	-
S 688	-	Bennett	J	10.4.17	-
B 1955	L/Cpl	Cartling	H	-	-
B 200681	Rfn	Benecke	H	11.4.17	-
S 20918	-	Conroy	A	-	-
Z 1569	-	Evans	H	10.4.17	-

Regt No.	Rank	Name		Date	Nature of Casualty
S26056	Rfn	Moyes	A	10.4.17	Wounded
B1784	L/Cpl	Allender	E	–	–
975	–	Smith	W	11.4.17	–
S26228	–	Dixon	E	12.4.17	–
S26275	Rfn	Westbrook	G	10.4.17	–
S27673	–	Aires	J	–	–
72	Sgt	Popejoy	B	–	–
S26003	Rfn	Sutton	W	–	–
S26158	–	Burgess	W	–	–
S14457	–	Tyler	W	–	–
S5675	–	Butterworth	G	11.4.17	–
S7639	Cpl	Mossen	H	–	–
S7445	–	Jarvis	J	–	– S.S.
B2802	Rfn	O'Brien	M	–	–
S12743	–	Coupe	A	12.4.17	–
S20278	–	Dorling	G	10.4.17	–
					Rejoined 16.4.17 }

30/4/17.

[signature]
Lt Col
Comdg 8th Bn Rifle Bde

Regt No	Rank	Name		Date	Nature of Casualty
S26056	Rfn	Myers	A	10.4.17	Wounded
B1754	L/Cpl	Allender	E	–	–
975	–	Smith	W	11.4.17	–
S26228	–	Dixon	E	12.4.17	–
S26275	Rfn	Westbrook	G	10.4.17	–
S27673	–	Airies	J	–	–
72	Sgt	Popejoy	B	–	–
S26003	Rfn	Sutton	W	–	–
S26158	–	Burgess	W	–	–
S14957	–	Tyler	W	–	–
S5675	–	Butterworth	G	11.4.17	–
S7639	Cpl	Missen	H	–	–
S7445	–	Jarvis	J	–	– S.S.
B2802	Rfn	O'Brien	M	–	–
S12743	–	Coupe	A	12.4.17	–
S20275	–	Darling	G	10.4.17	–

Rejoined 16.4.17 }

30/4/17.

[illegible] Lt Col

Comdg 8th Bn Rifle Bde

Regt No	Rank	Name		Date	Nature of Casualty
S 26288	Rfn	Hillman	W	11.4.17	Wounded
S 24500	-	Harvey	T	-	-
S 26547	-	Nyberg	A	-	-
Z 676	-	Whitehouse	G	-	-
S 21636	-	Edwards	E	-	-
S 29432	-	Bennett	J	-	-
S 23300	-	Evans	T	-	-
S 26072	-	Whypall	H	-	-
S 26242	-	Horne	F	-	-
S 25104	-	Taylor	C	-	-
S 26009	-	Turner	P	-	-
S 2145	L/Sgt	Pendlington	G	12.4.17	-
S 26002	L/Cpl	Sullivan	J	-	-
S 26019	Rfn	Winchester	H	-	-
S 20335	-	Bishop	J	-	-
S 6158	-	Jones	E	-	-
S 26251	-	Miles	W	-	-
S 15341	-	Taylor	T	-	-
S 15479	-	Plowright	E	-	-
S 12799	-	Hill	W	-	-
S 26588	-	Ward	J	-	-
S 26249	-	Marks S	W.	9.4.17	-
S 688	-	Bennett	J	10.4.17	-
B 1955	L/Cpl	Cuttling	H	-	-
B 200651	Rfn.	Benecke	H	11.4.17	-
S 20918	-	Conroy	A	-	-
Z 1569	-	Evans	H	10.4.17	-

3

Regt. No.	Rank	Name		Date	Nature of Casualty
S25486	Rfn	Potter	S	11.4.17	Killed
S26543	-	Mills	S	-	-
S26545	-	Naylor	H	-	-
S9823	-	Smith	W	-	-
S29428	-	Wright	A	-	-
S25567	-	Hensley	R	-	-
S26145	-	Capers	T	12.4.17	-
S29441	-	Shinn	E	-	-
S6253	Cpl	Holloway	W	11.4.17	-
S26254	Rfn	Parkes	A	-	-
B3072	-	Peet	A	-	-
S25998	-	Smith	S	-	-
S26165	-	Hawn	L	11.4.17	-
S26269	-	Williams	F	11.4.17	-
S26223	-	Brown	A	10.4.17	-
S4045	-	Boden	E	-	-
Z1409	L/Cpl.	Fryer	A	-	-
Z2504	Cpl.	French	F	9.4.17	-
S18063	Rfn	Dale	R	11.4.17	Missing
S16742	-	Clark	W	-	-
B1737	-	McCaffery	J	-	Wounded
S9457	-	Thompson	R	-	Missing
S25494	Rfn	Dando	W	11.4.17	Died at No. 6 Stationary Hospital from 'Peritonitis'

Regt No	Rank	Name		Date	Nature of Casualty
B4400	Rfn	Tappen	J	11.4.17	Wounded
B 92	Sgt	Clark	G	-	-
S12620	L/Cpl	Bates	A	-	-
S26515	-	Dutton	F	-	-
4531	-	Pattern	A	-	-
S29401	Rfn	Angel	W	-	-
S26205	-	Adams	A	-	-
S15596	-	Broughton	R	-	-
S4468	-	Betts	H	-	-
S27061	-	Church	H	-	-
S18537	-	Grimsdall	E	-	-
B 201	-	Johnson	J	-	-
S26048	-	Kelman	W	-	-
				11/4/17	Died at 96th FA }
P 323	-	Lovatt	H	-	Wounded
Z 336	L/Cpl	Bibby	W	-	-
S16623	Rfn	Morton	W	-	W -
S6460	-	Whitnough	F	-	-
S27122	-	Wicks	W	-	-
S3374	-	Tongue	D	-	-
S29425	-	Jackson	H	-	-
S17957	-	Golding	W	-	-
S17456	Cpl	Charlton	W	-	-
S1214	-	Bryant	S	-	-
S11132	-	Porter	E	-	-
S13300	L/Cpl	Grigg	E	-	-
B200667	-	Krajewek	S	-	-

Instructions regarding War Diaries and Intelligence Summaries are contained in F. S. Regs., Part II. and the Staff Manual respectively. Title pages will be prepared in manuscript.

WAR DIARY
or
~~INTELLIGENCE SUMMARY.~~
(Erase heading not required.)

Vol. 25 41/14 Vol 24

Army Form C. 2118.

8th Bn. The Rifle Brigade

Place	Date 1917	Hour	Summary of Events and Information	Remarks and references to Appendices
N.7.b 2.2 (51B France) O.19.c.2.9	May 1st		Fine. Batn. moved to N.15.c.4.4 commencing at 2.30 pm and rested there till 9.30 pm, at which hour Bn moved up to front line, taking over right half of front held by 7th Bn. K.R.R.C. Bn. H.Q. established in DUCK TRENCH (O.19 c 2.9). Heavy shelling during relief but no casualties. Relief complete 3.0. am 2nd. DJPB.	
	2nd		Disposition of Companies. 'D' in front line in IBIS and HERON Trenches. 'B' Co. in GANNET and EGRET. C Co. in EGRET and DUCK. 'A' Co. in BUZZARD and ALBATROSS trenches. Very little movement possible during day. Good deal of shelling. Unlucky shell causes eleven casualties to 'A' Company. Final attack orders issued at 4 pm. DJPB.	
	3rd		Battalion Headquarters move to advanced position immediately behind front line at 2.0. am (O.25.b.9.3). Battalion moved into position at 2.45 am and was disposed for the attack as follows:- B and D Coys. in front line, each in two waves, B left, D right. 'C' Co. in Support. A Co. in Reserve. At 3.45 am the three assaulting Companies moved forward. Barrage showing direction in the darkness. Barrage was an excellent one. NARROW TRENCH was reached with few casualties and it was found to be very lightly held. At 4.20 am 'D' Co. reported CHERISY on their right and at 4.35 am that they had passed that village. At 5 am this Company reported 'troops on right held up' and that they (D. Co.) were consolidating position on road left of ST MICHAEL'S STATUE. At 5.30 am 'B' Co. reported they were consolidating on BLUE LINE, but doubted being able to push on owing to machine gun fire from high ground on left, and rather behind Company line. B. Co. reported also that they had posted Lewis Gun team at Northern end of CHERISY main street. Situation in village uncertain, so a patrol was sent into the place and reported some enemy dead but none alive. At 6.40 am 'B' Co. reported that B & D Cos together with about a Company of East Surreys (18th DIV.) had crossed the SENSÉE RIVER and were digging in near RED LINE.	

A5834 Wt. W4973/M687 750,000 8/16 D. D. & L. Ltd. Forms/C.2118/13.

Instructions regarding War Diaries and Intelligence Summaries are contained in F. S. Regs., Part II. and the Staff Manual respectively. Title pages will be prepared in manuscript.

WAR DIARY VOL 25
or
~~INTELLIGENCE SUMMARY.~~

(Erase heading not required.)

Army Form C. 2118.

8th Bn. The Rifle Brigade

Place	Date 1917	Hour	Summary of Events and Information	Remarks and references to Appendices
	MAY 3rd (contd)		'D' Co. left flank in the air. Heavy machine gun fire probably from TRIANGLE WOOD. 'C' Co. digging in near ST MICHAEL'S STATUE. Position reached by front Companies 600 yards from ST MICHAEL'S STATUE across SENSÈE RIVER. For next 3 or 4 hours the situation remained unaltered, two Companies attempting to consolidate the position near the RED LINE and one Company consolidating on BLUE LINE. Both positions exposed to severe machine gun fire from left and BLUE LINE heavily shelled. Heavy shelling between BLUE LINE and our original front and between Battalion and Brigade Headquarters.	
			Report received from O.C. MIDDLESEX on right of EAST SURREYS that there was a large gap East and SOUTH of CHERISY. Orders given to Reserve Company to be ready to form a Defensive Flank towards CHERISY. Orders received from Brigade for reinforcements to be sent up to RED LINE, but before Reserve Company had moved off, word was brought that men were retiring all along the line. The retirement as far as we were concerned was carried out quietly and an attempt made to make a stand in NARROW TRENCH, but eventually the whole line came back to our original trenches. 'A' Co. had meanwhile occupied JACKDAW Trench and the remainder of the Battalion were distributed in IBIS and HERON. Cause of retirement from the RED LINE was the appearance of a strong force of the enemy advancing from the direction of VIS-EN-ARTOIS and encircling the advanced Companies from their left rear. This was simultaneous with an advance in front, and the possibility of an advance on the Right Flank, where the 18th DIVN. were no more. Touch was established with 8th Bn. K.R.R.C. and 42nd BDE on left and the EAST SURREYS and QUEENS on right. Remainder of the day was normal, except for entirely unexpected attack by the QUEENS in the evening.	
			Casualties:-	

	Killed	Wounded	Wounded & Missing	Missing	Total
Officers	2	2	1	2	7
O.R.	13	75	21	80	189

JPB.

A5834 Wt. W4973/M687 750,000 8/16 D. D. & L. Ltd. Forms/C.2118/13.

Instructions regarding War Diaries and Intelligence Summaries are contained in F. S. Regs., Part II. and the Staff Manual respectively. Title pages will be prepared in manuscript.

WAR DIARY
or
~~INTELLIGENCE SUMMARY.~~
(*Erase heading not required.*)

Army Form C. 2118.

8th Bn. The Rifle Brigade

Place	Date	Hour	Summary of Events and Information	Remarks and references to Appendices
	1917 MAY			
NEPAL TR.	4th		Battalion relieved at 1.0 am by 7th Bn. K.R.R.C. and returned to NEPAL TRENCH, where they rested for the day. Very hot. DJPB	
N.7.b.2.2	5th		Bn. arrived back in COJEUL SWITCH at 1.30 am. Party from MONCHIET rejoined Battn. during afternoon. Fine hot day with thunder in the evening. Draft of 15 other ranks joined Bn. Capt. F.E. YOUNG and 2/LT. E.G. MAGENTY joined Bn. DJPB	
	6th		Fine, and a little cooler. Battalion resting DJPB	
	7th		Fine. Lt & Q.Mr. F.H. Pryor rejoined from England. DJPB	
	8th		Fine. Working party of 3 officers and 100 other ranks salvaging wire and pickets under R.E. DJPB	
	9th		Fine. Quiet day. Portion of Bn. bathed at ACHICOURT. Heavy rain during night. DJPB	
	10th		Fine. Working party of 3 officers & 100 other ranks salvaging wire & pickets under R.E. Lt. H.A. TEAKLE and 5 other ranks to Summer Rest Camp at BOULOGNE. DJPB	
	11th		Fine. Orders received to relieve 43rd Bde. in the line on night 14/15th. 2/Lt. D. MEACOCK posted to 41st Trench Mortar Battery. DJPB	
	12th		Fine and very hot. 2/LT. W.A. SOLVEN joined Bn. Commanding Officer, Adjutant and Intelligence Officer reconnoitre SUPPORT LINE. DJPB	
	13th		Fine and hot. Company Officers reconnoitre line. Transport Camp moved from RONVILLE to a Camp at N.5.c.95.55. Draft of 68 other ranks arrive. DJPB	

A5834 Wt. W4973/M687 750,000 8/16 D. D. & L. Ltd. Forms/C.2118/13.

Instructions regarding War Diaries and Intelligence Summaries are contained in F. S. Regs., Part II. and the Staff Manual respectively. Title pages will be prepared in manuscript.

WAR DIARY
or
INTELLIGENCE SUMMARY.
(Erase heading not required.)

Army Form C. 2118.

Volume 25.

Place	Date	Hour	Summary of Events and Information	Remarks and references to Appendices
TELEGRAPH HILL	14th		Quiet day. 41st Inf Bde relieve 43rd Inf Bde in front of WANCOURT. Btn in Brigade Support in ALBATROS Trench – H.Q. established at N.24.c.0.5 (51b), relieving 6th D.C.L.I. Major (T/Lt Col) D.E. Prideaux Brune awarded D.S.O. } 2/Lt P.H. Wooding } T. O.F. Savege } awarded Military Cross } in connection with operations April 9–12th 1917. DEPB.	
N.24.c.0.5 (51b)	15.		Fine. Battalion working at night on communication trenches. Little movement possible during the day. Back areas shelled more or less continuously. DEPB.	
	16		Wet. Battalion again working at night on communication trenches. Trenches in very bad condition owing to wet. DEPB.	
	17		Dull. Work as for 15th & 16th. DEPB.	
	18.		Fine. Battalion still working as for previous days. DEPB.	
	19.		Fine. Battalion relieved the 9th R.B. in the front line, commencing at 11-0 p.m. Fairly quiet relief. Line held somewhat thinly owing to expected operation by 33rd DIV on our right. H.Q. of Batt at O.19.a.2.3. DEPB.	
O.19.a.2.3.	20		33rd Div attacked south of our front. Some retaliation on our trenches. Line thickened up at night – 2 Coys (B & C) in front line, D in support, A in reserve. Major G.V. Carey rejoins batt. from 5th K.S.L.I. DEPB.	

A5834 Wt. W4973/M687 750,000 8/16 D. D. & L. Ltd. Forms/C.2118/13.

Instructions regarding War Diaries and Intelligence Summaries are contained in F. S. Regs., Part II. and the Staff Manual respectively. Title pages will be prepared in manuscript.

WAR DIARY
or
INTELLIGENCE SUMMARY.
(Erase heading not required.)

Volume 25th

Army Form C. 2118.

Place	Date	Hour	Summary of Events and Information	Remarks and references to Appendices
O.19.a.2.3. (51b)	21.		Capture of prisoner belonging to 31st R.I.R. – one of a large patrol, who lost his way, remainder being dispersed. Usual shelling, mostly on support trenches. DSPB.	
	22.		Wet night & rain continued most of the day. Normal shelling. DSPB.	
	23		Fine & hot. Heavy shelling of Batt. H.Q. 2.15 to 2.45 a.m., by 5.9", coupled with a whizz-bang barrage on front line – no offensive action followed – trenches knocked about, but no casualties. DSPB.	
			~~Fine~~, ~~hot~~ Communication trenches still in a very bad condition owing to previous rain. A light trench mortar fired for the first time on our front & support line during the afternoon. Work, as on previous nights, consisting chiefly of wiring & patrolling. DSPB.	
	24.		Fine. Trench Mortars very active from 10.0 a.m. to 12.0 p.m. & 8.0 p.m. to 10 p.m. – trenches badly knocked about, casualties few. Relieved at night by 9th K.R.R.C. 42nd Inf Bde, commencing at 9.45 p.m. & complete at 1.0 a.m. Batt proceeded to COJEUL SWITCH for ~~the~~ 24 hours. DSPB.	
N.24.c.0.5.	25.		Fine & warm. Batt in DIVISIONAL Support during the day – relieved at night by the 6th Batt Somerset L.I. & proceeded to rest camp at M.10.d. (51b). DSPB.	

A5834 Wt. W4973/M687 750,000 8/16 D. D. & L. Ltd. Forms/C.2118/13.

Instructions regarding War Diaries and Intelligence Summaries are contained in F. S. Regs., Part II. and the Staff Manual respectively. Title pages will be prepared in manuscript.

WAR DIARY
or
INTELLIGENCE SUMMARY.
(*Erase heading not required.*)

Army Form C. 2118.

Volume 25

Place	Date	Hour	Summary of Events and Information	Remarks and references to Appendices
Rest Camp M.10.d (51b)	26		Fine & hot. Two companies use baths. Usual clothing & kit inspections. Lt E Poole, Lt D F Foxwell, S9762 Sgt McGinley J. S6844 a/cpl. Collins J. Z32 Rfn Dyke W. "Mentioned in Despatches". D.P.B.	London Gazette 25/5/17
	27		Fine. Parade Services for all denominations. D.P.B.	
	28		Fine. Battalion parade for purpose of clearing a parade & recreation ground. D.P.B.	
	29		Rain during the night. Dull day. Working party of 1 Officer & 70 O.R. for work on range under Brigade arrangements. Two Companies bathed. Regimental Courses started for training of Specialists. Draft of 30 O.R. D.P.B.	
	30		Fine. Working party of 2 Officers & 50 O.R. for range building at WAILLY. B1349 a/cpl Kingsbury T. S3175 a/cpl Waldron C. & S6427 Cpl Lawton (att 41st T.M.B.) awarded Military Medal. Very heavy thunderstorm 5–6 p.m. – camp more or less washed out. 2/Lt R.C. Dewhurst from Divisional Staff for duty. D.P.B.	
	31		Fine. 2 Parties for work at R.E. ground – each 1 Officer & 32 O.R. Corps Commander inspected the Battalion. D.P.B.	
			Strength – 32 Officers 814 O.R. (includes 59 at Depot)	
			Attached – 1 List of Officers 2 List of Casualties	

D. Pridsaux-Brune. Lt Col.
Comdg 8th Bn Rifle Bde

8th Bn. The Rifle Brigade.

Casualties - May 1917.

2/Lieut.G.C.Dalgoutte	Killed in Action 3/5/17.
2/Lieut.M.H.House	do.
2/Lieut.P.H.Wooding	Wounded 3/5/17 (rejoined 15/5/17)
2/Lieut.V.B.Nicol	Wounded do.
2/Lieut.W.H.Blades	Wounded and Missing. 3/5/17
2/Lieut.H.B.Oakley	Wounded and Missing. do.
2/Lieut.F.W.C.Reed	Wounded and Missing. do.

S 24674	Rfn.	Landsberg N.	"B" Coy.	1-5-17	Wounded (acc.) Died) 1/5/17)
S 11014	A/Cpl.	Smith J.	"A" Coy.	3-5-17	Killed in Action.
S 18006	Rfn.	Berryman A.	do.	do.	do.
S 20748	"	Allen E.	do.	do.	do.
S 22403	"	Barlow T.	do.	do.	do.
S 15672	"	Hollick A.	do.	do.	Wounded. (Died 4/5/17)
S 7374	A/Cpl.	Sexton H.	do.	do.	Wounded.
Z 2148	Rfn.	Nicholson R.	do.	do.	do.
S 26506	"	Clements R.	do.	do.	do.
S 27048	"	Lloyd C.	do.	do.	do.
S 22414	"	Hawkins F.	do.	do.	do.
S 15852	Sgt.	Gent T.	do.	3/5/17	Killed in Action.
B 1406	A/Sgt.	Parkes G.	do.	do.	do.
S 22426	Rfn.	McCarthy C.	do.	do.	do.
S 18534	"	West W.	do.	do.	do.
B 815	Cpl.	Clarkson J.	"B" Coy.	do.	do.
S 10322	A/Cpl.	Green J.	do.	do.	do.
B 1412	"	McCormack T.	do.	do.	do.
S 2249	Rfn.	Burt W.	do.	do.	do.
S 17286	"	Pert L.	"C" Coy.	do.	do.
S 18042	"	Twiner H.	do.	do.	do.
S 6372	Cpl.	Bates C.	"D" Coy.	do.	do.
S 12905	"	Sharples F.	do.	do.	do.
S 13728	Rfn.	Grey C.	do.	do.	do.
S 27032	"	Gausten A.	"A" Coy.	do.	Wounded.
3292	Sgt.	Benson C.	do.	do.	do.
S 9462	"	Norman C.	do.	do.	do. (rejoined 23th.)
S 31061	"	Youens H.	do.	do.	do.
S 26502	Cpl.	Cameron D.	do.	do.	do.
S 2345	A/Cpl.	Slee J.	do.	do.	do.
S 7346	"	Campbell A.	do.	do.	do.
S 11102	"	Boden J.	do.	do.	do.
S 23280	"	Jaffe S.	do.	do.	do.
S 10220	Rfn.	Kane G.	do.	do.	do.
Z 1544	"	Croxton W.	do.	do.	do.
S 6020	"	White P.	do.	do.	do.
S 27367	"	Seaton W.	do.	do.	do.
S 10233	"	Pomfret W.	do.	do.	do.
S 36244	"	Montague A.	do.	do.	do.
S 26514	"	Cleary G.	do.	do.	do.
S 22410	"	Morris G.	do.	do.	do.
S 16827	"	Betteridge A. (Betteridge)	do.	do.	do.
B 733	"	Harrison A.	do.	do.	do. (died 4/5/17)
8003	"	Jones F.	do.	do.	do.
S 17366	"	Kerswell A.	do.	do.	do.
6000	"	Parker E.	do.	do.	do.
4020	Sgt.	Bish J.	"B" Coy.	do.	do. (died 14/5/17)
4235	A/Sgt.	McCarthy R.	do.	do.	do.
S 10861	Cpl.	Looker S.	do.	do.	do.
S 2423	A/Cpl.	Barnes G.	do.	do.	do.
S 6617	"	Hazel G.	do.	do.	do.
S 13700	"	Thornhill C.	do.	do.	do.

S 26369	Rfn.	Bilton A.	"B" Coy.	3/5/17	Wounded.
S 26533	"	Greenhill W.	do.	do.	do.
S 26526	"	Hemmings W.	do.	do.	do.
S 26194	"	Henderson S.	do.	do.	do.
B 2470	"	Hobbs J.	do.	do.	do.
B 762	"	Holt J.	do.	do.	do.
S 26537	"	Johnstone J.	do.	do.	do.
S 26538	"	Luck G.	do.	do.	do.
S 15032	"	Spooner F.	do.	do.	do.
B 683	"	Warden H.	do.	do.	do.
S 26161	"	Chambers P.	do.	do.	do.
S 26284	"	Compson G.	do.	do.	do.
S 22436	"	Hunt G.	do.	do.	do.
B 1087	"	Ladd T.	do.	do.	do.
S 10888	"	Maughan G.	do.	do.	do.
B 3185	"	Smith G.V	do.	do.	do.
S 25225	"	Smith G.	do.	do.	do.
B 803	Sgt.	Snow G.	do.	do.	do.
S 16545	Cpl.	Collard E.	do.	do.	do.
S 26532	A/Cpl.	Ling S.	do.	do.	do.
B 1408	"	Williams T.	do.	do.	do.
B 545	Rfn.	Stafford W.	do.	do.	do.
S 26512	"	Fortune G.	do.	do.	do.
S 845	A/Sgt.	Batten H.	"C" Coy.	do.	do.
S 26204	Cpl.	Hansford A.	do.	do.	do.
S 12781	A/Cpl.	~~XXXXX~~ Howes A	do.	do.	do.
S 14701	Rfn.	Butler R.	do.	do.	do.
S 17956	"	Ellams W.	do.	do.	do.
S 21602	"	Lindfield T.	do.	do.	do.
S 25062	"	Merry R.	do.	do.	do.
S 25054	"	Millett R.	do.	do.	do.
S 2961	"	Mulvey W.	do.	do.	do.
S 10072	"	Thornley J.	dol	dol	dol
Z 1865	"	Waugh J.	do.	do.	do.
S 2618	"	Workman W.	do.	do.	do.
S 13435	"	Rushton E.	do.	do.	do.
S 18551	"	Barnes J.	do.	do.	do.
S 27022	"	Hampton F.	do.	do.	do.
S 26007	"	Trebble A.	do.	do.	do.
S 14200	"	Butler C.	do.	do.	do.
S 26147	"	Briggs G.	do.	do.	do.
S 23943	"	Chatterson C.	do.	do.	do.
S 19872	"	Collins S.	do.	do.	do.
S 12780	"	Ettery T.	do.	do.	do.
S 27042	"	King W.	do.	do.	do.
S 26172	"	Radford C.	do.	do.	do.
S 25297	"	Smith J.	do.	do.	do.
B 2384	Sgt.	Daws J.	"D" Coy.	do.	do.
B 3403	"	Thompson R.	do.	dol	do.
B 2296	Cpl.	Lawley E.	do.	do.	do.
S 2103	"	Bradley S.	do.	do.	do.
B200677	A/Cpl.	Marshall A.	do.	do.	do.
S 8604	"	May W.	do.	do.	do.
6/631	Rfn.	Dethridge J.	do.	do.	do.
S 23772	"	Dower T.	do.	do.	do.
S 13100	"	Jobling R.	do.	do.	do.
S 25393	"	Gatty C.	do.	do.	do.
S 8193	"	Williamson S.	do.	do.	do.
S 25263	"	Withers B.	do.	do.	do.
B200672	"	Fluck J.W.	do.	do.	do.
S 17443	"	Marson J.	do.	do.	do.
S 929	"	Mead W.	do.	do.	do.
S 23805	"	Pipe E.	do.	do.	do.
S 27552	"	Gill A.	do.	do.	do.
S 27538	"	Hurrell W.	do.	do.	do.
S 16636	"	Smith G.	do.	do.	do.
S 26264	"	Sharp W.	do.	do.	do.
S 11602	"	Adams G.	do.	do.	do.
S 8702	A/Cpl.	Pringle J.	do.	do.	do.
S 26063	"	Smith F.G.	do.	do.	do. (died 5/5/17)
3941	Sgt.	Foreman H	'C' Co.	do.	do.

S 26175	Rfn.	Smithson F.	"D" Coy.	3/5/17	Wounded.
S 12284	"	Barton E.	do.	do.	do.
S 17954	"	Loveday G.	do.	do.	do.
S 21714	"	Paine W.	do.	do.	do.
S 8992	"	Medcraft W.	do.	do.	do.
Z 1097	"	Tapscott M.	do.	do.	do. (attd. T.M.Bty.)
S 29429	"	Miller F.	"C" Coy.	do.	do.
S 6239	Cpl.	Bowers W.	"B" Coy.	do.	Missing.
B 777	A/Cpl.	Brooks F.	do.	do.	do.
S 17451	Rfn.	Bull J.	do.	do.	do.
S 28439	"	Cartter C.	do.	do.	do.
S 26225	"	Campbell E.	do.	do.	do.
S 23974	"	English G.	do.	do.	do.
S 26518	"	Forder A.	do.	do.	do.
S 20564	"	Hanchard A.	do.	do.	do.
S 20509	"	Harris S.	do.	do.	do.
S 26528	"	Henson A.	do.	do.	do.
S 26530	"	Hill A.	do.	do.	do.
S 28941	"	Inskip J.	do.	do.	do.
S 8966	"	Mileham G.	do.	do.	do.
S 10960	"	Murrall F.	do.	do.	do.
S 482	"	Pitchford C.	do.	do.	do.
S 23971	A/Cpl.	Cecil A.	"C" Coy.	do.	do.
S 25452	Rfn.	Attwood W.	do.	do.	do.
S 18676	"	Brown T.	do.	do.	do.
S 26150	"	Foster M.	do.	do.	do.
S 26170	"	Howarth J.	do.	do.	do.
S 24005	"	Jones R.	do.	do.	do.
S 13647	"	Jobson R.	do.	do.	do.
S 26959	"	Poole H.	do.	do.	do.
S 26173	"	Roff E.	do.	do.	do.
S 26155	"	Rose J.	do.	do.	do.
S 25301	"	Shipman H.	do.	do.	do.
S 23280	"	Suffield R.	do.	do.	do.
S 26064	"	Smith G.	do.	do.	do.
B 2092	"	Wale H.	do.	do.	do.
S 16084	"	Webster C.	do.	do.	do.
S 20719	"	Wiggs S.	do.	do.	do.
S 25862	A/Sgt.	Bloxham H.	"D" Coy.	do.	do.
S 835	Cpl.	Stanley F.	do.	do.	do.
S 5192	"	Stokes E.	do.	do.	do.
S 6140	"	Selser C.	do.	do.	do.
S 5394	A/Cpl.	Kemp G.	do.	do.	do.
S 28437	"	Finch S.	do.	do.	do.
S 2307	R"	Sowter W.	do.	do.	do.
S 8439	Rfn.	Barber E.	do.	do.	do.
S 28444	"	Eley G.	do.	do.	do.
S 15902	"	Scott W.	do.	do.	do.
S 26277	"	Withey A.G.	do.	do.	do.
S 10453	"	Wickens W.	do.	do.	do.
S 25268	"	Hanson G.S.	do.	do.	do.
B200678	"	Towndrow J.S.	do.	do.	do.
S 26177	"	White S.G.	do.	do.	do.
S 26058	"	Pearce C.	do.	do.	do.
S 20367	"	Nicholls G.	do.	do.	do
S 19501	"	Longman R.	do.	do.	r
S 12795	"	Farley A.	do.	do.	do.
S 26985	"	Green G.	do.	do.	do.
S 26023	"	Wright E.	do.	do.	do.
S 20742	"	Birkett A.	do.	do.	do.
S 27531	"	Crooks F.	do.	do.	do.
S 5977	"	Weed A.	do.	do	do.
S 26287	"	Burley S.C.	do.	r	do.
S 26267	"	Shepherd A.	do.	do.	do.
S 1791	"	Sands F.	do.	do.	do.
S 26145	"	Buchanan A.L.	do.	do.	do.

S	8536	Rfn.	Spurrier A.	"B" Coy.	3/5/17	Wounded and Missing.
S	2782	Sgt.	McGinley J.	"C" Coy.	do.	do.
S	XXXX					
S	17967	Rfn.	Barton C.	"C" Coy.	do.	do.
S	15656	"	Harding T.	do.	do.	do.
	5664	Cpl.	Baverstock T.	do.	do.	do.
B	1113	"	Mather S.	do.	do.	do.
S	13758	Rfn.	Chapman W.	do.	do.	do.
S	28434	"	Lee E.	do.	do.	do.
S	25942	"	Lockyer A.	do.	do.	do.
S	18001	"	Rothwell G.	do.	do.	do.
S	16135	"	Freeman S.	"D" Coy.	do.	do.
S	6477	Cpl.	Seabrook A.	do.	do.	do.
S	7639	"	Missen H.	do.	do.	do.
S	5652	A/Cpl.	Ward R.	do.	do.	do.
S	16200	Rfn.	Nicholls C.D.	do.	do.	do.
S	14216	"	Harford J.	do.	do.	do.
S	27674	"	Brooks A.	do.	do.	do.
S	26268	"	Smith J.A.	do.	do.	do.
S	16490	"	Thompson W.J.	do.	do.	do.
	6412	A/Cpl.	Saunders R.	"A" Coy.	9/5/17	Wounded (S.I.)
S	28660	Rfn.	Harold E.	do.	13/5/17.	Wounded (died 13/5/17)
S	5998	"	Brennan J.	"D" Coy.	16/5/17.	Wounded
S	14410	"	Turnham R.	do.	16/5/17	Wounded.
S	9072	"	Ellis T.	"C" Coy.	do.	do. (attd. T.M.Bty.)
S	6770	"	Miller H.	do.	do.	do. do.
S	3058	"	Speddy F	do.	do.	Killed in A. do.
B	9857	Sgt.	Austin T.	"D" Coy.	do.	Killed in Action.
S	23737	Rfn.	King J.	do.	19/5/17.	Wounded.
Z	2133	"	Vaughan F.	"B" Coy.	do.	do.
S	27522	"	Lowe E.	do.	do.	do.
S	29839	"	Dyer G.	do.	do.	do.
S	29408	"	McQueen J.	"A" Coy.	18/5/17.	Killed in Action.
Z	2188	"	Williams J.	"D" Coy.	do.	Wounded.
S	26239	"	Hardwick F.	"A" Coy.	do.	do. (died 22/5/17).
S	27812	"	Jollif J.	do.	do.	do.
S	2842	Cpl.	Farrell S.	"C" Coy.	20/5/17.	do.
S	6279	Rfn.	Palmer J.	do.	do.	do.
B	3132	"	Roberts B.	do.	do.	do.
B	415	"	McColloch G.	"B" Coy.	do.	do.
B	8	"	Beattie H.	"A" Coy.	21/5/17.	do.
Z	396	"	Wilson J.	"C" Coy.	do.	Killed. (attd. T.M.Bty.)
S	24021	"	Kratosky D.	do.	23/5/17.	Wounded.
S	18235	"	Bradley A.	"D" Coy.	do.	do.
S	23725	"	Hillier A.	"B" Coy.	do.	do. (died)
S	21630	"	Boothby G.	"A" Coy.	24/5/17.	do.
S	22808	"	Busby L.	do.	do.	do.
S	18402	A/Cpl.	Cole R.	do.	do.	do.
S	524	Sgt.	Newbury G.	"C" Coy.	do	do.
S	17485	Rfn.	Hallett W.	"D" Coy.	do.	do.
S	17482	"	Peaceful G.	do.	do.	do. (died 25/5/17)
S	11110	Cpl.	Skerritt R.	"C" Coy.	do.	Killed in Action,
S	27028	Rfn.	Gooding S.	do.	do.	do.

D. Prideaux-Brune

Lieut.Colonel.

31/5/17. Commanding 8th Bn. The Rifle Brigade.

Instructions regarding War Diaries and Intelligence Summaries are contained in F. S. Regs., Part II. and the Staff Manual respectively. Title pages will be prepared in manuscript.

WAR DIARY
or
INTELLIGENCE SUMMARY.
(Erase heading not required.)

Volume 26. 8 Rifle Bde Vol 25

Army Form C. 2118.

Place	Date	Hour	Summary of Events and Information	Remarks and references to Appendices
M 10 d (51 b)	June 1st		Fine. Firing carried out on 100 yards range at WAILLY. Lindy officer on leave. JPB.	
	2		Fine. Major A C SHEEPSHANKS D.S.O. to hospital. Baths allotted to battalion. Lewis Gunners on miniature range. JPB.	
	3.		Fine. Field firing practice cancelled after one company had fired & two companies were on the way to range. Voluntary Services for C of E & Wesleyans. JPB.	
	4.		Fine. Battalion left Rest Camp & proceeded to COJEUL SWITCH by platoons at five minutes interval, commencing at 7.15 p.m. Relief of 5th OX & BUCKS completed by 10.0 p.m. Accomodation found to be much improved since last visit. JPB.	
N 7 b 2 2 (51 b)	5.		Fine. 'A' Coy used miniature range at N19.a 2 5. Large working parties found for work on Corps ammunition dumps etc. JPB.	
	6		Fine. Large working parties again found. Draft of 21 O.R. under Lt T.A. BALDOCK joined. Lt W A CREBBIN awarded the Military Cross } London Gazette 5/6/17. B681 Rfn G KEELING " D.C.M. } JPB.	
	7		Some heavy showers, but fine for most part. Battalion again on working parties. Orders received that the Brigade would probably be relieved night of 9th/10th. JPB.	

A5834 Wt. W4973/M687 750,000 8/16 D. D. & L. Ltd. Forms/C.2118/13.

Instructions regarding War Diaries and Intelligence Summaries are contained in F. S. Regs., Part II. and the Staff Manual respectively. Title pages will be prepared in manuscript.

WAR DIARY
or
INTELLIGENCE SUMMARY.
(Erase heading not required.)

Volume 26

Army Form C. 2118.

Place	Date	Hour	Summary of Events and Information	Remarks and references to Appendices
N 7 b 22 (51 b)	June 8		Fine & very hot. Large working parties. JRPB	
	9		Fine. Battalion moves back to Rest Camp at M 10 d by platoons commencing at 8 p.m. Transport Lines at M 15 c JRPB	
	10		Fine & hot. Battalion bathes. Enemy shelled neighbourhood of camp slightly at 10 0 p.m. JRPB	
	11.		Rouse 2 30 a.m. Battalion marched off at 5 0 p.m. en route for MONCHIET. Heavy thunder & rain during the march. Arrived at MONCHIET at 8 15 a.m. Battalion accomodated in huts. 55240 Sergt ALLEN W. / 9859 L/cpl HAYES H } awarded the D.C.M. D.R.O. 449 d/- 11.6.17. JRPB	
MONCHIET	12		Fine & hot. Battalion moved off from MONCHIET at 8 0 a.m. & arrived at LAHERLIERE at 9 40 a.m. Billets exceedingly comfortable. JRPB	
LAHERLIERE	13.		Rouse 3 0 a.m. Battalion moved off at 5 0 a.m. en route for BERTRANCOURT, arriving at 9 30 a.m. Battalion accomodated in huts in LYNDHURST CAMP. Camp rather dirty, but plenty of room. Fine & hot. JRPB	
BERTRANCOURT	14		Fine. Battalion busy cleaning up & improving camp, cleaning up kit etc. JRPB	
	15		Fine & hot. Major A.C SHEEPSHANKS D.S.O. rejoined from hospital. Quiet day. JRPB	

A5834 Wt. W4973/M687 750,000 8/16 D. D. & L. Ltd. Forms/C.2118/13.

Instructions regarding War Diaries and Intelligence Summaries are contained in F. S. Regs., Part II. and the Staff Manual respectively. Title pages will be prepared in manuscript.

WAR DIARY
or
INTELLIGENCE SUMMARY.
(Erase heading not required.)

Volume 26

Army Form C. 2118.

Place	Date	Hour	Summary of Events and Information	Remarks and references to Appendices
BERTRANCOURT.	16		Fine & hot. Training commences. D Company employed on range construction. JRPB	
	17		Again very hot. Usual parade services for all denominations, including Jews. Comdg Officer returns from leave. Draft of 62 O.R. arrive. JRPB	
	18		Fine, after thunder during night. Comdg Officer inspects draft. Baths allotted to C & D Coys. 'D' again employed on range building – remaining Coys continue training. JRPB	
	19		Heavy thunderstorm during early morning with a good deal of rain – fine later. Range completed & ready for use. JRPB	
	20.		Showery, with fine intervals. 'B' Coy on range from 5.0 a.m. till 10.30 – 'D' Coy from 10.30 a.m. onwards. DIVISIONAL Gas N.C.O. inspects 1 platoon per Company in Gas drill & gives a very satisfactory report as to efficiency. All box respirators tested in Gas chamber. Baths allotted to H.Q. & Transport. Draft of 68 O.R under 2/Lt O.B. TABOR joined. JRPB	
	21		Good deal of rain during night. Dull day. 'C' & 'A' Coys on Range. Draft inspected by Medical Officer. JRPB	
	22.		A good deal of rain. B & C Coys on range. JRPB	
	23.		Fine, after a few showers first thing. Day devoted to Sports. Result of Inter-Company Competition – D Coy 38 points, H.Q. 27, 'B' 17, A 16 & 'C' Coy 14 points. Very successful day. JRPB	

A5834 Wt. W4973/M687 750,000 8/16 D. D. & L. Ltd. Forms/C.2118/13.

Instructions regarding War Diaries and Intelligence Summaries are contained in F. S. Regs., Part II. and the Staff Manual respectively. Title pages will be prepared in manuscript.

WAR DIARY
or
INTELLIGENCE SUMMARY.
(Erase heading not required.)

Volume 26

Army Form C. 2118.

Place	Date	Hour	Summary of Events and Information	Remarks and references to Appendices
BERTRANCOURT	24		Fine hot day. Usual parade services for all denominations. JRPB	
	25.		Fine. Officers parade for map reading, laying out trenches etc. Battalion parade under R.S.M for arm drill, ceremonial drill etc Proposed night operations cancelled owing to rain. JRPB	
	26.		Fine. Divisional Horse Show at MARIEUX – Battalion second in Cricket Competition JRPB	
	27.		Dull. Battalion parade for outpost duties, patrols etc. Brigade Military Events in the afternoon – Battalion secured first in Signalling, Stretcher Bearer & Bugler Competitions & Second in Lewis Gun Competition. JRPB	
	28.		Showery first thing – fine later. Rouse 4.0 a.m. Battalion parade at 5.45 a.m. for Brigade Tactical Scheme in neighbourhood of AUCHONVILLERS. Owing to rain, Brigade Scheme cancelled at last moment, but the Battalion carries out its part of the scheme. Terrific thunderstorm in the evening, with torrential rain. JRPB	

A5834 Wt. W4973/M687 750,000 8/16 D. D. & L. Ltd. Forms/C.2118/13.

Instructions regarding War Diaries and Intelligence Summaries are contained in F. S. Regs., Part II. and the Staff Manual respectively. Title pages will be prepared in manuscript.

WAR DIARY
or
INTELLIGENCE SUMMARY.
(Erase heading not required.)

Volume 26

Army Form C. 2118.

Place	Date	Hour	Summary of Events and Information	Remarks and references to Appendices
BERTRANCOURT	29		Fine. Battalion parade for ceremonial drill. Battalion first in Transport turnout & second in 'harnessing up' competition in Brigade Sports. JTB	
	30		Dull & wet. H R H the Duke of Connaught inspected the battalion, together with the 7th Battn. Inspection held in pouring rain. JTB	
			Strength - 32 Officers 962 O R, including 56 at Depot.	
			Attached 1 Roll of Officers	
			2 List of Casualties.	
			J. Pedraza Brown. Lt Col Comdg 8th Bttn The Rifle Bde	

A5834 Wt. W4973/M687 750,000 8/16 D. D. & L. Ltd. Forms/C.2118/13.

8th Bn. THE RIFLE BRIGADE.

Roll of Officers on Strength of the Battalion - June 1st 1917.

Lieut.Col.D.E.Prideaux-Brune D.S.O.	Commanding Officer.
Major A.C.Sheepshanks D.S.O.	Second in Command.
Major G.V.Carey	Commanding "B" Coy.
Capt. F.E.Young	Commanding "D" Coy.
Capt. C.H.Wenham	Commanding "A" Coy.
Capt. B.H.Bennett	Commanding "C" Coy.
Lieut. W.A.Crebbin	On Leave to England.
Lieut. J.R.Abbey	Lewis Gun Officer.
Lieut. E.Poole	Transport Officer.
Lieut. W.G.Spencer	
Lieut. W.A.Teakle	
2/Lieut. R.C.Dewhurst	
" M.A.Young	In Hospital.
" W.A.Solven	
" J.A.Gould	Bombing Officer.
" H.R.Hartley	
" E.A.F.Batty	Intelligence Officer.
" A.F.Newell	Acting Adjutant.
" W.W.Wines	In Hospital.
" O.F.Savege M.C.	VII Corps Inf. School (Course)
" W.G.Hanton	
" S.R.Evans	In Hospital.
" P.H.Wooding M.C.	Signalling Officer (On Leave)
" J.Greig	
" W.N.Sproston	In Hospital.
" E.R.Magenty	Attd. Trench Mortar Battery.
" G.J.Steptoe	
" J.S.Simpson	
" C.H.Slatford	
" H.Clayton	
" J.A.Webb	
Lieut. & Q.M. F.H.Pryor	
Capt. R.N.Hunter R.A.M.C. (attd.)	

D. Prideaux-Brune

Lieut.Colonel.
Commanding 8th Bn. The Rifle Brigade.

8th Bn. THE RIFLE BRIGADE.

Casualties - June 1917.

S 2333	A/Cpl.	Richardson G.	"A" Co.	Wounded	5.6.17	Rejd. 22nd.
S 10952	Rflmn.	Nash G.	"C" Co.	Gassed	25.6.17.	Att. 41st T.M.B.
S 26504	"	Castle A.	"C" Co.	Wounded	7.6.17.	Rejd. 8.6.17.
S 26208	A/Cpl.	Barry W.	"B" Co.	Wounded	8.6.17.	

J. Prideaux-Brune

Lt.Col.,

30.6.17. Cmdg. 8th Bn. The Rifle Brigade.

8th Bn. THE RIFLE BRIGADE.

ROLL OF OFFICERS.

Lieut.Col. D.E.Prideaux-Brune, D.S.O.	Commanding Officer.
Major A.C.Sheepshanks, D.S.O.	Second-in-Command.
Major G.V.Carey	Commanding "B" Company.
Capt. F.E.Young	Third Army School Course.
Capt. C.H.Wenham	Commanding "A" Company.
Capt. B.H.Bennett	Commanding "C" Company.
Lieut. W.A.Crebbin, M.C.	
Lieut. W.G.Spencer	
Lieut. T.A.Balcock.	
Lieut. J.R.Abbey	
Lieut. E.Poole	Transport Officer.
Lieut. W.A.Teakle	Commanding "D" Company.
2/Lieut. O.B.Tabor	
2/Lieut. R.C.Dewhurst	Lewis Gun Officer.
2/Lieut. W.A.Boiven	
2/Lieut. J.A.Gould	Bombing Officer.
2/Lieut. H.R.Hartley	
2/Lieut. E.A.F.Batty	Intelligence Officer.
2/Lieut. A.F.Newell	Acting Adjutant.
2/Lieut. O.F.Savege, M.C.	
2/Lieut. W.G.Hanton	
2/Lieut. W.W.Wines	Hospital
2/Lieut. P.H.Wooding, M.C.	Signals Officer.
2/Lieut. J.Greig	
2/Lieut. W.N.Sproston	Hospital.
2/Lieut. G.J.Steptoe	
2/Lieut. J.S.Simpson	
2/Lieut. C.H.Stafford	
2/Lieut. H.Clayton	Hospital.
2/Lieut. J.A.Webb	On Leave to England.
2/Lieut. E.R.Magenty	Attd. Trench Mortar Battery.
Lieut. & Quartermaster F.H.Pryor.	
Capt. R.N.Hunter, R.A.M.C.	Medical Officer.

D. Prideaux-Brune

Lieut.Colonel.
Commanding 8th Bn. The Rifle Brigade.

30/6/18.

Instructions regarding War Diaries and Intelligence Summaries are contained in F. S. Regs., Part II. and the Staff Manual respectively. Title pages will be prepared in manuscript.

WAR DIARY
or
~~INTELLIGENCE SUMMARY.~~
(Erase heading not required.)

8th Bn. The Rifle Brigade

Army Form C. 2118.

Volume 27

Vol 26

Place	Date 1917	Hour	Summary of Events and Information	Remarks and references to Appendices
BERTRANCOURT (SOMME)	JULY 1st		Dull. Parade services for C. of E. and Wesleyans. CAPT. A.R. BACKUS M.C. rejoined Bn. from England. 2/Lt. C.E. HADWEN, 2/Lt. A.F. RICHARDS and six other ranks joined Bn. JCPB	
"	2nd		Fine and warm. Two Companies bathed. Heats of Brigade Athletic Sports in afternoon. JCPB	
"	3rd		Fine and very hot. A full day holiday for the troops on account of Brigade Sports, which started at 9 am. and finished at 8 pm. 14th Divisional Band in attendance. JCPB	
"	4th		Wet morning. Two Companies bathed. Armourer Sgt. inspected Battalions rifles. Coys. under O.C. Coys. R.S.M. Fry rejoined Battn. JCPB	
"	5th		Fine & much cooler. Companies under O.C. Coys. for musketry and drill. Information received of probable move to IX Corps, Second Army. Draft of 29 other ranks arrived. JCPB	
"	6th		Fine. Short scheme in conjunction with 8th 60th. Transport and HQrs bathed. Enemy air raid during the night: several bombs dropped in the vicinity of the camp. No damage. JCPB	
"	7th		Fine-dull. Coys. under O.C. Coys. for Open Order work. Two Coys. bathe in afternoon. Battalion concert party show at night. Very heavy thunder storm during night. JCPB	

A5834 Wt. W4973/M687 750,000 8/16 D. D. & L. Ltd. Forms/C.2118/13.

Instructions regarding War Diaries and Intelligence Summaries are contained in F. S. Regs., Part II. and the Staff Manual respectively. Title pages will be prepared in manuscript.

VOLUME 27

WAR DIARY
or
INTELLIGENCE SUMMARY.
(Erase heading not required.)

8th BN THE RIFLE BRIGADE

Army Form C. 2118.

Place	Date 1917	Hour	Summary of Events and Information	Remarks and references to Appendices
BERTRANCOURT	JULY 8th		Wet. Church Parade Services cancelled in consequence. Voluntary Service in Canteen. 2/Lt E A F BATTY to Third Army Sniping School course. 2/Lt W N SPROSTON rejoins from Hospital. Draft of 2/Lt E R DYER and 38 OR join Bn. Warning Order that Bde would be transferred to IX Corps, Second Army received. Weather improving. JEPB.	
— " —	9th		Fine during day, light rain in evening. Battalion clean up camp. Move orders received. JEPB.	
TERRAMESNIL	10th		Fine. Bn, for the first time, called upon to find firing party to put a death sentence into execution. Bn marched out of BERTRANCOURT at 6 45am, arriving at TERRAMESNIL at 3 30pm + go into billets. Quarter Master proceeded by train with Brigade Advance Party to IX Corps Area. JEPB.	
— " —	11th		Fine. Battalion route march in morning. Advance party proceed to new area. 'D' Company find 100 OR for loading Brigade Transport on to train. JEPB.	
BERTHEN	12th		Fine. Bn move off at 8 45am marching to entraining station (DOULLENS SOUTH). Train leaves at 12 19 pm, arriving at GODEWAERSVELDE at 7pm. Transport and Battalion detrain very quickly and march to camp near BERTHEN arriving at 9 45 pm. Rear party (D Co.) on last train arrive in camp at 2 am 13th inst. Headquarters established in large farm on the BERTHEN – ST JANS CAPEL Road R. 28. b 5 5 (Sheet 27 Belgium + France). DIVISION now forms part of IX Corps, Second Army. JEPB.	
— " —	13th		Fine. Coys at disposal of O.C Companies. Bn rather split up. Companies being about one mile from Headquarters, and in two separate camps. JEPB.	

A5834 Wt. W4973/M687 750,000 8/16 D. D. & L. Ltd. Forms/C.2118/13.

VOLUME 27

Army Form C. 2118.

Instructions regarding War Diaries and Intelligence Summaries are contained in F. S. Regs., Part II. and the Staff Manual respectively. Title pages will be prepared in manuscript.

WAR DIARY
or
~~INTELLIGENCE SUMMARY.~~ 8th Bn The Rifle Brigade

(Erase heading not required.)

Place	Date 1917	Hour	Summary of Events and Information	Remarks and references to Appendices
BERTHEN	JULY 14th		Fine. Enemy aeroplanes drop bombs in the vicinity about 3 am. Companies training under O.C Company. Light rain in evening. JSPB	
–	15th		Fine. Divine Services. 'A' & 'B' Coys proceed to N.15 b 2.8 Sheet 28 Belgium & France, near KEMMEL, on detachment for work on roads under R.E. Major G.V. CAREY commanding detachment. Lieut H.R. ADAIR rejoins from wounds. 2/Lt R H LAST joins from England. JSPB	
–	16th		Fine. 'D' Co. find working party of 2 officers and 100 OR for work on Corps School Bayonet Fighting Course. 'C' Co training under O.C. Company. JSPB.	
–	17th		Fine. 'C' Co. find working party as 'D' on 16th. Two Coys & HQ bathed. Corps School training ground allotted Bn for practice with live Bombs and Rifle Grenades. Capt. C.H WENHAM goes on leave for one month. 2/Lt. O.F. SAVEGE MC to First Field Survey Company on months probation. Commanding Officer and Second in Cmd. reconnoitre the Ridge Defences. JSPB	
–	18th		Dull - some rain. 'C' Co. on Corps School range at MT. KOKEREELE. 'D' Co. find working party as on 16th. Lt J R ABBEY goes on leave. 2/Lt T D. ENGLAND joins Battalion. M. DAHANIS Belgian Interpreter attached to Bn. 'A' Co. on detachment lose 2 OR accidentally wounded while on digging party. JSPB.	
–	19th		Dull - blustery. Working party for Corps School reduced to 1 officer and 50 OR and found by 'C' Co. Bn. practice working in Box Respirators at night. Respirators continually worn for one hour. JSPB.	

A5834 Wt. W4973/M687 750,000 8/16 D. D. & L. Ltd. Forms/C.2118/13.

Instructions regarding War Diaries and Intelligence Summaries are contained in F. S. Regs., Part II. and the Staff Manual respectively. Title pages will be prepared in manuscript.

WAR DIARY
or
~~INTELLIGENCE SUMMARY.~~

(*Erase heading not required.*)

VOLUME 27

Army Form C. 2118.

8th Bn. The Rifle Brigade.

Place	Date	Hour	Summary of Events and Information	Remarks and references to Appendices
	1917 JULY			
BERTHEN.	20th		Fine - dull. Route march in morning. 'D' Co. find usual working party in afternoon. 'A' Co on detachment lose One Rfn. Killed and one wounded by shell fire. JLPB.	
–	21st		Fine. Signallers and 'Details' on route march. 'C' Co. find Corps School working party. Coys at disposal of O.C. Companies. 2/Lt. T.S. SIMPSON and 5 OR to IX Corps Signalling course. JLPB.	
–	22nd		Fine. Voluntary Church Services. 'C' and 'D' Coys. relieve A & B Coys on detachment. Capt. B.H. BENNETT now commanding detachment. Capt. C.E. SQUIRE rejoins Bn. from England and takes over command of 'A' Co. temporarily. 2/Lt. E A. F BATTY rejoins from Army Sniping School. Enemy aeroplanes active at night, dropping several bombs in the vicinity. JLPB.	
–	23rd		Dull. 2/Lt. W.N. SPROSTON to Second Army Trench Mortar Course. 'A' Co. in morning and 'B' Co in afternoon find working parties for Corps School. Four other ranks attached to Bde Machine Gun Company for duty. Three other ranks attached to 41st Trench Mortar Battery for duty. Lecture on the WATSON FAN held at Brigade Headquarters in the afternoon. JLPB.	
–	24th		Fine. Commanding Officer and Adjutant reconnoitre line. Draft of eleven OR arrive. 'B' Co. bathe. Detachment lose three other ranks killed, 2/Lt. E R. DYER and 5 OR wounded by shell fire. JLPB.	

A5834 Wt. W4973/M687 750,000 8/16 D. D. & L. Ltd. Forms/C.2118/13.

Instructions regarding War Diaries and Intelligence Summaries are contained in F. S. Regs., Part II. and the Staff Manual respectively. Title pages will be prepared in manuscript.

WAR DIARY
or
~~INTELLIGENCE SUMMARY.~~
(*Erase heading not required.*)

VOLUME 27

8th Bn. The Rifle Brigade

Army Form C. 2118.

Place	Date 1917	Hour	Summary of Events and Information	Remarks and references to Appendices
BERTHEN.	July 25th		Wet. 'A' and 'B' Companies on Rifle Range. 'A' Co. bathe. JRPB.	
-	26th		Fine. Commanding Officer, Second in Command, O.C. Companies, Signalling Officer, Intelligence Officer R.S.M. and N.C.O. i/c Runners reconnoitre trench area. Companies training under Coy arrangements. Master cook goes on refresher course. JRPB.	
-	27th		Fine. Working parties found in morning and afternoon for work at Corps School. One Company & H.Qrs. bathe. 'A' Co. on Corps School range in morning. 'B' Co. in afternoon. JRPB	
-	28th		Fine. Bn carry out scheme on the BAILLEUL Training Area. Signallers attend demonstration in use of the I.T. Three O.R. found for duty at IX Corps School. JRPB.	
-	29th		Wet. Divine Services cancelled owing to weather. Capt. F.E. YOUNG rejoins from THIRD ARMY SCHOOL. JRPB.	
-	30th		Fair. 'A' Co. find Corps School working party in morning. 'A' Co. on range at MT KOKEREELE in the morning, B. Co. in the afternoon. All available officers & senior N.C.Os attend lecture by Divnl. Gas Officer. 'C' and 'D' Coys. rejoin Bn. from detachment. Lieut. J.R. ABBEY from leave. 2/LT. H.R. HARTLEY goes on leave. 2/LT. HAROLD, EVERETT, MITCHELL joins Bn. for duty. JRPB.	Appendices attached (2)
-	31st		Fine, dull. Bn standing by ready to move forward at one hours notice. Inspector of Catering visits Bn. Bn Strength, - 41 Officers 946 O.R. Available for duty 32 Officers 787 O.R. JRPB.	

J. Pritzam Brune Lt. Col.
Cmdg 8th Bn. The Rifle Bde.

A5834 Wt. W4973/M687 750,000 8/16 D. D. & L. Ltd. Forms/C.2118/13.

8th Bn. The Rifle Brigade.

Roll of Officers on Strength.

Lieut. Col. D.E. Prideaux-Brune, D.S.O.	Commanding Officer.
Major A.C. Sheepshanks, D.S.O.	Second-in-Command.
Major G.V. Carey	Cmdg. "B" Company.
Capt. A.R. Backus, M.C.	A/Adjutant.
Capt. F.E. Young	Cmdg. "D" Company.
Capt. C.E. Squire	Cmdg. "A" Company.
Capt. C.H. Wenham	On Special leave.
Capt. B.H. Bennett	Cmdg. "C" Company.
Lieut. W.A. Crebbin, M.C.	
Lieut. W.G. Spencer	In Hospital.
Lieut. H.R. Adair	
Lieut. T.A. Baldock	
Lieut. J.R. Abbey	On leave.
Lieut. E. Poole	Transport Officer.
Lieut. W.A. Teakle	
2/Lieut. O.B. Tabor	
" R.C. Dewhurst	Lewis Gun Officer.
" W.A. Solven	
" T.D. England	
" J.A. Gould	Bombing Officer
" H.R. Hartley	On leave.
" E.A.F. Batty	Intelligence Officer
" W.W. Wines	
" A.F. Newell	
" O.F. Savege, M.C.	Attd. 1st Field Survey Company.
" W.G. Hanton	
" P.H. Wooding, M.C.	Signalling Officer.
" J. Greig	IX Corps Inf. Course
" W.N. Sproston	T.M. Course
" G.J. Steptoe	
" J.S. Simpson	IX Corps Signalling Course.
" C.H. Slatford	
" H. Clayton	In Hospital.
" E.R. Magenty	Attd. T.M. Bty.
" J.A. Webb	
" A.F. Richards	
" C.E. Hadwen	
" R.H. Last	
" H E MITCHELL	
Hon. Lieut. & Q.M. F.H. Pryor.	Quartermaster.
Captain R.N. Hunter (R.A.M.C.) attd.	Medical Officer

D. Prideaux Brune

Lieut. Colonel,
Commanding 8th Bn. The Rifle Brigade.

31-7-17

8th Bn. THE RIFLE BRIGADE.

Casualties - July 1917.

S 26511	Rfn.	Cox	J.W.	"A" Coy.	18-7-17	Wounded (acc.)
S 24659	"	Coleman	W.	do.	do.	do. do.
S 26207	A/Cpl.	Atkins	H.	do.	20-7-17	Killed in Action.
S 31514	Rfn.	Bowman	G.	do.	do.	Wounded in Action.
S 2465	Sgt.	Lephard	F.	"D" Coy.	24-7-17.	Killed in Action.
S 21547	Rfn.	Morris	G.	"C" Coy.	do.	do. do.
S 25468	"	Teesdale	F.	"D" Coy.	do.	do. do.
B 2226	"	Brooks	W.	"D" Coy.	do.	Wounded (S.S.)
S 6279	"	Palmer	J.	"C" Coy.	do.	Died of Wounds.
S 13687	"	Parsons	W.	do.	do.	do.
S 23939	"	Lawrence	G.	do.	do.	Wounded in Action.
2/Lieut.		E.R.DYER			do.	do. do.

J. Prideaux-Brune

Lieut.Colonel.
Commanding 8th Bn. The Rifle Brigade.

31/7/17.

C O N F I D E N T I A L.

W A R   D I A R Y

- of -

8th (S) Bn., T H E   R I F L E   B R I G A D E.

From: 1st August, 1917.
To: 31st August, 1917.

Volume XXVIII.

VOLUME 28

Army Form C. 2118.

Instructions regarding War Diaries and Intelligence Summaries are contained in F. S. Regs., Part II. and the Staff Manual respectively. Title pages will be prepared in manuscript.

WAR DIARY
or
INTELLIGENCE SUMMARY.
(*Erase heading not required.*)

8th Bn The Rifle Brigade

Place	Date 1917	Hour	Summary of Events and Information	Remarks and references to Appendices
BERTHEN	Aug. 1		Wet. Bn standing by ready to move forward at an hours notice. Order received at 2 pm cancelling the restriction. JRPB.	
–	2nd		Dull and overcast. Companies at the disposal of OC Companies for short route march or work near camp. JRPB.	
–	3rd		Wet. Companies do short route march in morning. Signallers tested and classified by Brigade Signal Officer. 2/Lt. W G HANTON goes on leave. Division is now in G H Q reserve. 2/Lt. REUBEN JOHN HOOK joined Battalion. Draft of Y OR joined Bn. Camp now in very muddy condition. JRPB.	
–	4th		Fine. Some sun. CAPT. A R BACKUS MC appointed Adjutant. Companies carry out short route marches. Commanding Officer inspects draft. Warning Order received that Brigade will move on the 6th inst. to the HONDEGHEM district. JRPB.	
–	5th		Fine. Sunny. Divine Services. Operation Orders for move received. JRPB.	
HONDEGHEM Area	6th		Bn moved off at 7 20 am marching via FLETRE and CAESTRE to the HONDEGHEM area. Billets here were very difficult to obtain and when Bn finally settled down Companies were a considerable distance apart. Bn. HQ established at 27 V 16 c 4 9. Brigade Headquarters in HONDEGHEM at 27 V 2 b 6 2. 2/Lt. H CLAYTON rejoined from hospital. JRPB.	
–	7th		Fine. Companies under OC Coys. for work. JRPB.	

A5834 Wt. W4973/M687 750,000 8/16 D. D. & L. Ltd. Forms/C.2118/13.

Instructions regarding War Diaries and Intelligence Summaries are contained in F. S. Regs., Part II. and the Staff Manual respectively. Title pages will be prepared in manuscript.

WAR DIARY
or
INTELLIGENCE SUMMARY.
(*Erase heading not required.*)

VOLUME 28

Army Form C. 2118.

8th Bn. The Rifle Brigade

Place	Date 1917	Hour	Summary of Events and Information	Remarks and references to Appendices
HAZEBROUCK Area	Aug 8		Fine Officers + senior N.C.Os on compass and map reading work. Companies at disposal of OC Coys for arm drill, close order drill, musketry &c. Afternoon devoted to recreational training. JRPB.	
–	9		Fine About 4 am Enemy aeroplanes bomb HAZEBROUCK. Bombs drop in vicinity of Bn. Billets. One direct hit on 'A' Coys. billet causes wounds to eleven other ranks. About 8.30 am enemy shell HAZEBROUCK with heavy long range guns. 2/Lt J. A GOULD goes on leave. Bn. carry out short route march map reading scheme. Each OC Coy being stationed at a separate rendezvous and one platoon from each Company marching to each of the rendezvous by various routes. Many refugees from HAZEBROUCK seek shelter in Bn. billets. JRPB	
–	10th		Dull. Between 3 and 4 am enemy aeroplanes pass over HAZEBROUCK and heavily bomb the railway between that town and BERGUETTE. Bn carry out an hours route march wearing small box respirators. Remainder of morning Coys practice with dummy bombs and rifle grenades. Enemy again shell HAZEBROUCK. Early part of night fine - rain later. JRPB.	
–	11th		Dull. 2/Lt H.R HARTLEY from leave. One platoon from each Coy. and one from HQ compete in drill competition. Competition judged by Maj Genl V. COUPER C.B. 'C' Co. win. Remainder of Bn. carry out route march. Rain in showers throughout day. JRPB.	
–	12th		Fine Divine Services. 130 OR inoculated. JRPB.	
–	13th		Fine Coys. under OC Companies. Officers + men who originally came out with the Bn attend the funeral of the late Brig. Gen. R C Maclachlan D.S.O. at LOCRE. JRPB.	

A5834 Wt. W4973/M687 750,000 8/16 D. D. & L. Ltd. Forms/C.2118/13.

Instructions regarding War Diaries and Intelligence Summaries are contained in F. S. Regs., Part II. and the Staff Manual respectively. Title pages will be prepared in manuscript.

WAR DIARY
or
~~INTELLIGENCE SUMMARY.~~
(Erase heading not required.)

VOLUME 28.

8th Bn. The Rifle Brigade

Army Form C. 2118.

Place	Date 1917	Hour	Summary of Events and Information	Remarks and references to Appendices
HAZEBROUCK	AUG 14th		Fine Coys under O.C. Coys. for practice with dummy bombs and rifle grenades. Warning order received that Brigade would move forward on 15th inst. Advance party proceeded to DICKIEBUSCH area. Bn organised in accordance with para XXX S.S. 135. JRPB	
-	15th		Fine. Bn clean up billets. Bn marched off at 8 pm to CAESTRE. Train late. Train eventually moved out at 2.30 am 16th inst. JRPB	
DICKIEBUSCH	16th		Fine Bn detrained at OUDERDUM at 4.30 am. Intense artillery fire seen to be in progress on the front. Bn marched to DICKIEBUSCH huts (28 - H.26.b.5.8) finally settling down about 7 am. Bn rest. About 8 pm orders received that Bn will move forward at 10.30 pm. Bn move forward to CHATEAU SEGARD area, arriving about 2.30 am 17th inst. JRPB	
-	17th		Fine. Capt. F.E. YOUNG, 2/Lt H.R. HARTLEY and N.C.O's left behind under para XXX proceed to 2nd Corps Advance Reinforcement Camp, at OUDEZEELE. Remainder left out stay at Transport Camp. Bn remained at CHATEAU SEGARD during the day, moving forward to Brigade Reserve in ZILLEBEKE BUND. Two OR. wounded JRPB	
-	18th		Fine. Great aeroplane activity, also artillery very active. One OR. wounded JRPB	

A5834 Wt. W4973/M687 750,000 8/16 D. D. & L. Ltd. Forms/C.2118/13.

VOLUME 28

Army Form C. 2118.

WAR DIARY
or
~~INTELLIGENCE SUMMARY.~~
(*Erase heading not required.*)

Instructions regarding War Diaries and Intelligence Summaries are contained in F. S. Regs., Part II. and the Staff Manual respectively. Title pages will be prepared in manuscript.

8th Bn. The Rifle Bde

Place	Date 1917	Hour	Summary of Events and Information	Remarks and references to Appendices
ZILLEBEKE	Aug. 19		Fine. Bn in Brigade Reserve. Enemy artillery active. Large number of gas shells used. Enemy aeroplanes bomb back area at night. DZPB	
	20th		Fine. Great aeroplane activity. One OR wounded. Bn relieved by 10th Bn D.L.I about 8.30pm & proceeded to DICKIEBUSCH Huts. Relief passed off quietly. DZPB	
DICKIEBUSCH	21st		Fine. Bn resting. Capt H R ADAIR on leave. Commanding Officer attends conference at Brigade HQ. Enemy aeroplanes less active at night but more shelling of back areas. DZPB	
	22nd		Fine. Bn left camp at about 2pm & marched to ZILLEBEKE BUND where they came under orders of the 43rd Inf. Bde. Reported to Brig Genl P. WOOD CB at DORMY HOUSE. 8th KRRC and this Bn ordered to take over the line tonight on the North and South of the MENIN Rd respectively with the object of attacking and gaining final objectives, - Strong point 28-J14b 25.30 FITZCLARENCE Fm - HERENTHAGE CHAU at 4am 24th inst. This was cancelled by Division. DZPB	
	23rd		8th Bn KRRC ordered to relieve us at ZILLEBEKE. DZPB	
	24th		Waited for relief all night. Finally two and half companies KRRC relieved 'C', 'D' & half 'A' Coys 8th R Bde, who marched back to DICKIEBUSCH Huts. Enemy counter attacked at 6am and at 10.45am. troops at ZILLEBEKE ordered to be prepared to move up to reinforce front line. At 1.10pm orders received for all troops in ZILLEBEKE BUND to reinforce original front line. Lt Col. DE PRIDEAUX-BRUNE D.S.O. cmdg 1½ Coys 8th Bn Rifle Brigade and 2½ Coys. KRRC to report to OC 10th D.L.I. at CLAPHAM JUNCTION 28-J.13d 85.85. Moved up through intense barrage. Casualties, - 2/Lt. W.W. Wines killed. Capt. B.H. Bennett, 2/Lt T.D. England and about 40 OR wounded.	

A5834 Wt. W4973/M687 750,000 8/16 D. D. & L. Ltd. Forms/C.2118/13.

VOLUME 28

Army Form C. 2118.

Instructions regarding War Diaries and Intelligence Summaries are contained in F. S. Regs., Part II. and the Staff Manual respectively. Title pages will be prepared in manuscript.

WAR DIARY
or
~~INTELLIGENCE SUMMARY.~~ 8th Bn. The Rifle Brigade

(Erase heading not required.)

Place	Date	Hour	Summary of Events and Information	Remarks and references to Appendices
	1917			
INVERNESS COPSE	AUG 24		Capt. C.E. SQUIRE with half 'A' Co and 2/Lt W.N. SPROSTON and 2/Lt T.D. ENGLAND with their platoons of 'C' Co. ordered to re-occupy western edge of INVERNESS COPSE. They were held up by machine gun fire about 300 yards short of edge of wood – Here they occupied a line of shell holes astride the MENIN Rd. and parallel to the western edge of the copse. Here 2/Lt ENGLAND was wounded. At dusk 2/Lt W.N. SPROSTON with both platoons of 'C' Co reoccupy western edge of copse and consolidate. ~~A~~ ~~right~~ defensive flank being formed along JASPER AVENUE, composed of elements of all Bns in 43rd Inf. Bde., to join up with XXIV Divn.	
			At 3 am 1½ Coys relieved by 7th Bn Rifle Brigade and returned to BUND. Meanwhile 2½ Coys under Lieut H.A. CREBBIN M.C. had moved from camp to ECOLE and then relieved 5th Ox & Bucks L.I. in GLENCORSE WOOD on the left of the 7th 60th.	J.L.P.B.
	25th		41st Inf. Bde took over whole Divisional line. HQ and One and half Coys moved up from BUND to HOOGE TUNNEL. Quiet relief. The Brigade ordered to put out a line of outposts 100 yards in front of our position roughly on the line J.14.a.7.3 – J.14.c.4.8 – J.14.c.45.55. This was reported complete at 2.45 am 26th inst	J.L.P.B.
	26th		The enemy attacked at 4.45 am with Flammenwerfer. The attack was repulsed in GLENCORSE WOOD but succeeded in driving in the outpost at J.14.c.4.8. The enemy kept up a heavy barrage on the MENIN Road from 4.30 am to 8.30 am. Remainder of day quiet. Orders came in at 7.30 pm that the Brigade is to attack on a three platoon front assisted by four tanks. The objective being J.14.a.55.15 – Strong point J.14.c.4.9 – J.14.c.6.6. 2/Lt W.N. SPROSTON and platoon from 'C' Co. chosen to make this attack.	J.L.P.B.

A5834 Wt. W4973/M687 750,000 8/16 D. D. & L. Ltd. Forms/C.2118/13.

Instructions regarding War Diaries and Intelligence Summaries are contained in F. S. Regs., Part II. and the Staff Manual respectively. Title pages will be prepared in manuscript.

WAR DIARY VOLUME 28
or
~~INTELLIGENCE~~ SUMMARY.
(Erase heading not required.)

8th Bn. The Rifle Brigade

Army Form C. 2118.

Place	Date 1917	Hour	Summary of Events and Information	Remarks and references to Appendices
INVERNESS COPSE	Aug 27		Rain all night. 2/Lt SPROSTON moved off from Bn. HQ at 3 20 am. Most of his platoon became casualties on the way up and he was reinforced by 14 platoon. The state of the ground would not allow tanks to operate and the attack did not develope. The enemy kept up a terrific barrage from 4 am till 9 am. Rest of day quiet. Rained all day. Relieved by two Coys 8th K.O.Y.L.I. (23rd Div.) Heavy barrage during relief from 8pm - 9.30 pm. incoming troops suffered many casualties. Relief complete 5.15 am 28th inst. Casualties for tour Officers - Killed 1 Wounded 2 OR - K 12 M 9 W 91	
DICKIEBUSCH	28		Fine. Bn. resting at DICKIEBUSCH HUTS. Lt. H G SPENCER rejoined from hospital. D.R.P.B. 2/Lt C. L. EMY joined Bn. D.R.P.B.	
METEREN	29		Wet. Bn. left camp at 1.20 pm and proceeded to billets in METEREN arriving about 6 pm. D.R.P.B.	Appendices 2
- -	30th		Fine. Companies at disposal of O.C. Companies, for refitting and cleaning up. D.R.P.B.	
- . -	31st		Showery. Companies under OC Companies. Training of specialists commenced to bring Bn up to strength in Lewis Gunners, Bombers, Rifle Grenadiers, Stretcher Bearers, Snipers &c. D.R.P.B.	

J. Pritchard Brame
Lt Col
Cmdg 8th Bn The Rifle Brigade

A5834 Wt. W4973/M687 750,000 8/16 D. D. & L. Ltd. Forms/C.2118/13.

8th. Bn. The Rifle Brigade.

Nominal Roll of Officers serving with the Battalion.

Lieut.Col.D.E.Prideaux-Brune, D.S.O.	Commanding Officer.
Major A.C.Sheepshanks, D.S.O.	2nd. in Command.
Major G.V.Carey	O.C. "B" Company.
Capt. A.R.Backus, M.C.	Adjutant
Capt. F.E.Young	G.H.Q. Lewis Gun Course
Capt. C.E.Squire	O.C. "A" Company.
Lieut. W.A.Crebbin, M.C.	
Lieut. W.G.Spencer	
Lieut. H.R.Adair	On leave to England.
Lieut. T.A.Baldock	2nd. Army Inf. School.
Lieut. J.R.Abbey	
Lieut. E.Poole	Transport Officer.
Lieut. W.A.Teakle	
2nd.Lieut. O.B.Tabor	
2nd.Lieut. R.C.Dewhurst	Lewis GunOfficer.
2nd.Lieut. W.A.Solven	
2nd.Lieut. J.A.Gould	
2nd.Lieut. H.R.Hartley	
2nd.Lieut. E.A.F.Batty	Intelligence Officer.
2nd.Lieut. A.F.Newell	A/Adjt. Div. Depot.
2nd.Lieut. O.F.Savege, M.C.	1st. Field Survey Coy.
2ndmLieut. W.G.Hanton	
2nd.Lieut. P.H.Wooding, M.C.	Signalling Officer.
2nd.Lieut. J.Grieg	
2nd.Lieut. W.N.Sproston	
2nd.Lieut. G.J.Steptoe	
2nd.Lieut. J.S.Simpson	1X Corps Signal Course.
2nd.Lieut. C.H.Slatford	
2nd.Lieut. H.Clayton	
2nd.Lieut. E.R.Magenty	T.M.B.
2nd.Lieut. J.A.Webb	
2nd.Lieut. A.F.Richards	
2nd.Lieut. C.E.Hadwen	
2nd.Lieut. R.H.Last	
2nd.Lieut. C.L.Emy	
2nd.Lieut. R.J.Hook	
2nd.Lieut. H.E.Mitchell	
Lieut. & Q.M. F.H.Pryor	Quartermaster.

J. Prideaux Brune

Lieut.Col.

31/8/17.

Cmdg. 8th. Bn. The Rifle Brigade.

In the Field. Sheet 2. 31/8/17.

S 26280	Rfn.	Kitching A.	8th Bn. R.B.	Wounded	24/8/17	C
S 17908	Cpl.	Norman J.	do.	do.	26/8/17	C
S 25264	Rfn.	Matthews N.	do.	do.	24/8/17.	C
S 30095	"	Nicholls G.	do.	do.	do.	C
S 26290	"	Ormerod E.	do.	do.	do.	C
B200516	L/Cpl.	Neville W.	do.	do.	do.	C.
S 31041	Rfn.	Turner J.	do.	do.	27/8/17.	C.
S 25323	"	Woodward E.	do.	do.	24/8/17	C
5928	"	Ellis	do.	do.	do.	C
S 21537	"	Reed T.	do.	do.	25/8/17	D
S 20984	"	Bridges J.	do.	do.	do.	D
S 28443	"	Hill G.	do.	do.	do.	D
S 26050	"	Ludlow A.	do.	do.	do.	D
304635	"	Ross L.	do.	do.	do.	D
S 14854	"	Gillett W.	do.	do.	do.	D
S 10363	"	Newman G.	do.	do.	do.	D
S 17443	"	Morson J.	do.	do.	do.	D
S 20727	"	Aldridge A.	do.	do.	do.	D
S 12984	"	Bartoh E.	do.	do.	do.	D
B200121	"	Smith J.	do.	do.	do.	D
S 22813	"	Richards H.	do.	do.	do.	D
8545	"	McDonald H.	do.	do.	do.	D
S 26176	"	Tait W.	do.	do.	do.	D
B200665	"	Salter F.	do.	do.	do.	D
B200876	"	Taylor E.	do.	do.	do.	D
S 14670	"	Green W.	do.	do.	do.	D
B200210	"	Stevens V.	do.	do.	do.	D
S 13100	"	Jobling R.	do.	do.	do.	D
S 26248	"	Thurston F.	do.	do.	do.	D
S 6924	L/Cpl.	Watson J.	do.	do.	do.	D
S 30684	Rfn.	Creighton S.	do.	do.	do.	D
S 23737	"	King J.	do.	do.	do.	D
S 28821	"	Clary G.	do.	do.	do.	D
S 5982	"	Everett G.	do.	do.	do.	D
S 8193	"	Williamson S.	do.	do.	do.	D
S 26029	"	Woods S.	do.	do.	do.	D
B203331	"	Hilditch J.	do.	do.	do.	D
B 341	"	Lyons W.	do.	do.	do.	B
S 17925	"	Griffen J.	do.	do.	do.	B
S 24021	"	Kratosky	do.	do.	do.	C
S 21991	"	KMXXMXK Johnson	do.	do.	do.	C
S 18554	"	Chapman	do.	do.	do.	C
S 26510	L/Cpl.	Creswick	do.	do.	do.	A
B200850	Rfn.	Lewis W.	do.	Missing.	24/8/17	A
306242	"	Sheridan E.	do.	do.	do.	A
S 18073	"	Brown T.	do.	do.	do.	A
S 14701	"	Butler R.	do.	do.	do.	C
S 23108	"	Gordon S.	do.	do.	do.	C
S 13213	"	Hicks W.	do.	Missing b. K.	do.	C
S 25997	"	Smith J.	do.	Missing	27/8/17	C
S 12720	"	Ettery T.	do.	do.	24/8/17	C
B 2232	"	Davies H.	do.	Missing b. K.	do.	D

A.R. Backus Capt & Adjt.
for O.C. 8th Bn. The Rifle Brigade

8th Bn. The Rifle Brigade

Casualties Aug 1917

In the Field. ~~XXXXXXX~~ 31.8.17.

No.	Rank	Name	Unit	Casualty	Date	Coy.
	2/Lieut.	W.W. WINES	8th Bn. R.B.	Killed in A.	24/8/17	
	2/Lieut.	T.D. ENGLAND	do.	Wounded	do.	
	Capt.	B.H. BENNETT	do.	do.	do.	
S 31773	Rfn.	Stretton S.	do.	Killed in A.	26/8/17	"B"
S 26536	"	Jaques W.	do.	do.	27/8/17	B
6581	Sgt.	Emmett H.	do.	do.	24/8/17	C
S 31539	L/Cpl.	Wiles L.	do.	do.	do.	C
S 6196	Rfn.	Williams T.	do.	do.	do.	C
B200184	"	Freeman H.	do.	do.	do.	C
S 24366	"	Gibson A.	do.	do.	25/8/17	D
S 31221	"	Willis W.	do.	do.	do.	D
S 28045	"	Grinyer E.	do.	do.	do.	D
305240	"	Bishop B.	do.	do.	do.	D
305320	"	Baker W.	do.	do.	do.	D
304663	"	Winkworth H.	do.	do.	do.	D
S 17993	"	Mills G.	do.	Wounded	23/8/17	A
S 15062	"	Muckle T.	do.	" (bel.K.)	24/8/17	A
S 31548	"	Stumbles A.	do.	do.	do.	A
913	Sgt.	Rideout G.	do.	do.	27/8/17.	A
B 141	Rfn.	Anderberg A.	do.	do.	do.	A
S 26492	L/Cpl.	Bonnie J.	do.	do.	24/8/17	A
S 26235	Rfn.	Green H.	do.	do.	do.	A
S 7278	"	Hanley F.	do.	do.	26/8/17	A
S 23062	"	Martin W.	do.	do.	24/8/17.	A
S 24644	"	Mates A.	do.	do.	do.	A
S 16871	"	Nutkins H.	do.	do.	27/8/17	A
B200853	"	Lee N.	do.	do.	24/8/17	A
B200881	"	Willis J.	do.	do.	27/8/17	A
B200879	"	Wildman W.	do.	do.	do.	A
305294	"	Trout C.	do.	do.	do.	A
Z 1098	"	Robertson F.	do.	do.	do.	A
6412	"	Sanders R.	do.	do.	do.	A
S 9684	"	Cooper S.	do.	do. (Gas)	do.	A
305294	"	Page W.	do.	do.	24/8/17	A
S 30855	"	Smith G.	do.	do.	27/8/17	A
S 975	A/C.S.M.	Childe H.	do.	do.	do.	B
4258	Sgt.	Pevalin W.	do.	do.	26/8/17	B
S 26260	L/Cpl.	Cannell O.	do.	do.	do.	B
S 26520	Rfn.	Foster A.	do.	do.	do.	B
S 2399	"	Guy W.	do.	do.	do.	B
S 26519	"	Fortune C.	do.	do.	do.	B
S 29891	"	Crowhurst G.	do.	do.	do.	B
S 25682	"	Pears W.	do.	do.	do.	B
S 31358	"	Savoie R.	do.	do.	do.	B
S 26529	"	Holding G.	do.	do.	27/8/17	B
S 26523	"	Garrett A.	do.	do.	do.	B
S 23999	"	Fish A.	do.	do.	do.	B
S 26280	"	Hodges T.	do.	do.	do.	B
S 22435	"	Wallen F.	do.	do.	do.	B
B 545	"	Stafford W.	do.	do.	24/8/17	B
S 8445	"	Baker R.	do.	do.	do.	C
B 1507	"	Bliss J.	do.	do.	do.	C
4753	L/Cpl.	Bennett V.	do.	do.	26/8/17	C
S 208	Rfn.	Brock S.	do.	do.	24[illegible]	C
S 29915	"	Carter G.	do.	do.	[illegible]	
S 20278	"	Dorling S.	do.	do.	[illegible]	
S 31526	"	Franklin W.	do.	do.	[illegible]	
S 1[illegible]08	"	Griffiths R.	do.	do.	[illegible]	

Instructions regarding War Diaries and Intelligence Summaries are contained in F. S. Regs., Part II. and the Staff Manual respectively. Title pages will be prepared in manuscript.

WAR DIARY
or
~~INTELLIGENCE SUMMARY.~~

(Erase heading not required.)

VOLUME 29

Army Form C. 2118.

8th Bn The Rifle Brigade

Vol 28

Place	Date 1917	Hour	Summary of Events and Information	Remarks and references to Appendices
METEREN	Sept 1st		Fine. Companies under O.C. Coys. Specialist Officers training men to bring Bn. up to strength in specialists. Two Coys. & HQ. bathe. Operation Orders received that the Dvn will relieve 30th DIVN in the line from LA DOUVE RIVER to DELPORTE Fm. on night 2nd/3rd. GL	
	2nd		Showery. Voluntary Church Services in morning. At 1.30pm Bn marched out of METEREN to camp at 28-T. 14 d 5 4 (NEUVE EGLISE), arriving about 5pm. BN HQ in huts, remainder of BN under canvas. Enemy aeroplanes extremely active, dropping bombs throughout night and early morning. GL	
NEUVE EGLISE	3rd		Fine. BN. cleaning up and draining camp. Training of specialists continued. Enemy aeroplanes again active at night. GL	
	4th		Fine. A and B Coys on range. Specialists training continued. Five OR to Fifth Army Rest Camp. BN employed on improving the camp. Working party of 1 Off. & 30 OR found for loading RE material. Commanding Officer and Second in Command reconnoitre line. Draft of 10 OR arrive. Enemy aeroplanes again active. GL	
	5th		Fine. Specialists continue training. D Co. on range. 'C' Co. bathe. Coys. at disposal of O.C. Coys. GL	
	6th		Fine. Coys at disposal of O.C. Coys. 'D' Co. bathe. Heavy thunder storm at night. GL	

A5834 Wt. W4973/M687 750,000 8/16 D. D. & L. Ltd. Forms/C.2118/13.

Instructions regarding War Diaries and Intelligence Summaries are contained in F. S. Regs., Part II. and the Staff Manual respectively. Title pages will be prepared in manuscript.

WAR DIARY
or
~~INTELLIGENCE SUMMARY.~~
(Erase heading not required.)

VOLUME 29.

8th Bn. The Rifle Brigade

Army Form C. 2118.

Place	Date	Hour	Summary of Events and Information	Remarks and references to Appendices
	1917			
NEUVE EGLISE	Sept. 7th		Fine. Coys under O.C. Coys. Armourer Sgt. inspects rifles and fits new muzzle protectors. Company Officers Signal Officer & Intelligence Officer go round line with Commanding Officer. Maj. G.V. CAREY rejoins from leave. Warning ~~off~~ Order received that Bn will go into front line on 10th inst. Enemy shell back areas at night, less aeroplane activity. GM	
	8th		Dull. Coys under O.C. Companies. 2/Lt. HEBB and 5 O.R. to Second Army Rest Camp (Divn now forming part of VIII Corps, Second Army). Quiet night. GM	
	9th		Fine. Companies at disposal of O.C. Companies. Bn clean up camp. GM	
	10th		Fine. 2/Lt. C.H. SLATFORD to Base Depot to take up duties as instructor. B611 R.S.M. W.C. FRY to Base for transfer to Home Establishment. Bn move off by platoons at 200 yards interval starting at 5.30 A.M. and relieve 3 Coys. 9th K.R.R.C. in support. Relief complete at 9 am. 'B' Co relieve one Coy 5th K.S.L.I. in Reserve at 9 pm. A, C, D and HQ relieve 5th K.S.L.I. in front line by 10 pm. Quiet relief. GM	
Trenches N.E. of MESSINES	11th		Fine. Some shelling during day, but quiet generally. One O.R. wounded. GM	
	12th		Fine. Very quiet day. Considerable air activity on both sides. GM	
	13th		Fine. Intermittent shelling throughout day. One O.R. wounded. 2/Lt. J. GREIG rejoins from leave. Officers from 9th K.R.R.C. reconnoitre front line. GM	

A5834 Wt. W4973/M687 750,000 8/16 D. D. & L. Ltd. Forms/C.2118/13.

Instructions regarding War Diaries and Intelligence Summaries are contained in F. S. Regs., Part II. and the Staff Manual respectively. Title pages will be prepared in manuscript.

WAR DIARY
or
~~INTELLIGENCE~~ SUMMARY.

(Erase heading not required.)

VOLUME 29

Army Form C. 2118.

8th Bn. The Rifle Brigade.

Place	Date 1917	Hour	Summary of Events and Information	Remarks and references to Appendices
Trenches N.E. MESSINES	SEP. 14		Fine. Quiet throughout day. At 7.30 pm our artillery opened out and kept up a steady fire until 2 am 15th inst. At 11.30 pm gas was released from front line. Enemy replied with 5.9s & Trench Mortars. One OR killed. One OR wounded. 2/Lt. C.E. HADWEN 'C' Co. established advanced post at night in trench previously occupied by the enemy. Lt-Col. D.E. PRIDEAUX-BRUNE proceeds on one months leave. GM	
	15th		Fine. Gas shells in early morning around Bn. HQ. and Reserve Company. Our artillery kept up a steady fire throughout the day. Enemy Quiet. Small enemy raid about 5.40 am on post of 8th K.R.R.C. just on our right. GM	
	16th		Fine. About 9.30 am our artillery opened rapid fire which continued till 10.40 am. Enemy replied with 5.9s. Bn relieved at night by 7th 60th about 10 pm and took over the Support Line. GM	
	17th		Fine. Bn in Support. Quiet day. About 250 all ranks found for working parties at night. GM	
	18th		Fine. Quiet day. Artillery barraged enemy's line from 8 pm to 9 pm. Working parties of 7 off. and 200 OR found for carrying R.E. material & work on Corps Line. Capt. F.E. YOUNG and Capt. W.A. TEAKLE go on leave. GM	
	19th		Fine. Situation quiet. Usual working parties at night. GM	

A5834 Wt. W4973/M687 750,000 8/16 D. D. & L. Ltd. Forms/C.2118/13.

Instructions regarding War Diaries and Intelligence Summaries are contained in F. S. Regs., Part II. and the Staff Manual respectively. Title pages will be prepared in manuscript.

WAR DIARY or ~~INTELLIGENCE SUMMARY.~~

(Erase heading not required.)

VOLUME 29

Army Form C. 2118.

8th Bn. The Rifle Brigade

Place	Date 1917	Hour	Summary of Events and Information	Remarks and references to Appendices
Support N.E. MESSINES	Sept 20		Dull. Right rain improving later. At 5.40 am 7th Bn. The Rifle Brigade raided enemy's line. Bn. relieved by 3 Coys 10th Bn. D.L.I. and One Coy. 6th D.C.L.I. commencing at 2 pm. Bn. proceeded to camp at 28. T. 14 c 5.4. GM	
NEUVE EGLISE	21st		Fine. Bn. cleaning up. Coys at disposal of O.C. Coys. Working parties found at night for carrying for Bns in the line and work on Corps Line. 4 Officers and 150 OR employed. GM	
	22		Fine. Coys at disposal of O.C. Coys. Working parties found for work in the forward area. 7 Officers and 270 OR employed. LIEUT W.G. SPENCER on leave. Notification of following awards appear in Divisional Routine Orders. 2/LT W.N. SPROSTON – Military Cross. 8005 A/R.S.M. HARWOOD H. – Bar to Distinguished Conduct Medal. GM	
	23rd		Fine. Capt and Adjt. A.R. BACKUS M.C. died of injuries received in bicycle accident. Parade Church Services. GM	
	24th		Fine. 'A' Co. on range all day. Remaining Companies bathe. Regimental Class in Boxing and Lewis Gun commenced. GM	
	25th		Fine. Coys at disposal of O.C. Coys. 'A' Co. bathe. Officers and 150 OR attend funeral of the late Capt. A.R. BACKUS M.C., buried at Military Cemetery 28. T 19 a 1.9. GM	
	26th		Fine. Coys at disposal of O.C. Coys. 'B' Co on range. Working parties up to 8 Officers and 400 OR found for work in forward area. Major A.C. SHEEPSHANKS D.S.O. leaves Bn to take over Command of 10th Bn. K.R.R.C. Major G.V. CAREY assumes command of the Battalion. GM	

Army Form C. 2118.

Instructions regarding War Diaries and Intelligence Summaries are contained in F. S. Regs., Part II. and the Staff Manual respectively. Title pages will be prepared in manuscript.

WAR DIARY VOLUME 29
or
~~INTELLIGENCE SUMMARY.~~
(*Erase heading not required.*)

8th Bn. The Rifle Brigade

Place	Date	Hour	Summary of Events and Information	Remarks and references to Appendices
NEUVE EGLISE	1917 Sept 26		2/LT. A F NEWELL rejoins from Depot Bn. and takes up duty as acting adjutant. 2/LT. J. S. SIMPSON on leave. Men in possession of new box respirators tested in gas. GM	
	27		Fine. Coys at disposal of O.C. Coys. 'C' Co. on range. Armourer inspects rifles of A & B Coys. H.Qrs inoculated. ~~Working parties of 7 Officers and 320 OR found~~ GM Enemy aeroplanes active at night GM	
	28		Fine. 2/LT. H.A. SOLVEN and Sgt. JAMESON proceed to England for course of musketry instruction at HAYLING ISLAND. 'D' Co. on range. Armourer inspects Lewis Guns and rifles of 'D' Co. Working parties of 7 Officers and 320 OR found GM	
	29		Fine. 'D' Co. on range. Coys under O.C. Coys. Specialists classes carried on in morning. Bn attend Gas Drill Demonstration in afternoon. Draft of 27 OR arrive. Enemy aeroplanes extremely active at night bombing camps &c GM	
	30		Fine. Divine Services. Capt. F.E. YOUNG rejoins from leave. Working parties of 7 Officers and 275 OR found Bn Strength, - 36 Officers 816 OR Available Strength 26 " 741 " GM	

G M [signature] Major
Cmdg 8th Bn. The Rifle Brigade

A5834 Wt. W4973/M687 750,000 8/16 D. D. & L. Ltd. Forms/C.2118/13.

<u>8th Bn. THE RIFLE BRIGADE.</u>

<u>Appendix to War Diary.</u>

<u>September 1917.</u>

<u>Roll of Officers on Strength.</u>

Lieut.Col.D.E.Prideaux-Brune, D.S.O.	Commanding Officer. (On Leave)
Major G.V.Carey	In Temp. Command of Bn.
Captain F.E.Young	Commanding "D" Company.
Captain C.E.Squire	In Hospital.
Lieut. W.A.Crebbin M.C.	Commanding "B" Company.
Lieut. W.G.Spencer	On Leave.
Lieut.(A/Capt.)H.R.Adair	Fourth Army Inf. School Course.
Lieut. T.A.Baldock	Commanding "C" Company.
Lieut. J.R.Abbey	Commanding "A" Company.
Lieut. E.Poole	Battalion Transport Officer.
Lieut.(A/Capt.)W.A.Teakle	On Leave.
2/Lieut. O.B.Tabor	In Hospital.
" R.C.Dewhurst	Battalion Lewis Gun Officer.
" W.A.Solven	School of Musketry, HYTHE.
" J.A.Gould	Battalion Bombing Officer.
" H.R.Hartley	
E.A.F. E.A.F.Batty	Bn. Intelligence Officer.
" A.F.Newell	Acting Adjutant.
" O.F.Savege, M.C.	1st Field Survey Company.
" W.G.Hanton	
" P.H.Wooding, M.C.	Battalion Signal Officer.
" J.Greig	
" W.N.Sproston, M.C.	
" G.J.Steptoe	
" J.S.Simpson	On Leave.
" C.H.Slatford	Central Training School, LE HAVRE (Instructor)
" H.Clayton	
" E.R.Magenty	41st Trench Mortar Battery
" J.A.Webb	
" A.F.Richards	
" C.E.Hadwen	
" R.H.Last	
" C.L.Emy	
R.J R.J.Hook	
" H.E.Mitchell	

Hon.Lieut. & Quartermaster, F.H.Pryor.

Captain R.N.Hunter,(R.A.M.C)	Medical Officer.

G.V.Carey

Major,
Commanding 8th Bn. The Rifle Brigade.

30th Sept.1917.

8th Bn. THE RIFLE BRIGADE.

Appendix to War Diary.

September 1917.

Casualties.

11th	S 26212	Cpl.	Barden G.	"A" Co.	Wounded in Action.
13th	S 26291	Rfn.	Smith H.	"D" Co.	do. (at duty)
14th	B 2521	A/C.	Allston C.	do.	Killed in Action.
	S 20367	Rfn.	Atkins R.	"C" Co.	Wounded in Action (Died of wounds 16th)
15th	S 21974	"	Stedman E.	"B" Co.	Wounded in Action.
	S 27503	"	Kain J.	"A" Co.	Missing.
16th	S 26183	"	Allen G.	do.	Wounded in Action.
	S 27673	"	Aires J.n	"D" Co.	do.
	S 31572	"	Imms E.	"A" Co.	do. (Gas)
	S 25993	"	Smith A.	do.	do. (Gas) Died - 18th)
17th	S 25996	"	Smith G.	"B" Co.	Killed in Action.
18th	S 21682	L/C.	Cox J.	"A" Co.	Wounded in Action.
	S 7711	Sgt.	Phillips R.	"D" Co.	do.
	S 31262	Rfn.	Taylor A.	do.	do.
	S 5455	"	Cryer V.	do.	do.
	B200868	"	Sharp A.	do.	do.
	B200524	"	Knights A.	do.	do.
	S 24655	"	Chandler A.	do.	do.
	867	A/Sgt.	Stevens C.	do.	do.
	S 29440	Rfn.	Read W.	do.	do. (Died of wounds 19th)
	B200671	L/C.	Mitchell G.	"C" Co.	Wounded in Action.
19th	2487	Cpl.	Irving S.	"D" Co.	do.
	304650	Rfn.	Tomlinson F.	"D" Co.	do.
	S 2052	L/C.	Forster F.	do.	do.
23rd		Captain	A.R.BACKUS M.C.		Killed (accidentally).

[signature]

Major,

30th Sept. 1917. Commanding 8th Bn. The Rifle Brigade.

Instructions regarding War Diaries and Intelligence Summaries are contained in F. S. Regs., Part II. and the Staff Manual respectively. Title pages will be prepared in manuscript.

WAR DIARY
or
~~INTELLIGENCE SUMMARY.~~
(Erase heading not required.)

VOLUME 30

October 1917

8th Bn The Rifle Brigade

Army Form C. 2118.

WR 29

Place	Date OCT 1917	Hour	Summary of Events and Information	Remarks and references to Appendices
NEUVE EGLISE	1		Fine. Companies at disposal of O C Coys. Divnl Train Sports. Bn enter team for relay race but do not win. 2/Lt C.H. SLATFORD rejoins from employ at 41st Inf Base Depot. JPPB	
	2		Fine. Capt W.A. TEAKLE from leave. 'C' and 'D' Coys on range. Medical Officer inspects 'A' Co. Divnl Band play for Bn from 4 pm to 6 pm. Commanding Officer, Adjutant and two Company Officers reconnoitre right Bn forward area. Aeroplanes less active. 2/Lt H.R. HARTLEY to Corps Bombing Course. 2/Lt J.A. WEBB to Corps Lewis Gun course. JPPB	
	3		Dull. 'A' Co. and Lewis Gunners on range. 2 OR on Pigoneer's course. Working parties of 7 officers and 305 OR found. 40 OR inoculated. Lieut T.A. BALDOCK on leave. JPPB	
	4		Dull. Lewis Gunners on range. N.C.O's attend course of instruction in U framing. 2/Lt A.F. RICHARDS and 8 N.C.O's to revetting course. 'A' and 'B' Coys bathe. JPPB	
	5		Showery. Remainder of Bn bathe. Operation Orders received that Bde will relieve 43rd Inf Bde in the line on the night of 6/7th. At 5 pm Operation Orders cancelled. Warning Order received that Divn will relieve 33rd Divn in X Corps. 41st Inf Bde to move on 6th inst. JPPB	
RENINGHELST	6		Showery. Bn move off at 1 pm and march to camp near RENINGHELST. Enemy bombing planes active at night. JPPB	
	7		Dull. cold. Church Services. JPPB	
	8		Fine. cold wind. Companies at Disposal of O.C. Coys. 2/Lt J.S. SIMPSON from leave. JPPB	

A5834 Wt. W4973/M687 750,000 8/16 D. D. & L. Ltd. Forms/C.2118/13.

Instructions regarding War Diaries and Intelligence Summaries are contained in F. S. Regs., Part II. and the Staff Manual respectively. Title pages will be prepared in manuscript.

WAR DIARY or ~~INTELLIGENCE SUMMARY~~.

(Erase heading not required.)

VOLUME 30

Army Form C. 2118.

8th Bn. The Rifle Brigade

Place	Date 1917	Hour	Summary of Events and Information	Remarks and references to Appendices
DICKIEBUSCH Area	Oct 9		Dull - light rain. Bn marched out of camp at 8 30pm and proceeded to camp in DICKIEBUSCH area. On arrival no accommodation for Bn at all. During afternoon tents were obtained and camp pitched. 2/Lt H. CLAYTON proceeded on leave. JRPB.	
	10		Dull and rainy. Bn left camp at 9 30 am and proceeded to RIDGE WOOD. Dinners served here and packs dumped. Bn (less personnel left out under para XXX SS 135) left at 1 30pm and marched by Companies to BEDFORD HOUSE (28-I 26 a.9 2). Teas served here. Some enemy shelling. One OR wounded. No guides from 5th Div arrived as arranged. At 6pm Bn moved off to take up position as Brigade Reserve. Brigade holding line immediately left of the MENIN ROAD. Bn marched via SHRAPNEL CORNER - ZILLEBEKE - to TOR TOP (Brigade HQ). Here guides met Bn and took it by tracks through SANCTUARY WOOD. Guides did not know the way! Result - Bn marched around for two hours in an endeavour to find destination. Some enemy shelling. Ground a mass of shell holes and mud thigh deep in places. Possibly the worst relief ever experienced by the Bn. Eventually Bn HQ established in concrete dugout near STIRLING CASTLE, and Companies in trenches close by. 2 OR wounded during relief. Brigade holding line with right on MENIN ROAD. Disposition, - Left front, 7th Bn Rifle Brigade; Right front, 9th Bn K.R.R.C. Support 8th Bn. K.R.R.C. Reserve, 8th Bn. The Rifle Brigade. JRPB.	
STIRLING CASTLE (Bde Reserve)	11th		Commanding Officer (Major G.V. Carey) and officers from each Co reconnoitre approaches to Support Bn HQrs - via INVERNESS COPSE. Our artillery put down a practice barrage at 5.15pm for 22 minutes. Enemy retaliation slight. 3 OR killed. Enemy shelled vicinity of Bn HQ throughout the night. JRPB.	

Instructions regarding War Diaries and Intelligence Summaries are contained in F. S. Regs., Part II. and the Staff Manual respectively. Title pages will be prepared in manuscript.

WAR DIARY
or
~~INTELLIGENCE~~ SUMMARY.
(Erase heading not required.)

VOLUME 30

8th Bn The Rifle Brigade

Army Form C. 2118.

Place	Date	Hour	Summary of Events and Information	Remarks and references to Appendices
	1917			
STRLING CASTLE	Oct 12		Heavy shelling on both sides about dawn lasting till 8.30 am. Rain during afternoon. Practice barrages by our artillery at 10 pm and 10.11 pm lasting 6 minutes each. Quiet night. 2/LT C.F. HADWEN wounded. JPPB	
	13		Fine - turning to rain in afternoon. Practice barrage by our artillery at 5.15 am lasting 51 minutes. Enemy heavily shelled vicinity of TOR TOP. Several casualties among ration parties. JPPB	
	14		Bn HQ heavily shelled by various calibres during early morning - some gas shells. Intermittent shelling throughout day. German aeroplanes very active. S.O.S signalled on sector adjoining Bn right at 11.15 pm. Bn 'stood to' at 11.30 am. 'Stand down' ordered about midnight. From midnight to 5 am 15th enemy heavily shelled Bn area with gas shells, causing several gas casualties. Lieut T.A. BALDOCK rejoined from leave. JPPB	
	15		Fine. Usual shelling of Bn area by enemy. 'A' Co carrying rations for 4/60th in front line caught in barrage near CLAPHAM JUNCTION. Several casualties. All rations safely delivered. Lt Col D.E. PRIDEAUX-BRUNE rejoined from leave. JPPB	
	16		Heavy enemy shelling throughout night. About 3 am shell burst in front of HQrs dugout killing the sentry. The Bn were relieved by 9th BN. The Rifle Brigade about 8 am and proceeded to BEDFORD HOUSE. 2/LT E.A.F. BATTY and 15 Runners left behind to assist relieving Bn in reconnaissance of area. Fairly quiet relief. Rather uncomfortable camp. Work at once started to improve this. JPPB	

A5834 Wt. W4973/M687 750,000 8/16 D. D. & L. Ltd. Forms/C.2118/13.

Army Form C. 2118.

Instructions regarding War Diaries and Intelligence Summaries are contained in F. S. Regs., Part II. and the Staff Manual respectively. Title pages will be prepared in manuscript.

WAR DIARY
or
~~INTELLIGENCE SUMMARY.~~
(Erase heading not required.)

VOLUME 30

8th Bn. The Rifle Brigade

Place	Date 1917	Hour	Summary of Events and Information	Remarks and references to Appendices
BEDFORD HOUSE	Oct 17		Fine 2/Lt E A F BATTY and party (less one casualty) rejoin Bn Work on camp improvement continued 2/Lt C H SLATFORD goes on leave JEPB.	
	18		Wet Working party of 250 found for carrying from the CULVERT under 11th Kings (Liverpool) Rgt Left camp about 3 am returning at 9.30 am 10 OR casualties on party Brigadier General Commanding visits camp Enemy shell vicinity of camp about 3 pm as transport was arriving with rations One driver mortally wounded Lieut J R ABBEY and 2/Lt G J STEPTOE to hospital as result of gas shelling during night 14th/15th and 15th/16th JEPB.	
	19		Working party of 100 OR found as on 18th Also 150 OR for work under R.E. Party of 80 OR under R.S.M. continue work on camp improvement G.O.C and C.R.E visit camp. Relieved by 7th Bn K.R.R.C. during afternoon and proceeded to camp in RIDGE WOOD. Enemy bombing planes active at night. One OR wounded Capt & Qr Mr. F H PRYOR on leave Total Casualties for tour 4 Officers wounded ~~10~~ 11 OR killed 1 OR missing 78 wounded JEPB.	
RIDGE WOOD	20		Fine Bn at RIDGE WOOD cleaning up Enemy bombing machines very active at night JEPB.	
	21		Fine Church Services. Enemy bombing planes active in early morning. Operation Orders received that Bn will proceed to camp at 28 N 5 c 5.4 on 22nd inst. JEPB.	

Instructions regarding War Diaries and Intelligence Summaries are contained in F. S. Regs., Part II. and the Staff Manual respectively. Title pages will be prepared in manuscript.

WAR DIARY or ~~INTELLIGENCE SUMMARY.~~

VOLUME 30

Army Form C. 2118.

(Erase heading not required.)

8th Bn. The Rifle Brigade.

Place	Date	Hour	Summary of Events and Information	Remarks and references to Appendices
RENINGHELST	1917 Oct 22		Showery Bn march out of camp at 10 am and proceed to CHIPPAWA Camp near RENINGHELST. Enemy bombing aeroplanes active at night. JPPB.	
METEREN	23rd		Dull Bn proceed by Route march to billets just North of METEREN Billets very scattered and accommodation poor. JPPB.	
-	24th		Fine. Bn clearing up and refitting. JPPB.	
-	25th		Fine Bn finish refitting. Two Coys bathe 2/Lt O B TABOR rejoins from hospital. Bn Concert party give a concert in the YMCA, METEREN. JPPB.	
-	26th		Showery 'A' Co. bathe. 'D' Co. Lewis Gunners on L.G range. 'A' Co. on rifle range. Training of Lewis Gunners and Rifle Grenadiers commenced to bring Bn. up to strength in in specialists. 9 to 10 am Companies under O.C. Coys for March discipline, steady drill &c 10.30 am to 12.30 pm Lewis Gunners train with gun - remainder of Coys. do Musketry, Arm Drill, Squad and Gas Drill Afternoon devoted to sports. Inter platoon football competition started. JPPB.	
-	27th		Fine 'C' Co. on range 'B' Coys. Lewis Gunners on L.G. range Other parades as on 26th. Armourer inspects rifles of A & B Coys. Afternoon devoted to football. 2/Lt. HERBERT STUART BOWYER joined Bn and posted to 'A' Co. JPPB.	

A5834 Wt. W4973/M687 750,000 8/16 D. D. & L. Ltd. Forms/C.2118/13.

Instructions regarding War Diaries and Intelligence Summaries are contained in F. S. Regs., Part II. and the Staff Manual respectively. Title pages will be prepared in manuscript.

WAR DIARY
or
~~INTELLIGENCE SUMMARY.~~
(*Erase heading not required.*)

VOLUME 30

8th Bn. The Rifle Brigade

Army Form C. 2118.

Place	Date 1917	Hour	Summary of Events and Information	Remarks and references to Appendices
METEREN	Oct 28		Fine. Church Services. Inter-platoon football matches in afternoon. JPPB.	
	29		Fine. 'B' Co. on range. Other parades as on 26th. Football in afternoon. Concert party give concert at 2nd Army Sniping School. Commanding Officer inspects 'A' Co. Enemy aeroplanes active at night. JPPB.	
	30		Blustery. Commanding Officer inspects 'B' Co. 'D' Co. on range. Other parades as usual. Football in afternoon. JPPB.	
	31st		Fine. Commanding Officer inspects Headquarter Company. Parades as usual up to 11.30 am. At 11.45 am Bn. attend demonstration in Assault and Counter Attack practice. Afternoon devoted to football. JPPB.	

J. P. Pickersgill-Browne
Lt. Col.
Cmdg. 8th Bn. The Rifle Brigade

A5834 Wt. W4973/M687 750,000 8/16 D. D. & L. Ltd. Forms/C.2118/13.

8th Bn. THE RIFLE BRIGADE.

Appendix to WAR DIARY - October 1917.

Roll of Officers.

Lieut.Col.D.E.Prideaux-Brune, D.S.O.	Commanding Officer.
Major G.V.Carey	A/Second in Command.
Captain F.E.Young	Commanding "D" Company.
Captain C.E.Squire	In Hospital (Sick).
Captain E.Poole	Transport Officer.
Lieut. W.A.Crebbin, M.C.	Commanding "B" Company.
Lieut. W.G.Spencer	
Lieut.(A/Capt.)H.R.Adair	Fourth Army Inf.School Course.
Lieut. T.A.Baldock	Commanding "A" Company.
Lieut.(A/Capt.)W.A.Teakle	Commanding "C" Company.
Lieut. R.C.Dewhurst	Lewis Gun Officer.
Lieut. W.A.Solven	On Leave to U.K.
Lieut. J.A.Gould	
Lieut. H.R.Hartley	
2/Lieut.O.B.Tabor	
" E.A.F.Batty	Intelligence Officer.
" A.F.Newell (Act.Capt.)	A/Adjutant.
" O.F.Savege, M.C.	1st Field Survey Company.
" W.G.Hanton	X Corps Infantry School Course.
" P.H.Wooding, M.C.	Signals Officer (On Leave).
" J.Greig	
" W.N.Sproston, M.C.	
" J.S.Simpson	
" C.H.Slatford	In Hospital (Sick)
" H.Clayton	
" E.R.Magenty	41st T.M.Bty.
" J.A.Webb	
" A.F.Richards	
" C.L.Emy	
" R.J.Hook	
" H.E.Mitchell	In Hospital (Sick)
" H.S.Bowyer	
Hon. Captain & Q.M. F.H.Pryor	On Leave to U.K.
Captain R.N.Hunter, R.A.M.C.	Medical Officer (Attd.)

J. Prideaux-Brune.

Lieut.Colonel,
Commanding 8th Bn. The Rifle Brigade.

1/11/17.

8th Bn. THE RIFLE BRIGADE.

Appendix to WAR DIARY - October 1917.

Casualties.

1st.	S 6207	Rfn.	Jessup G.	"A" Co.	Killed in Action.
	B200848	"	Gledhill J.	do.	Wounded.
	B200847	"	Freeman C.	do.	do.
	S 11409	"	Hawkes W.	do.	do.
10th.	S 17926	"	Abrahams W.	do.	do.
	S 26152	"	Pearce W.	"C" Co.	do.
11th.	B200275	"	Taylor C.	"A" Co.	do.
	S 22794	A/C.	Humm F.	"B" Co.	Killed in Action.
	S 27711	Rfn.	Hennessy J.	do.	do.
	S 25499	"	Knapp J.	do.	do.
	4395	A/C.	Vaughan A.	"C" Co.	Wounded.
12th	Z 1017	Sgt.	Andrew G.	"A" Co.	Killed in Action.
	S 26265	A/C.	Styants G.	"D" Co.	Wounded.
	S 27043	Rfn.	Lucas W.	do.	do.
	B200672	"	Elbourne W.	"C" Co.	do.
	S 26185	"	Bogard J.	do.	do.
	6/158	"	Franklin W.	do.	do.
	S 17759	"	Thompson R.	"D" Co.	do.
	Z 2299	"	Fretter F.	do.	do.
	B200680	A/C.	Dyer A.	do.	do.
	S 8009	"	Spragg C.	do.	do.
	S 25444	Rfn.	Fergerson J.	do.	do.
	2487	Cpl.	Irving S.	do.	do.
	S 25263	Rfn.	Withers B.	do.	do.
	S 32732	"	Whiting C.	"A" Co.	do.
	S 24655	"	Chandler A.	"D" Co.	do.
	S 31528	"	Jeffries G.	do.	do.
	S 16561	Sgt.	Field A.	do.	do.
	305281	Rfn.	Brooks G.	do.	do.
		2/Lieut.	C.E.HADWEN		do.
	3161	C.S.M.	Rosser E.	"A" Co.	do. (at duty).
	S 26171	Rfn.	Lelliott B.	"B" Co.	do.
	S 25500	"	Squire C.	"D" Co.	do.
	S 27078	"	Bentley W.	"C" Co.	do.
	B 734	"	Mack T.	"A" Co.	Killed in Action.
	S 13229	"	Townsend W.	do.	Wounded.
13th.	S 18516	"	Parkes C.	"B" Co.	do.
	Z 1098	"	Robertson T.	"A" Co.	do. (S.I.)
	S 273	"	Sail H.	"D" Co.	do.
	S 32222	"	Wheeler F.	do.	do.
	S 32536	"	Ward W.	do.	do.
	S 27788	"	Oakley S.	"C" Co.	do.
	S 46	"	Woods F.	"B" Co.	do.
14th.	S 17879	"	Walters H.	"C" Co.	do.
	5928	"	Ellis A.	do.	do.
15th.		2/Lieut.	R.H.LAST		do. (Gas).
		Lieut.	J.R.ABBEY		do. (Gas).
		2/Lieut.	G.J.STEPTOE		do. (Gas).
	S 32483	Rfn.	Langan S.	"A" Co.	do. (Gas).
	S 29418	"	Simmonds G.	do.	do. (Gas).
	B200872	"	Spencer F.	do.	do. (Gas).
	S 26191	"	Friend G.	do.	do. (Gas).
	S 26495	"	Bright H.	do.	do. (Gas).
	S 31422	"	Burt A.	"B" Co.	do. (Gas).
	S 13731	Cpl.	Baker A.	do.	Killed in Action.
	S 26521	Rfn.	Fulcher J.	do.	Wounded (Gas).
	S 11157	"	West R.	do.	do. (Gas).

Instructions regarding War Diaries and Intelligence Summaries are contained in F. S. Regs., Part II. and the Staff Manual respectively. Title pages will be prepared in manuscript.

WAR DIARY VOLUME 31
or
~~INTELLIGENCE SUMMARY.~~
(Erase heading not required.)

Army Form C. 2118.

8th Bn THE RIFLE BRIGADE

Vol 30

Place	Date 1917	Hour	Summary of Events and Information	Remarks and references to Appendices
METEREN	Nov. 1		Fine. Major G.V. CAREY to X Corps HQ on attachment. Inter-platoon drill competition in morning judged by Brig Genl P.C.B. SKINNER D.S.O. Final of inter-platoon football competition played in afternoon. Draft of 30 OR arrived. JPB.	
"	2		Fine dull. Bn carry out a platoon route march and map reading scheme. Commanding Officer inspects Transport and Signallers. Afternoon draft inspected by Commanding Officer and Medical Officer. Medical Officer inspects H.Qr. Company. JPB.	
"	3rd		Fine. Commanding Officer inspects 'C' Company. Other parades as usual. JPB	
"	4th		Fine. Divine Services. Two Coys bathe. Bn play 7th Bn football in afternoon. JPB.	
"	5th		Fine. Commanding Officer inspects 'D' Co. 3 N.C.Os attend gas course at Bde H.Q. Other parades as usual. JPB.	
"	6th		Fine. Companies under O.C. Coys. for usual training. Snipers on range. JPB.	
"	7th		Fine. Companies training under Company Commanders. JPB.	
"	8th		Dull. Platoon Commanders parade for instruction under the Commanding Officer. Bn. do route march. Warning Order received that Bde will move to TATINAHEM area on 13th inst. JPB.	

A5834 Wt. W4973/M687 750,000 8/16 D. D. & L. Ltd. Forms/C.2118/13.

Instructions regarding War Diaries and Intelligence Summaries are contained in F. S. Regs., Part II. and the Staff Manual respectively. Title pages will be prepared in manuscript.

WAR DIARY or ~~INTELLIGENCE SUMMARY.~~

VOLUME 31

Army Form C. 2118.

(Erase heading not required.)

8th Bn. The Rifle Brigade

Place	Date 1917	Hour	Summary of Events and Information	Remarks and references to Appendices
METEREN	Nov 9th		Dull 2/Lt F.W. RICHARDS joined Bn. Companies parade as usual. Notification received that Brigade will move on 11th inst. JPB	
	10th		Wet. Following officers join Bn. and posted to A, B, C and D Coys. respectively 2/Lt J. D. DAVIDSON, 2/Lt W. G. F. DEWAR, 2/Lt D. F. HAMPSON, 2/Lt G. BROWN. Lieut N. A. SOLVEN admitted to Field Ambulance JPB	
ST MARTIN-AU-LAERT	11th		Dull and rainy. Bn. left METEREN at 6.45 am, marched to CAESTRE and entrained for WIZERNES, arriving about 1.30 pm. Bn. march to billets at ST MARTIN-AU-LAERT. Companies rather scattered. Transport move by road under 2/Lt P. H. WOODING M.C. JPB	
-	12th		Fine. Coys. at disposal of O.C. Coys. cleaning up. Commanding Officer holds conference to arrange training programme. JPB	
-	13th		Fine. Programme of work issued for period 15th - 23rd. Coys. at disposal of O.C. Coys. Sgts. Mess formed. JPB	
-	14th		Dull. Battalion practice on Rifle Range. JPB	
-	15th		Fine. cold. Adjutant proceeds on leave. Lieut R. C. DEWHURST takes over duties JPB	

A5834 Wt. W4973/M687 750,000 8/16 D. D. & L. Ltd. Forms/C.2118/13.

Army Form C. 2118.

WAR DIARY VOLUME 31.
or
~~INTELLIGENCE SUMMARY.~~ 8th Bn. The Rifle Brigade.

(*Erase heading not required.*)

Instructions regarding War Diaries and Intelligence Summaries are contained in F. S. Regs., Part II. and the Staff Manual respectively. Title pages will be prepared in manuscript.

Place	Date 1917	Hour	Summary of Events and Information	Remarks and references to Appendices
ST MARTIN-AU-LAERT	Nov 16		Fine. 2/Lt F W HUME and 2/Lt J. F. SMITH join Bn. Coys. under O.C. Coys. in morning. Afternoon devoted to football and running. JPPB	
–	17th		Dull - cold. Coys. training as usual. A and C Coys. on Miniature range. 2/Lt P. H. WOODING M.C. attached to IX Corps Signals. JPPB	
–	18th		Dull. Divine Services. Bn. football match in afternoon against 7th 60th. JPPB	
–	19th		Fine. A and C Coys. on Miniature range. B and D. Coys. under O.C. Coys. for Company drill, gas drill &c. JPPB	
–	20th		Fine. Coys. at disposal of O.C. Coys. Bn. football in afternoon. Bn. versus 8th 60th. JPPB	
–	21st		Rainy. B and D. Coys. on range. A and C Coys. take part in Brigade Scheme. JPPB	
–	22nd		Fine. Bn. present at demonstration by 'C' Co., shewing the co-operation of all weapons at the disposal of the platoon commander in an attack on a strong point. G.O.C. and ~~B. G. C.~~ JPPB present. JPPB	
–	23rd		Fine. Brigade Cross Country Run. Each Coy. enter team of 100 men. Cross country course of 3½ miles. 340 men complete course in 35 minutes – time stipulated. The whole of 'D' Co. included in this number. JPPB	

A5834 Wt. W4973/M687 750,000 8/16 D. D. & L. Ltd. Forms/C.2118/13.

Instructions regarding War Diaries and Intelligence Summaries are contained in F. S. Regs., Part II. and the Staff Manual respectively. Title pages will be prepared in manuscript.

WAR DIARY or ~~INTELLIGENCE SUMMARY.~~

(Erase heading not required.)

VOLUME 31

Army Form C. 2118.

8th Bn. The Rifle Brigade

Place	Date 1917	Hour	Summary of Events and Information	Remarks and references to Appendices
St. MARTIN-AU-LAERT	Nov 24th		Fine. Commanding Officer and other officers inspect the Ordnance Workshop and Bakery at CALAIS. Usual parades. RPB.	
-	25th		Fine. Divine Services. Football in afternoon. 2/LT. E.A.F. BATTY to 41st Inf. Bde. HQ to take up duties as Bde. Intelligence Officer. RPB.	
-	26th		Fine - cold. Commanding Officer reconnoitres the line at PASSCHENDAELE. RPB.	
-	27th		Fine. Coys. training under O.C. Companies. RPB.	
-	28th		Dull and blustery. Corps Commander inspects the Bn. at work, and expresses his appreciation of the manner in which a demonstration was carried out showing the co-operation of all weapons at the disposal of the Platoon Commander in an attack on a strong point. Warning Order received that the Transport will move on the 29th and the Bn. on the 30th. RPB.	
-	29		Fine. Coys at disposal of O.C. Coys. Bn. win Brigade Road Relay Race. 2/LT. J. HOGG and 2/LT. W.L. FAIRWEATHER join Bn. 2/LT. W.G. HANTON returns from X Corps Infantry School Course. Transport proceed by road to new area. Destination - GOLDFISH CHATEAU. RPB.	

A5834 Wt. W4973/M687 750,000 8/16 D. D. & L. Ltd. Forms/C.2118/13.

Instructions regarding War Diaries and Intelligence Summaries are contained in F. S. Regs., Part II. and the Staff Manual respectively. Title pages will be prepared in manuscript.

~~WAR DIARY~~ VOLUME 31

or

~~INTELLIGENCE~~ SUMMARY. 8th Bn. The Rifle Brigade.

(*Erase heading not required.*)

Army Form C. 2118.

Place	Date 1917	Hour	Summary of Events and Information	Remarks and references to Appendices
BRANDHOEK	No. 30		Showery. Bn. march out of billets at 9 am. and proceed to WIZERNES, entraining here at about 11 am. Bn. arrived at BRANDHOEK and take over camp at about 4 pm. 2/LT W. G HANTON proceeds to HQ RFC on probation as observer. [illegible]	

[illegible]

Lt. Col

Cmdg. 8th Bn. The Rifle Bde.

A5834 Wt. W4973/M687 750,000 8/16 D. D. & L. Ltd. Forms/C.2118/13.

8th Bn. THE RIFLE BRIGADE.

Appendix to WAR DIARY - November 1917.

Roll of Officers.

Lieut.Col.D.E.Prideaux-Brune, D.S.O.	Commanding Officer.
Major G.V.Carey	Attd. 53rd Sqdrn. R.F.C.
Capt. F.E.Young	Commanding "D" Company.
Capt. C.E.Squire	On Leave.
Capt. W.A.Crebbin, M.C.	Commanding "B" Company.
Capt. E.Poole	Transport Officer.
Lieut.W.G.Spencer	
Lieut.(A/Capt.)H.R.Adair	
Lieut. T.A.Baldock	Commanding "A" Company.
Lieut.(A/Capt.)W.A.Teakle	Commanding "C" Company.
Lieut. R.C.Dewhurst	Lewis Gun Officer.
Lieut. J.A.Gould	Second Army Inf. School.
Lieut. H.R.Hartley	
2/Lieut.O.B.Tabor	
" E.A.F.Batty	41st Inf. Bde. I.O.
" (A/Capt.)A.F.Newell	Adjutant.
" W.G.Hanton	Attd. R.F.C.
" P.H.Wooding, M.C.	Attd. IX Corps Signals.
" J.Greig.	
" W.N.Sproston, M.C.	II Corps Inf. School.
" J.S.Simpson	Signalling Officer.
" C.H.Slatford	In Hospital.
" H.Clayton	
" E.R.Magenty	Attd. 41st T.M.Bty.
" J.A.Webb	On Leave.
" A.F.Richards	
" C.L.Emy	
" R.J.Hook	On Leave.
" H.E.Mitchell	In Hospital.
" H.S.Bowyer	Intelligence Officer.
" F.W.Richards	
" J.D.Davidson	
" G.Brown	
" D.F.Hampson	
" W.G.F.Dewar	
" F.W.Hume	
" J.F.Smith	
" J.Hogg	
" W.L.Fairweather	
Hon. Capt. & Q.M. F.H.Pryor	

D. Prideaux Brune

Lieut.Colonel,
Cmdg. 8th Bn. The Rifle Brigade.

30/11/17.

Casualties (Continued).

15th (contd.)	S 22339	Rfn.	Cove G.	"B" Co.	Wounded	(Gas)
	S 29438	"	Bolton S.	do.	do.	(Gas)
	S 31531	"	Fuller E.	"A" Co.	do.	(Gas)
	S 27530	"	Doughty D.	do.	do.	(Gas)
	S 32526	"	Sawyer G.	do.	do.	(Gas)
	S 24688	Cpl.	Best W.	do.	do.	
	S 12016	"	Vize A.	do.	do.	
	S 3121	Rfn.	Beasley J.	"B" Co.	do.	
	S 32719	"	Robinson G.	"A" Co.	Killed in Action.	
	S 23579	"	Boddington E.	do.	Wounded	
	305297	"	Page W.	do.	do.	
	B200860	"	Peck J.	do.	do.	
	B200869	"	Smith A.	do.	do.	
	9501	"	Wheatley G.	do.	dok	
	B200850	A/C.	Green E.	do.	do.	
	S 25994	Rfn.	Smith E.	"B" Co.	do.	(Gas)
	S 28424	"	Dorrell H.	"A" Co.	do.	(Gas)
	B200846	"	Fletcher W.	do.	do.	(Gas)
	S 29419	"	Hayes A.	do.	do.	(Gas)
	4531	"	Patten H.	do.	do.	(Gas)
	S 25872	Sgt.	Cook W.	"C" Co.	do.	(Gas)
	S 32495	Rfn.	Clewes R.	do.	do.	(Gas)
	XXXXXXXX	X/X.	XXXXXXXXXXX.			
16th	S 27613	Rfn.	Sumner A.	"C" Co.	Killed in Action.	
	S 32237	"	Shute B.	do.	do.	
	S 9721	A/C.	Futter J.	do.	do.	
	S 22454	Rfn.	Mayoss J.	do.	Wounded.	
	S 23277	"	Gregory J.	do.	do.	
17th	B200327	A/C.	Bathurst R.	"A"Co.	do.	
18th	S 32486	Rfn.	Bischoff C.	"D" Co.	do.	
	B200870	"	Smith F.	do.	do.	
	S 28445	"	Pipe G.	do.	do.	
	S 24655	"	Chandler A.	do.	Missing.	
	Z 1671	"	Finch J.	"A" Com	Wounded.	
	P 266	"	Haward H.	do.	do.	
	305332	"	Allen F.	"C" Co.	Killed in Action.	
	S 27751	"	Cooper A.	do.	Wounded.	
	S 25997	"	Smith J.	do.	do.	(S.S.)
	S 1110	"	Simpson G.	"D" Co.	do.	(Died - same day)
	S 26505	"	Castell A.	"C" Co.	do.	(Gas)
19th	B 3139	"	Roberts B.	"C" Co.	do.	(Gas)
	S 29705	"	Stone J.	"D" Co.	do.	(Aerial Bomb)
	B					

J. Pedrans Brune [signature]

Lieut.Colonel,
Commanding 8th Bn. The Rifle Brigade.

1/11/17.

Instructions regarding War Diaries and Intelligence Summaries are contained in F. S. Regs., Part II. and the Staff Manual respectively. Title pages will be prepared in manuscript.

WAR DIARY or ~~INTELLIGENCE~~ SUMMARY.

(Erase heading not required.)

VOLUME 32 4/14

Army Form C. 2118.

8th Bn The Rifle Brigade

Vol 31

Place	Date 1917	Hour	Summary of Events and Information	Remarks and references to Appendices
BRANDHOEK	DEC 1		Fine Cold. Battalion resting at RIDGE CAMP, BRANDHOEK [initials]	
PASSCHENDAELE	2nd		Fine Cold Bn less details move out of Camp at 7 am and entrain at BRANDHOEK siding for ST JEAN On arrival at ST JEAN Bn march to CAPRICORN CAMP (28. C 18. c central) where they rest all day At 7 pm Bn moves off by platoons and relieves 2nd Bn The Rifle Brigade and 2nd Bn Lincoln Regt in the front line at PASSCHENDAELE Relief reported complete at 1.40 am 3rd inst. 2/Lt J. HOGG killed Lieut T.A. BALDOCK mortally wounded (A Co. Cmdr.) 2/Lt J. D DAVIDSON assumes command of A Co and completes a very difficult Company relief Estimated OR casualties 25 2/Lt H R HARTLEY to hospital sick [initials]	
	3rd		Fine Cold Artillery on both sides very active Enemy pay particular attention to main road from MOSSELMARK to KANSAS CORNER 2/Lt F W HUME wounded 10 OR casualties [initials]	
	4th		Cold Little snow and hail Sharp frost Enemy machine guns very active at night Artillery on both sides very active Capt. W A TEAKLE to hospital (O C C Co) Lieut W G SPENCER assumes Command of Company [initials]	
	5th		Fine Frost Usual heavy artillery fire Bn relieved in front line by the 7th Bn The Rifle Brigade Relief completed about midnight A and C Coys take up position in immediate support B D and HQ Coys at CAPRICORN CAMP Main road from MOSSELMARK to KANSAS Corner heavily shelled, especially from WATERLOO to KANSAS Enemy aeroplanes very active throughout day [initials]	

Instructions regarding War Diaries and Intelligence Summaries are contained in F. S. Regs., Part II. and the Staff Manual respectively. Title pages will be prepared in manuscript.

WAR DIARY
or
~~INTELLIGENCE~~ SUMMARY.
(Erase heading not required.)

VOLUME 32

Army Form C. 2118.

8th Bn The Rifle Brigade

Place	Date 1917	Hour	Summary of Events and Information	Remarks and references to Appendices
PASSCHENDAELE	DEC 6		Fine Cold About 11 30 am enemy artillery heavily shell gun positions near camp, causing 11 7 OR casualties At 5 30 pm enemy bombing planes drop bombs on surrounding country. RPB	
	7		Fine Frost Situation generally quiet. Capt. N.A TEAKLE rejoins Detail Camp from HOSPITAL Lieut Col W. MERRICK (6th Bn East Surrey Regt.) reports at Detail Camp for attachment under instruction RPB	
	8		Fine Cold B, D + HQ Coys move out of camp at 4 pm and marched to ST JEAN Station, entraining at 5 30 pm for BRANDHOEK and marched to WARRINGTON CAMP arriving about 7 30 pm RPB	
BRANDHOEK	9		Fine Frost During night 8/9th A and C Coys relieved in immediate support by two Companies of 43rd Inf Bde, and marched to ST JEAN, entraining here for BRANDHOEK. These two Coys arrive in Camp at 9 30 am RPB Bn resting and cleaning up throughout day.	
	10		Dull Cold Bn cleaning up and improving camp, which was taken over in a very bad condition Enemy bombing planes active at night Lieut N.G. SPENCER and 2/Lt C.H SLATFORD proceed to join 47th Division for duty RPB	
	11		Cold Bn bathe at baths at CANAL BANK Working party of One officer and 25 OR found for work under 62nd Field Co. R.E Enemy shell vicinity of camp with H.V. gun at night. Enemy bombing planes again active at night. Capt N.A. TEAKLE to leave RPB	

A5834 Wt. W4973/M687 750,000 8/16 D. D. & L. Ltd. Forms/C.2118/13.

Instructions regarding War Diaries and Intelligence Summaries are contained in F. S. Regs., Part II. and the Staff Manual respectively. Title pages will be prepared in manuscript.

WAR DIARY *or* ~~INTELLIGENCE SUMMARY.~~ VOLUME 32

(Erase heading not required.)

8th Bn. The Rifle Brigade

Army Form C. 2118.

Place	Date 1917	Hour	Summary of Events and Information	Remarks and references to Appendices
BRANDHOEK	DEC 12		Fine. Dull. Bn. find working party of 5 officers and 220 OR for work on Light Railways in forward area. Every available man taken to make up numbers. Parade for work at 4 am., returning at 3pm. HPB	
	13th		Fine - dull. Working party of 3 officers and 100 OR found for work on R.F.A Horse lines. Remainder of Bn. employed on camp improvements. 2/Lt. R.J. HOOK proceeds to H.Q. Royal Flying Corps on probation. Lieut. F.A. KINGSHELL attached for duty from 7th Rifle Bde. and posted to Command of 'A' Co. HPB	
	14th		Dull. Bn. supplies working party of 2 Officers and 100 O.R. for work on forward railways. Remainder of Bn. continues work of drainage and cleaning of Camp. Signallers under the Regtl. Sgt Major, dig defensive Shell-holes for practice purposes. HPB	
	15th		Fine - Strong N. Wind. Bn. training in Shell-hole warfare, and construction of shell-hole defences. Medical Officer inspects Companies. S.B.Rs tested. Gas drill. Drainage of Camp Continued. Capt H.R. ADAIR goes on leave. HPB	
	16th		Dull. Slight snow. Working party of 3 Officers & 100 O.R. found for work on forward railways. Remainder of Bn. cleaning & draining Camp. HPB	
	17th		Fine. Companies under O.C. Coys. for practice in Shell-hole warfare & construction of Shell-hole defences. Gas drill & inspections. Camp drainage work continued. Sharp frost at night. HPB	

A5834 Wt. W4973/M687 750,000 8/16 D. D. & L. Ltd. Forms/C.2118/13.

Instructions regarding War Diaries and Intelligence Summaries are contained in F. S. Regs., Part II. and the Staff Manual respectively. Title pages will be prepared in manuscript.

WAR DIARY
or
~~INTELLIGENCE~~ SUMMARY.
(*Erase heading not required.*)

Army Form C. 2118.

Volume 32

8th Bn The Rifle Brigade

Place	Date	Hour	Summary of Events and Information	Remarks and references to Appendices
Nr BRANDHOEK	Dec 18		Fine. Frosty. Commanding Officer goes on 6 days leave to Paris. Major F.E. YOUNG in command of Bn during Colonel's absence. Bn training by Companies, in Shell-hole warfare - uses of Camouflage - reliefs - Communications. Gas drill. Arm drill & physical drill. Drainage & general camp improvement continued. JEPB	
	19		Fine. The Bn left WARRINGTON CAMP at 4 pm. Marched to ST JEAN area, relieving the 5th Bn Shropshire L.I. about 6.30 pm. "A" & "C" Coys. at CALIFORNIA Camp, and "B" & "D" Coys at CAPRICORN Camp. Bn H.Q at CAPRICORN Camp. Situation quiet. JEPB	
Nr ST JEAN	20		Sharp frost and mist. Situation very quiet. Working party of 150 O.R supplied for carrying R.E material. JEPB	
	21		Sharp frost and mist. Situation quiet. JEPB	
Nr PASSCHENDAELE	22		Fine and frosty. Enemy artillery active, with aerial observation. JEPB At 8 PM the Bn. (less "B" Coy.) relieved 5th Bn K.S.L.I. (3 Coys.) at BELLEVUE (Support) "B" Coy. relieved 1 Coy. 5th Bn. K.S.L.I. in immediate Support. Very satisfactory relief. 3 O.R casualties	JEPB
	23		Frost & fine. Quiet during day, artillery and machine guns (our own & enemy) active at night. Bn. supplied parties for taking up rations to front line Bns. Heavy bombing of back areas by hostile aircraft at night - specially in neighbourhood of GOLDFISH CHATEAU.	JEPB
	24		Mist and rain. Quiet during day except for usual enemy shelling of main roads and tracks. Rations carried to front-line Battalions. JEPB	

A5834 Wt. W4973/M687 750,000 8/16 D. D. & L. Ltd. Forms/C.2118/13.

Instructions regarding War Diaries and Intelligence Summaries are contained in F. S. Regs., Part II. and the Staff Manual respectively. Title pages will be prepared in manuscript.

WAR DIARY
or
INTELLIGENCE SUMMARY.
(Erase heading not required.)

Army Form C. 2118.

VOLUME 32

8th Bn The Rifle Brigade

Place	Date	Hour	Summary of Events and Information	Remarks and references to Appendices
Nr PASSCHENDAELE	25.		Snow. Enemy artillery very active, especially on WOLF COPSE, from 4 - 5 PM. Also usual shelling of main roads and tracks. Rations carried to front-line Battalions. JRPB	
	26.		Snow. Enemy aeroplanes very active, directing artillery fire. Enemy artillery very active throughout whole of day. About 8 PM, the relief of front line Bns having commenced, the Enemy opened heavy barrage (artillery + M.G.). On the S.O.S signal being sent up, our artillery opened severe barrage, neutralising enemy fire, + about 9 PM situation became normal.	
			"A" "C", "D" + HQ relieved by 3 Coys. Sherwood Foresters at 10 PM. "B" Coy. in immediate Support, relieved by 1 Coy. 2nd Bn. East Lancashire R. at 9.45 PM. No casualties during relief.	
			Bn. arrived at Camp at 28-C.27.C.2.8 about 11.45 pm. JRPB	
	27		Bn. entrained at WIELTJE at 12.30 pm for WIZERNES, arriving at 5.30 pm, and proceeded by 'bus to billets at ESQUERDES. Reaching which place about 6.30 pm. JRPB	
ESQUERDES	28		Fine and cold. Companies at disposal of O.C. Coys for cleaning up, refitting etc	
			Major-Genl V.A Couper + the Brigadier visited HQ. Very satisfied as to work done by Bn during recent tour. Messages of thanks also received from the other Battalions of the Brigade — rations being successfully delivered to Bns in front line each night without any loss whatever, either of rations or by casualties, under difficult circumstances — the nights being particularly bright and snow on the ground. Capt C E SQUIRE to Command of "A" Coy. JRPB	
ESQUERDES.	29.		Fine + frost holds. 2/Lt H S BOWYER to Fourth Army School of Sniping, and 2/Lt H. CLAYTON to Fourth Army Infantry School. Bn. Team practising for Brigade tobogganing Competition. JRPB	

A5834 Wt. W4973/M687 750,000 8/16 D. D. & L. Ltd. Forms/C.2118/13.

Instructions regarding War Diaries and Intelligence Summaries are contained in F. S. Regs., Part II. and the Staff Manual respectively. Title pages will be prepared in manuscript.

WAR DIARY
or
INTELLIGENCE SUMMARY.
(Erase heading not required.)

Army Form C. 2118.

VOLUME 32

8th Bn The Rifle Brigade

Place	Date	Hour	Summary of Events and Information	Remarks and references to Appendices
ESQUERDES	DEC. 30		Slight thaw. Dull. No tobogganing possible. 2/Lt J.S. SIMPSON transferred to 47th Division. JPB	
	31		Dull. Slight thaw continues. Orders received that the Division is to be transferred to Fifth Army, and will move to neighbourhood of BRAY-SUR-SOMME in a few days. "A" & "D" Companies have their Christmas Dinner. – At the conclusion of which, the Commanding Officer proposed a resolution to be forwarded to Mrs R.C. Maclachlan; of sympathy with her in the loss of her husband Brig-Genl R.C. Maclachlan, D.S.O, who commanded the Bn for so long, and of thanks to her for all she had done, and was doing, for the comfort of the Bn; from Officers, N.C.Os and men of this Battalion. JPB	

TOTAL CASUALTIES during month:–

	Of	O.R
Killed	1	16
Died of Wounds	1	2
Wounded.	1	59
Wounded S.I		2
Missing.		3
	3	82

J. Pretor-Brown [?] Lt Col.
Cmdg 8th Bn The Rifle Brigade

A5834 Wt. W4973/M687 750,000 8/16 D. D. & L. Ltd. Forms/C.2118/13.

8th. Bn. The Rifle Brigade.

Appendix to War Diary.

Casualties during December 1917.

Dec.2	2/Lieut.J.HOGG.	Killed in Action.
"	Lieut.T.A.BALDOCK.	Wounded (died of wounds 3/12/17)
"	S 17436 Rfn. Mercer G.	Killed in Action
"	S 28651 " Whittle E.	" "
"	S 32555 " Robertson D.	" "
"	S 25945 " Wood J.	" "
"	S 32758 " Holmes E.	" "
"	S 1795 " Clarry G.	Wounded
"	S 25073 " Hawkins T.	"
"	S 14126 " Molden A.	" (Died of W)
"	B 2311 " Searle E.	"
"	B200864 " Sagar W.	"
"	305235 " Harold W.	"
"	S 27380 " Read W.	"
"	S 8960 " Perkins C.	"
"	S 21868 " Janes J.	"
"	S 400 " Lovegrove H.	"
"	Z 2018 " Moss P.	"
"	S 681 " Keeling G.	"
"	S 17685 " Baker W.	"
"	S 28445 " Pipe T.	"
"	S 4727 " Dudley F.	"
"	S 16761 " Collins P.	" S.I.
"	6423 " Hendy W.	"
"	S 18802 " Penfold G.	" S.I.
"		
Dec.3	S 30994 A/C. Curtis G.	Killed in Action.
"	S 27741 Rfn. Denton W.	" "
"	2/Lieut.F.W.HUME.	Wounded.
"	4835 Rfn. Brown F.	"
"	S 11222 " Shewring E.	"
"	S 31187 " Thomas R.	"
"	6/644 Cpl. Pevalin H.	"
"	S 17430 Rfn. Cross G.	"
"	S 975 C.S.M. Childe H.	"
"	S 31017 Rfn. Brindley E.	"
"	S 24984 " Weekes C.	"
"	S 25132 " Luckins H.	"
"	S 23267 " Cooper S.	"
"	S 29430 " Oliver A.	" (Died of W.)
"	S 5347 A/C. Rennard T.	"
"	S 23946 Rfn. How H.	"
"		
Dec.4	S 18536 Rfn. Rushman W.	Killed in Action.
"	S 14474 A/C. Lowe G.	" "
"	5/8394 Rfn. Barnett H.	" "
"	S 8428 " Godfrey W.	" "
"	S 10323 " Ashbolt E.	Wounded
"	S 15204 " Libby L.	"
"	S 28443 " Hill G.	"
"	S 208 " Brook G.	"
"	S 29727 " Beaney E.	"
"	S 29327 " Smith B.	"
"		
Dec.5	S 11346 A/C. Meech H.	Wounded
"	S 30003 Rfn. Botwright F.	"
"	S 12790 " Hill W.	"
"	B200873 " Stow W.	Missing.

8th. Bn. The Rifle Brigade.

Appendix to War Diary.

Roll of Officers.

Lieut.Col.D.E.Prideaux-Brune, D.S.O.	Commanding.
Major G.V.Carey.	53rd.Squadron R.F.C.
Capt.(Actg.Major) F.E.Young.	2nd. in Command.
Capt.C.E.Squire.	O.C. "A" Company.
Capt.E.Poole.	Transport Officer.
Capt.W.A.Crebbin, M.C.	O.C. "B" Company.
Lieut.F.A.Kingswell.	
Lieut.(A/Capt.) H.R.Adair.	O.C. "D" Company.
Lieut.(A/Capt.) W.A.Teakle.	Leave to U.K.
Lieut.R.C.Dewhurst.	Lewis Gun Officer.
Lieut.J.A.Gould.	Leave to U.K.
Lieut.H.R.Hartley.	Hospital.
2/Lieut.E.A.F.Batty.	41st. Bde.Intelligence.
2/Lieut.P.H.Wooding, M.C.	Attd. IX Corps Signals.
2/Lieut.J.Grieg.	Leave to U.K.
2/Lieut.W.N.Sproston, M.C.	Leave to U.K.
2/Lieut.H.Clayton.	Fourth Army Inf. School.
2/LieutJ.A.Webb.	
2/Lieut.A.F.Richards.	Fifth Army Musketry. School.
2/LieutC.L.Emy.	Temp. O.C. "C" Company.
2/Lieut.H.S.Bowyer.	Fourth Army Sniping and Observation Course.
2/Lieut.F.W.Richards.	
2/Lieut.J.D.Davidson, M.C.	
2/Lieut.G.Brown.	
2/Lieut.D.F.Hampson	
2/Lieut.W.G.F.Dewar.	
2/Lieut.J.F.Smith.	
2/Lieut.W.L.Fairweather.	
2/Lieut.E.T.Jones	
2/Lieut.T.Grant	
2/Lieut.C. Randall.	
2/Lieut.S.D.Brown.	
A/Capt.A.F.Newell.	Adjutant.
Capt.R.N.Hunter, R.A.M.C.	Attached.

J. Prideaux Brune.

Lieut.Col.
Commdg. 8th. Bn. The Rifle Brigade.

Dec.31/1917.

Sheet 2.

Dec.6	S 16425	Rfn.	Locke J.	Killed in Action.
"	S 30868	"	Reader C.	Wounded
"	S 21974	"	Stedman E.	"
"	S 26558	"	Luck G.	"
"	S 20283	"	Burrell F.	"
"	S 22013	"	Meader J.	"
"	S 20434	"	Cole S.	"
"	S 27548	"	Mills E.	"
"	S 30823	"	Browne S.	"
"	S 10280	"	Tomkinson C.	"
"	S 27525	"	Lefevre A.	"
"	S 32479	"	Benson A.	"
"	S 13214	"	Blencowe J.	"
"	S 30762	"	Glasspool F.	"
"	Z 2024	"	Griffen L.	"
"	S 12058	"	Merritt E.	"
"	S 24286	"	Kalinsky A.	"
"	S 26202	"	Lewis J.	Missing
Dec.7	B 1318	Rfn.	Fenson P.	Killed in Action
"	B200840	"	Gorden F.	" "
"	S 27781	"	Sweet T.	Wounded
"	S 25871	"	Collins G.	"
"	S 20957	"	Haynes A.	"
"	S 16083	"	Cox G.	"
Dec.8.	S 24021	Rfn.	Kratosky D.	Killed in Action
"	B203331	"	Hilditch G.	Wounded
Dec.22	B 146	Rfn.	Searle H.	Killedin Action
"	305313	"	Coleman C.	Wounded
Dec.26	S 8541	Rfn.	Greenwood J.	Wounded.
Dec.2	B 3198	Sgt.	Jameson J.	Missing

[illegible signature]

Lieut.Col.,
Cmdg., 8th. Bn. The Rifle Brigade.

Dec.31/1917.

Instructions regarding War Diaries and Intelligence Summaries are contained in F. S. Regs., Part II. and the Staff Manual respectively. Title pages will be prepared in manuscript.

WAR DIARY VOLUME 33
or
INTELLIGENCE SUMMARY. 8th Bn THE RIFLE BRIGADE

(*Erase heading not required.*)

Army Form C. 2118.

41/14

Vol 32

Place	Date	Hour	Summary of Events and Information	Remarks and references to Appendices
	1918			
ESQUERDES	JAN 1		Bright and frosty. Companies at disposal of O C Coys	
	2		Dull - some raid. Advance party under Lt R C DEWHURST proceeded to SAILLEY le SEC. Bn cleaning up billets &c.	
SAILLEY le SEC	3		Some snow. Bn move out of ESQUERDES at 4 am and march to St OMER. Entrain here at 8 am. Arrive at BUIRE at 4.30pm and march to billets at SAILLEY le SEC. Bn reported in at 9.30 pm. A very hard march owing to snow and frost. Division now form party of FIFTH ARMY.	
	4		Fine. Hard frost. Battalion resting. Lt J A GOULD from leave	
	5		Fine. Cold. Coys at disposal of O C Coys cleaning up and improving billets	
	6		Dull. Divine Services. Capt C R GORELL BARNES D.S.O., M.C. rejoins Bn and is appointed to Command of 'D' Company. Bn receives following awards in New Years Honours Gazette. Capt W A TEAKLE - Military Cross; B3444 Rfn WILLICOMBE. H. - D C M.; B2873 Sgt. POPE. E C - M S M.	
	7		Dull - some rain. Coys at disposal of O.C. Coys for inspections, drill, gas drill and Recreational training	
	8		Snow. Coys at disposal of O.C. Coys as on 7th inst.	

A5834 Wt. W4973/M687 750,000 8/16 D. D. & L. Ltd. Forms/C.2118/13.

Instructions regarding War Diaries and Intelligence Summaries are contained in F. S. Regs., Part II. and the Staff Manual respectively. Title pages will be prepared in manuscript.

WAR DIARY VOLUME 33
or
~~INTELLIGENCE SUMMARY.~~ 8th Bn The Rifle Brigade
(*Erase heading not required.*)

Army Form C. 2118.

Place	Date 1918	Hour	Summary of Events and Information	Remarks and references to Appendices
SAILLY le SEC.	Jan 9th		Dull. Draft of 31 other ranks arrive. Coys continue training under Company Commanders. Rain at night.	
	10		Rain and thaw. A and D Coys bathe. Companies at disposal of O.C. Companies. Following officers join Bn - 2/Lieuts, - J COOK; A.R. GRAY; R. CONDIE; M. McC. MARTIN; A.W. McCRORIE; J R GIBSON.	
	11		Thaw continues. Coys at disposal of O.C. Coys. Army Commander visits Brigade.	
	12		Some snow. Coys at disposal of Company Commanders for thorough inspection of kit, equipment &c. Commanding Officer proceeds to England on leave. Capt. C.R. GORELL BARNES D.S.O., M.C., assumes temporary Command of Bn. Course for training Reserve Signallers assembles at Divnl. Depot. Bn. Bn. find two instructors and send twelve students.	
	13		Fine. Divine Services. Bn. play 7th 60th in Brigade football competition - lost 2-0. 'D' Co. give concert at night.	
	14		Dull. B and C Coys bathe. Armourer inspects rifles of C and D Companies. Coys. at disposal of O.C. Cos.	
	15		Rainy. Headquarters bathe. Bn. Small Box Respirators re-tested in gas. Draft of 90 other ranks arrive.	

A5834 Wt. W4973/M687 750,000 8/16 D. D. & L. Ltd. Forms/C.2118/13.

Instructions regarding War Diaries and Intelligence Summaries are contained in F. S. Regs., Part II. and the Staff Manual respectively. Title pages will be prepared in manuscript.

WAR DIARY VOLUME 33
or
~~INTELLIGENCE SUMMARY.~~ 8th Bn. The Rifle Brigade

(Erase heading not required.)

Army Form C. 2118.

Place	Date 1918	Hour	Summary of Events and Information	Remarks and references to Appendices
SAILLY le SEC	Jan 16		Rain. Inter-platoon A.R.A competition No 6 platoon win & selected to represent Bn in Brigade Competition. Commanding Officer and Medical Officer inspect new draft - not a good lot.	
	17		Rain. Brigade inter-platoon A.R.A competition won by 7th/60th. Coys at disposal of O.C Coys. in morning. Bn. attend concert given by the Staff of 41st Stny. Hospital in afternoon.	
	18		Showery. Coys. continue training under Company Commanders. Draft of 47 OR. arrive.	
	19		Dull. Commanding Officer and Medical Officer inspect draft. Coys. at disposal of O.C Coys. for thorough inspection of kits &c. Head Qr. Company give concert at night. Major F.E. YOUNG rejoins from leave and assumes Command of Bn.	
	20		Fine. Church Services. Warning Order received that Bn. will move on 22nd inst.	
	21		Rain. Bn. cleaning up billets.	
MEZIERES	22		Showery. Bn. march out of SAILLY le SEC at 8.45 am & proceed by route march to MEZIERES arriving at 3 p.m. Hard march, but only two men fell out.	

Instructions regarding War Diaries and Intelligence Summaries are contained in F. S. Regs., Part II. and the Staff Manual respectively. Title pages will be prepared in manuscript.

WAR DIARY or ~~INTELLIGENCE SUMMARY.~~ VOLUME 33

8th Bn. The Rifle Brigade

Army Form C. 2[illegible]

(Erase heading not required.)

Place	Date 1918	Hour	Summary of Events and Information	Remarks and references to Appendices
ROYE	JAN 23		Dull - fine. Bn continue march, leaving MEZIERES at 8 am and arriving in billets at ROYE at 2 pm. Billets good. March of 13 miles with no-one falling out. TH.	
BEINES	24		Fine - dull. March continued. Bn. leave ROYE at 9 am and proceed to billets at BEINES. Dinners on route. Billets good. March of 17 miles with only one man falling out. TH.	
CLASTRES	25		Fine. Bn march out of BEINES at 12.30 pm and proceed to CLASTRES by route march arriving about 6 pm. Village destroyed. Headquarters and Support & Reserve Companies accommodated in huts at CLASTRES. Two Companies for front line accommodated at LIZEROLLES. TH.	
URVILLERS	26		Fine. Bn resting throughout day. March out of Camp at 6 pm and proceed to front line, taking over from portions of the 413th and 416th French Regiments. Front extends from Sheet 66c N.H. B 30 c. 5. 4 to B 29 b. 5. 9. Disposition. - 'D' Co on left front. 'A' Co. right front. 'C' Co. in support on Sunken Road West of URVILLERS. 'B' Co. in reserve at ESSIGNY. Bn HQ established in Support Line at 66c N.H. H. 4 b. 5. 5. Reserve Company is too far away. TH.	
- . -	27		Fine. Very quiet. Commanding Officer thoroughly reconnoitres line. Large amount of work required to be done on wiring, fire bays and C.T's. B.G.C. visits line. TH.	

Instructions regarding War Diaries and Intelligence Summaries are contained in F. S. Regs., Part II. and the Staff Manual respectively. Title pages will be prepared in manuscript.

WAR DIARY VOLUME 33

or

~~INTELLIGENCE SUMMARY.~~ 8th Bn The Rifle Brigade

(*Erase heading not required.*)

Army Form C. 2118.

Place	Date 1918	Hour	Summary of Events and Information	Remarks and references to Appendices
LINE URVILLERS	Jan 28		Fine - frost. Quiet. Enemy aeroplanes very active - flying low. Some bombs dropped on back areas at night. Commanding Officer alters his dispositions. Bringing Reserve Company from ESSIGNY to position in Route 44. This Company is now Company in Support. Former Company in Support remains in Original Position and becomes Reserve Company. [initials]	
-	29		Fine - frost. Quiet day. Enemy aeroplanes again very active. Work on trench defences & improvements commenced. Fire bays being put into better condition. C.T's deepened and trench boarded. One OR wounded. Lt. & Qr Mr A. H. COLLIER joined Bn. for duty. [initials]	
-	30		Fine. frost. Enemy aeroplanes very active throughout day. Intermittent shelling of Bn area from 10 am to 5 pm. chiefly about Route 44. Working parties from Reserve and Support Coys. assist front line Coys. on improving fire bays and forward C.T's. Inter-Company relief at night completed by 12.30 am. New disposition 'B' Co. Right Front. 'C' Co. left front. 'A' Co. Support. 'D' Co. Reserve. [initials]	
-	31st		Fine - frost. Very quiet day. Lt Col. D.E. PRIDEAUX-BRUNE D.S.O. rejoins from leave. [initials]	

F. S. Young Major for Comdg. 8th Bn The Rifle Bde

APPENDIX TO WAR DIARY

8th Bn. The Rifle Brigade

Casualty List for January 1918

S 25062	Rfn	BUTT	T	'B' Co		Died 9-1-18
S 34750	-	HAYES	T	'A'	-	Accidentally wounded 27th
S 34267	-	WHITE	F	'A'	-	Wounded 29th

T. S. Young Major
for O. Cmdg 8th Bn The Rifle Bde

31/1/18

8th. Bn. The Rifle Brigade.

Nominal roll of Officers serving with Bn. January 31st, 1918.

Lieut.Col.D.E.Prideaux-Brune, D.S.O.	Commanding Officer.
Major F.E.Young	Second in Command.
Captain C.R.Gorell Barnes, D.S.O., M.C.	O.C. "D" Company.
Captain C.E.Squire	O.C. "A" Company.
Captain W.A.Crebbin, M.C.	O.C. "B" Company.
Captain E.Poole	Transport Officer.
Lieut.(A/Captain)W.A.Teakle, M.C.	O.C. "C" Company.
Lieut.(A/Captain)H.R.Adair	
Lieut. R.C.Dewhurst	Lewis Gun Officer.
Lieut. J.A.Gould	
Lieut. F.A.Kingswell	
2/Lieut.E.A.F.Batty	Attd. 41st. Inf. Bde.
2/Lieut.P.H.Wooding, M.C.	Attd. X Corps Signals.
2/Lieut.J.Grieg	Attd. 14th.Div.H.Q.
2/Lieut.W.N.Sproston, M.C.	
2/Lieut.H.Clayton	Fourth Army Inf.School.
2/Lieut.J.A.Webb	
2/Lieut.A.F.Richards	
2/Lieut.C.L.Emy	VII Corps Bombing Course.
2/Lieut.H.S.Bowyer	On leave to U.K.
2/Lieut.F.W.Richards	
2/Lieut.J.D.Davidson, M.C.	Fifth Army Musk. Course.
2/Lieut.G.Brown	
2/Lieut.D.F.Hampson	
2/Lieut.W.G.F.Dewar	
2/Lieut.J.F.Smith	
2/Lieut.W.L.Fairweather	
2/Lieut.E.T.Jones	
2/Lieut.T.Grant	
2/Lieut.C.Randall	Hospital
2/Lieut.S.D.Brown	
2/Lieut.J.Cook	
2/Lieut.A.R.Gray	
2/Lieut.R.Condie	
2/Lieut.M.McC.Martin	
2/Lieut.A.W.McCrorie	
2/Lieut.J.R.Gibson	
Captain & Adjutant A.F.Newell	Adjutant
Lieut. & Quartermaster A.H.Collier	Quartermaster.

F.E.Young Major,

31/1/18. for O. Commanding 8th. Bn. The Rifle Brigade.

Instructions regarding War Diaries and Intelligence Summaries are contained in F. S. Regs., Part II. and the Staff Manual respectively. Title pages will be prepared in manuscript.

WAR DIARY VOLUME 35
or
~~INTELLIGENCE SUMMARY.~~

(Erase heading not required.)

8th Bn. The Rifle Brigade

Army Form C. 2118.

Vol 33

Place	Date 1918	Hour	Summary of Events and Information	Remarks and references to Appendices
Trenches near ITANCOURT	Feb 1		Fine. Very quiet day. Support Companies find working parties to assist in work on front line trenches. ZFM	
	2nd		Fine clear. Enemy intermittently shell Bn. Area throughout day. At 4.40pm enemy obtain direct hit on trench outside Bn. H.Q. dugout with 5.9. One OR wounded. Enemy aeroplanes very active all day. Bombing 'planes come over about 6pm and proceed Westwards. Rather more M.G. fire than usual at night. ZFM	
	3rd		Fine clear. Bn. relieved by the 7th Bn. The Rifle Brigade and proceed to Brigade Support being disposed as under. H.Q. and B Co. at CLASTRES. A and C Cos. in the Railway Cutting at ESSIGNY. D Co. at LA SABLERIE. Quiet relief. ZFM	
CLASTRES	4th		Fine. Bn resting and cleaning up. 2/Lt. J.S. SIMPSON (London Regt.) rejoins from duty with 47th Div. and resumes position of Bn. Signalling Officer. ZFM	
	5th		Fine. Enemy bombing machines active about CLASTRES at 7am. Working parties of 4 Officers and 150 O.R. found for work in forward area. ZFM	
	6th		Fine. B Co and H.Q. bathe. Our aeroplanes very active. First time in evidence since Bn has been in this area. Companies work under Coy. Commanders. ZFM	
	7th		Dull. Some rain. Two officers and 2 N.C.Os per Company reconnoitre Left Front Bn. Area. Companies at disposal of OC Coys. ZFM	

A5834 Wt. W4973/M687 750,000 8/16 D. D. & L. Ltd. Forms/C.2118/13.

Instructions regarding War Diaries and Intelligence Summaries are contained in F. S. Regs., Part II. and the Staff Manual respectively. Title pages will be prepared in manuscript.

WAR DIARY VOLUME 35

or

~~INTELLIGENCE~~ SUMMARY. 8th Bn The Rifle Brigade

(Erase heading not required.)

Army Form C. 2118.

Place	Date 1918	Hour	Summary of Events and Information	Remarks and references to Appendices
CLASTRES	Feb. 8th		Dull some rain Similar reconnoitring party as on 7th inst. go forward. Draft of 11 OR arrive	
Trenches near ITANCOURT	9th		Dull some rain Bn relieve 8th Bn K.R.R.C. in Brigade Left Front Sector Quiet relief completed at 10.45 pm Lt. Col. D.E. Prideaux Brune DSO proceeds to Army R.F.C. HQ on 5 days course Major F.E. YOUNG in temporary Command of Bn	
–	10th		Fine Quiet day Our aeroplanes worry enemy throughout day. Bn commence work on strengthening defences of area Considerable amount of work necessary	
–	11th		Fine. Quiet throughout day Aeroplanes active on both sides. Enemy shell URVILLERS with gas shells in evening. One OR wounded (S.I.)	
–	12th		Fine In the early morning enemy attempt to raid SPHINX POST, held by D Co. The bombing is heard by Lieut J.A. GOULD who is out with a patrol. He at once faces his patrol about with the object of cutting off the enemy. A fierce fight ensues. The enemy who has superior numbers manages to retreat taking his wounded with him; leaving one wounded and one unwounded prisoner in our hands. N.C.O. in charge of enemy party subsequently found dead on our wire. Two infernal machines for blowing up dugouts also captured from the enemy Casualties to our patrol One OR wounded. Casualties in front line – Capt H.R. ADAIR and 2/Lt G. BROWN wounded. One OR killed, 5 OR wounded, 3 OR missing.	

A5834 Wt. W4973/M687 750,000 8/16 D. D. & L. Ltd. Forms/C.2118/13.

Army Form C. 2118.

Instructions regarding War Diaries and Intelligence Summaries are contained in F. S. Regs., Part II. and the Staff Manual respectively. Title pages will be prepared in manuscript.

WAR DIARY VOLUME 35
or
~~INTELLIGENCE SUMMARY.~~ 8th Bn The Rifle Brigade

(*Erase heading not required.*)

Place	Date 1918	Hour	Summary of Events and Information	Remarks and references to Appendices
Trenches near ITANCOURT	Feb 13th		Some rain. Quiet throughout day. Fighting patrol out from right Company fail to meet any enemy. Work on defences of area continued. [initials]	
	14th		Fine - frost. Very Quiet day. Aeroplanes active on both sides. [initials]	
	15th		Fine - frost. Quiet day. 'B' Co. from Reserve Co. relieve 'A' Co. as Right Front Co. and vice versa. [initials]	
	16th		Fine - frost. Quiet day. 'C' Co. from Support Co. relieve 'D' Co. on Right Front and vice versa. The 1st Bn. Royal Irish Fusiliers on our left and the 8th Bn. K.R.R.C. on our right take over small portions of the Bn. front. Bn. now holds front line from 66c B 23 d. 35 35 to B 17. c 70. 40. At night 'C' Co. capture two escaped German prisoners who were making their way back to their own lines. Capt. B H BENNETT rejoins Bn. at Transport Lines. Draft of 81 OR. joins Bn. [initials]	
	17th		Fine. Very Quiet day. [initials]	
	18th		Fine. Capt. B.H. BENNETT assumes Command of 'C' Co. Quiet day. Few gas shells near Bn. HQ. about 5pm. Heavy bombardment heard in progress to the South. [initials]	
	19th		Fine. Very quiet. Enemy aeroplanes very active. [initials]	

A5834 Wt. W4973/M687 750,000 8/16 D. D. & L. Ltd. Forms/C.2118/13.

Instructions regarding War Diaries and Intelligence Summaries are contained in F. S. Regs., Part II. and the Staff Manual respectively. Title pages will be prepared in manuscript.

WAR DIARY or ~~INTELLIGENCE SUMMARY.~~ VOLUME 35

(Erase heading not required.)

8th Bn. The Rifle Brigade

Army Form C. 2118.

Place	Date 1918	Hour	Summary of Events and Information	Remarks and references to Appendices
ITANCOURT	FEB. 20th		Some rain. Enemy shell LA SABLIERE heavily during day. Quiet in the line. 1 OR. wounded [initials]	
	21st		Fine. Quiet day. Between 5pm and 6pm our guns carry out a concentrated shoot on enemy Bn. HQrs. Bn. relieved at night by 7th Bn. The Rifle Brigade. HQ, B and D Cos. proceed to ESSIGNY CUTTING. 'A' Co to LA SABLIERE and 'C' Co to CLASTRES. Bn. reported all in at 1.40 am 22nd inst. [initials]	
ESSIGNY	22nd		Dull. Bn. cleaning up. Accommodation in new area very good. [initials]	
	23rd		Dull. Whole Bn employed on strengthening and constructing defences in the Battle Zone. HQ, A and C. Companies bathe [initials]	
	24th		Some rain. Party of 33 OR under 2/Lt A.W. McCROIRIE attached to 61st Fd. Co. R.E. for work. Bn. continue work on Battle Zone defences. [initials]	
	25th		Fine. Keen North wind. Our aeroplanes very active. Bn. continues work as on previous days [initials]	
	26th		Fine. Strong North wind. Work on Battle Zone continued. Heavy bombardment heard in progress on left at night. [initials]	

Instructions regarding War Diaries and Intelligence Summaries are contained in F. S. Regs., Part II. and the Staff Manual respectively. Title pages will be prepared in manuscript.

WAR DIARY or INTELLIGENCE SUMMARY. VOLUME 35

Army Form C. 2118.

8th Bn The Rifle Brigade

(Erase heading not required.)

Place	Date	Hour	Summary of Events and Information	Remarks and references to Appendices
	1918			
ESSIGNY	Feb 27th		Dull. Some rain. Enemy shell ESSIGNY during afternoon with 4.2 and 5.9s. Working parties held up by rain during day and by Gas shells and rain at night. Draft of 65 OR join Depot Bn. FEY	
	28th		Dull. Working parties as usual. Lewis Gun range built near Bn HQ. At 12.45 pm message received "Battle Zone take Precautionary Action". Bn stand by ready to move at 15 minutes notice. Working parties come in. Personnel to be left out under para XXX stand by to return to Transport Camp. At 5.20 pm message from Brigade, orders Bn to be ready to move at one hours notice instead of 15 minutes. 'A' Co. working at LA SABLIERE to continue work on defences, other Companies to cease work and stand by. FEY	

F.E. Young Mjr for Lt Col
Cmdg. 8th Bn The Rifle Brigade

2353 Wt. W2544/1454 700,000 5/15 D. D. & L. A.D.S.S./Forms/C. 2118.

8th Bn. THE RIFLE BRIGADE.

CASUALTIES. WAR DIARY - February 1918. - Appendix

Feby. 2.	S 34089	Rfn.	Jevans H.	Wounded.
	S 26097	L/C.	Fletcher J.	Wounded (accidentally)
10.	305299	Rfn.	Richards A.	Wounded.
	S 34210	"	Overton W.	Wounded (S.I.)
12.		A/Capt.	H.R.ADAIR	Wounded.
		2/Lieut.	G.BROWN	Wounded.
	S 31180	Rfn.	Arnold C.	"
	O 324	"	Ridpath A.	"
	S 32533	"	Bazell C.	"
	S 32235	"	Thomas F.	"
	S 6644	"	Renham J.	"
	P 1391	"	Staveley S.	"
	O 328	"	Snow A.	Killed in Action.
	O 329	"	Stimson E.	Missing.
	S 34297	"	Edgar H.	"
	S 18451	"	Mellor H.	"
16.	S 9055	Rfn.	Cheffey E.	Killed in Action.
20.	S 1140	Rfn.	Halifax W.	Wounded.

28/2/18.

T. E. Young Major Lieut.Colonel,
Commanding 8th Bn. The Rifle Brigade.

41st Brigade

14th Division.

8th BATTAION

THE RIFLE BRIGADE

M A R C H 1 9 1 8

41/14

CONFIDENTIAL.

WAR DIARY

of

8th. Bn. THE RIFLE BRIGADE.

From : 1st March. 1918.
To : 31st. March. 1918

VOLUME XXXVI

Army Form C. 2118.

Instructions regarding War Diaries and Intelligence Summaries are contained in F. S. Regs., Part II. and the Staff Manual respectively. Title pages will be prepared in manuscript.

WAR DIARY or ~~INTELLIGENCE SUMMARY.~~ VOLUME 36

(Erase heading not required.)

8th Bn The Rifle Brigade

Place	Date 1918	Hour	Summary of Events and Information	Remarks and references to Appendices
ESSIGNY	Mar 1		Dull. some rain 'C' Co move from CLASTRES to ESSIGNY at 8 25 pm Bn employed on work in Battle Zone. At 8 25 pm enemy open very heavy bombardment on Right Divisional Sector. Bombardment continued till 9 20 pm Our artillery also open out in response to S.O.S. Signals from front line Night passed off quietly. [initials]	
"	2nd		Snow. At 5 pm Bn receive message "TEST BATTLE ZONE". Para XXX stand fast. Companies move off to Battle Positions. Telephonic communication poor, - otherwise test satisfactory [initials]	
	3rd		Thaw Bn continue work on defences around ESSIGNY. Two Coys bathe. 2/LT J GOOK and 2/LT J.R. GIBSON to III Corps Inf. School. [initials]	
"	4th		Some rain Two Coys. bathe. Dugouts in CUTTING thoroughly cleaned out and disinfected. [initials]	
"	5th		Fine Dull. Bn relieve 7th Bn. The Rifle Brigade in the line. Companies disposed as follows 'B' Co. left front, 'C' Co. right front 'A' Co Support 'D' Co. Reserve. [initials]	
Trenches URVILLERS	6th		Fine Quiet day 2/LT H.S BOWYER proceeds on Aeroplane Photo. course. [initials]	

2353 Wt. W2544/1454 700,000 5/15 D. D. & L. A.D.S.S./Forms/C. 2118.

Instructions regarding War Diaries and Intelligence Summaries are contained in F. S. Regs., Part II. and the Staff Manual respectively. Title pages will be prepared in manuscript.

WAR DIARY VOLUME 30
or
~~INTELLIGENCE SUMMARY.~~ 8th Bn. The Rifle Brigade

(Erase heading not required.)

Army Form C. 2118.

Place	Date 1918	Hour	Summary of Events and Information	Remarks and references to Appendices
Trenches near URVILLERS	Mar. 7th		Fine Quiet Aeroplanes on both sides active. Capt W A CREBBIN M.C. and Capt & Adjt. A.F. NEWALL proceed to Transport Lines prior to proceeding on leave. Capt C.R. GORELL BARNES DSO, MC takes over Adjutants duties ZH	
–	8th		Fine Quiet BGC visits line. Aeroplanes active day and night. 2/Lt R.C. COOK joins Bn from the 2nd Bn The Rifle Brigade and is posted to D. Co. At 10.40 pm enemy shell URVILLERS with gas shells ZH	
–	9th		Fine Bright Aeroplanes active. At 11.45 am front line Co. report enemy artillery engaged in wire cutting on SPHINX POST. Night passed quietly on our front. Heavy artillery action throughout night on our left. Company relief carried out. ZH	
–	10th		Fine Quiet. Aeroplanes active Our artillery active throughout day. At 10 pm enemy heavily shell Bn on our left ZH	
–	11th		Fine 2/Lt A R GRAY wounded by G.S. in chest. Patrols active at night but met with no enemy ZH	
–	12th		Fine Enemy aeroplanes drop bombs on our trenches about 10 am. Quiet day. 'A' Co send out a fighting patrol under 2/Lt H G F DEWAR ZH	

Instructions regarding War Diaries and Intelligence Summaries are contained in F. S. Regs., Part II. and the Staff Manual respectively. Title pages will be prepared in manuscript.

WAR DIARY or ~~INTELLIGENCE~~ SUMMARY.

(Erase heading not required.)

VOLUME 36.

8th Bn. The Rifle Bde

Place	Date 1918	Hour	Summary of Events and Information	Remarks and references to Appendices
Trenches				
URVILLERS	Mar 12		Patrol out 7 hours, and locate an enemy post. Post not attacked as men were not in a fit condition after their long patrol in the cold.	
-	13th		Fine. Bn. relief put off for 5 hours in order to allow 'A' Co. to raid enemy post located on 12th inst. Enemy's trenches entered but no personnel found in occupation. Bn relieved by 8th Bn. K.R.R.C. and proceeded to CLASTRES.	
CLASTRES	14th		Fine. Bn. reported all in at 6 am and rests throughout day.	
-	15th		Fine. Two Coys digging cable trench under Div. Signal Co. Two Coys and HQ bathe. Medical Officer inspects 'A' Co. Armourer inspects rifles of A + D. Cos.	
-	16th		Fine. Two Coys. digging cable trench. Parties of 1 Off. + 20 OR; 1 Off. + 20 OR and 1 N.C.O. and 10 OR found for work on new Brigade HQrs.	
-	17th		Fine. Voluntary Divine Services. Three Coys digging cable trench under R.E. One platoon constructing rifle range. 12 OR working under 47th Bde. R.F.A. Enemy aeroplane over about 8 am one bomb dropped. Junior N.C.O.s class started. Bn. HQ reorganised on New War Establishment.	
-	18th		Fine. Three Coys digging cable trench.	

2353 Wt. W2544/1454 700,000 5/15 D. D. & L. A.D.S.S./Forms/C. 2118.

8th Rifle Brigade

22nd March 1918

Line 1. Is "Sassy"

meant for "Jussy". There is no "Sassy" on map.

5.1.25. H. R. Davies

Instructions regarding War Diaries and Intelligence Summaries are contained in F. S. Regs., Part II. and the Staff Manual respectively. Title pages will be prepared in manuscript.

WAR DIARY
or
~~INTELLIGENCE SUMMARY~~.
(Erase heading not required.)

VOLUME 36

Army Form C. 2118.

8th Bn The Rifle Brigade

Place	Date 1918	Hour	Summary of Events and Information	Remarks and references to Appendices
CLASTRES	Mar 19th		Wet. Three Coys digging cable trench under Div Signal Co. 24 O.R. working on new Bde HQrs at LA FAY farm.	
X –	20th		Fine. Whole Bn engaged on digging cable trench.	
–	21st		Dull – Misty. At 4.30 am enemy open out heavy bombardment on forward and back areas. Bn. occupy Battle Positions in Brigade Reserve being disposed in FREDDY and FANNY trenches. Enemy attack in force about 10 am. Situation in forward area rather obscure. At 11.30 pm orders received for Bn to retire via CLASTRES to Canal Bank at (JUSSY) 'D' Co fight rearguard action to cover retirement of Bn.	
JUSSY	22nd	X	Bn in position North of SASSY on Canal Bank disposed as follows on a front of about 2700 yds 'A' Co. on right, 'C' Co centre, 'D' Co left, 'B' Co in Reserve at FLAVY le MARTEL. In touch on the left with the 20th DIVISION and on the right with 5th Lancers and 43rd Inf Bde. Enemy appear about 7 am. Two platoons of 'B' (Reserve) Co. brought into front line between 'C' and 'D' Cos. Other two platoons take up position ~~between~~ along CHATEAU Road.	

2353 Wt. W2544/1454 700,000 5/15 D. D. & L. A.D.S.S./Forms/C. 2118.

Instructions regarding War Diaries and Intelligence Summaries are contained in F. S. Regs., Part II. and the Staff Manual respectively. Title pages will be prepared in manuscript.

WAR DIARY ~~VOLUME 53~~
or
~~INTELLIGENCE SUMMARY.~~
(Erase heading not required.)

8th Bn The Rifle Brigade

Army Form C. 2118.

Place	Date 1918	Hour	Summary of Events and Information	Remarks and references to Appendices
JUSSY	March 22nd		At 9am enemy patrol attempted to cross canal but driven off. Enemy put down a heavy Machine Gun barrage all day especially down CHATEAU Road and enfilading Canal Bank. During the afternoon enemy artillery shelled area between Canal Bank and FLAVY. Heavy casualties to Bn. At dusk enemy attempted to cross Canal in force, but were driven off by 'D' Co with Lewis Guns. Enemy sustain heavy casualties. About midnight enemy patrol crossed Canal. Three of the patrol captured remainder killed.	
FLAVY	23rd		Germans Cross Canal. Line taken up by us as follows from LEFT to RIGHT. 'D' Co CANAL BANK. 8th Bn K.R.R.C., 7th Bn The Rifle Bde, 11th Kings Rgt. Half 'B' Co.; 'A' Co. 9th Bn The Rifle Bde. Half 'C' Co (SUCRERIE). Half 'C' and half B Cos in Support near Bn HQrs. Line of Railway to Sucrerie. Enemy open bombardment at 6 am, and advance in force on FLAVY Station. At 10 am Bn withdraw to FLAVY - PETIT DETROIT Road - with rearguard under Capt C.R GORELL BARNES D.S.O, M.C in FLAVY.	

2353 Wt. W2544/1454 700,000 5/15 D. D. & L. A.D.S.S./Forms/C. 2118.

Instructions regarding War Diaries and Intelligence Summaries are contained in F. S. Regs., Part II. and the Staff Manual respectively. Title pages will be prepared in manuscript.

WAR DIARY VOLUME 38. Army Form C. 2118.

or

~~INTELLIGENCE SUMMARY.~~

(Erase heading not required.)

8th Bn. The Rifle Brigade

Place	Date 1918	Hour	Summary of Events and Information	Remarks and references to Appendices
FLAVY	March 23rd		Capt F.E. YOUNG with personnel left out under Para XXX and details from Bn. HQrs and Stores take up position on the FLAVY – CUGNY Road About 3pm enemy had worked round both our flanks making a withdrawal necessary. Withdrawal carried out under heavy machine gun fire. Withdrawal through French on CUGNY – LA NEUVILLE road covered by good resistance of Major F.E. YOUNG and Capt C.E. SQUIRE on LE HAUT BOIS. At 7 pm Major F.E. YOUNG and Capt C.E. SQUIRE forced to withdraw N.W. through 1st and 2nd Bns Royal Irish Rifles. Situation 7.30 pm 36 Divn – CUGNY 14th DIV and 329th French Rgt to BOIS de GENLIS, which was held by 1st French Cav Divn 10 pm enemy attack CUGNY and drive back 36th DIV to high ground West of CUGNY. Major F.E. YOUNG with details under his Command join 36th DIVN. 2M	
CUGNY	24th		Situation. Gap on left between French in front of LE RIEZ de CUGNY and French & 36th DIV. near BEAULIEU 11 am orders received to withdraw and reform behind the French at 90 BEINES Fm	

2353 Wt. W2544/1454 700,000 5/15 D. D. & L. A.D.S.S./Forms/C. 2118.

Instructions regarding War Diaries and Intelligence Summaries are contained in F. S. Regs., Part II. and the Staff Manual respectively. Title pages will be prepared in manuscript.

WAR DIARY
or
INTELLIGENCE SUMMARY.
(Erase heading not required.)

8th Bn. The Rifle Brigade

Place	Date 1918	Hour	Summary of Events and Information	Remarks and references to Appendices
BEINES	March 24th		Whilst this was being carried out the French were driven back and we took up a form of hollow square and dug in on high ground North of BEINES About 2pm orders received to withdraw and concentrate near BUCHOIRE. Rations sent up here but enemy aeroplanes stop concentration. Enemy artillery open with 5.9s. In the middle of this B.G.C. arrives and orders concentration on CRISSOLLES. - We move across country to QUESMY where H.V. gun shoots at us. Arrive CRISSOLLES 7.45pm men make themselves comfortable in straw near SUCRERIE. At 10.20pm we move on to LA VIGNETTE arriving about 3am 25th inst. ~~25th~~	
LA VIGNETTE	25th		Major F.E. YOUNG and party rejoin us. Support positions to 42nd and 43rd Inf. Bde taken up in front of NOYON - ROYE, with second line on forward slopes of MONT de PORQUERICOURT. Most interesting position as we could see the French fighting East of Canal near BUSSY and CRISOLLES GENVRY. French suddenly retired about 5.30pm Orders received to remain in position until 42nd and 43rd Brigades had	

2353 Wt. W2544/1454 700,000 5/15 D. D. & L. A.D.S.S./Forms/C. 2118.

Instructions regarding War Diaries and Intelligence Summaries are contained in F. S. Regs., Part II. and the Staff Manual respectively. Title pages will be prepared in manuscript.

WAR DIARY
or
~~INTELLIGENCE SUMMARY.~~

(Erase heading not required.)

8th Bn. The Rifle Brigade

Place	Date 1918	Hour	Summary of Events and Information	Remarks and references to Appendices
	March			
THIESCOURT	25th		got to their new Battle Zone on high ground in front of DIVE LE FRANCE. No enemy met and when within half mile of DIVE LE FRANCE B.G.C. met us and told us to proceed to THIESCOURT. Here we spent the night. FH	
	26th		8 am moved to position in wood just West of THIESCOURT.	
			9 am Moved to high ground round LÉCOUVILLON. Orders received to take up a defensive position. On reconnoitring we found three Coys of the 61st French Chasseurs occupying positions allotted to us.	
			6 pm formed rear guard to Division, which concentrated in neighbouronghood of ELINCOURT. Very comfortable night. FH	
ESTREES ST DENIS	27th		Moved to DISTILLERIE near ESTREES ST DENIS. Comfortable night. Transport rejoined Bn. FH	
GOURNAY	28th		Bn took up a defensive position on high ground South of GOURNAY. About 5 pm Bn marched off to CINQUEUX. Long bad march. 1½ hours halt in pouring rain near BAZINCOURT. Billets poor FH	

Instructions regarding War Diaries and Intelligence Summaries are contained in F. S. Regs., Part II. and the Staff Manual respectively. Title pages will be prepared in manuscript.

WAR DIARY
or
~~INTELLIGENCE SUMMARY.~~
(Erase heading not required.)

8th Bn. The Rifle Brigade

Place	Date 1918	Hour	Summary of Events and Information	Remarks and references to Appendices
	March			
NOGENI	29th		At 10 am Bn moved off to NOGENI and passed the day in a field at 11 pm Bn embussed for HEBECOURT	
HEBECOURT	30th		Bn arrived at HEBECOURT at 4 am and breakfasted. At 11 am Bn moved off marching to billets at VERS.	
VERS.	31st		Easter Day. Comfortable day at VERS. 7th Bn K.O.Y.L.I join Bn for duty.	
			3 Officers and 130 OR (Lt D.E.C. CROWTHER, 2/Lt. W. LOFTUS, " A. GRAY)	
			Casualties for period 21/3/18 – 31/3/18 16 Officers 354 OR	

F. E. Young Major
Cmdg 8th Bn The Rifle Brigade

2353 Wt. W2544/1454 700,000 5/15 D. D. & L. A.D.S.S./Forms/C. 2118.

41st Inf.Bde.
14th Div.

WAR
DIARY

8th BATTN. THE RIFLE BRIGADE.

A P R I L

1 9 1 8

C O N F I D E N T I A L.

W A R D I A R Y

- of -

8th (S) Bn., T H E R I F L E B R I G A D E.

From: 1st April, 1918.
To: 30th April, 1918.

Volume XXXVI.

Instructions regarding War Diaries and Intelligence Summaries are contained in F. S. Regs., Part II. and the Staff Manual respectively. Title pages will be prepared in manuscript.

WAR DIARY Volume 36
or
~~INTELLIGENCE SUMMARY.~~
(Erase heading not required.)

Army Form C. 2118.

8th Bn. The Rifle Bde

Place	Date 1918	Hour	Summary of Events and Information	Remarks and references to Appendices
HOURGES	1		Bn embussed at VERS at 8am and proceeded to St. NICOLAS. Bn moved forward at night and took over line from 6th Dragoons in front of HOURGES.	JPB.
	2nd		At 3 30 pm Warning Order received to attack and establish a line along the MOREUIL – DEMUIN Road in conjunction with the French. This order cancelled at 5 pm. Bn relieved by French at night. Relief completed at 2 am and Bn proceeded to BOIS de BLANGY.	JPB.
BLANGY	3rd		Day spent in BOIS de BLANGY. At 8pm Bn proceeded to relieve the 18th Hussars holding positions in front of WARFUSÉE - ABANCOURT. Relief complete at 12.30 am	JPB.
BOIS d'ACEROCHE	4th		Bn disposed as follows, - front line - 'B', 'C' & 'D' Cos, with 'A' Co. in close support in BOIS d'ACEROCHE and Bn HQrs in quarry at Cross Roads WARFUSÉE - FOUILLOY - and HAMEL - MARCELCAVE.	JPB
		5 AM	at 5 AM the enemy put down an extremely heavy barrage on the front line which lasted about one and half hours. At 6.30am he repeatedly attacked, but was driven off. Eventually he succeeded in penetrating our position and reached Bn HQrs in the Quarry. Here a stand was made and the enemy held up for about 1½ hours, a line being re-established about	

2353 Wt. W2544/1454 700,000 5/15 D. D. & L. A.D.S.S./Forms/C. 2118.

Instructions regarding War Diaries and Intelligence Summaries are contained in F. S. Regs., Part II. and the Staff Manual respectively. Title pages will be prepared in manuscript.

WAR DIARY Volume 36
or
~~INTELLIGENCE SUMMARY.~~ 8th Bn. The Rifle Bde

(*Erase heading not required.*)

Army Form C. 2118.

Place	Date 1918	Hour	Summary of Events and Information	Remarks and references to Appendices
	April 4th		200 yards in rear of Bn. HQrs. JEPR.	
AUBIGNY	5th		About 2 am Bn. was relieved by details of the 9th Scottish Rifles and M.G. Corps, and proceeded to take up a defensive position at AUBIGNY JEPR.	
-	6th		Fine Bn remain in reserve in positions near AUBIGNY Quiet day Men refitted with greatcoats and given clean change of underclothes JEPR.	
-	7th		Fine Bn. remain in position all day and proceed to billets at SAINT FUCIEN at night. Bn. rejoined by transport. Billets very bad. JEPR.	
ST FUCIEN	8th		Wet. Bn. rest and clean up JEPR.	
-	9th		Wet Bn. reorganised into two Companies JEPR.	
-	10th		Fine. Bn. entrain at SALEUX at 9am at proceed to GAMACHES detraining here at 3 pm. Bn proceed by route march to billets at DARGNIES. Billets good. 2/Lt W.A SEAMAN (7th Bn. K.O.Y.L.I) joined Bn. JEPR.	
-	11th		Fine. Bn. resting. Following officers proceed to join 2nd Bn The Rifle Brigade for duty, - Lt Col W. MERRICK (6th East Surreys att) 2/Lt. W LOFTUS (7th Bn KOYLI) 2/Lt. W.A SEAMAN (7th Bn KOYLI) and 2/Lt. H.E. MITCHELL. JEPR	
-	12th		Fine At 6.30 am Bn march to FEUQUIERES entraining here for	

2353 Wt. W2544/1454 700,000 5/15 D. D. & L. A.D.S.S./Forms/C. 2118.

Army Form C. 2118.

Instructions regarding War Diaries and Intelligence Summaries are contained in F. S. Regs., Part II. and the Staff Manual respectively. Title pages will be prepared in manuscript.

WAR DIARY
or
~~INTELLIGENCE SUMMARY.~~
(Erase heading not required.)

VOLUME 36

8th Bn. The Rifle Bde

Place	Date 1918	Hour	Summary of Events and Information	Remarks and references to Appendices
COUPELE VIEILLE	Apl 12th		MARESQUEL. Bn. detrain about Noon and proceed to COUPELE VIEILLE by route march. Long and tedious march. Billets scattered but fairly good. JEPR.	
-	13th		Fine Orders received that Bn. less transport will form a company of a Composite Battalion and come under orders of 43rd Inf. Bde. on 14th inst. This order is postponed for one day JEPR.	
LISBOURG	14th		Fine Bn. proceed by route march to LISBOURG. A Company of 6 officers and 280 O.R. formed to become 'C' Co of 'D' Composite Bn. 43rd Inf. Bde. This brings Bn. strength down to 2 Officers and 90 other ranks, including transport personnel. JEPR.	
-	15th		Company as above under Major F.E. YOUNG proceed to join 43rd Inf. Bde at MOLINGHEM. Remainder of Bn. stay at LISBOURG. JEPR.	
-	16th		Bn. Transport thoroughly cleaned up. Bn. Company with Composite Bn. work on defensive position just East of the railway JEPR.	
-	17th		Bn. training. Squad drill - musketry &c. Detached Co. on defences. JEPR.	
-	18th		Bn. move to SAINS les FRESSIN by route march. Billets poor. Detached Co.	

2353 Wt. W2544/1454 700,000 5/15 D. D. & L. A.D.S.S./Forms/C. 2118.

Instructions regarding War Diaries and Intelligence Summaries are contained in F. S. Regs., Part II. and the Staff Manual respectively. Title pages will be prepared in manuscript.

WAR DIARY or ~~INTELLIGENCE SUMMARY.~~

Volume 6

8th Bn. The Rifle Bde

(Erase heading not required.)

Army Form C. 2118.

Place	Date 1918	Hour	Summary of Events and Information	Remarks and references to Appendices
SAINS les FRESSIN	April 18		working as usual. JPPB.	
	19th		Bn training. All equipment thoroughly cleaned. Comany Composite Bn working as usual. JPPB.	
	20th		As on 19th. A Training Staff consisting of 10 Officers and 49 OR selected from Bn. Transport personnel reduced to War Establishment. JPPB.	
	21st		Bn training. Company Composite Bn move from MOLINGHEM to GUARBECQUE taking over billets from Composite Company of 9th Bn K.R.R.C. JPPB.	
	22nd		Composite Co work on defences in front of GUARBECQUE. JPPB.	
	23rd		As for 22nd. JPPB.	
FRESSIN	24th		Bn move from SAINS les FRESSIN to FRESSIN. Composite Co working as usual. JPPB.	
	25th		All personnel not included on Training Staff or Transport Establishment proceed by bus to join Composite Company at GUARBECQUE. JPPB.	

A5834 Wt. W4973/M687 750,000 8/16 D. D. & L. Ltd. Forms/C.2118/13.

Instructions regarding War Diaries and Intelligence Summaries are contained in F. S. Regs., Part II. and the Staff Manual respectively. Title pages will be prepared in manuscript.

WAR DIARY
or
~~INTELLIGENCE SUMMARY.~~
(*Erase heading not required.*)

VOLUME 36

Army Form C. 2118.

8th Bn The Rifle Brigade

Place	Date 1918	Hour	Summary of Events and Information	Remarks and references to Appendices
FRESSIN GUARBECQUE	Apl 26		Fine Composite Company working as usual. JTPB	
	27th		Fine. All personnel excluding Training Staff and Transport, transferred to 'J' Inf Base Depot, ETAPLES as reinforcements. JTPB	
LISBOURG	28th		Training Staff still remaining at GUARBECQUE proceed by route march to LISBOURG. Musketry Instructors and L.G.O. proceed to First Army Musketry School Course. JTPB	
FRESSIN	29th		Training Staff continue their march to FRESSIN and join transport. JTPB	
—	30th		Bn training. Bn Strength now is 10 Officers 87 other ranks. JTPB	

J. Purdon Browne Lt Col. ~~Major~~
Cmdg 8th Bn. The Rifle Brigade

A5834 Wt. W4973/M687 750,000 8/16 D. D. & L. Ltd. Forms/C.2118/13.

CONFIDENTIAL.

WAR DIARY.

- of -

8th (S) Bn., THE RIFLE BRIGADE.

From: 1st May, 1918.
To: 31st May, 1918.

Volume XXXVII.

Vol 36

Instructions regarding War Diaries and Intelligence Summaries are contained in F. S. Regs., Part II. and the Staff Manual respectively. Title pages will be prepared in manuscript.

WAR DIARY
or
~~INTELLIGENCE SUMMARY.~~

(*Erase heading not required.*)

Volume 37

8th Bn The Rifle Brigade

Army Form C. 2118.

Place	Date 1918	Hour	Summary of Events and Information	Remarks and references to Appendices
FRESSIN	MAY 1st		Fine. Temp Capt M.S HEYCOCK M.C, 9th Bn The Rifle Brigade taken on strength of Training Staff as Scout Officer. F.E.Y.	
EMBRY	2nd		Fine Training Staff proceed by route march to billets at EMBRY. Billets central and good F.E.Y.	
	3rd		Fine Gas N.C.Os attend Gas Course at Brigade HQrs Remainder of staff do Physical Training and inspections F.E.Y.	
	4th		Classes continued as on 3rd inst. F.E.Y.	
	5th		Classes as on 4th Rifle range fitted up. Staff practice on range F.E.Y.	
	6th		Commanding Officer Lt Col D.E PRIDEAUX-BRUNE D.S.O proceeds to II Corps Infantry School as Commandant. Major F.E Young assumes Command F.E.Y.	
	7th		List of Honours awarded to Officers & men of Bn. for gallantry during operations of March 21st to April 4th published,– Lt Col D.E Prideaux Brune D.S.O – Bar to D.S.O Major F.E. YOUNG and Capt C.E SQUIRE – Military Cross. 5415 C.S.M. WARREN W – D.C.M 5/261 L/Cpl Davis G – Bar to M.M. S1116 Rfn BARRETT J. – M.M. S8641 Rfn MODDER V. – M.M. S26278 Rfn WEBB G.A – M.M B3139 Rfn ROBERTS B. ITALIAN Bronze Medal for Military Valour F.E.Y.	

2353 Wt. W2544/1454 700,000 5/15 D. D. & L. A.D.S.S./Forms/C. 2118.

Instructions regarding War Diaries and Intelligence Summaries are contained in F. S. Regs., Part II. and the Staff Manual respectively. Title pages will be prepared in manuscript.

WAR DIARY Volume 37
or
~~INTELLIGENCE SUMMARY.~~ 8th Bn. The Rifle Brigade
(Erase heading not required.)

Army Form C. 2118.

Place	Date 1918	Hour	Summary of Events and Information	Remarks and references to Appendices
EMBRY	May 8		Training Staff continue usual parades of Musketry, Physical Training, Gas Drill &c. FEY	
	9		Usual parades. FEY	
	10		Usual parades FEY	
	11		Usual parades 2/Lt. J. COOK proceeds to I Inf Base Depot. FEY	
	12th		Transport and personnel proceed by route march to CUCQ Camp under 2/Lt. A.F. RICHARDS Training Staff is now left complete with 10 officers and 51 OR. and Transport as per Establishment. FEY	
	13th		Fine. Usual parades Capt. C.H. WENHAM joins from England. FEY	
	14th		Usual parades. FEY	
STEENBECQUE	15th		Fine. Training Staff proceed by lorry to STEENBECQUE area to administer troops in that area. On arrival Major F.E. YOUNG M.C. assumes Temp. Command of the 7/8th Bn. ROYAL INNISKILLING FUSLIERS (Reinforcing Battalion) Battalion consists of details of the 16th DIVISION made up from the following regiments:- Connaught Rangers, Royal Inniskilling Fusliers, Royal Irish Regt., Royal Irish Rifles and Leinster Regt. Bn. organised on a three Company basis. Capt. E Poole posted to command of 'A' Co. (R. Inniskilling Fusliers)	

2353 Wt. W2544/1454 700,000 5/15 D. D. & L. A.D.S.S./Forms/C. 2118.

Instructions regarding War Diaries and Intelligence Summaries are contained in F. S. Regs., Part II. and the Staff Manual respectively. Title pages will be prepared in manuscript.

WAR DIARY Volume 37
or
~~INTELLIGENCE SUMMARY.~~ 8th Bn The Rifle Brigade
(*Erase heading not required.*)

Army Form C. 2118.

Place	Date 1918	Hour	Summary of Events and Information	Remarks and references to Appendices
STEENBECQUE	May 15		Capt. C H WENHAM ~~[illegible]~~ posted to Command of B Co (R Irish Rifles, R Irish Regt. Lunsters) Capt. M.S. HEYCOCK posted to Command of 'C' Co (Connaught Rangers) Strength of Battalion less Training Staff. 11 officers 707 OR. [illegible]	
	16th		Bn employed on work on defensive system between THIENNE and STEENBECQUE. Whole Bn employed. Enemy aeroplanes active at night bombing AIRE and district. [illegible]	
	17th		Fine. – Bn employed as on 16th inst. Aeroplanes again very active at night [illegible]	
	18th		Fine – Usual working parties. Aeroplanes active bombing at night [illegible]	
	19th		Fine – Usual working parties, Lieut. R.C. DEWHURST rejoins Division as A D C to G.O.C. Enemy bombing machines cause lare fire at ST. OMER [illegible]	
	20th		Fine. Usual working parties. Enemy bombing machines active [illegible]	
	21st		Fine. Working parties as usual. Bn Provisional Defence Scheme issued in conjunction with Brigade Divisional Defence Scheme. Bn role – To take up a position near STEENBECQUE in support of PORTUGUESE troops. Training Staff Personal acting as guides to reinforcements and stragglers. [illegible]	
	22nd		Fine. Usual working parties. Training Staff Guides reconnoitre Defensive position. [illegible]	

2353 Wt. W2544/1454 700,000 5/15 D. D. & L. A.D.S.S./Forms/C. 2118.

Instructions regarding War Diaries and Intelligence Summaries are contained in F. S. Regs., Part II. and the Staff Manual respectively. Title pages will be prepared in manuscript.

WAR DIARY
or
~~INTELLIGENCE SUMMARY.~~ 8th Bn. The Rifle Bde

Volume 37

Army Form C. 2118.

(*Erase heading not required.*)

Place	Date 1918	Hour	Summary of Events and Information	Remarks and references to Appendices
STEENBECQUE	May 23rd		Fine. Working parties as usual. Enemy bombers active at night. [initials]	
	24th		Rain throughout day. Working parties suspended [initials]	
	25th		Fine. Working parties resumed as usual. Enemy planes less active at night [initials]	
	26th		Fine. Sunday. work as usual. Capt. M.S. HEYCOCK M.C. proceeds to XI Corps Gas School. Following officers (category B1 & B2) join Reinforcing Bn	
			Capt. J. WYPER . H.L.I. (B.1)	
			Lieut (A/Capt) M. FITZPATRICK Lincolns (B.1)	
			Lieut. R. H. WALLACE Royal Scots (B.2)	
			Lieut E. BURGESS Gordon Highlanders (B.2)	
			2/Lt. J. TURNER Notts. & Derbys (B.1)	
			2/Lt. E. J. ANDERSON Essex Regt (B.2)	
			2/Lt. G. W. WESTGARTH South Staffs (B.1)	
			Junior officers suffering from 'Shell Shock' very nervous. [initials]	
	27th		Fine. Usual working parties. Following 'category' officers join unit	
			2/Lt J.B LAMONT A & S Highlanders (B.2) 2/Lt A FOTHERINGHAM H.L.I. (B2)	

2353 Wt. W2544/1454 700,000 5/15 D. D. & L. A.D.S.S./Forms/C. 2118.

Instructions regarding War Diaries and Intelligence Summaries are contained in F. S. Regs., Part II. and the Staff Manual respectively. Title pages will be prepared in manuscript.

WAR DIARY Volume 37
or
~~INTELLIGENCE SUMMARY.~~ 8th Bn. The Rifle Brigade

(Erase heading not required.)

Army Form C. 2118.

Place	Date 1918	Hour	Summary of Events and Information	Remarks and references to Appendices
	May			
STEENBECQUE	27		2/LT R.G. HEWLAND - Gordon Highlanders (B.1) 2/LT F KERSHAW - Leicester Regt (B.1)	F.E.Y.
	28th		Fine. Following officers reposted & proceed to join units as follows.-	
			2/LT A.C. DAVIES to 11th Bn ESSEX REGT 2/LT J.E.S. TAYLOR to 2nd Bn ESSEX REGT	
			2/LT P.M. EVERETT to 2nd Bn. ESSEX REGT Following officers join unit	
			2/LT H.G. MAY - South Staff. (B.2) Lieut R.T. BOARDLEY - Lincoln Regt (B.2)	
			Lieut E. CAMERON - 7th Camerons (B.1) Sub. Lt E POLITZER - Naval Divn (B.2)	
			Working parties as usual Enemy shell near working party at STEENBECQUE STN	F.E.Y.
	29		Fine Working parties as usual. Training Staff training in map work &c	
			LT J.R. BYERS - Notts & Derby Regt. to hospital Enemy aircraft active at night	
			Enemy 'plane brings down balloon in vicinity of camp. F.E.Y.	
	30		Fine Working parties as usual. Training Staff working on maps & message	
			writing. 2/LT R.G. HEWLAND - Gordon Highlanders - to hospital Enemy bomb	
			STEENBECQUE at night. F.E.Y.	
	31		Fine Usual working parties. Training Staff training with the compass. F.E.Y.	

F.E. Young Major
Comdg. 8th Bn. The Rifle Brigade

4

Instructions regarding War Diaries and Intelligence Summaries are contained in F. S. Regs., Part II. and the Staff Manual respectively. Title pages will be prepared in manuscript.

WAR DIARY
or
~~INTELLIGENCE SUMMARY.~~
(Erase heading not required.)

Volume 38

8th Bn The Rifle Brigade

Army Form C. 2118.

14

Vol 37

Place	Date 1918	Hour	Summary of Events and Information	Remarks and references to Appendices
STEENBECQUE	June 1		Fine Companies at work on defensive line in front of STEENBECQUE	
	2		Fine Divine Services Battalion Sports	
	3		Fine Usual working parties out Training Staff do map reading	
	4		Fine Working parties as usual	
	5		Fine Working parties as usual. Commanding Officer inspects Training Staff. Major Keith attends F.G.C.M. at 7th R.B. H.Q.	
	6th		Fine Working parties as usual B.G. Comdg 41st Inf. Bde inspects Training Staff.	
	7th		Fine Work as usual Commanding Officer inspects kits of Staff and one platoon of Bn.	
	8th		Fine Draft of 84 OR join Reinforcing Bn. S7382 Sgt HAMMOND H awarded Distinguished Conduct Medal (London Gazette)	
	9th		Fine Divine Services	
	10th		Fine G.O. Comdg 14th (L) Divn inspects Training Staff	
	11th		Fine Work as usual Bn take over Guards & Piquet at ISBERGUES - 6 N.C.Os 18 men One Company left off work & do training	

2353 Wt. W2544/1454 700,000 5/15 D. D. & L. A.D.S.S./Forms/C. 2118.

Instructions regarding War Diaries and Intelligence Summaries are contained in F. S. Regs., Part II. and the Staff Manual respectively. Title pages will be prepared in manuscript.

WAR DIARY Volume 38
or
~~INTELLIGENCE SUMMARY.~~ 8th Bn The Rifle Bde

(*Erase heading not required.*)

Army Form C. 2118.

Place	Date 1918	Hour	Summary of Events and Information	Remarks and references to Appendices
STEENBECQUE	June 11		under instructors of Training Staff. Inter platoon football tournament commences	
	12th		Fine. Three Coys working, one Coy training. Draft 12 OR join Reinforcing Bn.	
	13th		Fine. Work & training as usual	
	14th		Fine. Work & training as usual	
	15th		Fine. Work & training as usual	
	16th		Fine. R.C. Service in STEENBECQUE Church. 41st Inf Bde HQ & 7th Bn The Rifle Bde Training Staff entrain at AIRE en route for ENGLAND. Bn Training Staff now directly under 14th DIV. 'Q' for administration	
	17th		Fine. Usual working parties. Portuguese troops now administered by 1st Portuguese Divn. New Defence Scheme issued	
	18th		Fine. Work & training as usual	
	19th		Heavy rain in morning. Working parties cancelled	
	20th		Fine. Work resumed as usual.	
	21st		Fine. Work and training as usual. B/3502 RQMS Jackson G. awarded the Meritorious Service Medal.	

2353 Wt. W2544/1454 700,000 5/15 D. D. & L. A.D.S.S./Forms/C. 2118.

Instructions regarding War Diaries and Intelligence Summaries are contained in F. S. Regs., Part II. and the Staff Manual respectively. Title pages will be prepared in manuscript.

WAR DIARY
or
~~INTELLIGENCE SUMMARY.~~

Volume 38

8th Bn The Rifle Bde

(*Erase heading not required.*)

Army Form C. 2118.

Place	Date	Hour	Summary of Events and Information	Remarks and references to Appendices
	1918			
STEENBECQUE	June 22nd		Fine. Medical Officer inspects 'C' Co. (Connaught Rangers). Sick parades rather large - a good deal of fever about. Following personnel from Training Staff proceed for attachment to 59th Div. Capt. C.H. WENHAM Bombing Instructor, One Gas N.C.O. and two Musketry Instructors.	
—	23rd		Fine. Divine Services.	
—	24th		Dull, with some rain in afternoon. Medical Officer inspects "B" Coy. (Royal Irish Regt). Working Parties and one Company Training, as usual.	
—	25th		Fine — Usual Working parties under R.E., and one Company Training. Four Officers from Reinforcements administered by 8th Bn KRRC Training Staff, join 7/8th (Reinfg) Bn R Inniskilling Fus. Warning order, received, to be prepared to move at short notice.	
—	26th		Two of the Officers joining yesterday, rejoin Reinforcements administered by 8th Bn KRRC, and three more Officers join. (All Category B Officers). Lieut-Col F.E. YOUNG, M.C. is President of F.G.C.M. assembled at H.Q. Training Staff of 7/8th Bn R Inniskilling Fus. arrive about 4.30 pm and take over administration of 7/8th (Reinforcing) Bn R Inniskilling Fusiliers at midnight 26th/27th inst.	
—	27th		Training Staff, 8th Bn The Rifle Brigade (less Transport), leaves at 9.30 am in four lorries and proceed to SAMER area to assist in Training 80th American Divisions. Transport proceeds by Road, staying for night at FAUQUEMBERGUES.	

2353 Wt. W2544/1454 700,000 5/15 D. D. & L. A.D.S.S./Forms/C. 2118.

Instructions regarding War Diaries and Intelligence Summaries are contained in F. S. Regs., Part II. and the Staff Manual respectively. Title pages will be prepared in manuscript.

WAR DIARY

~~or~~

~~INTELLIGENCE SUMMARY~~.

(Erase heading not required.)

Volume 38

8th Bn. The Rifle Brigade.

Army Form C. 2118.

Place	Date	Hour	Summary of Events and Information	Remarks and references to Appendices
BERNIEULLES	1918 June 27 (contd.)		The Training Staff is divided for instructional purposes as follows:- Lt-Col. F.E. YOUNG, M.C., Major J.H. KEITH, Capt J.E.C. CROWTHER, 2/Lts. J.A. WEBB and E.T. JONES with certain of the Staff to BERNIEULLES with Headquarters, 318th Inf. Regt. (American E.F.). One C.S.M., CQMS, Musketry, Lewis Gun and Gas Instructors to CORMONT with 1st Battalion; Capt. E. POOLE and Instructors as above to ROLET with 2nd Battalion; Instructors as above to ENGUINEHAUT with 3rd Battalion. The Training Staffs are administered by 39th Division. FEY	
–	28th		Fine and very hot. Transport, under 2/Lt J.A. WEBB, arrives. Some bombing by Enemy aeroplanes in the district at night FEY	
–	29th		Very fine – hot. The Commanding Officer inspects the Combined Training Staffs of 8th Bn The Rifle Brigade and 5th Bn N. Staffs Regt. at the American Headquarters to which they are attached (viz. BERNIEULLES, CORMONT, ROLET and ENGUINEHAUT.) FEY	
–	30th		Very fine. Establishment of Training Cadre increased – Each Battalion Cadre by 7 other ranks, making Establishment 10 Officers and 58 other Ranks. FEY	

F.E. Young Lieut. Col.
Cmdg. 8th Bn. The Rifle Brigade (T.C.)

To

Brig-Gen. R.C.Maclachlan, D.S.O.

From

All ranks of the 8th Bn. The Rifle Brigade. :-

"The Battalion wish to express what a lasting debt they owe to you for the skill, energy, and devotion with which you have trained and nursed them in their early days, and led them and inspired them in active service.

We feel that any success that has fallen to the Battalion has been founded on your example and leadership. Those who have served under you will never forget what you have done for them, and will strive to pass on the high tradition of the Regiment which you have established in the 8th Battalion.

All ranks unite in wishing you happiness and the highest success in your new Command and in any higher post to which you may be called."

Instructions regarding War Diaries and Intelligence Summaries are contained in F. S. Regs., Part II. and the Staff Manual respectively. Title pages will be prepared in manuscript.

WAR DIARY
or
~~INTELLIGENCE SUMMARY.~~
(Erase heading not required.)

Army Form C. 2118.

Volume 39

~~8~~ Rifle Bde

Vol 38

Place	Date	Hour	Summary of Events and Information	Remarks and references to Appendices
	1918 July			
BERNIEULLES	1		Fine & hot. Rifle Inspection of whole of Training Staff carried out daily. F.E.Y.	
	2		Very fine. Capt D.E.C. CROWTHER (A/Adjt) proceeds on leave; 2/Lt J.A. WEBB as A/Adjt in his place. The Commanding Officer visits 1st & 3rd Battalions of 318th Inf. Regt (80th American Division) F.E.Y.	
	3.		Dull – fine later. Training for 80th (American) Division ceases today, in view of the fact that a 'move' of the Division is imminent. F.E.Y.	
	4.		The Commanding Officer (A/Lt.Col. F.E. YOUNG, MC) is gazetted as Temp. Major. He proceeds to England on leave. Major J.H. KEITH (Scottish Rifles) in temporary Command of the Unit. F.E.Y.	
	5		Dull. 80th (American) Division leaves for Third Army Area. F.E.Y.	
	6		Fine. The Bn. is now in VII Corps – Second Army. F.E.Y.	
	7		Very brilliant day. Capt. E. POOLE and 16 Instructors of the Training Staff go on Courses at VII Corps School. F.E.Y.	
	8.		Fine – thunderstorm in afternoon. Usual inspections in the morning. F.E.Y.	
	9.		Fine. C.Q.M.S. Lloyd entered as Competitor in the cross-country race in connection with the Cup offered for competition between the Second Army and the Belgian Army, by the Princess CARAMAN-CHIMAY. F.E.Y.	
	10.		Fine – Showery. Strength of Training Staff is now 7 Officers and 49 Other Ranks. (Exclusive of Orderly Room Sgt at the Base, who is Supernumerary to Establishment.) F.E.Y.	

2353 Wt. W2544/1454 700,000 5/15 D. D. & L. A.D.S.S./Forms/C. 2118.

Instructions regarding War Diaries and Intelligence Summaries are contained in F. S. Regs., Part II. and the Staff Manual respectively. Title pages will be prepared in manuscript.

WAR DIARY

or

~~INTELLIGENCE SUMMARY~~.

(Erase heading not required.)

Army Form C. 2118.

VOLUME 39

Place	Date	Hour	Summary of Events and Information	Remarks and references to Appendices
	July			
BERNIEULLES	11.		Showery. The 117th Inf. Bde. eliminating run for competitors in the CARAMAN-CHIMAY Cross-Country runs took place today. Length of course – 10 Km. Starting and finishing at SAMER. 84 competitors entered from the Brigade. B/727 C.Q.M.S. Lloyd C. of the Bn. won the race by approximately 100 yards. 2/Lt. J.A. WEBB proceeds on leave. Much rain during night. [illegible]	
	12.		Rainy with fine intervals. 2/Lt. E.T. JONES as A/Adjt. [illegible]	
	13.		Fine. 5502 A/Cpl. Lee T. (Signals) awarded M.S.M. [illegible]	
	14.		Dull. N.C.Os and men granted days passes to PARIS-PLAGE. 2/1228 C.S.M. Walker from VII Corps Sch. to Second Army Musketry School [illegible]	
	15.		Fine. Divisional eliminating run to select competitors to represent Second Army against the Belgian Army takes place at NORDAUSQUES. CQMS Lloyd (first in Brigade run) represents the Bn. but fails to get a place owing to an attack of "stitch". The Commanding Officer is granted two days extension of leave to visit the Reserve Bns. Captain C.H. WENHAM and 4 Instructors rejoined from attachment to 59th Division. [illegible]	
	16		Heavy storm between 5 and 6 am. Local crops greatly damaged. Very fine but later. [illegible]	
	17		Exceptionally hot day – very heavy thunderstorm in the evening. Captain C.H. WENHAM to Hospital. [illegible]	

Instructions regarding War Diaries and Intelligence Summaries are contained in F. S. Regs., Part II. and the Staff Manual respectively. Title Pages will be prepared in manuscript.

WAR DIARY
or
INTELLIGENCE SUMMARY
(Erase heading not required.)

Army Form C. 2118

Place	Date	Hour	Summary of Events and Information	Remarks and references to Appendices
RIVIERE	18.		Snow & sleet. Very large working parties. 2/Lt O.F. Savage & draft of 73 O.R. arrive. Most of the latter had seen active service with various battalions of the Regiment.	
	19.		Dull. For the first time for many months the battalion has now its full complement of Officers & is almost up to strength in O.R. Working parties found up to our whole available strength.	
	20.		Dull. All the men employed in working parties up to the line. Comdg. Officer inspects the draft, who test their box respirators in gas.	
	21.		Cold & fine. Batt. relieve 7th R.B. in the line, relief being rather late owing to cross relief with garrison of the keeps, otherwise without incident. Disposition Right to Left C, A, D, B Coy in Reserve. German plane flew low over the Quarry, followed shortly after by one of our aeroplanes, which fired into the enemy trenches. Z1283 Sgt Every D. killed by direct hit from a Vane bomb.	
Trenches P23 (51C)	22.		Cold & dull. Enemy more active with Vane bombs.	
	23		Fine & frosty. Good deal of aerial activity. 2/Lt. H.G. Hanlon arrives.	
	~~23~~. 24.		Fine evening after sharp frost. For the first time since the battalion came up into this sector, the enemy has shown activity with 90 pounder T.M's. 2/Lt J. Greig 2/Lt V.B. Steel & draft of 93 O.R. arrives at Transport Camp to remain there until relief.	

Instructions regarding War Diaries and Intelligence Summaries are contained in F. S. Regs., Part II. and the Staff Manual respectively. Title pages will be prepared in manuscript.

WAR DIARY Volume 39

~~or~~

~~INTELLIGENCE SUMMARY~~.

(Erase heading not required.)

Army Form C. 2118.

Place	Date	Hour	Summary of Events and Information	Remarks and references to Appendices
BERNIEULLES (Pas-de-C.)	18.		Fine. Capt. D.E.C. CROWTHER returns from leave. [initials]	
	19		Fine. Shooting match arranged for today with 8th Bn R.R.R.C. had to be postponed as the latter were unable to come. [initials]	
	20.		Fine very hot. Usual morning rifle inspection. [initials]	
	21		Fine. Captain E POOLE and 15 Instructors rejoin from courses at VII Corps School. 5415 A/RSM Warren to Second Army Inf. School, WISQUES. [initials]	
	22		Fine. Commanding Officer returned from leave. Captain C.H. WENHAM rejoined from Hospital [initials]	
	23.		Wet all day. Headquarters of a Cavalry Brigade – 2nd Cavalry Division quartered in the village [initials]	
	24		Fine. Usual rifle inspection followed by three hours training for Instructors. P.T. & B.F. Musketry & Gas. [initials]	
	25		Fine. Instructors training in morning. [initials] S/9738 Rfn Brooks R awarded M.M.	
	26		Stormy. 117th Inf Bde. with certain units leaves the area. The Bn. comes under the administration of O.C. 16th Divisional Train, and under the orders of the Adjutant-General [initials]	
	27.		Dull & showery. Commanding Officer and Major J.N. Keith attend Machine Gun Demonstration at CAMIERS. 2/Lt E.T. JONES to Second Army S.O.S. Course. [initials]	

2353 Wt. W2544/1454 700,000 5/15 D. D. & L. A.D.S.S./Forms/C. 2118.

Instructions regarding War Diaries and Intelligence Summaries are contained in F. S. Regs., Part II. and the Staff Manual respectively. Title pages will be prepared in manuscript.

WAR DIARY
or
~~INTELLIGENCE SUMMARY.~~
(Erase heading not required.)

Volume 39

Army Form C. 2118.

Place	Date	Hour	Summary of Events and Information	Remarks and references to Appendices
	July			
BERNIEULLES (P-de-C.)	28		Fine. N.C.Os + men granted day passes to PARIS-PLAGE. Voluntary Service in village School in the evening. Draft of six other ranks joined – including Sgt. Musketry Instructor. F.E.Y.	
	29		Fine. Hot. Usual rifle inspection at 9 am. Kit inspection at 11.30 am F.E.Y.	
	30		Very hot. Three hours training for Instructors in the morning. F.E.Y.	
	31		Fine weather continues. Route march, for Instructors, in the morning – Dress, Fighting Order. Third anniversary yesterday of what is perhaps the most memorable day in the history of the Battalion – the enemy 'flammenwerfer' attack at HOOGE – when, only two months out from England, it lost in the enemy attack and subsequent magnificent but impossible counter-attack, the majority of the splendid Officers, N.COs + men of which it was composed; and gained the first V.C. and the first D.S.O. in the New Armies – the former being the posthumous award to 2/Lt. S.C WOODROFFE and the latter to Major (then Capt.) A.C. SHEEPSHANKS (Commanding D. Coy). Only six N.COs + men who were actually in the line on that day, now remain with the Bn. F.E.Y.	

F.E. Young Lieut. Colonel
Commanding 8th Bn. The Rifle Brigade.

2353 Wt. W2544/1454 700,000 5/15 D. D. & L. A.D.S.S./Forms/C. 2118

8th Bn. The Rifle Brigade.

Apendix to WAR DIARY - July 1918.

Roll of Officers.

Lieut.Col.F.E.Young, M.C.
Major J.H.Keith (Scottish Rifles).
Captain E.Poole
Captain C.H.Wenham
Captain D.E.C.Crowther (K.O.Y.L.I) - A/Adjt.
Lieut. J.A.Webb
2/Lieut.E.T.Jones.

Captain & A/Adjutant,
31/7/18. for O.C. 8th Bn. The Rifle Brigade.

D.A.G.,
3rd Echelon.

Herewith WAR DIARY for the month of July 1918 for this Battalion.

F E Young Lieut.Col.,
31/7/18. Commanding 8th Bn. The Rifle Brigade.

www.ingramcontent.com/pod-product-compliance
Lightning Source LLC
Chambersburg PA
CBHW081045020526
44114CB00044B/2325